The Arts Therapies

The separate arts therapies – drama, art, music and dance – are becoming available to increasing numbers of clients, as mental health professionals discover the potential of the arts therapies to reach and help people. But what are the arts therapies, and what do they offer clients? *The Arts Therapies* provides, in one volume, a guide to the different disciplines and their current practice and thinking. It presents:

- a clear analysis of the relationship between therapist, client and art form;
- exploration of the practice and key contributions made to the field by practitioners internationally and within many different contexts;
- discussion of how the arts therapies relate to established health services.

The Arts Therapies: A Revolution in Healthcare is a unique book that provides a thorough and up-to-date overview of the arts therapies. It will prove invaluable to arts therapists who wish to learn more about the whole field, and to health professionals who want to know what the arts therapies can offer their clients.

Phil Jones, MA course leader of Childhood and Community, Leeds Metropolitan University, has held the posts of Principal Lecturer on Masters programmes in Drama and Art Therapy, and course leader of Advanced Training in Art Therapy and Dramatherapy, Postgraduate Diploma in Dramatherapy and Foundations in Art, Drama and Dance Movement Therapy. He is also author of *Drama as Therapy: Theatre as Living*.

The Arts Therapies
A revolution in healthcare

Phil Jones

Brunner-Routledge
Taylor & Francis Group

HOVE AND NEW YORK

First published 2005 by Brunner-Routledge
27 Church Road, Hove, East Sussex, BN3 2FA

Simultaneously published in the USA and Canada
by Brunner-Routledge Press Inc
29 West 35th Street, New York, NY 10001

Brunner-Routledge is an imprint of the Taylor & Francis Group

Copyright © 2005 Phil Jones

Typeset in Times by RefineCatch Limited, Bungay, Suffolk
Printed and bound in Great Britain by
TJ International, Padstow, Cornwall

Cover design by Sandra Heath
Cover art by Helena Ivins

This publication has been produced with paper manufactured to strict
environmental standards and with pulp derived from sustainable
forests.

British Library Cataloguing in Publication Data
A catalogue record for this book is available from the British Library

Library of Congress Cataloging-in-Publication Data
Jones, Phil, 1958–
    The arts therapies: a revolution in healthcare / Phil Jones.
        p. cm.
    Includes bibliographical references and index.
    ISBN 1-58391-813-2 (hardback : alk. paper) – ISBN 1-58391-812-4
(pbk. : alk. paper)
    1. Arts–Therapeutic use.   2. Art therapy.   3. Psychotherapist and
patient.   I. Title.

RC489.A72J66 2004
615.8′515–dc22   2004007553

ISBN 1-58391-813-2 (Hbk)
ISBN 1-58391-812-4 (Pbk)

Dedicated to Neil Walters, Mark Blann, Helena Ivins, Carol and Pete Gamble and Mary Jane Rust for their support during my mother's death and the completion of this book

'But how can you tread that path with thought? How measure the moon from the fish?'

Conference of the Birds, Fard ud-bin Attar, twelfth century AD

Contents

Foreword

This book attempts to draw together strands of work and ideas developed over many years by many individuals and groups. The primary focus is on those who have been involved in the arts therapies as clients or as therapists. However, others who contribute to our understanding of the development and current state of the field are included: from Surrealists in France of the 1920s to dramatists in Africa.

My aim is to provide a broad introduction to ideas and work, whilst providing specific insights into particular moments in the therapy room from all the arts therapies. I've drawn on published accounts and research along with interviews of arts therapists at work, from Taipei to New York, from Johannesburg to London.

It is a book that can be looked into for specific topics. It is also a book that intends, as a whole, to be a first book for finding out about the arts therapies. One of the most pleasurable aspects of creating my book, *Drama As Therapy* (1996), was of meeting people who have discovered it in bookshops as far away as Italy and Korea, and who have gone on to train as arts therapists. I hope that this book, too, will provide a good first contact for people who would like to know more.

In addition, though, it is intended for those already involved in one of the arts therapies. For them I hope it can open up the connections between their particular discipline and the other arts therapies – to see both connection and difference. This is in part inspired by my twenty years of working alongside other arts therapists who are often curious about but shy of each other's disciplines. Along with many others Read Johnson has noticed the lack of interdisciplinary references and exchange within the individual arts therapies trainings and writings. Commenting on his time as the editor of the international journal, the *Arts in Psychotherapy*, he says, 'I was frequently exposed to parallel formulations of theory and practice among the modalities, though rarely did authors make reference to similar scholarship in the other modalities' (Johnson, 1999: 9). In some ways, my writing is a response to the challenge set up by him in this comment.

Though my background is in dramatherapy, this book has been written in the spirit of curiosity, to find out and to try to make sense of other disciplines.

I have experienced the other arts therapies as client in art therapy, and co-worker with dance movement and music therapists. This is an enterprise full of pitfalls – to try to speak of the disciplines together. I have tried to bring my experiences and ideas into contact with others – so, though this book is the work of one person, it has drawn inspiration and accounts from many people. I hope that it can now, in turn, be read by practitioners who will develop its work into further investigations of the relationships between the arts therapies. I hope, also, that this book will encourage the investigation of the questions that are at its heart: what are the arts therapies, do they have anything new to offer, and how can we gain a sense of whether and how they are effective?

Dr Phil Jones
Spread Eagle House, Settle
January 2004

Acknowledgements

The development of this book has involved twenty years of therapeutic work, study and lecturing in a number of countries. It bears the traces of insights gained from many clients, colleagues and students. The ideas and dialogues are often referenced to those whose work has been published, but there are many others from the postgraduate trainings in the arts therapies and from various hospitals, clinics and schools who are not referenced in the ways that written texts can be. To all of these people, from special schools in Inner London, to psychiatrists in St John, Newfoundland, from art therapy foundation students in England to MA and Ph.D. students in Athens, I offer my thanks for the stimulation and challenges that have added to this book.

Though, of course, he can't read, it would seem ungrateful not to mention Woof, who has contributed a great deal to this book by accompanying me on many walks in the Dales whilst I was thinking through chapters and struggling with ideas.

I would like to name some individuals who have worked with me over the years or whose work has been influential in my thinking and practice. Thanks go to Michael Barham, Bruce Bayley, Philippa Brown, Isabel Cristina Calheiros, Caroline Case, John Casson, Petruska Clarkson, Ayad Chebib, Ditty Dokter, Janek Dubowski, Lesley Kerr Edwards, John Evans, Zigi Fibert, Manolis Fillipakis, Nicky Gavron, Alida Gersie, Ruth Goodman, Hank Guilickx, Jonathan Glover, Roger Grainger, Sue Jennings, Ragnar Johnson, David Read Johnson, Rea Karageourgou-Short, Vikki Karkou, Robert Landy, Leah Lewis, Deborah Loveridge, Jenny Mark, Ann McGuire, Annie, Zoe and Pavlos Nowak, Patsy Nowell Hall, Helen Payne, Pat Place, Rosemary Sanctuary, Joy Schaverien, Jan Stirling, Richard Wainwright and Michelle Wood. I would also like to thank Helen Pritt, Joanne Forshaw and Sue Dickinson for their editorial help.

I would like to thank the copyright holders for permission to reproduce illustrations in my book as follows:
Louise Bourgeois's I DO, I UNDO, I REDO (1999) installed in the inaugural exhibition of the Tate Modern at Turbine Hall in 2000. Collection of the Artist, courtesy Cheim & Read, New York. Photo: Marcus Leith © Tate, London.
André Masson's ARIADNE'S THREAD. Copyright © ADAGP, Paris and DACS, London 2004.
Permission to publish all other images has been obtained.

Part I
Introductions

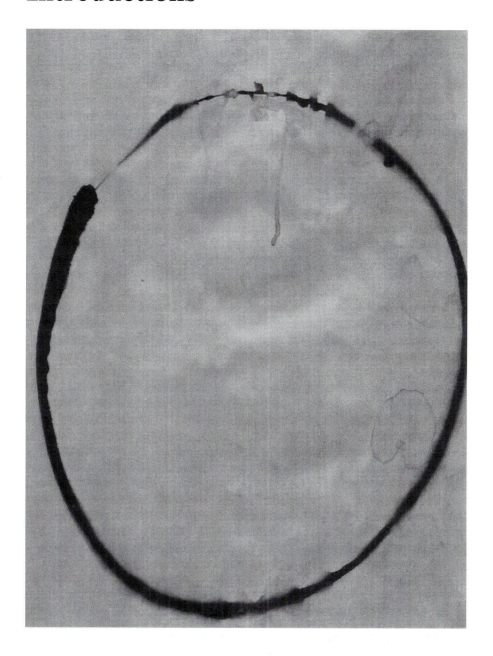

As in Ecchoes by reflection . . . where we know the thing we see is in one place; the appearance in another. And though at some certain distance the real, the very object seems invested with the very fancy it begets in us; yet still the object is one thing, the image or fancy is another.

T. Hobbes in *Leviathan* (1651: 86)

1 An introduction to *The Arts Therapies*

This chapter introduces the areas covered by *The Arts Therapies*, and looks at the main topics and themes within each of the different sections.

Introduction to Part II

Chapters 2 to 7

From one perspective, the arts therapies are a continuation, a development of ideas and ways of working which have had different forms and manifestations over centuries. Looked at another way, though, the arts therapies mark a revolution in the way the arts and healthcare can be seen and experienced. This book will describe that revolution.

Despite an extensive prehistory of connections between the arts and health, the arts therapies have emerged as distinct, coherent disciplines and professions since the 1940s. In a number of countries art, music, drama and dance movement therapy have become recognised as formal disciplines and professions within existing health and care provision. The past half-century has witnessed a massive shift from a situation where there were virtually no arts therapists, with no professional identity, specific theory or established ways of practising, to one where there is a contemporary flourishing of practice, training, published research and theory with developing recognition by state medical providers in a number of countries. One of the very first academic professional trainings, for example, was established in music therapy, at the University of Kansas, USA, in 1946. The National Association of Music Therapy in the US followed in 1950. By the end of the twentieth century there were almost seventy degree courses approved by the National Association and its partner organisation the American Association of Music Therapy (Bunt, 1997: 250). Now there are over 3,000 music therapists practising in the USA, with recorded music therapy initiatives occurring in over thirty countries. This is an example of the advance of the arts therapies from their comparatively recent beginnings. Part II, 'The arts therapies: definitions and developments', describes the different arts therapies and their aims. It looks at organisations and associations that oversee training and practice in many parts of the world, referring to arts therapists from the USA to Taiwan, from the UK to South Africa. Chapter 2 gives an overview of the process of definition, and each subsequent chapter deals with one of the main modalities: art; music; drama; and dance movement. Specific definitions of each discipline are given in Chapters 3 to 6, though examples of the ways the arts therapies are practised are also contained throughout the book. This book focuses on art, music, drama and dance movement therapy, as they are the main ways in which the arts therapies are currently offered. Other areas such as the expressive arts therapies, where all art forms are brought together, are referred to, however. The commonalities and differences between art, music, drama and dance movement therapies are described and looked at in terms of what they can offer to clients. Whilst Chapters 3 to 6 describe each discipline, Chapter 7 looks at the relationship between the different arts therapies, as well as that between the arts therapies and the arts-in-health movement.

Introduction to Part III

Chapters 8 to 10

A part of the arts therapies revolution in the use of the arts can be linked to developments in art, theatre, dance and music at the end of the nineteenth century and early years of the twentieth century. These movements are widespread and vary enormously. They include the Surrealists, the revolt in theatre in the Soviet Union and Germany, through to the dance experiments of Laban, from Diaghilev's and Nijinsky's productions such as the *Rite of Spring* through to developments in jazz. Part III, 'Backgrounds, histories and encounters: from the first happening to the shadow of logic', describes and analyses initiatives from this period. It focuses on two specific examples, as a way of sampling many other similar occurrences. Chapter 8 looks at Black Mountain College in the USA, a place of experimentation and interdisciplinary discovery. Chapter 9 looks at one of the early meetings between those involved in the arts therapies, on 30 April 1960 in London.

The movements and experiments referred to above resulted in particular ways of viewing creativity, the imagination, the roles of the artist and of the art form. These arts movements examined areas of expression and experience which had hitherto been seen to be outside the range of what was considered suitable for artistic attention. Lyotard presents this as the central tenet of modern representation: 'To make visible that there is something which can be conceived and which can neither be seen nor made visible' (Lyotard, 1983: 16). The movements often included an interest in artistic products of people with mental health problems, for example, and the use of techniques devised to free the imagination and to increase spontaneity.

The first performance in 1896 of Albert Jarry's play *Ubu Roi* is an example of such work, reflecting these concerns in its conception and realisation. It was met by an audience uproar – almost bringing the production to a halt.

The audience was in such a state of disruption that violence nearly erupted (Innes, 1993). Riotous arguments in the audience almost drowned out the players. This performance has been described as a seminal moment in modern culture, a formative influence on the twentieth-century avant-garde.

What was so disturbing? What caused people to revolt? A key to this lies in both the content and form of the performance. The central character, Ubu, is a manifestation of basic, repressed, amoral instincts: his character is an unleashing of parts of the self normally hidden or censored. The play combines obscenity, moral taboos crossed, actions performed by dreamlike, puppet-like characters.

In this world kingship means eating as many sausages as you want, wearing big hats, slaughtering at whim. As drawings by Jarry show, the figure of Ubu is not meant to be realistic: rather he is an abstract, a suggestive form, a king from a nightmare, rather than from a bourgeois drawing-room or royal castle. Part of Jarry's intent was to explore 'the power of base appetites' (Jarry, cited in Innes, 1993: 24). The plays in this cycle can be seen to be in line with Jarry's 'Pataphysics', which he defined as a system devoted to unreason, 'a science of imaginary solutions' (Jarry, cited in Innes, 1993: 26). On a theatre stage in Paris he was trying to break down the relationship between everyday perception and hallucination:

> You will see doors open onto snow-covered plains under blue skies, mantelpieces with clocks on them swinging open to turn into doorways, and palm trees flourishing at the foot of beds so that little elephants perching on book shelves can graze on them.
>
> (Jarry, 1965: 77)

This concern was echoed within other experimental art forms of the time. These involved attempts to reach beyond surface reality, to explore through the arts what was thought of as 'inner' nature: dreams, the subliminal, the unconscious. The stage or gallery becomes a place for dreams to become concrete, for the mind to reveal previously hidden thoughts and experiences, for the concerns of the unconscious, rather than the rational, to be played out.

Taylor could have been referring to Jarry's work when he draws parallels between the avant-garde in twentieth-century art and the kind of work produced in arts therapies, 'During this period avant garde artists became able to do through the activity of painting what therapists today do with their patients – namely explore aspects of feeling that are often not accessible by other means' (Taylor, 1998: 21).

As this book will demonstrate, the arts therapies are much *more* than such a process of exploration. However, Taylor's reference indicates one of the connections that created the context for the arts therapies to emerge: that of the fascination of the experimental arts with emerging ideas of the unconscious and extreme states of mind. As we will see later in this book, the work of groups such as the Surrealists, or the experiments at places such as

Black Mountain College, described in Chapter 8, 'The first happening', were all part of this upheaval or experimentation. Their challenging of boundaries between different disciplines, such as psychology and the arts, would enable the arts therapies to emerge. Arts therapist McNiff has said that Surrealism may be the clearest link between the arts and arts therapy: 'During the surrealist era many of the values that currently guide art as medicine began to take shape' (McNiff, 1992: 44).

The emergence of work from behind asylum walls has also been credited with helping to challenge and widen the notion of what can be described as 'art'. Arts practice had occurred within hospitals for centuries. Pioneers such as Reil (1759–1813) had worked in an asylum setting, with staff acting out patients' fantasies in staged plays seen as part of the treatment (Jones, 1996). Patients with what would now be described as mental health problems were involved in singing, music groups and art activities (Edwards, 1989: 82). This kind of practice was not typical, however. In the twentieth century, interest and concern with such areas of the arts developed and increased dramatically. One of the most well-known examples of this concerns the initiative begun by Prinzhorn, a doctor in the Heidelberg Psychiatric Clinic, who collected art work made by patients in asylums and published them in *Bilnerei der Geiteskranken* (Prinzhorn, 1922). He believed that these pictures could be viewed as a new art form, previously neither acknowledged nor valued. As we will see, this opening of the asylum doors fed into growing concerns in the experimental arts through movements such as Art Brut and the Surrealists. However, the growing interest in the area was not only influential within artistic circles: over the next decades, it helped raise awareness of the ways in which arts products could assist in understanding, communicating with and, eventually, working therapeutically with patients and their conditions. For example, at the international meeting of psychiatrists in Barcelona in 1958, a section on psychiatric art raised such interest that an International Society for Psychopathological Art was established the next year in Paris (Pickford in O'Hare, 1981: 279). Within the next two decades the flowing tide of interest had resulted in a surge of activity and the unprecedented rise of new organisations, ways of working, professions, training and benefits for users of health services. The International Society is only one example of the many initiatives that were beginning to link the arts and therapy. In Chapter 9, I will look closely at such a forming link: the speeches and ideas of people coming together for a Conference of the Society of Music Therapy and Remedial Music in 1960.

These experiments and developments enhanced the awareness of connections vital to the notion of the arts as therapy. They created some of the foundations that the arts therapies would develop from. Part III gives a flavour of the awareness of potential relationships between arts making and arts products, the unconscious and change which began to emerge in a way that made the idea of the arts therapies possible.

Introduction to Part IV

Chapters 11 to 13

The movements and meetings described in Part III can be considered as a foregrounding of particular concerns to do with the ways in which the arts and therapeutic change are related. They reflect the connections between the arts and discoveries and ideas emerging from sciences such as psychology, the fields of psychoanalysis, psychotherapy and education. These connections are analysed further in Part IV, 'Agents of transformation'. Here three of the main areas that are brought together by much arts therapies practice are looked at: the arts, the unconscious and play. They are, in some arts therapists' eyes, key 'agents', or forces at work, within the arts therapies.

Artists' fascination with the meeting points of the unconscious, the apprehension of their media and their own identity was accompanied by shifts in the ideas of what was suitable for artists to consider as subject matter and form. The unconscious came to the fore in all the arts. This, as described above, was accompanied by the increased appreciation of art produced by those previously disenfranchised from the public showing of the products they created. The hidden worlds of those whose minds and experiences were deemed invalid received more public exposure through their arts products than ever before. Many artistic movements of the early and mid-twentieth century gave credence and value to such experiences and voices, shifting them from the private worlds of asylum, dreams and nightmares onto canvas, stage, gallery and concert hall in an unprecedented fashion. Such innovations will be analysed in Chapter 12, 'The sensuous encounter: the arts therapies and the unconscious'.

This was not just one-way traffic – of the arts as practised by patients in asylums affecting the general world of the arts, for example. The introduction of the arts into hospitals also led to discoveries about the ways the arts seemed to affect patients within the hospitals. The experience of the arts in mental health contexts, for example, led to people seeing that the arts seemed to impact positively on the problems being experienced by patients. In addition, the effects of these revolutionary exchanges between the arts and areas such as psychoanalysis were not confined to the arts practice alone. Crucial to the arts therapies are the ways in which the arts influenced and featured within the development of psychoanalysis and psychotherapy, as well as changes in the field of education.

This book will review the varieties of arts processes within the arts therapies, and the ways in which the discoveries about arts processes being made have an impact on the development and formation of the arts in the arts therapies. In particular, Chapter 11, 'The arts in the arts therapies', will focus on this range. It will also, in Chapter 13, 'Playing, development and change', explore the interaction between fields such as psychology and education in the development and current practice of the arts therapies.

Introduction to Part V

Chapters 14 to 17

In her 'map of major traditions in psychotherapy', Clarkson identifies three major schools: psychoanalytic, behavioural and humanistic-existential (Clarkson and Pokorney, 1994). The dates she gives for the inception, or active development, of each of these are 1893, 1902 and 1908 respectively: the key founders being Freud, Pavlov and Moreno. Any such definition of psychotherapy's areas of concern is notoriously complex because of the diversity and variety of its theories and practice. Many attempts draw upon a distinction between the verbal and physical. They propose that psycho-therapy is a form of treatment for emotional and psychiatric disorders that relies on talking and on the relationship between patient and therapist. This is contrasted with other treatments that rely on physical means such as drugs or electroconvulsive therapy (Brown and Peddar, 1979; Holmes and Lidley, 1989).

Clarkson attempts a wide definition that does not rely on this dichotomy between verbal and physical. She advises that the most definite we can be in looking at psychotherapy in all its various forms is to say that it relies on the bringing about of changes in the personality and manner of a person's relat-ing by the uses of psychologically based techniques (Clarkson and Pokorney, 1994: 4). Since the turn of the twentieth century there has been a massive expansion within areas such as psychotherapy and parallel disciplines such as counselling, psychiatry and psychology. Their forms and ways of working have been adapted within diverse cultural frameworks. The diversity and extent of their practice has expanded through health services and practices all over the world, and their ideas and discoveries have echoed through many other fields. How does this growth relate to the emergence of the arts therapies?

The full nature of this relationship and its relevance to the arts therapies will be discussed throughout this book, but especially in Part V, 'The client–therapist relationship: paradigms, dialogues and discoveries'. At this point I want to consider briefly some of the key aspects of the development and emergence of the field in relation to the formation of the arts therapies as a way of reflecting the themes in Part V. Put most simply, the arts therapies can be identified historically, philosophically and methodologically as a part of this development. The emergence of areas such as psychotherapy is relevant to the arts therapies as they share a common background. The background has three main components:

1   A general root of ideas and assumptions
2   The establishing of therapy as treatment
3   Specific aspects of the field that start to discover links between therapeutic change and the arts.

The shared roots concern the variety of ideas and notions emerging as the fields of psychoanalysis and psychotherapy developed. The explorations and discoveries about identity, change and the therapeutic relationship affected many fields, as we have seen, including the arts. As mentioned earlier in this chapter, the arts showed influence from analysis and therapy. Was this mutual? Did the arts have any impact upon the emergence and formation of psychotherapy and psychoanalysis?

Kuhn (1983) describes the relationship between analysis and the arts as a revolution. He says that the main components of this revolution are Freud's theory of psychic life and his method of interpreting psychological events. These had a profound effect upon the 'creation, use and appreciation of works of art' (Kuhn, 1983: 2). The development of Freud's theories are linked to his 'discovery' that important works of art dealt with the 'deep psychological problems he encountered as part of his clinical work' (Kuhn, 1983: 2–3). Kuhn's critique of Freud says that he didn't adequately follow up his own thoughts about the arts: there was no systematic exposition of an explicit psychoanalytic theory of art. The emphasis is upon the arts as indicators of repression, as manifestations of psychic problems.

Most arts therapists would echo Jung in saying: 'Psychology and the study of art will always have to turn to one another for help, and the one will not invalidate the other' (Jung in Ghiselin, 1952: 209). What could this turning towards each other involve?

It is possible to say that the 'therapeutic roots' of significant aspects of the arts therapies relate to different areas of discovery and development in the field of therapy. As this book will illustrate, dialogue and mutual discovery is occurring between the arts therapies and different approaches to therapy, from the psychoanalytic, humanistic, to the developmental and cognitive. This will be looked at in detail in Chapters 14 and 15 of this book, which focus on different aspects of the client–therapist relationship.

Both the *Handbook of Dramatherapy* (Jennings *et al.*, 1994: 15) and the *Handbook of Art Therapy* (Case and Dalley, 1992: 59) in their sections on the process of therapy in the arts therapies refer to the same material from psychotherapist Cox and his definition of therapy as: 'A process in which the patient is enabled to do for himself what he cannot do on his own. The therapist does not do it for him, but he cannot do it without the therapist' (1978: 45). Both Handbooks have independently drawn attention to this, as it is of central importance to the ways many arts therapists understand their practice. However, the arts therapies have made a number of discoveries about how arts processes and art forms create new opportunities and reveal new aspects of this relationship. This has led to innovative ways of working and to new opportunities for clients to make use of in therapy. Chapter 17 will focus on the processes that are at the heart of these discoveries and innovations.

The history of the development of the arts therapies has not always been a smooth or easy progress of their entry into the field of medicine and healthcare. Indeed, for some practitioners, any notion of assimilation is problematic. They see the arts therapies emergence as questioning the medical model. McNiff, for example, says that the field of the arts therapies:

> can revolutionise therapy, and its transformative impact will be realised only if it continuously offers a radically different paradigm. The excessive reliance on chemical therapies, hierarchical control, and other institutional practices of 'health' have to be looked at from a completely foreign perspective in order to be seen.
>
> (McNiff, 1992: 11)

This would echo Clarkson's point about change: that it can come from the most unlikely of connections and unexpected directions. She adds that change demands that the areas that something connects to and emerges from become different: 'A characteristic of revolutionary change is that the starting conditions and basic components of the system have to be changed, and (these) may even appear out of the regions of probable predictions' (Clarkson, 1994: 10). One of the tensions which has been present in writing about the arts therapies concerns whether and how the arts therapies offer a radical challenge to mainstream health services, or whether they should work within existing systems and adopt their languages and therapeutic frameworks to assist clients. McNiff argues that once the arts therapies accommodate themselves to these approaches and systems, and become assimilated into them, they lose their ability to provide a radical perspective.

Others have worked hard and long to enable arts therapists to practise within the major systems of healthcare provision. As this book will describe, there is now extensive provision offered to clients in the mainstream healthcare systems within many countries. This is dealt with in Chapter 10, 'Art and science: the rise of the medical model and the shadow of logic', but is also considered in Chapters 14 and 15 which examine the nature of the therapeutic relationship within the arts therapies. Chapter 16 will continue the debate about the nature of the dialogue between arts and therapy practice, as it looks at the ways in which change in the arts therapies can be understood, accounted for and communicated, in 'Efficacy: what works in the art gallery? What works in the clinic?'

Chapter 17, which completes the book, summarises the unique processes that the arts therapies offer. It reviews the many ways of working, and, within the diversity of art, music, drama and dance movement therapy, proposes a set of common-core processes: 'From the triangular relationship to the active witness'. It argues that these are the essential, different opportunities offered to clients by the arts therapies.

Overview

Over the past century, then, a series of connections have developed into a particular form: the arts therapies. This book will look at the way clients are offered new opportunities, of using the therapy space to work creatively, to develop and to change. The arts therapies have emerged from an explosion of experimentation and exploration. We can say that the current situation of the established practice of the arts therapies is both an evolution and a revolution in healthcare and the arts. This book will now go on to look at the development, practice and ideas within the emerging fields of art, music, drama and dance movement therapy.

Part II

The arts therapies: definitions and developments

We know that words can be used in many ways: to say what we mean, what we think we mean, what we think we ought to mean, what we deliberately do not mean and so on.

M. North in Personality Assessment through Movement (1972: 6)

2 Definitions in flux: contexts and aims

INTRODUCTION

A single definition for the arts therapies wouldn't be useful to anyone. There must be different definitions in response to different demands. This is not an indication of confusion, or a lack of clarity. Rather, it's a recognition that a national or international accreditation board or a client and arts therapist working together in a day centre have different needs in terms of definitions. A music therapist beginning practice in India and one in Ireland may have aspects of a definition of music therapy in common, for example. However, they may also have needs that must be met differently in terms of defining what it is they do, and how it can offer change to meet local conditions. As we will see, my research has not discovered a single overarching definition that has become widely used. The situation is one where there is a lively, rigorous diversity meeting different situations and needs.

Within this diversity, though, the development of the arts therapies within health services in the second half of the twentieth century has seen two main needs met in terms of definition.

1   One need has been for *global definitions* that fit national or international demands. This has been in response to the establishment of services and organisations functioning within national health services, or to define a broad spectrum of practice covering all the disciplines of music, art, drama and dance. This kind of definition marks the coming together of smaller groupings to form large coalitions: necessary in establishing standards of professional training and practice at a state, national or international level.
2   The second relates to smaller, more *focused definitions*. These serve the needs of particular client contexts such as forensic or educational services, or individual health centres, and even particular groups run in such settings.

By paying attention to these different levels of definition we can gain some sense both of the ways the arts therapies are seen: not only from a countrywide or international perspective, but also at a grass-roots level. This way of look-ing at definitions of the arts therapies will show how the broadest of pictures can be created and, at the opposite end of the spectrum, we will also under-stand some of the ways clients and therapists in different countries see their specific practice.

This is not to say these need to be vastly at odds with each other, but, as we will see, different things about the arts therapies show through in these vari-ous approaches to answering the same question: what are the arts therapies?

ARRIVING AT DEFINITIONS

The National Coalition of Creative Arts Therapies Associations (NCCATA) in the USA goes about answering the question with one of the broadest of definitions: the arts therapies consist of:

> Arts modalities and creative processes during intentional intervention in therapeutic, rehabilitative, community, or educational settings to foster health, communication, and expression; [they] promote the integration of physical, emotional, cognitive, and social functioning; enhance self awareness; and facilitate change.
>
> (NCCATA website)

Here are many of the themes that can be found in most of the definitions – art forms are linked to approaches to healing, with some of the intended out-comes stated. This definition tries to meet the needs of finding common ground between different art forms – it has to cover music, art, drama, dance movement and poetry, as well as serving an enormous range of health con-texts and kinds of provision. Hence it gives a sense of the overall processes at work.

Similar wide-ranging definitions come from organisations and profes-sionals who work across disciplines: music, art, drama and dance movement therapy. In some countries, such as the USA and the Netherlands, organisa-tions covering all art forms operate in parallel to others focusing on specific disciplines such as music or art therapy. In the early 1960s, for example, the Nederlandse Vereniging voor Kreatieve Therapie (Netherlands Society for Creative Therapy) was formed alongside the Netherlands Art Therapy Society (Jones, 1996: 93). YAHAT, the Israeli Association of Creative and Expressive Therapies, says simply that 'creative and expressive therapies is an overall name used to describe creative and expressive processes from the fields of art used in treating emotional, developmental and organic disorders' (YAHAT website). Another example of a broad approach is that taken by the US National Expressive Therapy Association (USNETA), founded in the 1970s. This Association focuses on what it calls 'expressive therapy' and 'expressive arts therapy' rather than the individual arts therapies (USNETA website). Here all the arts are brought together under one umbrella, their common quality described as 'expressive'. The NCCATA, by contrast, doesn't claim that all arts therapies can be included in this way; it, rather, notes connection and difference: 'Although unique and distinct from one another, the creative arts therapies share related processes and goals. Participation in all the creative arts therapies provides people with ... ways to express themselves that may not be possible through more traditional therapies' (NCCATA website 2). As we will see, this echoes the stance taken in many countries, where the arts therapies are divided into separate, but related, professions of art, music, drama or dance movement therapy.

There are arts therapists practising round the world. In different countries there are diverse levels of training and practice within the disciplines. The recognition and status of the arts therapies within health services also varies enormously. This can have a bearing on how arts therapy practice is seen and described. The range is considerable – from Brazil, for example, where music therapists have been training since the 1970s, and there were 1,500 music therapy graduates by 2003 (Smith, 2003), to Korea where, by the same date, 15 music therapists who have trained abroad were working (Kim, 2002).

One of the earliest associations of arts therapists was founded in 1950: the US National Association for Music Therapy. Fifty years later there were over 3,800 music therapists holding membership in the USA. The American Dance Therapy Association (ADTA), formed in 1966, notes that by the start of the twenty-first century its membership included over 1,200 dance movement therapists in 46 states of the USA and 29 foreign countries (ADTA website). Each of these associations have developed in response to individuals coming together and forming groups – from the smallest initial meetings of people exploring the potentials of the field to these much larger, established associations. Definitions are the outcome of these groupings negotiating with each other, and with clients and organisations who will use their services. Some have evolved their own definitions; others have adapted or adopted existing ones. One of the newest definitions created by such a grouping of individuals has emerged from Taiwan. In 2003 Taiwanese Dramatherapists have developed this definition for their use:

> Dramatherapy is an involvement in drama with the intention to facilitate growth and changes based on individual needs. Dramatherapy is deeply rooted in the therapeutic aspects of drama. Dramatherapy uses the human potential for expression. The expression here is both the process and the aim of dramatherapy. It enables the client to achieve a new relationship towards the problem or life experience.
>
> (Chang, interview, 2003)

This definition is a part of the process of creating a Dramatherapy Association for the first time in Taiwan. In interview Chih Hao Chang revealed the way in which, after reaching a definition, he and others who wish to form an association recognised by the Taiwanese government need to follow specific procedures:

> If we want to use the word 'therapy' in the title of our Association we have to find twenty doctors to be our members. If we want to call ourselves an Association, for example, The Taiwanese Association of Dramatherapy, we also have to find thirty members who have backgrounds in dramatherapy.
>
> (Chang, interview, 2003)

Here we see a snapshot of the pattern that has emerged in different countries as the arts therapies have grown. A small group of interested and trained people are gathering together to develop definitions, identities and professional governance relating to their discipline and practice.

In similar ways, different subgroups or professional groupings of arts therapists have arrived at their own descriptions. Some of these are identified by their theoretical orientation – for example 'art psychotherapy' (Wadeson, 1980). Malchiodi, for example, has written about the development of art therapy in relation to people dealing with physical illness. She defines the term '*medical* art therapy' as the 'use of expression and imagery with individuals who are physically ill, experiencing trauma to the body, or who are undergoing aggressive medical treatment such as surgery or chemotherapy' (Malchiodi, 1993: 66). Others are generated by their practice context – such as prisons or education. It's interesting to look at some of these, as they give an indication of the way in which different contexts refine the broader strokes of the national or international definitions.

A document created by the UK Standing Committee on the Arts in Prisons (SCAP), for example, says that:

> The Arts Therapies provide a radical way of using the arts as rehabilitative as opposed to occupational services for offenders. The forensic nature of our work lies in our potential to facilitate creative investigations with inmates as our clients.
>
> (SCAP, 1997: 6).

The arts therapies are talked about as a whole in the document, as well as being differentiated as art, dance movement, drama or music. These arts therapists acknowledge that whilst they share theoretical foundations, the 'specialisms' differ in the ways in which therapeutic aims are achieved. In the quote above, you can see how the idea that those within the prison system can have therapy made available to them as a specific *rehabilitative* process is focused on, and also the notion of creativity as an 'investigation'. All of these facets of the definition show how particular aspects of the arts therapies can be foregrounded to relate to a context. In this instance they are the ways in which the arts can be used to rehabilitate and to investigate issues as part of the work of a forensic setting.

One of the points I'm making is that a definition in the arts therapies shouldn't be something set in stone, that is immovable. The arts therapies – like any form connected to the arts – naturally need to evolve and change. As disciplines in the early years of their establishment within contemporary health services, we are still discovering much about what they can do and how and why they are effective. So any definitions must be still *in process* – they are developing maps that show where the disciplines have been, where they are now, and where the arts therapies are going. That is why the following sections answer the question: 'What are the arts therapies?' by taking definitions and asking *what they show us* about different contexts, ways of working and developments, rather than simply *reporting* what they say.

SETTINGS AND CONTEXTS: AN OVERVIEW

All the arts therapies work with groups and individuals. Arts therapists work on their own or in departments, in multidisciplinary teams and in a freelance capacity. The size of arts therapies groups varies: they are normally between three and twelve, though, as we will see, in some countries groups can be as large as fifty or more. All the arts therapies stress that they can be used by anyone, and are not in any way oriented towards those perceived to have talent or interest in the art form, or that referral is for those whose issues are seemingly related to the area of artistic expression. As Payne points out, a common misconception about dance movement therapy (DMT), for example, is that it is 'only for those clients with physical difficulties such as co-ordination problems; that only people with a natural talent for rhythm or movement should attend DMT' (Payne, 1992: 5).

Broadly speaking, arts therapists work in a wide variety of settings the world over. Most aspects of healthcare and educational provision have been worked in, and are documented in recorded practice. From the early days when the arts therapies were focused in areas such as mental health or learning disability, their work has expanded into most aspects of the human condition, from pre-school to work with the elderly, from medical wards to prison rehabilitation, from private practice to state provision. The American Art Therapy Association (AATA) lists an extremely diverse range of contexts: from hospitals, outpatient clinics and schools, to halfway houses and pain centres. Work has taken place with people with addictions, living with cancer, and those who have been bereaved. As this book will show, the arts therapies have proved flexible and adaptable, meeting the capacities and needs of a broad range of clients, from people with learning difficulties or attention deficit disorders, to those with mental heath problems such as psychosis or schizophrenia. The extent of practice can be limited by attitude, availability of therapists and systems of healthcare, alongside the economic and political situation. Kim (2002: 1) notes that in Korea, for example, the existing music therapists face opposition not only from sceptical and defensive professionals in related fields, but also from the effects of the economic collapse within the country, and the recoil of political instability:

> We do not have a secure well-established welfare system and our national health insurance does not cover for alternative and creative therapies. Therefore, most clients for music therapy are privately funded. Many psychiatric hospitals in Korea have some form of creative arts therapy program, especially music therapy, but social workers and nurses run most of these programs. However, gradually, institutions are opening up towards the music therapy profession more readily than ever before.
>
> (Kim, 2002: 1)

Okazaki-Sakaue reflects that in Japan the general attitude is that you need to be extremely ill to receive therapy, and that, though the need for psychiatric treatment in urban areas is increasing, psychotherapeutic approaches are not well accepted. He notes that the approach to music therapy, for example, tends towards a medical or behavioural approach, with little music-centred or psychodynamic work taking place. He says that goals tend to be group- or family-orientated, not in the service of an individual. He also refers to practice where some music therapists work with as many as 50 people in a group and call it a therapy session. Okazaki-Sakaue points to other cultural issues:

> I have found that there are also some cultural and social issues with seniority rules both in clinical practice and training. For example, children do not call their therapists by their own names, but rather as 'Sensei' (Teacher) and this does impact on aspects of the therapeutic relationship. Also grown ups are expected to control their emotions and not express them openly. This sometimes works against the typical therapeutic goal of 'promoting self-expression'.
>
> (Okazaki-Sakaue, 2003: 2)

Here we can see illustrated the way the arts therapies try not only to respond to local needs and frameworks of health, but also to some of the tensions between different attitudes and understandings. Okazaki-Sakaue is drawing our attention to some of the tension experienced between a therapeutic goal and the culture he is working within. Arts therapists such as Boston and Short would see such issues as rooted in differences between cultural concepts such as identity, the arts and change. Some of the issues described by Okazaki-Sakaue are paralleled in their definition of an Afrocentric, in contrast to a Eurocentric, position on the arts therapies. In general terms they typify the Eurocentric world view as stressing individuality, uniqueness and differences, the Afrocentric as being represented by 'groupness, sameness and communality. The values and customs are co-operation, collective responsibility and interdependence' (Boston and Short, 1998: 37). They discuss this in the context of African American clients and therapists, and the importance of art therapy recognising the impact of 'the African American heritage of the tribe, slavery, the need for practical application of therapy that acknowledges and validates the unique ethnic background of clients' (Boston and Short, 1998: 47). So, one way of seeing Okazaki-Sakaue's comments regarding the definition and the provision of arts therapies is to understand them in the context of different cultural issues within a society, concerning how therapy should be provided. Some of these are to do with fundamental areas such as views on identity, the expression of feelings and the way the need for therapeutic help is seen. Rackstraw speaks of how she organised her art therapy practice according to the specific needs of settlements and townships outside Cape Town, South Africa. There are no art therapy posts, and work is funded by Rackstraw's own efforts. Her work includes practice focusing on the after-effects of *apartheid*, people dealing with rape, abuse or HIV:

> I work in various school settings, chosen because they are safe and accessible for the children, in townships or informal settings outside of Cape Town. When I work with adults this will usually be in a community clinic or hall. I seek out the client group by getting referrals from various organisations and agencies . . . these communities are both marginalised and poor . . . often this will be their first experience of a service which offers psychological support.
>
> (Interview with Rackstraw, 2003)

Given that the arts therapies are now practised in many different cultural arenas, as these illustrations show, it is unlikely that one definition will satisfy the range of needs such contexts require. The following sections try to include definitions from a number of contexts in recognition of this diversity.

Arts therapists such as Boston and Short (1998), and others (Clarkson, 2002b), have pointed out that the connections between issues concerning spiritual or religious matters are often left out of considerations to do with client and therapist experiences within therapy:

> many agencies are very clear to keep religion out of sessions, out of schools and out of government as much as possible. In the African American community, religion is prevalent and it is just as prevalent in the art work as religious symbols and topics often surface spontaneously in art therapy sessions.
>
> (Boston and Short, 1998: 46)

They echo comments saying that clinical work is flawed if spiritual matters are not addressed. Clarkson argues for the importance of acknowledging the 'spiritual, mystical, transcendent or numinous' aspects of living and areas within the therapeutic relationship. She adds that this is especially important as 'there can be no multicultural psychotherapy without some kind of respectful relationship with the religious and spiritual practices in which many, if not most, cultures are steeped' (Clarkson, 2002b: 8–9). For the arts therapies these are especially important points to hear, given the relationships between art, music, drama and dance and many forms of religious experience and practices. The arts therapeutic relationship, some would argue, is also connected to the ways in which participation in arts processes such as dancing, or making music, may connect to spiritual matters for client and therapist alike.

DIFFERENT MODALITIES

Whilst arts therapists practise in similar settings, there can be differences in emphasis across the different modalities. Within the UK, for example, Karkou's small-scale research seems to indicate that for dance movement therapists educational settings are the main working environment, whereas for music therapists they are the second most common, and for dramatherapists the third. There are proportionally far more therapists from these disciplines practising in education than art therapists (Karkou, 1999: 64). The main employment setting for art therapists was within health services.

Ways of working within settings also have many similarities, but also some differences. Again, Karkou points out that from a small sample of arts therapists within education only 50 per cent of art therapists worked with groups compared to 80.6 per cent and 87.5 per cent for music therapy and dance movement therapy and 100 per cent for dramatherapy (Karkou, 1999: 66).

So, whilst contexts are broadly similar across disciplines, there may often be specific differences in the extent and nature of some of the ways arts therapists practise according to their modality. As we will see, these different concepts can produce different emphases within definitions.

What, then, are the differences and similarities between the different arts therapies? The next chapters explore definitions and ways of working in each of the arts therapies.

3   What is art therapy?

DEFINITIONS

The American Art Therapy Association roots its approach to art therapy in a belief that the creative process involved in the making of art is healing and life-enhancing (AATA website). It defines art therapy as:

> The therapeutic use of art making, within a professional relationship, by people who experience illness, trauma, or challenges in living, and by people who seek personal development. Through creating art and reflecting on the art products and processes, people can increase awareness of self and others, cope with symptoms, stress and traumatic experiences; enhance cognitive abilities; and enjoy the life affirming pleasures of making art.
>
> (AATA website)

The PROFAC Centre de Psychologie Appliquée defines art therapy as follows: 'L'Art-thérapie est une methode basée sur l'expression artistique. Elle n'exclut pas le langage oral mais offre d'autres voies en rapport avec ce que Michel Ledoux appelle "Les souvenirs du corps". La matière pictoriale, la danse, le chant, l'argile . . . sont considérés comme autant d'objets médiateurs dans la relation thérapeutique. L'Art thérapie s'appuie sur une mobilisation des capacités créatrices individuelles et sur la dynamique créative des groupes' (PROFAC website). [Art therapy is a method based on artistic expression. While it does not exclude oral language, it offers other ways to gain rapport through what Michel Ledoux calls 'body memories'. Images, dance, song, clay . . . are all considered as so many mediatory objects in the therapeutic relationship. Arts therapy depends on mobilisation of both the creative capacity of the individual and the creative dynamics of the group.]

Art therapy has changed significantly since its early beginnings. Within the UK, for example, there is a strong influence from psychoanalytic and psycho-dynamic theory in contemporary practice (Schaverien, 1992; Karkou, 1999). This is mirrored by the Art Therapy Association of Colorado (ATAC), which offers as its definition, 'art therapy brings together psychotherapy and the healing qualities of the creative process' (ATAC website) and the Canadian Art Therapy Association (CATA) definition, which allies art directly to psychotherapy: 'Art Therapy combines visual art and psychotherapy in a creative process using the created image as a foundation for self-exploration and understanding' (CATA website).

The Canadian Association emphasises the way thoughts and feelings often reach expression in images rather than words, and places this process within a psychotherapeutic model of change where 'feelings and inner conflicts can be projected into visual form. In the creative act, conflict is re-experienced, resolved and integrated' (CATA website). Here, then, the emphasis is on the notion of inner conflict and on art as a projective means through which re-experiencing is connected to resolution. Differences in the definition and practice of art therapy exist both within and between individual countries. In German the general term in use is similar to the English 'art therapy': *Kunsttherapie*; but there are other terms used, such as *Maltherapie* (painting therapy), *Kunstpsychotherapie* (art psychotherapy) and *Therapie durch Medien* (therapy through media) (Herrmann, 2000: 19). These indicate different approaches or ideas about change within the overall discipline.

The definition of the British Association of Art Therapists (BAAT) reflects a broader and more evenly inclusive approach to defining art therapy. It first stresses the use of materials, the process and the relationship, giving no immediate allegiance to a particular model such as the psychodynamic or cognitive: 'Art therapy is the use of art materials for self expression and reflection in the presence of a trained art therapist.' After declaring that clients do not need to have experience or skill in art, it makes a statement that marks a difference from art therapy practice which emphasises the diagnostic use of imagery:

> The art therapist is not primarily concerned with making an aesthetic or diagnostic assessment of the client's image. The overall aim of its practitioners is to enable a client to effect change and growth on a personal level through the use of art materials in a safe and facilitating environment.
>
> (BAAT website)

The relationship between therapist and client is treated as central, and the difference from other psychological therapies is cited in terms of its being a 'three-way process', involving the crucial presence of the image or artefact. From early theory and practice, through to contemporary attitudes, this triad has been a developing theme in defining art therapy. In 1958, for example, Naumburg described work in this way: 'The images produced are a form of communication between patient and therapist; [they] constitute symbolic speech' (Naumburg, 1958: 561).

The art in art therapy is often defined in a broad way: 'this activity ranges from the child scribbling to express himself, to . . . working with clay to the graphic painting by a woman deeply depressed' (Dalley, 1984: 97). The art materials can vary widely depending on factors such as artistic choice or availability. Waller, for example, makes the point that within the introduction of art therapy practice in Bulgarian contexts, 'traditional' art materials were both scarce and expensive: 'Instead, scrap material, such as old boxes, magazines, string, wool, old toys and clothes, were assembled and decorators' shops were located where useful oxides, tints, glues, large tubs of emulsion paints and brushes etc. provided the basic source of colour' (Waller, 1995: 230). Malchiodi and McLeod have written on the uses of new technology, of computers, software and the creation of a 'virtual art studio' (McLeod, 1999; Malchiodi, 2000). The art form within art therapy is still developing, creating and responding to new cultural forms.

AIMS OF ART THERAPY

The diversity of definition is reflected in the variety of ways that aims are formulated. As with the definition of what art therapy is, aims can vary from being related to a specific context of practice, through to a much broader, national perspective. An example of aims specific to a setting are those defined by Wald in relation to her work in a rehabilitation context with clients who have had strokes. She says that art therapy goals for 'stroke survivors' include:

- improving the patient's awareness of individual problems
- teaching compensatory techniques to deal with deficits
- improving functional, manipulative ability
- assisting the patient to mourn, grieve and accept change in body image
- supporting a patient's efforts to work through their emotional reaction to their losses and limitations
- providing a non-verbal visual means of communication, self-expression and interpersonal exchange

(from Wald, 1999: 36)

The aims above are edited down from the list Wald devised. These few, however, illustrate the wide range of attention given, including areas relating to physical rehabilitation, through to the exploration of feelings, perceptions and relationships. They show an awareness of, and a response to, the particular therapeutic needs of a specific client population.

Members of CATA talk of the broad, general aims of art therapy as using 'simple materials' to help individuals in the following ways:

- Expressing feelings too difficult to talk about
- Increasing self-esteem and confidence
- Developing healthy coping skills
- Identifying feelings and blocks to emotional expression and growth
- Providing an avenue for communication
- Making verbal expression more accessible

(Art Therapy in Canada Homepage, website 1)

Such general aims emphasise the capacity of art in therapy to express and communicate feelings, to work with, and through, areas of difficulty and to facilitate reflection and discussion. Art therapist Cameron talks about her work in conflict resolution with people who were homeless in New York City in a way that illustrates these aims.

She sees homelessness in a broad context including the breakdown of the family, a lack of skills or education, unemployment, despair and the availability of guns and drugs. These 'all contribute to the inability to sustain a home' (Cameron, 1996: 183). The therapy took place in a setting working with 'street homeless' who have been living in parks and subways. Art therapy was part of a broad arts programme within a structured rehabilitation process. The rehabilitation recognised that for many of the clients homelessness, trauma and violence were interconnected, and that after basic needs such as food and shelter were addressed, there was a need for 'healing, insight, creative problem solving and conflict resolution' (Cameron, 1996: 185).

She notes that for some of the participants the traumatic experiences meant that they could not risk failure, and had developed what she calls 'self-destructive ways of coping'. One of the facets of this noted by her was a common pattern of conflict in their relationships with others. The aims of the art therapy were to relieve stress, to teach participants to express themselves through different art media, and to 'process' problems, violent reactions and self-destructive thoughts. The group involved ten participants, lasted for six weeks and was funded under a 'Stop the Violence' initiative. The practice involved a variety of ways of working and included directive use of image making. Cameron, for example, says that she wanted to find out what 'Stop the Violence' meant to each participant:

> In two sessions I expressly asked them to depict a violent episode, and I also reminded them intermittently to include any altercations from their week. However, I always left the first piece of each session open in order to find out how they were being affected, if at all, by this art experience, what their real issues were, and how they personally related to violence ... This was followed by a stress reduction exercise, then they painted

another piece and the group ended with sharing and discussion. At this point we noted the differences between the pieces, how their states of mind related to their everyday living, and their relationship with themselves and others.

(Cameron, 1996: 188)

The close of the sessions was marked by an exhibition of work, along with the final statements of the participants, written on cards by one of the group. Comments included:

It has opened up a channel of my life that is inspirational.

Painting made me aware of options that I couldn't see when I started to paint.

I felt the art class put me in control of my situation without criticism. I am always being viewed and judged, but this time I was doing the viewing . . . I got a chance to explore my ideas and what I feel.

(Cameron, 1996: 204–5)

If we look at the aims of the work they can be summarised as relating to a combination of the art therapy having an effect on behaviour, offering opportunities for insight and reflection, and teaching clients art language and processes. The client feedback seems to indicate that their experiences reflect these aims, in that they write of being given access to painting, and that this is linked to reflecting on their lives, and to being inspired.

The ways Cameron works include sessions in which she gives a structure – there is painting followed by stress-reduction exercises, followed by more painting and reflection. She also introduces activities with an instruction on the broad topic, or theme, of painting activity, in order to assist clients and herself focus on the area for which the group is created through funding and identified need.

Here the artwork produced by clients is created by a given direction. The properties of art making are seen as relevant to therapy as a way of enabling clients to access aspects of their experience, and to facilitate change. Difficulties within the clients' lives are focused on by the therapist – first through the nature of referral and the brief for the group, and secondly through a direct invitation to explore material on a given theme through image making. Images produced are reflected on, by the individual who made them, and by others within the group – both therapist and clients. There is seen to be value in the creation of images as a way of exploring difficulties, the process of being within a group, the relationship with a therapist, along with opportunities for reflection on the connections between images, the clients' life experiences and change. It's interesting to note the way one of the clients quoted describes the sessions as an art 'class'. This is not uncommon within the arts therapies, in that it might indicate a client trying to describe the work in the more familiar terms of teaching. Perhaps it was also an indication of the client feeling more at ease with the notion of attending sessions orientated towards learning art skills rather then personal exploration. Perhaps, also, the approach taken by Cameron felt akin to a directive approach that teaching can take in classes, rather than the more open-ended approaches of non-directive art therapy where subjects, activities and reflection are much less likely to be provided by the therapist. The work culminates in an exhibition of words and images. Though Cameron doesn't comment on the therapeutic purpose of this, other art therapists have pointed to exhibiting work as an option within art therapy.

Some art therapists see aims and ways of working rather differently from this therapeutic approach. They would argue that if the therapist structures the art therapy session by deciding factors such as when and for how long the individual, or group, should paint, the therapist is in danger of being 'too controlling and thus interfering with the transference' (Skaife, 1990: 238). Skaife gives an example of a different approach in a group art therapy context. The description comes from the fifteenth month of the group. There were six members and one member of the group was absent, some were late:

> R told S, as the last person in the group to know, that he was leaving. He gave his reasons as financial; his changing circumstances meant that he could no longer afford both group and individual therapy. He was keeping on the individual therapy as he needed some support and he felt the group could not offer enough of it. E asked if he was disappointed in the group. R said that he was mainly disappointed in himself, but he was disappointed that there was not more painting in the group and he reminded everyone that he had said this all along. E said that she too would like to do more painting and that she had joined the group so that she would have the opportunity to express herself by painting. There was a general moan about the difficulty of getting down to painting. I said that I felt there was a wish in the group that I should tell them when to paint and to offer more structure to the group. Perhaps this seemed even more frustrating since I had made a rule about B and S not meeting before the group. I wondered if the recent absenteeism and lateness might be a means of getting me to lay down more rules. B said he'd hate me to be like a mum telling them what to do. H contradicted my interpretation and said that the lateness and absenteeism must be to do with R leaving . . .
>
> They returned to the subject of painting. H said that I should be telling them 'how to do it'. What was the point of my being in the group? They could have anyone in off the street if they had to do it themselves. H said that she felt I was withholding my special knowledge.
>
> (Skaife, 1990: 240)

The group continue to discuss painting and not painting. Issues are raised – such as the time after painting being valuable to talk, how frustrating some members find not having time to discuss all the images. Skaife reminds them that it is possible to return to images the following week, and refers back to the previous week's creation of images of biting mouths. One of the clients says that she is afraid to paint because she fears the chaos, and it makes her feel that she understands nothing. The therapist notes to the group that each member had said that they wanted to paint, and that some had suggested painting, but that no one seemed to want to follow anyone's lead. She offers an interpretation that this might be due to some competitiveness in the group, perhaps concerning envy if one person's idea is taken up. A suggestion comes from the group, B saying that he didn't want to steal H's idea, and supports the idea of a group painting. The clients go about this:

> They set to and painted with lots of energy . . . They were very aware of each other . . . B, although he started painting boldly in his own space, soon left it and was merged with the others. There was lots of red paint going on and they kept painting over each other's work. At first S appeared to be the only one painting figuratively. R looked very excited and was playing with black paint. H kept in her own space and painted a skyscape and a Scottie dog on it.
>
> All of a sudden they stopped as if they were afraid of the language of the paint taking over. E complained that her crocodile had been sub-merged: its biting jaws had been painted over by R, who said he had not been aware that it was a crocodile.
>
> (Skaife, 1990: 241)

Skaife shows here how, by not taking a directive approach to starting or stopping painting, or giving subject matter to the group directly, areas of group and individual process open up. Themes such as group members caring about others' opinions and issues of power are engendered and explored. These come to the fore, 'by my taking an analytic role rather than a leadership role' (Skaife, 1990: 242). The area is seen by her as being to do with clients giving up dependent patterns and taking on power. Themes are identified by Skaife as including a challenge to the therapist, being directly angry, whilst at the same time being afraid of abandonment and being left to the aggressive impulses of one another. Isolation and merging are seen as possible themes within the group. Skaife describes S's voiced fears of being isolated in the picture making, and that no one would come near her; she created an image that protected her face with surrounded crosses. Skaife notes, 'Merging with others, while on the one hand relieving one from feelings of isolation, also involves a loss of individuality' (Skaife, 1990: 243). She argues that by allowing the group to make decisions on how and when they should change activity, issues such as the use of time, being alone and being part of the group are brought into focus. The group's experience of its own process becomes highlighted through this way of working with 'a dual emphasis on the self determination of group members, since this is expressed not only through their paintings but also through the form that the group takes' (Skaife, 1990: 244).

In both examples we can see illustrated one of the defining characteristics of art therapy: the relationship between client, therapist and art object or process. Evans (1982) bases his description of art therapy on this:

> The art process and the way it is used in therapy is central and an essence of the practice. For in my definition of art therapy the art process is engaged with in the presence of, and to some extent, in response to . . . the therapist. This takes outside of art therapy that which some have called 'spontaneous art therapy', where individuals have discovered art/image making and found it therapeutic without the intermediary of the therapist . . . It also excludes . . . persons bringing imagery into [psycho] therapy for analysis and comment.
>
> (Evans, 1982: 114–15)

The issue of directive compared to non-directive approaches is one that receives a good deal of attention in art therapy writing and definition. Practitioners vary – some therapists working mainly with one or the other approach, whilst others modify their practice within sessions, or within the process of work, depending on the needs of the client or client group. For example, Murphy (1998) conducted research through questionnaires with British art therapists working with sexually abused children and young people. She was exploring, in part, the methods and approaches used. Of the therapists responding, most were engaged in individual work, with a quarter also offering groupwork. Of these therapists, 60 per cent said that they worked in a way that was described as non-directive. The rationale behind working non-directively was that the sexually abused client needed to feel in control, and that direction from the therapist could feel intrusive. In addition, respondents said that clients making their own choices of art materials developed self-confidence and taking control, and formed part of the therapeutic process. Others have said that a directive approach can help in addressing issues. Murphy refers to Hagood, who 'warns that unless some directive therapy is used, issues concerning sexual abuse tend to be avoided' (Hagood, 1992, in Murphy 1998: 11). Prokofiev (1998) also says that the art therapist needs to be more active and to provide more structure when working with some children because this enables a greater feeling of safety (Prokofiev, 1997). Here we can see the ways in which differences in approach are understood to offer clients different opportunities. The art therapist's role, the therapy space and the art form are not offered to the client from one approach only.

Some have noted a difference in emphasis within much art therapy practised within the USA compared to that within the UK. Woddis (1986, in

Gilroy and Skaife, 1997: 57) noted what she thought was an orientation towards a pragmatic, problem-solving approach in the USA, with a tendency to use imagery for diagnostic purposes. She, along with Gilroy and Skaife a decade later, compares this to the model they say is predominant in the UK which is rooted in 'the making of images within the context of a dynamically-orientated relationship' (Gilroy and Skaife, 1997: 58). They locate this difference as being rooted in the US healthcare system and its influence in the training of US art therapists. They see art therapy in the USA as being used to elicit material for diagnosis, prognosis and treatment on the one hand while, on the other, art is seen as inherently healing 'via a shamanic, spiritual and soul-making, studio-based tradition' (Gilroy and Skaife, 1997: 58).

AATA sees its members' approach to practice as wide-ranging. It says that art therapy utilises art media, images, the creative art process and client responses to products as reflections of an individual's development, abilities, personality, interests, concerns and conflicts. It says the knowledge underpinning the work is rooted in a variety of sources and includes developmental and psychological theory, educational, psychodynamic, cognitive, and transpersonal perspectives. It states the broad aims as 'reconciling emotional conflicts, fostering self awareness, developing social skills, managing behaviour, solving problems, reducing anxiety, aiding reality orientation and increasing self esteem' (AATA website FAQs).

Bromberg's survey of 386 members of the AATA in the New York area seems to echo much of the Association's recognition of diverse approaches and ways of working. The survey asked about practice with cancer patients. Part of it looked at the 'theoretical approaches' of art therapy practitioners in this area of work. It revealed that no one theoretical approach was preferred. The diversity of theoretical approach indicated gestalt, behavioural, cognitive, psychoanalytic, Jungian and object relations being cited at similar levels (Bromberg, 2000). This variety of orientation in practice is echoed in BAAT's description of an art therapist. This refers to key areas of the training of an art therapist as including the psychology of mark making and symbolism, non-verbal communication, a psychotherapeutic understanding of child development and family dynamics. The art therapists draw on their knowledge of these diverse areas to enable change for the people they work with.

Lanham captures something present in all these definitions when he argues that the products of art therapy, though they may not be seen in public, are as *essential* as any 'great' work of art in art galleries:

> They may, even when kept in a drawer, have a real life and meaning for the person or group involved in their creation and through this make a greater contribution to our society ... this broader concept of art, including all creative utterances by all people, is not a new one. It is only within the development of Western civilisation, where the artist has

achieved the status of myth in his own right, that the art of the unknown
or anonymous person has been ignored by society.

(Lanham, 1989: 21)

The examples we've looked at have shown us that art therapy can enable this
'broader concept of art' and the relationship between client, art process and
product and therapist to develop in many different ways in diverse settings.
Aldridge gives an interesting example of this flexibility and ingenuity in terms
of art therapy occurring in a sink.

Tom, aged seven, was attending an art therapy group as part of social
services care and is described as living in a situation of poverty. He:

> liked to paint the large sink in the art room with his brown mixture
> made of all the paints mixed together. He respected the boundary
> imposed of only painting on the tiles and sink. He mixed the colours with
> the group and then painted the sink; when he'd finished he'd name the
> sink according to the colour – they were called shit, vomit, diarrhoea,
> piss, sick. These sinks took nearly three quarters of an hour to complete
> as they were very carefully painted so that none of the white showed
> through.

(Aldridge, 1998: 2–9)

We can say, then, that the ways in which art therapy occurs varies according
to the client/patient group or individual, the context and the therapist.

This recognises the reality of the working situations of many arts therapists: they may work in settings with different orientations, whose clients may
be best served by a particular approach. Some art therapists work within a
particular therapeutic framework, whilst others, as the survey showed, maintain a dialogue with different theories. However, as the BAAT definition
recognises, a common denominator is that there is always an emphasis on
creativity and the therapeutic relationship.

4 What is music therapy?

DEFINITIONS

Blair points out a number of different aspects of music that are relevant to music therapy. He describes one of these elements as music's impact on 'the affective sides of our minds' (Blair, 1987: 5). By this he means the ways music can affect mood, how it can relieve or create tension, for example. Another quality concerns music's capacity to express 'instincts' and 'complexes' for the maker or composer, and also for the listener. Music as a form is open to the individual's own interpretation and it can powerfully evoke 'imagery of many kinds – realistic, fanciful or even hallucinatory – which may enable him temporarily to escape from the unacceptable world or reality' (Blair, 1987: 5). Music also can be associated with important experiences in someone's life, including ones that may have been forgotten or repressed. Music can revive such memories, whether remembered or hidden. He refers to music's association with community, and with its role in affecting relationships between people. In many societies music is associated with its capacity to 'foster feelings of mysticism and reverence mak[ing] its use almost indispensable in religious rituals of all kinds' (Blair, 1987: 5). He sees it as an important 'agent' of non-verbal communication and interpersonal relationships. In this respect he highlights, in particular, its capacity to arouse empathy between people and to increase self-esteem and enhance social contact.

These qualities of music would be recognised by many clients and professionals involved with music therapy. They are touched on in the different definitions and uses of music in therapy. Priestley's definition is simple and wide-ranging: 'Music therapy is an art, and as such, a very personal and creative form of work' (Priestley, 1975: 15). He says that there are three main activities in music therapy: musical sound and expression on instruments or with the voice, listening to music with the therapist, and movement to music.

This broad range of activity is reflected in several definitions. For example the New Zealand Society for Music Therapy (NZSMT) says that music therapy is 'the planned use of music to assist the healing and personal growth of people with identified emotional, intellectual, physical or social needs'. The Society emphasises the potentials of music within a therapeutic relationship to develop communication, extend language and intellectual development, and to give support in times of emotional challenge. The range extends from music's role in rehabilitation, to improving movement and physical coordination, through to music's capacity in therapy to assist memory, imagination and thought, and to enhance spiritual and cultural identity (NZSMT website). The Florida Association for Music Therapy (FAMT) echoes many of these ideas in its definition of 'music and music activities both in treatment programs which address the physical, emotional, social and cognitive challenges faced by children and adults with diverse illnesses and special needs, and in wellness programs which promote the maintenance of good health in the general population' (FAMT website).

The American Music Therapy Association (AMTA) takes a similar, broad approach, saying that music therapists design music sessions for individuals and groups using music improvisation, receptive music listening, song writing, lyric discussion, music and imagery, music performance and learning through music (AMTA website).

The British Society for Music Therapy (BSMT) foregrounds the therapeutic relationship, contrasting with these explanations that focus on outcomes and method:

> There are different approaches to the use of music therapy. Depending on the needs of the client and the orientation of the therapist, different aspects of the work may be emphasised. Fundamental to all approaches, however, is the development of a relationship between the client and the therapist. Music making forms the basis for communication in the relationship.
>
> (BSMT website)

The UK Standing Committee of Arts Therapies Professions (SCATP) also emphasises relationship, stating that music therapy:

> provides a framework for the building of a mutual relationship between client and therapist through which the music therapist will communicate with the client, finding a musical idiom . . . [that] . . . enables change to occur . . . By using skilled and creative musicianship in a clinical setting, the therapist seeks to establish an interaction – a shared musical experience – leading to the pursuit of therapeutic goals.
>
> (SCATP, 1989: 6)

The Ambito de Docencia e Investigación en Musicterapia (ADIMU) cooperating with the Department of Music Therapy at the Centro Regional de Salud Mental (University Psychiatric Hospital) of Rosario, Argentina, emphasises communication, seeing music therapy as making use of the sounds of conventional and non-conventional musical instruments, of everyday materials, the human voice and sounds made through the body along with movement and body language, 'as a non-verbal means of communication in the therapeutic process, in which all kinds of sounds and noises, even pre-natal acoustic experiences are taken into consideration' (Centre for Training and Research in Music Therapy, ADIMU website). Their approach to music therapy is rooted in the ideas that each individual presents themselves according to their current 'mental tempo', and that this can be connected to their pre-natal, early childhood, family, social and cultural background. It is also linked to the idea that musical instruments are 'transitional objects' and enhance both communication and process within therapy 'without triggering fright or a stress situation in the client' (ADIMU website).

Practitioners such as Newham have focused upon the voice and therapy. Here, the voice is seen as an expression of 'who we are and how we feel . . . by transforming and enhancing the way we sound, we can transform and enhance the way we perceive our self' (Newham, 1997; 1999). Frohne-Hagemann (1998) talks about work with women in East Berlin based in the ways in which the emotional meaning of experiences, events and memories are connected with music in the client's life. Music was used as a stimulus to reflection and verbal discussion, but also to conduct improvisations seen as therapeutic in communicating and working with client experiences.

All these potentials are seen to be available to anyone, irrespective of musical skill. Wigram echoes Payne's earlier point about dance movement therapy, as he notes that it is not uncommon for people to assume that musical ability is necessary for referral to music therapy: 'some people may still think they are referring someone to music therapy for musical activities, development of musical skills, or just to make them happy' (Wigram, 2002: 13). The capacity to make music is one that is assumed to be a potential in *anyone*, and the ways in which music can feature in their therapy can reflect a broad variety of therapeutic needs and aims. Participation need not be connected to any perceived inclination to be able to create music.

AIMS OF MUSIC THERAPY

What kinds of aims does music therapy have? These vary widely, as we have seen with art therapy, but here are illustrations from Japan, Northern Ireland and Australia, which also draw on interviews with music therapists by Skewes (2002) in New York to illustrate something of the ways in which music therapy aims are seen.

Music therapy is cited, for example, as being used to help alleviate pain in conjunction with anaesthesia or pain medication, in counteracting depression, in promoting movement in rehabilitation settings, to stimulate intellectual, social or emotional functioning and memory, to strengthen communication and coordination, to explore personal feelings and to resolve conflicts (Bunt, 1997).

The Mostar Music Centre (MMC) cites the aims of music therapy as being to engage individuals in growth, development and behavioural change, and to transfer musical and non-musical skills to other aspects of their lives. They stress the potential for music to help bring people from isolation into active engagement with their world. They say that music therapy aims to:

- facilitate creative expression in people who are either non-verbal or who have deficits in communication skills
- provide the opportunity for experiences that can open the way for and motivate learning in all domains of functioning
- create the opportunity for positive, successful and pleasurable social experiences not otherwise available to them
- develop awareness of self, others and environment and improve functioning on all levels, enhancing well-being and fostering independent living

Here we can see an emphasis on enabling communication, providing reparative or motivating experiences, and increasing functioning or awareness. These aims are orientated towards well-being, contact and independence. It's interesting that the language and process of music seems absent here; the emphasis is on the language of behavioural change (MMC website).

Aims vary from those that focus on music's relationship with physiological change, to those relating to the capacity Blair speaks of in terms of music's effect on relationships, and to those concerning processes relating to exploring emotions, memories and personal experiences from the present or past.

Tateno and Ikuko (1982) describe work starting in 1970 in Japan using the potential of singing and whistling in conjunction with breathing exercises. It aimed to relieve the physical symptoms for children with asthma. This was developed into work using singing, and taped music to help children develop their breathing and response to respiratory attacks (Tateno and Ikuko, 1982: 2–10). Okazaki-Sakaue makes a general point about this perspective: he states that the approaches within Japan emphasise medical/ biological and behavioural aspects of practice, with little evidence of what he calls psychodynamic or music-centred approaches (Okazaki-Sakaue, 2003: 2).

Cosgriff, working in Northern Ireland with people with Parkinsonism, collaborated with a consultant neurologist and a physiotherapist. Parkinsonism is cited as resulting in neurophysiological disturbances such as muscular rigidity and tremor, facial immobility, difficulties in moving and walking, and restlessness. Music therapy aimed to assess the effect of music on walking, movement, tremor and speech. It was observed that music provided motivation and rhythmic stimulus to initiate movement, increase mobility and assist in the control of voluntary movements. The therapy also aimed to use

music to induce a state of relaxation that could reduce involuntary movements and permit increased control of voluntary movement (Cosgriff, 1986:
14). Meetings lasted for two hours over a number of weeks. Improvised piano
music along with guided imagery was used. A series of movements for upper
limb functioning, standing, balancing, turning and dancing was used along
with group singing and the use of percussive instruments. It was found that
'group dynamics and the use of instruments promoted activity beyond many
people's described capabilities. Whilst playing percussion instruments all the
participants were able to extend upper limb function considerably'. Group
members used music outside the session to accompany activities – having
discovered that music seemed to assist them. Playing music whilst shaving, for
example, impeded 'freezing' (Cosgriff, 1986: 17). The emphasis of this work
is on behavioural, physical effect.

Australian music therapist Dawes (1987) talks about music therapy in a
way that encompasses the wider range of aims spoken of earlier by Blair and
Bunt. Her work encompasses goals that relate to physical, intellectual and
psychosocial functioning. She says that the aims particularly try to address
the needs of clients who would 'benefit from an alternative approach in counselling, involving increased opportunities for non-verbal expression of
emotional responses to their life situation' (Dawes, 1987: 4). This is linked to
three distinct approaches to counselling-orientated music therapy, environmental music and activity-orientated music therapy. Environmental music
aims to influence and enhance the environment of the clients. She cites a
series of tapes created by the music therapist to assist in the reduction of
'general agitation and choreic movements' (Dawes, 1987: 4).

The aims of the activity-orientated music therapy are to improve and
maintain physical, intellectual and psychosocial functioning. The emphasis
here is on non-verbal and verbal communication, or cognitive skills such as
memory, concentration, relaxation and social interaction. The therapy might
involve listening to music, singing or musical games and activities. One such
example is conducted by a music therapist and a physiotherapist. The music
therapist provides improvised music on a piano and piano-accordion 'to
support the dynamics of movement and to create an appropriate atmosphere.
The music is designed to elicit individual responses from members of
the group and the essence of the movement generated by one person (in
particular activities) for the group to take up' (Dawes, 1987: 8).

The aim of the counselling-orientated music therapy is to 'improve/
maintain levels of psychosocial functioning' (1987: 4), emphasising communication, self-expression and self-esteem in work with individuals and
groups. One of the examples of this she gives is for people who are sustaining
loss of physical and intellectual capacities, loss of a job or spouse, or a
deterioration of relationships with friends, family members and familiar or
meaningful activities. A common phenomenon is the loss and decreasing
ability to communicate verbally – areas such as the client's emotional
response to their life situation.

In group therapy within her practice, a typical session might consist of an activity encouraging group members to identify with one another, and to create a supportive atmosphere. This might be an opening song chosen by the group, or a physical warm-up to music with a strong rhythm. After this, the structure is relatively free form – songs might be introduced by the group or by an individual. Dawes says that the choice of song reflects the group or individual's emotional state. Emotions and issues raised by songs – for example, by lyrics – are discussed. An example of this might be the ending of relationships. The choice of song material might then be directed by the therapist to encourage participants to analyse their response to issues raised. Later sessions tended to have a larger component of improvisational music. This is seen to express emotion non-verbally; the therapist may offer interpretations of the music. It is stressed that interpretations are suggestions, and can be accepted or rejected:

> Music is used as a catalyst for discussion and emotional out-pouring; a vehicle for emotional expression . . . Sessions tend to follow a pattern of confrontation, followed by reflection, then recreation . . . expressed by music. Comments by members of such groups have indicated that they find the atmosphere of these sessions makes it easier to 'share together', and that they can participate on differing individual levels both verbally and non-verbally.
>
> (Dawes, 1987: 6).

Music therapy group improvisation is described by Skewes (2002) as 'a powerful tool for working with groups of clients who do not communicate successfully using verbal means' and for 'gaining insight into self and their relationships with others' (Skewes, 2002: 46). She interviewed nine music therapists in New York. Some of the aims behind the ways of working in New York mirror the examples from Japan, Northern Ireland and Australia. Group improvisation in music was seen by the New York therapists to encourage people to express themselves freely and spontaneously, to create interaction and to result in a unique manner of interacting with other group members. This was seen to allow members to discover new aspects of themselves, and to express something of themselves musically that might be new and surprising. Participants could use musical improvisation, and the relationship it created with others, to role-rehearse new behaviours within the group. Music here is seen to provide an opportunity to do and experience different things. As with Blair's comments on evoking 'instincts' or 'complexes', the therapists say that within music making it is possible to use the momentum of the group sound to move through a range of emotional states and feelings, and to achieve benefit in acknowledging and expressing these aspects of the self. Making music is seen as an expression of the self, and this individual self-expression as an important aspect of music therapy (Skewes, 2002: 49–50). The awareness of the connections between the client's sense of self, the music and the relationship with the therapist enhances the possibility of learning and growing from experience. The therapists observed that 'where words are specific and exact, music offers the opportunity to express abstract ideas and amorphous feelings', and can help express things that 'have not been worked out yet' (Skewes, 2002: 49).

What do these definitions tell us? The examples and descriptions assert that music can offer safety because of its complementarity to words; it can contain and express powerful feelings; music can link to spiritual matters, the 'transpersonal world of the soul' (Skewes, 2002: 49). Music has its own meaning and relationship to feelings: fluidity between physical, emotional and cognitive can be aimed for and achieved. It allows participants to live in the moment and to allow permissions outside their normal experience of themselves. In focus group activity relating to Bunt, Burns and Turton's work, clients gave feedback on their experiences of music therapy. It reflected many of the key themes this review has touched on. It included comments that changes of mood within music being listened to had a 'knock-on' effect both emotionally and physically; that playing music enabled people to feel more confident, fresher after the experience. They also said that playing was powerful, energising and releasing for some, relaxing for other group members, and that participating with others created positive effects, helping people to sense what others were feeling and thinking (Bunt *et al.*, 2000: 67).

5   What is dramatherapy?

DEFINITIONS

Casson's research looked at dramatherapy with clients with mental health problems who were encountering auditory hallucinations, and who had a variety of diagnoses including schizophrenia and paranoid schizophrenia. They were asked about their opinions of their ongoing dramatherapy work. Their comments included:

> *Cheryll:*   It's active, fun, motivating – when you're down, or have low self-esteem it's uplifting and brings you out of your shell.

> *Dave:* The great thing about these groups . . . is that you are free to be what you want – an adult, a child, thoughtful, flippant, sad, happy, you have freedom gained from shared and directed trust to be anything . . . I haven't played since a small child feeling intimidated, scared, guilty; responsible and alone . . . if voices are stress related then by alleviating the stress as happens in the group, then it's very useful . . . one of the problems with medication is that it flattens your emotions; it induces a tranquillity of sorts but this is more like a numbness or hollow feeling . . . writing, painting or John Casson's dramatherapy group are important to maintain your sense of self as a human being and to realise that emotions can be expressed in a positive way without having to suppress everything and resulting in even more emotional flattening and long term psycho-logical illness . . .

> *Gloria:* Only when I started dramatherapy was I able to state how I felt . . . [dramatherapy] helps you to do the healing yourself, to be instrumental in helping yourself, empowering rather than just taking medication.
>
> (Casson, 2001: 23–4)

Many of these clients stress the active, physically participatory nature of the therapy as being one of the key aspects they feel to have been important in change for them. This is echoed, in part, in the US National Association for

Drama Therapy's (NADT) description of dramatherapy as an active, experiential approach:

Dramatherapy facilitates the client to:

- tell his/her story
- solve problems
- set goals
- express feelings appropriately
- achieve catharsis
- extend the depth and breadth of inner experience
- improve interpersonal skills and relationships
- strengthen the ability to perform personal life roles while increasing flexibility between roles

(NADT website)

Its broad definition sees dramatherapy as working towards symptom relief, emotional and physical integration and personal growth (NADT website). There is an emphasis on setting goals, solving problems, finding how to express feelings appropriately, interpersonal skills and performing roles with more flexibility. Many would see this as foregrounding processes that tend towards a cognitive approach to change, with its emphasis on determining goals, problem solving and performing roles and expressing feelings 'appropriately'. Other languages of therapy are reflected, however, in the general areas of exploration and 'inner experience' cited. The British Association of Dramatherapists (BADth) gives a broad definition that emphasises the healing potentials present in drama and theatre, with the therapeutic process being described in terms of creativity, imagination, learning, insight and growth (BADth website). It describes dramatherapy as forming the meeting point between psychology and drama, based on the capacity of drama to heal and reorganise human awareness.

Some have stressed the role of creativity within dramatherapy as being at the heart of change: 'It is the client's creativity as developed, expressed and explored within the therapeutic framework, and the focused dramatic processes, which provide the opportunity for health and . . . change' (Jones, 1996: 5). Dramatherapy facilitates change through drama processes. It uses the potential of drama to reflect and transform life experiences to enable clients to express and work through problems they are encountering, or to maintain a client's well-being and health. A connection is made between the client's inner world, problematic situation or life experience and the activity in the dramatherapy session. 'Clients make use of the content of drama activities, the process of creating enactments, and the relationships formed between those taking part in the work within a therapeutic framework' (Jones, 1996: 6).

Valente and Fontana's research consulted UK dramatherapists on their views and ways of working. Part of this concerned factors that therapists considered relevant for final assessment in dramatherapy. This gives us an overall idea of the kinds of areas seen by them as connected to change or outcomes. Those most frequently indicated were as follows:

- Self-esteem
- Self-awareness
- Self-acceptance
- Self-confidence
- Hope
- Communication
- Trust
- Self–other awareness
- Spontaneity
- Social interaction

(Valente and Fontana, 1993; 1997)

Valente and Fontana draw attention to the cluster of variables to do with 'the self'. Part of their conclusions based on the research is that the general goals of dramatherapy place an emphasis on the client's achieving emotional openness, perception, creativity and self-acceptance. The researchers say that this can be seen as giving an indication of what UK therapists feel is most amenable to change through dramatherapy.

The drama methods and processes used in dramatherapy are broadly similar from Greece to the UK, from the USA to the Netherlands. Andersen-Warren and Grainger have said that 'dramatherapy means the therapy that is in drama itself – all drama – and not merely the use of some aspects of drama as therapeutic tools' (Andersen-Warren and Grainger, 2000: 15). Areas within the realm of drama include improvisation, play-based processes, role-play, mask, puppetry, drama games, voice work and script. Some forms such as role-play and those rooted in psychodrama emphasise a direct replaying of reality. Others using story, myth, image and movement stress the creation of metaphors or symbols to enable the client to explore material. Of this latter type the Sesame approach, developed by Lindkvist in the UK, is typical (Jones, 1996). It aims to work obliquely through metaphor; the emphasis is on recognising and dealing with client material through indirect expression.

AIMS OF DRAMATHERAPY

The Irish Association of Creative Arts Therapists (IACAT) gives the general aims of dramatherapy as being to:

- stimulate imagination and the development of personal expressive skills in an enjoyable way
- creatively explore ideas, issues and problems by using drama activities
- explore real-life relationships and social situations through the fictional mode of drama
- promote multisensory learning
- foster developments of positive communication, cooperative sharing and social skills
- develop concepts of responsibility for the self and other in relationships, so as to promote increased self-esteem, confidence and changed ways of functioning

(IACAT)

This definition of aims tends towards a cognitive or behavioural approach to change, with its emphasis on learning, or the development of skills or capacities and problem resolution in five out of the six aims. Creativity is linked to learning, and seen as a means of changing ways of functioning in terms of self-esteem, cooperation, social skills and communication. Notions of positivity and enjoyment within the work are seen, within this definition of aims, as a part of stimulating and assisting learning-based and developmental processes in therapy.

Dramatherapist Dokter saw clients for group dramatherapy in an eating disorder unit. She had asked clients initially to look at their expectations or fears and ran an assessment activity, to look at their situation and interpersonal relationships:

> Clients select objects from a basket with shells, stones, wood and other natural objects. The objects represent significant people in their life and themselves. They then sculpt these objects in relation to each other; close, far, on top etc. . . . The sculpt is threefold; present, a significant past moment and some time in the hoped-for future (the client decides how far ahead this future is). I then . . . asked [for] the first small change clients might wish for in the near future. This provided a good stepping stone to discuss the client's aims for themselves.
>
> (Dokter, 1996: 186)

The work included what Dokter describes as *projective* techniques such as sculpting, poetry and storytelling. She sees part of her approach as linked to a developmental understanding of her clients and their issues. She considers this as a way of looking at how the clients' difficulties can be linked to a block or difficulty to do with development, and also in selecting a dramatic language and process to assist in revisiting and reworking the block the client originally encountered:

> Johnson proposes that movement, drama and verbalisation correspond with the sensorimotor, symbolic and reflective stages. This developmental perspective is useful for those clients who have been blocked in their development. For clients with eating disorders this blocking of their autonomy and difficulty with verbalisation certainly applies . . . [it] can . . . supply a guide for selecting the most appropriate structures and techniques.
>
> (Dokter, 1996: 188)

In addition, the work acknowledged that for many clients with eating disorders, what has been expressed non-verbally through the body can be very threatening to express externally in words: 'The threat is to experience emotions often deadened by the obsessive preoccupation with food and body shape and/or the physical effects of "starvation and over-activity" ' (Dokter, 1996: 190). Once the 'pain' is externalised, she argues, engagement with the underlying issues can begin.

> Clients used little figures to sculpt some of the important interpersonal events of their past week. The theme arising from these sculpts was . . . the clients' total preoccupation with caring for others, losing themselves within the process. I suggested a continuum line, one pole the totally caring for others, the other pole total caring for oneself. I asked clients to select their preferred and feared places along the continuum and write some scenes connected with these points (past and present life events). These stories were then shared.
>
> (Dokter, 1996: 189)

A continuum involves the therapist creating an imaginary line across a room. The two poles of the line represent two different extremes on an issue. The continuum line, for example, might indicate anxiety on entering a new group. One end of the continuum might indicate an extremely high level of anxiety, the other no anxiety at all. Clients place themselves to communicate their own response. Dokter says that the continuum was used for the clients to explore their life and issues, rather than to rely on the therapist's interpretation. It encouraged clients to look at alternative perceptions and interpretations made by the group, by the clients themselves. She says that her role primarily involved containment, and that too much direction would link to feelings of being controlled or manipulated.

The model is influenced both by a developmental and an insight-orientated approach to change. Dramatherapy here helps the clients to create perspective, to explore and make connections with material that would be difficult to access through words alone, and then to work through areas of their experiences which are developmentally needed. So, for example, issues to do with caring – being cared for, and caring for others – are explored. Past experiences can be re-connected with, explored dramatically, and the client can gain insight and a new relationship to issues underlying the eating disorder.

Here dramatherapy is seen as a way of powerfully evoking issues, experiences and areas within a client's life. Enactment enables feelings to be actively expressed and explored, but the dramatic language of using objects and stories enables the client to feel able to achieve enough distance to explore and acknowledge sensitive material. The exploration, once worked with in this way, can then be discussed or acknowledged and owned, rather than denied and acted out through the body.

Landy's work in individual dramatherapy illustrates another approach to defining what dramatherapy can be, and how it offers change to a client. As part of ongoing work with 'Sam', Landy (1997) describes the exploration of the client's experience through looking at what he describes as 'Sam's role system'. The work took place weekly for 50 minutes each session over a 3-year period.

Some of the issues brought by Sam to therapy included his relationship with his father. He had become mentally and physically ill, and abandoned his family when Sam was aged 8, dying when Sam was in his early twenties. His mother had, in Sam's terms, expected him to fulfil his father's role in the family. Sam had been brought up within a fundamentalist Christian religion. He was suffering a breakdown in his marriage and was incapable of leaving owing, in part, to his religious beliefs.

Initially Landy uses a combination of story making, where the client makes up a story spontaneously, playing with small figures and objects in sand, choosing masks or puppets, and creating roles. Within this, the client and therapist begin to look for themes or roles that reflect problematic areas for the client. The created roles are seen as a way of exploring Sam's 'inner life', and the system of different roles gives an indication of the past and present concerns of the client. Issues emerge in this way and are summarised by Landy as: 'the murderous, exploitative father who is not what he appears, of women who are split into children, seductresses, and aggressors, of bravery and fear, of gatekeeping and setting boundaries' (Landy, 1997: 131). The aim of the therapy, at its simplest, Landy states as being to help the client to explore their imaginative world of roles, and to relate it to their everyday life, to visit and revisit what Landy calls unsafe inner territory:

> Sam played out many versions of heroes and villains, and saints and sinners, and bad fathers who tried to be good, and beautiful women who turned out to be beastly. A recurring image was that of the double, the disguise, the face beneath the mask. Sam created the sinning saint, based on the pastor who abandoned the church and maybe even based upon his

father who abandoned him at the age of eight. He created the image of a flower with a long stem that was attached to a box containing an explosive charge. A detonator stuck out of the box, ready to discharge its explosive contents. He created, in a story, one of his most powerful characters, Rupert Stosh, the good man who liked to do bad. Stosh, a demonic Nazi-type, appeared to be a wealthy, kindly philanthropist, but actually operated an underground slave labour nuclear plant. During this early stage, Sam and I became familiar with those role types that would dominate his psyche.

(Landy, 1997: 133)

The client plays out many parts, exploring these roles and their relationship to himself. Over time the playing of roles allows the client to gain insight into the past and present, and ways in which these roles reflect himself. He experiments with the roles, exploring different ways of relating, seeing himself and being with others. For example, Landy describes how this happens through the creation and exploration of dramas around characters such as Rupert Stosh, or another role, Farmer Sam. Towards the end of the therapy Landy notes, for example: 'During our final months together, Sam was able to understand that farmer Sam and Rupert Stosh, the secretly brutal men, though based upon his confusing parents, were fearful and shameful parts of himself' (Landy, 1997: 138). Landy sees this as a key moment in change, as the client is no longer in 'denial' of his problematic relationships, his fear and shame. At the end of therapy, Landy says that Sam had discovered a way to integrate his 'many confusions and reconstruct a viable role system'. He says that Sam came to mourn the loss of his denied childhood, and of his own father; he was able, through the therapy, to express feelings rather than to act them out in explosive, manic episodes, or implosive depressive ones.

Landy concludes that, for Sam, drama became 'a safe craft for many therapeutic voyages: it proffers an alternative reality, that of images and reflections, through its imaginary walls of distance shaped by fictional characters and stylised actions' (Landy, 1997: 141). Here we can see at work a number of the facets referred to at the beginning of this section, and identified by Casson's clients: the process is active, as Sam engages imaginatively and physically in playing out roles; this in turn allows insight and the permission to try out being free to play roles differently. The work also validates the client's sense of identity by dramatically exploring different aspects of the self, and people important to the client. By experimenting in playing different roles, or by playing roles differently, the therapy creates opportunities for emotions to become more positively expressed.

It is possible to see, then, that active participation in encountering this dramatic world, of creating an alternative reality through the enactment of roles, or playing with objects, can empower the client. The qualities of drama to reflect reality through playing or acting are utilised to enable clients to work actively through dramatic representations of their lives.

6 What is dance movement therapy?

DEFINITIONS

Payne writes that 'at its very simplest, dance movement therapy is the use of creative movement and dance in a therapeutic relationship' (Payne, 1992: 4). Stanton-Jones (1992) and Meekums (2002) have attempted to summarise the theoretical principles underlying dance movement therapy. Their definitions include the following:

- The mind and body are in constant interaction
- Movement reflects personality: this includes psychological developmental processes as well as psychopathology and interpersonal patterns of relating
- The therapeutic relationship includes a non-verbal dimension
- Movement is symbolic, and evidences unconscious processes
- Improvisation in movement allows clients to experiment with new ways of being and relating
- Creative processes in free movement are inherently therapeutic

(Stanton-Jones, 1992: 10; Meekums, 2002: 8)

The UK Standing Committee for Arts Therapies Professions (SCATP) defines dance movement therapy (DMT) as focusing on the use of movement and dance as a means of engaging in 'personal integration and growth'. At the heart of the discipline is the notion that 'there is a relationship between motion and emotion and that by exploring a more varied vocabulary of movement people experience the possibility of becoming more securely balanced yet increasingly spontaneous and adaptable' (SCATP, 1989). An often-stated notion is that the 'inner world' of the client is expressed through dance and movement, and that things that might be difficult to say become visible through dance. The therapy space becomes one where these areas can be discovered, expressed and worked with. This is often accompanied by the idea that aspects of the client's experiences or identity that have become split or buried can become integrated. Both the Irish and American Associations use this idea. For example, the American Dance Therapy Association (ADTA) defines DMT as 'the psychotherapeutic use of movement as a process which furthers the emotional, cognitive, social and physical integration of the individual' (ADTA website). The Irish Association of Creative Arts Therapists' (IACAT) definition echoes this:

> Dance movement therapy is a means of expression within a psycho-therapeutic relationship, founded on the principle that movement reflects an individual's patterns of thinking and feeling – the person is enabled creatively in a process of personal integration and growth. In acknowledging and supporting the movements of clients, therapy encourages development of new, adaptive movement patterns, together with the emotional experiences that accompany such changes.

These definitions, then, are rooted in the idea that through movement and dance, the client's inner emotional world becomes tangible. This bodily expression is seen as the making visible of personal symbols and relationships (IACAT website (dance therapy)).

Jawole Willa Jo Zollar of the Urban Bush Women has linked improvisation, dance and African and African-derived music as an inspiration for her work with adults and children, particularly with black women. She says that 'improvisation can be empowering to those who have been disenfranchised, for it can teach people how to be independent and "to move through situations, to structure a path" ' (Zollar, 1994: 343). MacLow has similar concerns. She says that 'If you dance, your body is your instrument and you intuit connections between mind and body. Improvisation communicates that most eloquently, because everything about you is reacting immediately to the situation at hand. And you can push the limits of your physical body. That's important for people to do or see' (MacLow, 1994: 345). These understandings of the way dance, improvisation, change and the self relate are at the heart of much dance movement therapy practice.

In the 1940s dance was being used in psychiatric settings, and went on to be developed across different areas of provision. In the USA ADTA was established in 1966. By the early 1990s the Association had 1,500 members (Payne, 1992: 13). In the UK in the mid-1970s groups began to offer informal trainings, which in turn developed into the Sesame course in movement and drama, and Laban's one-year course on dance in special education.

As in the other arts therapies, different countries are at different stages in developing the profession. The IACAT website, for example, notes in 2003 that DMT is still in its infancy in Ireland with no full-time posts. Practice was on a sessional basis in day centres for people with disabilities, the elderly, people who have had strokes, survivors of sexual abuse, those with eating disorders and those seeking personal growth (IACAT website (dance therapy)).

Some dance movement therapists stress the importance of creating an atmosphere of safety and security, as this is seen as enhancing the clients' use of improvised movement. Often the sessions follow a pattern of initial warm-up led by the therapist, a section where material is explored through movement, and a reflection period and closure. They might have a theme selected by the client, together with the therapist, or might link back to material from previous work. As with other arts therapies, it might be directive or non-directive, and there may be verbal reflection within the session.

AIMS OF DANCE MOVEMENT THERAPY

The UK Association for Dance Movement Therapy (ADMT), when describing the potential benefits of dance movement therapy, focuses upon different kinds of *connection*. These include DMT's capacity to enable links between thought, feelings and actions, inner and outer reality, physical, emotional and/or cognitive shifts. There is also an emphasis on DMT's capacity to expand or develop the client's potential in 'increasing self-awareness, self-esteem and personal autonomy', or maximising an individual's capacity for communication or social interaction. Reality testing and learning or re-learning in a safe environment also feature. Examples of this include increasing and rehearsing adaptive coping behaviours; expressing and managing overwhelming thoughts and behaviours; testing the 'impact' of self on others, and developing trusting relationships (ADMT website).

Stanton-Jones, in her work with outpatients in a psychiatric ward, speaks of the aims of DMT in this way:

> • To activate and motivate patients to use movement as a means with which to experience new ways of interacting with others
> • To explore imagery emerging from and through the movement
> • To extend the patient's expressive range of movement in planes, shapes and qualities
>
> (Stanton-Jones, 1992: 126)

She underpins these aims with the assumption that the imagery emerging from movement can be interpreted as evidence of unconscious processes within the group and 'the communication contained within the quality of movement can be reflected back to the clients by the therapist' (Stanton-Jones, 1992: 126). Other approaches and goals reflect physical and emotional change. The US Administration on Aging, Department of Health and Human Services gave a research grant, for example, looking at DMT work with older individuals who have sustained neurological insult. The findings of the study framed change in terms of the functional abilities of individuals – these included balance, rhythmic discrimination, mood, social interaction and increased energy levels (ADTA website).

In group work in a setting for clients with mental health problems UK dance movement therapist Steiner talks about DMT and its aims in a similar way. She allies her work to jazz: 'The beginning and the end are fixed, all the rest is improvisation. Everyone gets a chance for a solo whilst being supported by the rest of the band' (Steiner, 1992: 150). Themes emerge from warm-ups or discussion, and then a focus may emerge that reflects a group theme, or relates to an individual. She says that these often take the form of images that 'arise from the pooled group unconscious, triggered off by the common group activity'. The group exploration aims to recognise and acknowledge these, to understand them and to become more aware of these 'unconscious forces', and to develop mutual support (Steiner, 1992: 150).

She illustrates this process: a group of seven psychotic or borderline residents 'at various stages on the continuum between sanity, coping, and breakdown' (Steiner, 1992: 161), meet weekly for one-and-a-half hours:

> When Jeremy complained of obsessive thoughts, which prevented him from stopping talking, I asked him to translate them into movements. His response was a crescendo of fists, shaking violently, and kicking movements. So he found ways of physical outlet for his nervous mental energy and was eventually able to contact some of the depression that was underneath his anger. Then he could even allow the group to hold him in the middle of the circle and rock him soothingly.
>
> (Steiner, 1992: 158–9)

Movement is seen here as the vehicle for creating a structure to hold the powerful projections of the clients and the fear of further breakdown. Movement aided the process of grounding and centring, and opened possibilities for symbolic expression, communication and interaction.

Some forms of DMT, such as those above, use verbal analysis, interpretation and reflection. Other forms focus on movement without the therapist offering such analysis, with the therapist at most only making a verbal acknowledgement of the movement made. In discussing her work in a special school for pupils with emotional and behavioural difficulties, Payne deliberately practises in this way: 'there is no attempt at interpretation of the child's feelings or thoughts but an active focus on the movement material presented' (Payne, 1992: 63). This intends to convey a recognition and acceptance of what is going on, to support interaction and to encourage the child to talk. The aims are to promote differentiation of experiences, and information processing – these are seen as especially important for children with 'chaotic thinking'.

In dance movement therapy the therapist often moves with, and can be physically engaged with, the client. Payne says that through such physical engagement and movement the therapist is able to influence the form and expression in the direction of therapeutic aims. She can also model possibilities in movement, can open a path to communication at a preverbal level, and can encourage the client in movement by showing what is possible.

These examples show the variety of ways in which the use of creative movement and dance in a therapeutic relationship can work to meet the needs of different client groups. Different aspects of movement and dance are used to explore and resolve client issues, emphasising the relationship between the physical and the emotional, the body and psyche.

7   Between the arts therapies

INTRODUCTION: DIFFERENCES AND SIMILARITIES

One of the debates within the arts therapies has been concerned with whether the art forms and processes should be divided into separate services and professions with distinct identities and ways of working, or whether there should be one discipline which makes use of a variety of art forms and processes. There is a long tradition within different cultures of forms that combine the arts. Massey and Massey say that 'Bharata, the father of Indian aesthetics, saw all artistic forms as expressions of the same creative urge' (Massey and Massey, 1987: 115), pointing out that in Bharata's writing drama, music and dance were employed together as a matter of course. In early Hindu plays music, poetry, dance and costume 'were equal members of the same body'. They point out how ingrained in culture this is, linking it to the wide appeal of Indian film. Others have pointed to the fact that children do not naturally differentiate between expressive forms and that, especially in arts therapies work with children as clients, such division does not suit the expressive language of the child. We can see this reflected in writing such as Matthews's study of children's early representation and the ways children construct meaning:

> the forming and transforming nature of art materials has great facilities for representing ... events, but the child employs many other materials and activities to consolidate these understandings. Emerging conceptual understandings are 'transported' ... from one medium to another. From enacting, for example, the motion of cars, aeroplanes and people ... running in circles in the playground, synchronising these movements with agonistic facial expressions and noisy vocalisations, the child may go on to enact these trajectories in drawing and so map them into 2D.
>
> (Matthews, 1986: 13)

The arguments about this tend to revolve around issues to do with the nature of the arts, cultural differences, and the relationship between the arts and therapy in the arts therapies.

Art, music, drama and dance within the European and American traditions of education and practice are often separated in a number of ways. Examples of this separateness can be seen in the way identities are formed – dramatist, musician or painter, for example, or in the way subjects are taught from early education to university level. There are practitioners who work in a manner that does not recognise this separation, or who work in disciplines that do not separate out forms in this way. Examples of this are the stage musical, for example, or emergent disciplines such as the video art of Bill Viola (Viola, 2002). However, the main tradition that the arts therapies have drawn on to date has been one that separates each art form through training, methods and processes that are distinct. These are seen to be specific to the art form and are separate from one another.

There are examples of arts therapists within this tradition using aspects of the arts outside their own 'domain'. This tends to involve using a part of the language of another art and drawing it into their own art form. For example, a dance movement therapist would use music but this would be to facilitate movement process through rhythm, or to use sound as an inspiration to promote the clients' dance improvisation. Or a dramatherapist might ask a client to produce images, but this would normally be as a part of drama: to create access to dramatic form, perhaps using the images as cues.

Arts therapies that work in this way are extant throughout the world. The Health Professions Council, for example, regulates training in the UK, and this involves distinct demarcation and separation.

This has a knock-on effect for the client. Arts therapies that operate in this way give the client access to only one art form in their sessions. Arts therapists of one discipline would not be seen to be qualified to work with other arts processes as a primary method in their work, nor would most arts therapists consider themselves able to facilitate other art forms in this way. Art therapists, for example, would not consider themselves able to facilitate music therapy assessment processes within their sessions.

Another issue connected to the separation into different arts modalities within the arts therapies concerns cultural difference. As mentioned earlier, for some cultures, such as the Western tradition, the arts tend to have evolved in a way that has involved certain expressive forms such as the theatre play, painting, sculpture, ballet or dance. These tend to be replicated in forms of practice and the identity of practitioners who create them. Not all cultures replicate this division. Hence, people whose culture of origin does not recognise the division may find the separation of the arts restrictive, alien and even racist in its assumptions. Here some would say power-based issues arise when the therapist holds the framework of the language and form of the arts tradition. Looked at in this way, their sense of professional identity and artistic values and training does not deem them equipped to respond to cultural forms that do not replicate their cultural division of artistic experience into art, music, drama and dance movement.

Auriel Warwick and music therapy

MS: Had you heard of music therapy in New Zealand?
AW: No, I hadn't. But I had had an experience when I was teaching, when I had no piano to practise on and needed creative outlet. I turned to drama and theatre. We had a very fine amateur theatre in the city . . . and the wife of the resident professional producer had been an actress with the Bristol Old Vic Company in England . . . I found her method of working (which was to start with complete relaxation of the body to music before going into vocal exercises) so incredibly refreshing. After one particularly bad day I went to her to try to cry off the session but she wouldn't let me. After that hour I felt so refreshed that I said to her, 'Why isn't this done with people with psychiatric problems?' and she smiled wisely and said, 'When you get to England you will probably find that it is.' So, in a sense, it was perhaps the concept of dramatherapy, but with the use of music, that planted the germ of the idea. But it certainly wasn't conscious at that stage.

(Simmons, 2001: 44)

It's interesting that some of the early developers of arts therapies showed an awareness of the therapeutic potentials of art forms other than the one they specialised in, and also of mutuality. In 2001 music therapist Warwick was interviewed by Simmons about her early experiences in New Zealand and about how she came to music therapy (see above). She had initially trained to be a teacher at Auckland Training College.

Some, such as Petzold and Ilse have continued this awareness of mutuality, and have argued for an integrative approach where arts therapists work with all art forms depending on the client's needs. They argue that the individual arts therapies such as art therapy or music therapy do not constitute approaches in their own right, but are only *methods* (Petzold and Ilse, 1990).

Arts therapists might see what they do as a dialogue – they follow the way the client expresses themselves, or indicate interest – but many would see themselves as not professionally able to follow into certain areas of artistic creativity.

However, some who argue against this separation practise in a way that is directly different from the approach described above. Levine and Levine, for example, describe such an orientation: 'Expressive arts therapy is grounded not in particular techniques or media but in the capacity of the arts to respond to human suffering.' The expressive arts therapist must have an ability to use 'appropriate media for therapeutic purposes' (Levine and Levine, 1999: 11). Arts therapists who use a variety of art forms within their work tend to see the role of the arts as being interconnected, and to emphasise the importance of creativity as primary within the process, overriding the division into separate arts disciplines. Some work brings together a fascinating mix of activities reflecting local needs and resources. For example, Danev talks of the 'Library project' in work with children, supporting them after the impact of the war in Croatia (1991–5). This used the library-building as a cultural and therapeutic resource for children, initially in Zagreb. It was called 'Step by Step to Recovery' and described as 'an expressive [art therapy] intervention technique offered through a multi-media programme of creative activities' (Danev, 1998: 133). The initiative was designed to be adapted in several locations in Croatia, using whatever resources were available: 'the multi-media combination of creative techniques and materials, depending . . . on the equipment available and the abilities of the local project leader . . . painting, bibliotherapy, music therapy, video therapy, movement therapy (non-verbal), and selected computer games . . . as therapeutic media' (Danev, 1998: 135). This description illustrates the issue, described earlier, of how the division of the arts can be seen as a cultural imposition. You can feel Danev's language struggling here, not only with the use of English in translation, but also in finding words to describe the different segments of the whole that she and her colleagues and the children involved were creating!

Others, such as Mertens (1996) and Herrmann (2000), have argued against the notion of an integrative arts therapies approach or profession. Herrmann, for example, says that 'As far as merging all the arts therapies into one profession . . . [it] is doomed to lose the expertise that each form of art in therapy requires' (Herrmann, 2000: 27).

HOW DIFFERENT IS DIFFERENT? HOW SIMILAR IS SIMILAR?

Wigram raises the issue of referral, saying that it is common in many countries for professionals from other disciplines to be unaware of why they should refer someone to music therapy. Such comments are equally relevant in relation to client self-referral. Looked at in this way, it is important to have referral criteria that communicate clearly to people who are not familiar with the arts therapies. He gives an example of referral criteria developed from his work with people with autism:

- Difficulties with social interaction at verbal and non-verbal level
- Lack of understanding or motivation for communication
- Rigid and repetitive patterns of activity and play
- Poor relationships
- Hypersensitivity to sounds
- Lack of ability or interest in sharing experiences
- Significant difficulties in coping with change
- Apparent lack of ability to learn from experiences
- Lack of emotional reciprocity and empathy
- Poor sense of self

(Wigram, 2002)

Such referral criteria attempt to reflect a service's experience of the needs of the person likely to attend the setting, and to anticipate why they might come to an arts therapy such as music therapy. In addition, the criteria contain a basic notion of the areas likely to be featured in the music therapy in terms of expression, development and change. Wigram (2002) follows referral by an initial assessment period, and a period of work to identify the needs of the client and the direction of the therapy. What is interesting to me is that the way in which the referral criteria described above could easily relate across the arts therapies: to art, drama, movement or music.

Wigram then creates a series of five areas of 'expectation' that the therapy might look at. These are: developing communication, developing social interaction, meeting emotional needs, cognitive development and 'areas of therapy specific to autism'. I want to examine two of these areas in some detail, to look at what is common to all the arts therapies and what is specific to music therapy. These two areas are the development of communication, and the 'areas of therapy specific to autism'.

Development of communication is subdivided by Wigram into five points – activating intersubjective behaviours, spontaneous initiation of contact, development of meaningful gestures and signs, development of communicative vocalisation and emergence of language in song. Areas of therapy specific to autism are described as the tolerance of sounds, meaningful use of objects – from stereotyped and unimaginative use of part-objects, and seeking to divert clients away from habitual, stereotyped, ritualistic, perseverative or obsessive behaviours (Wigram, 2002: 15).

This way of looking at therapy is orientated towards considering how change can occur from a behaviourally orientated framework, concerning aspects of 'physical, social and emotional behaviour' (Wigram, 2002: 14). The definition of these two areas of referral and the expectations of therapy are interesting in that they could be seen to be the same or similar for dance movement, drama or art therapy practising within such a framework. Some of the areas of expectation, though, seems to be orientated specifically towards music. In 'Developing communication', for example 'language in song', and in 'Areas of therapy specific to autism', 'tolerance of sounds' seems to be unique to music. Even here, though, the second example concerning 'tolerating sound' could be seen as relevant to the other arts therapies in terms of speech, or the sound of music and instruments, or vocalisation in drama or dance movement therapy. The rest of the expectations of the therapy and the referral could be seen as just as appropriate for all the arts therapies.

Wigram goes on to describe events within a therapy session based on these areas and expectations. He talks about the responses and interactions between himself and an individual client diagnosed as autistic. He analyses in detail an assessment session designed to help ascertain whether music therapy can help. He describes this as aiming to build up a picture of the client's strengths and needs in order to be as clear as possible, 'as to the precise nature and severity of his social and communication impairment' (Wigram, 2002:

14). The assessment includes a variety of activities. At the start of the session therapist and client together improvise a piano duet. Wigram notes that the client matches his own tempo and rhythm, and also moderates tempo and volume, at times taking over the melody. This is followed by a drum duet, drums and piano playing together, dropping drumsticks on the drum, copying rhythmic patterns, singing together with instruments, with the therapist using a microphone, and the client making up his own words in solo singing, and saying and singing hello. There is a game of pretending to go to sleep, waking up and having breakfast, where the therapist models exclaiming 'Ugghh' when eating his drumstick, along with sharing a drink of imaginary tea.

Here, apart from the last game, the therapy is clearly rooted and primarily articulated in music. Wigram links each event to the music therapy 'expectations' and 'referral areas' as described earlier. So, for example, the client singing and saying 'hello' is connected to the development of communication. Activities are seen as examples of spontaneous initiation of contact, intersubjective behaviour and the development of communicative vocalisation.

So, whilst the areas of referral and the expectations of therapy could be common to all the arts therapies, the description of the *events* or *activities* within the therapy, and the *response* and *interaction* between client, therapist and art form are seen by Wigram to be clearly in the language and process of music. This is an important point, and one that can be seen across much of the practice analysed and described in this book. It is possible to argue that the broad aims and directions of therapy, along with its general outcomes, are largely common to all the arts therapies. It is in the language and the interactions within the therapy itself that the differences fully emerge. What the arts therapies have in common is their aims, and broad benefits to be brought: it is in the particular, the specifics of form and interactions of the individual sessions, that the differences of language and process emerge.

The importance of this is that it creates a framework from which to see commonality and difference. In the broad understanding of change, in the assumptions about what enables change to occur, and in the broad views about what change is and how it happens, the arts therapies have much in common. In the language and process of the specific sessions we have some areas of commonality, but it is here that the differences emerge: in the languages that realise these broad aims and understanding of change, in the processes that create response and interaction between clients and therapist.

ARTS THERAPIES AND ARTS IN HEALTH

It's important to differentiate between arts practised in health settings and the arts therapies. Arts in health settings tend to be devoted to two main areas. The first is creating access for those who have been disenfranchised from participating in the arts, whether as makers or consumers. The second area is where the arts are practised in ways that complement health practice concerning the commissioning of art in hospitals, or the use of the arts in health promotion. Initiatives in these areas have occurred at local, national and international levels.

On a local level, for example, the 'Good Medicine' Report in the early 1990s looked at arts in health initiatives practised in the West Midlands region of Britain. It concluded that managers of hospitals and healthcare settings had a growing awareness of the ways in which the arts could be of great benefit to the health sector. The focus is on improving healthcare environments, for example, by making them more 'friendly or interesting' and involving the local community in arts that are 'socially relevant' (Roberts and Bund, 1993: 2). It notes that participatory arts run by professional artists have a different purpose from arts therapies though they can have an indirect therapeutic effect:

> There are radical changes taking place in the way in which the medical profession views its role with a growing emphasis on prevention. The arts already play a big part in this process of change . . . Health promotion clinics are now an everyday part of the work of most GP practices. Developmental arts in health work are taking place in the primary sector in the region.
>
> (Roberts and Bund, 1993: 13)

It cites as examples theatre in education projects raising awareness about HIV and Aids, and substance abuse. Environmental arts reflecting the culture, history of local people involving local artists and the community are seen to give a 'sense of place and interest to all those who use the building' (Roberts and Bund, 1993: 26). Residencies in the visual arts, film and video, writing, dance and theatre are all included:

> Arts workshops are run by professional practising artists and are not intended, in any way, to be used in a clinical context for direct diagnostic or treatment purposes. They are not to be confused with the work of the professional arts therapist; nor the work more closely associated with Occupational Therapists and a programme of diversional therapy. The purpose of the participatory arts is to bring fun, enjoyment, involvement and an opportunity to find a means of self-expression and discovery: all this may contribute to a beneficial, therapeutic effect. It is not, however, therapy in the clinically defined sense of the word.
>
> (Roberts and Bund, 1993: 28)

The scope for the arts therapies is in direct therapeutic work as part of the clinical provision, whilst arts activities create 'access to the arts for thousands of people who would not otherwise have the opportunity to be involved, whether as audience or participants' (Senior and Croall, 1993: 7). I would concur with Senior and Croall (1993) who note the potential for cooperation between arts practitioners in health contexts and arts therapists. They recognise the two areas as different but complementary.

PROFESSIONAL IDENTITY

In a number of countries, as described earlier in this chapter, arts therapies associations have come into existence to develop relations between training institutions, clinical settings and legislative or regulatory bodies concerning educational, professional and ethical standards for members and practice. The Canadian Art Therapy Association (CATA) was formed in 1977, for example, and sees as one of its key objectives 'to promote and maintain national standards of training, practice and professional registration' (CATA website).

Many associations focus on specific disciplines, either within a coalition consisting of one overall association that connects individual disciplines, or associations focusing on one area such as dance or art. The National Association for Drama Therapy (NADT), for example, was formed in 1979 in the USA and is also a member organisation of the National Coalition of Creative Arts Therapies Associations (NCCATA) aligned with art, music, dance and poetry therapies.

Associations promote the arts therapies through information and research, and lobby and make representations to statutory and governmental bodies regarding recognition and provision. They also often oversee requirements that must be met to enable individuals to qualify and practise as arts therapists. Each association or organisation tends to have an approval and monitoring process, a code of ethics and standards of clinical practice often including a role for overseeing and regulating clinical supervision and professional development (see Appendix for association details).

Examples of this include the National Association for Music Therapy that was founded in 1950, and the American Association for Music Therapy founded in 1971. These joined together in 1998 to form the American Music Therapy Association (AMTA). The Irish Association of Drama, Art and Music Therapists was founded in 1992, changing its name in 1998 to the Irish Association of Creative Arts Therapists (IACAT), developing out of a core of arts therapists who had trained abroad, and who were developing practice and the profession in their own country.

The nature of such associations and organisations varies across countries. Within Europe the European Consortium of Arts Therapies Educators (Ecarte), was developed in the 1980s to encourage communication and cooperation across member states. In the USA Art Therapy Registration (ATR) is granted upon completion of graduate education and postgraduate supervised experience. Board Certification (ATR-BC) is granted to registered art therapists who pass a written examination, and is maintained through continuing education. Some states regulate the practice of art therapy and in some states art therapists can become licensed as counsellors or mental health therapists. For example, in Kentucky art therapists are certified as 'Certified Professional Art Therapists' and are considered qualified providers of Medicaid, special needs adoptions and crisis intervention (AATA website, State Legislative Information).

In the UK, in 1980 the Department for Health and Social Services (DHSS) recognised that no one could be employed as an art therapist without having completed a recognised postgraduate course. In 1997 state registration in the UK was granted for music, art and dramatherapists under the Council for Professions Supplementary to Medicine (subsequently titled the Health Professions Council: HPC). This meant that only music, art or drama therapists registered with the HPC could legally practise. Attached to this is a range of requirements including training, ethical and professional standards. This standardisation is by no means the norm. Herrmann, for example, says, as late as 2000, that in Germany 'a doctor, psychologist, psychiatrist, artist or any other professional, without any qualification in art therapy or art, could practise under the term "art therapy" ' (Herrmann, 2000: 19). This was the case even though training was well established, with 30 programmes related to art therapy ranging from postgraduate trainings in academies of fine art and private training institutions. Herrmann and others called for clarity in minimal standards in training and a legally sanctioned single professional association for Germany. In countries where the arts therapies are less established, associations may not exist, or may be in the early stages of development. In this situation relationships with other professional associations may be sought. Dramatherapist Kurgan speaks of such a situation in South Africa:

Interview with South African dramatherapist, Anna Kurgan, 2003

There are so few of us arts therapists practising in this country . . . The country lacks facilities for arts therapies training at present, and therefore lacks the experience of the arts therapies as a treatment model . . . To my knowledge there are only five dramatherapists in the whole of South Africa and, to my knowledge, no therapeutic facility that has more than one arts therapist employed as a member of its staff team. There are no statistics as yet. South Africa is, indeed, pioneering turf for arts therapists. The arts therapies are very new to this country, a country which is rebuilding itself, and is in the midst of social, political and economic change. South Africa has become part of what is termed the 'African Renaissance', which is characterised by the constantly changing dynamics of its people, who face feelings such as the fear, joy and freedom integral to the process of re-integration within a continent inhabited by a myriad of different cultures . . . The Health Professions Council of South Africa (HPCSA) has very firm standards that need to be met before it registers an arts therapist who has, necessarily, qualified in another country. This registration is a process which all arts therapists wishing to practise as such in this country need to undergo. It is a means of not only accrediting and validating such a qualified practitioner, but is also a process involving the conversion of a 'foreign' course and their qualifications into the recognised South African framework. All standards of practice, such as ethics, laid down by the HPCSA, apply to all healthcare practitioners in this country.

This illustrates that the patterns of registration and monitoring of arts therapist practitioners varies widely, with different countries evolving different routes towards establishing standards and professionalisation.

The processes of standardisation, approval and professionalisation in the arts therapies have seen impressive milestones passed in the last twenty years in a number of countries. However, much remains to be done to develop the full professional potential and recognition of the disciplines.

CONCLUSION: FROM DEFINITION TO EXPLORATION

At the start of Part II I said that the definitions were pictures that would give us information. Each chapter looked at the pictures given by a different modality. There are many parallels between art, music, drama and dance movement arts therapies, both in terms of process and aims, and even of language. There are undoubtedly differences, but, in the pictures the definitions enabled us to begin to see, there are common themes that will be present in the next chapters in this book. These include the particular ways in which arts media and processes within the arts therapies allow clients to communicate, the effect the art form has upon the therapeutic relationship, and the particular ways in which arts languages and processes allow clients to explore and develop the material they bring to the therapeutic space.

Read Johnson says that the arts therapies 'have not developed in the mid twentieth century by accident. They are the result of historical processes, and serve some function for our culture now and in the future. We must understand that function and find a way to articulate it meaningfully' (Read Johnson, 1999: 72). In Part III we will begin to look at some of the ways in which these areas started to make links. This will serve as a way to begin to explore how the processes of the arts and therapy came together to form a new, powerful tool for change.

Part III

Backgrounds, histories and encounters: from the first happening to the shadow of logic

Tens of thousands of years ago, long before the word art had entered the language system of any culture, there existed a human need for creative expression beyond that required for the completion of utilitarian tasks. That which we now call art (involved) the making of events or objects of contemplation through an act of the imagination, displayed or performed in special environments . . . the traditional artist fashioned images of an alternative reality, that of the imagination, different from the one given by nature and taken in through the five senses.

R. Landy in 'Establishing a Model of Communication between
Artists and Creative Arts Therapists' (2001: 22–3)

8   From the first happening

INTRODUCTION: HISTORIES

Many accounts of the origins of the arts therapies draw on two kinds of history. The first is seen as an ancient lineage, linking healing and the arts through processes such as ritual or a tradition of healers, rather like the one quoted at the start of Part III. The other concerns the emergence in the twentieth century of the professions and practice of the arts therapies within contemporary health and care-related settings such as hospitals, schools and private practice.

The Irish Association of Creative Arts Therapists (IACAT) puts this history in a multicultural context of the healing 'virtues' of arts activities. It relates the origins of the arts therapies to accounts of visions and dreams, and to art objects linked to shamanic ritual or healing practices. This is often echoed by a number of authors and in various accounts. The American Music Therapy Association (AMTA), for example, says the notion that music is a healing influence that can impact on health and behaviour is at least as old as the writings of Plato and Aristotle. One of the oldest texts in English concerning the healing effects of music was printed in 1729: *Medicina Musica or A Mechanical Essay on the Effects of Singing, Musick and Dancing on Human Bodies* (Darrow *et al.*, 1985: 18). Walker's research acknowledges parallels across different cultures:

> A belief common to practically all cultures appears to be that concerning the power of musical sound to exert some influence over our physical and mental states. A ubiquitous version of this is the belief in the power of songs to heal physical and mental sickness; equally pervasive is the belief that certain sounds are inextricably linked in some way to the character, or ethos, of an object, person, tribe, nation or other group of people.
>
> (Walker, 1990: 180)

The idea that artistic activity and exposure to art forms are intrinsically beneficial is not accepted by all. The idea that the arts can harm as well as heal has been expressed. Hamm (1979) cites a psychiatrist who says that rock and roll is a 'communicable disease' (Hamm, 1979: 180). In 1961 a classical cellist, for example, described rock and roll as 'a poison put to sound – a raucous distillation of the ugliness of our times . . . It is against art, against life. It leads away from the exultation and elevation of spirit that should naturally spring from all good music' (in Hamm, 1979: 400). Jazz in the 1920s was seen by some as 'doing a vast amount of harm to young minds and bodies not yet developed': it was 'an activity which may be analysed as a combination of nervousness, lawlessness, primitive and savage animalism and lasciviousness' (Merriam, 1964: 242, in Walker, 1990: 181).

However, the potentials in the arts for healing are seen across cultures and across historical periods. This background is often referred to in linking current practices named as 'arts therapies', initially developed mainly in the Netherlands, USA and UK, during the twentieth century, and practices within other cultural contexts or historical periods.

A common perception is that this connection between the arts and health-care was diminished in many cultures, especially in Western medicine, until its revival or rediscovery in the twentieth century. A major review of the arts and healthcare in the UK funded by the Calouste Gulbenkian Foundation says, for example: 'In many cultures the connection between the arts and health-care has been a strong one in the past. In more recent times it has been largely lost sight of' (Senior and Croall, 1993: 3).

The Irish Association's account similarly refers to a *re-emergence*, as a 'rich melting pot of influences came together, and art therapy emerged as a way of focusing this power in modern psychological healing methods'. They include in this 'melting pot' the development of child-centred approaches in educa-tion which emphasised the importance of each individual's unique potential and creativity, interests in the art work of people with mental health problems and in particular:

> the many modern art movements; expressionism, surrealism and symbol-ism [which] were concerned with the subjective, rather than objective experience. The burgeoning psychoanalytic movement was generating new insights into human motivation and behaviour, and new models of the psyche.
>
> (IACAT website (art therapy))

The AMTA account also supports this idea of a re-emergence, saying that the impetus behind the twentieth-century discipline began after the two world wars when community musicians went to veterans' hospitals to play for people, including those suffering emotional and physical trauma from the conflicts. The responses led to musicians being hired by hospitals, developing a need for training. One of the earliest music therapy training degree programmes in the world was founded at Michigan State University in 1944. The first documented use of the term 'dramatherapy' also occurs in a paper written around this time by Peter Slade for the British Medical Association in 1939 (Jones, 1996: 44, 82).

I want to present two snapshots to illustrate something of this history. The first is from the exciting developments in post-Second World War North America at the Black Mountain College, as a way of illustrating how the 'climate' for the arts therapies was emerging. This setting, its atmosphere and opportunities, stands in for many other places and occasions in the twentieth century when potent mixtures of people, ideas and practices were fermenting. The second is from the Society for Music Therapy and Remedial Music's One Day Conference on Music Therapy, in London on 30 April 1960. It represents many other meetings in the 1950s and '60s when the arts therapies were emerging in their own right, and gives us a picture of the changes in thinking and work taking place at this time.

THE FIRST HAPPENING AND BLACK MOUNTAIN COLLEGE

On Monday 27 November 1933, speaking little English, Josef Albers arrived at Black Mountain College, North Carolina, USA on the Southern railway. His work with the revolutionary Bauhaus arts movement had been abruptly halted, following raids by Nazi stormtroopers and by the City Council firing him from his post in what they described as 'a germ cell of Bolshevism' (Wingler, 1969: 1880). Within a few weeks he had been elected Professor of Art at the Black Mountain College. He and others, pioneers in the avant-garde and refugees from fascist Germany, came into contact at Black Mountain College with artistic revolutionaries such as musician Cage, artist Rauschenberg, Perls, an innovator of Gestalt therapy, and dancer Cunningham. Its advisory council included Carl Jung, Albert Einstein, John Dewey, Walter Gropius and Franz Kline – all key names in the revolution of ideas in areas such as psychology and the arts in the twentieth century.

Black Mountain College was founded by a group of people, many of whom had become unemployed in the Great Depression of the early 1930s. Harris (2001) has described it as founded in the spirit of experimentation, idealism and international turmoil. The origins of the approaches of the college had their roots both in the revolution in art in America, and also in the artistic revolt that had begun in Europe. However, as the varied composition of the advisory council hints, the connections occurring at Black Mountain were more complex than this.

I want to use the story of the Black Mountain College to illustrate the ways in which the fervour and combustion of different realms of experimentation created the catalyst for the arts therapies. The thinkers and practitioners at the college were at the forefront of radicalism in the areas of arts, of psychology, and of ideas about the individual and society.

My point is that Black Mountain was not unique in this, but it is an example of places and groupings where the collisions and connections that created the arts therapies started to occur. Previously held notions and practices were challenged in ways which show how the time was right for the ideas and ways of working to emerge *which would make the arts therapies possible.* Albers, for example, was an advocate of abstract art. Working with him were people such as Drier, brought up in a New York household in a family devoted to the arts, social action, women's emancipation and improved conditions for people with mental health problems: all influences which he brought into his participation in the forming of Black Mountain College.

A combination of new ideas about education was at the core of the venture. The emphasis was on creating a college where the arts could be explored as an experimental, improvisatory active process, rather than as a place for passive learning. Work undertaken by students respected individual capacities and interests and the 'creative spirit' of the individual was fostered. The education focused on dramatics, music and the fine arts. There was a declared emphasis on the value of being sensitised to movement, form, sound and other media, and on their effect on the self and the environment. The arts were seen 'as a force penetrating to the deepest levels of community life' (Harris, 2001: 16). One of those involved described the college as 'total freedom to experiment, to perform, to get feedback' (June Rice interview, Harris, 2001: 182). The place was engaged with the advanced edge of thinking and movements of the time: of Jung, Sauer and Artaud; of Gestalt and jazz.

Though the College did not advocate one specific method or ideology, certain themes were echoed or shared. Musician Cage 'considered art and life to be the same, though art is distinguished from life by being set aside as "a special occasion" ' (Harris, 2001: 182). For artist Rauschenberg, 'Painting relates to both art and life. Neither can be made. (I try to act in that gap between the two)' (Rauschenberg, 1959: 2). Here is a parallel concern with living and art, or art as living. The 1952 Bulletin of Black Mountain College emphasises a search for the primary energies or propelling forces at the heart of both art and life. Goodman, contributor in creative writing and drama at Black Mountain, reflects yet another angle on the relationship between living and art. He brings together directly the fields of art and therapy. Whilst at Black Mountain Goodman was working with Perls and Hefferline on the seminal text *Gestalt Therapy* (Goodman *et al.*, 1951). Goodman, in his teaching, drew on Gestalt and his knowledge of Reichian therapy. In art classes, for example, Goodman asked students to draw on their own feelings and experiences through Reichian exercises in relaxation, to increase aware-ness and free the body from tension (Harris, 2001: 212). It is not too great a step to see this approach as foreshadowing the art therapy practices of Cam-eron fifty years later as described in Chapter 3. Her work also combined relaxation activities, image making and personal awareness but in the context of conflict resolution with people who were homeless in New York City.

Theatre tutor and practitioner Olson was seeking, in artistic work, 'an expression the equal of the original fact'. Harris cites that art as a medium for change through an 'alchemical process of transformation' emerged as a groundbreaking concern within much practice at Black Mountain (Harris, 2001: 182). Punning on avant-garde, 'Advance-Guard Writing', Goodman, for example, wrote about the crucial need in society for the artist, and the necessity for art in community experience. He spoke of its important function in mediating key aspects of individual and social life – at birth and death, for example. His ideas concerned a search for a way of working which vitally connected the creative act and the community (Goodman, 1951: 376).

THEATRE PIECE NO. 1

This combustible mix at Black Mountain saw Schawinsky create what has been described as the first examples of performance art, linked to Bauhaus ideas of non-narrative form, using music, lights and movement, emphasising ritual over verbal text. This is documented in his sketches for *Spectodrama: Play, Life, Illusion* (first published 1936). At the same time Leger gave demonstrations and classes on his ideas of Ballet Méchanique (Harris, 2001: 78). The work of Graham and influences of Laban in movement were present in the work that was undertaken at the college. Merce Cunningham improvised with John Cage (Harris, 2001: 156), combining elements of Hindu dance and I Ching, in particular identifying ways of releasing conscious control and breaking habitual patterns of creating – a method of composition that attempted to challenge concepts of logic and meaning in art.

Theatre Piece No. 1

Black College is often cited as the site of the first 'happening' staged by John Cage in 1952. Cage staged the improvised Theatre Piece No 1 (Harris, 2001: 40). He conceived the piece after lunch and it was performed that evening. Each performer was given a time bracket that had been arrived at by chance procedures. In this period they had to enact a particular activity. Cage had a rough idea of what they should do, but nothing specific. The people didn't play fictional characters but were themselves. The work took place with no rehearsal, script or costume.

Emphasis was on chance, on the integration of audience and performer, on the freedom to determine one's own work. Action took place all over an auditorium: in the aisles and in the areas between the chairs. Some of Rauschenberg's all-white paintings hung in a cross from the rafters, along with a painting by Kline. There were many foci within the performance: Cage reading aloud on a ladder, whilst others did so from other ladders, Cunningham dancing in and around the chairs was joined by his dog. Rauschenberg stood by his paintings, or played Edith Piaf records at double speed, Tudor played a piano and a radio. Films and still pictures were projected upside down and on angled surfaces. Coffee was served in ashtrays used as cups.

The arts were seen as essential to life and their role that of a generative force in a culture rather than 'distraction' or entertainment. Albers said that art should not be a 'beauty shop', or an imitation of nature, an embellishment or entertainment, but rather 'a spiritual documentation of life ... real art is essential life and essential life is art' (Albers, 1935: 111.1).

The point I'm making is that this kind of exploration and pushing of boundaries in the arts, and in therapy, was happening in a variety of places. Ideas were stretching out, making new contacts: the particular ways that experimentation in different disciplines was taking shape created opportunities for discoveries to occur. The social and political upheavals and the increased opportunities for communication, such as the displacement of individuals caused by the rise of fascism or the 1930s Depression, are witnessed in the above-created connections. The concerns at the heart of these revolutions and innovations in separate disciplines meant that the ground was ripe for the arts therapies to emerge.

What are these concerns and connections? In the above description we see the following practices and preoccupations:

- artists who are paying attention to the importance of *process*, on the effects of the *making* of art as compared to the primacy of the finished product;
- concerns about the *effects of this process on people*, the ways in which the arts can function to affect people in their lives, in the way they encounter key stages in their individual and collective lives – such as birth or death;
- an educative philosophy and the creation of methods that emphasise the development of the individual and the importance of their potential – arts as education developing the student's *potentials* rather than being taught existing material within a strict curriculum;
- experiments with the new opportunities which artistic expression is offered from *improvisation and spontaneity*, with interest in the immediate and unplanned rather than the rehearsed and planned;
- individuals writing about, and discovering, ways of working and understanding identity and therapy whilst being involved in the arts – Goodman, Perls and Jung, for example.

Painters, theatre practitioners, dancers, musicians, psychologists, therapists came together and were working within an environment that was conducive to interdisciplinarity and to the breaking down of boundaries. Hence experimentation in one area was open to the repercussions brought from discoveries made within other fields. Discoveries about spontaneity and the arts were reflected in the findings and practice of Gestalt therapy, for example. Actors and dramatists were adapting therapy-influenced techniques in their preparation, artists were making use of the ideas about consciousness to work with improvisation and discovery. Arts therapists such as Byrne (1995) have pointed to the ways in which such revolutions in the arts influenced the development of the arts therapies.

A part of this is well summed up by Read Johnson:

> Improvisation is a relatively late development in the arts and seems to have emerged in all art forms in the twentieth century, in jazz, in expressionist painting, modern dance and improvisational theatre. The stretching and altering of rigid artistic forms seems a characteristic of this century's art, and clearly created the conditions under which the creative arts therapies could develop.
>
> (Johnson, 1999: 25)

Movements such as surrealism, modernism, abstract expressionism, Arte Povera with their interests in the unconscious, automatism, dreams, inner feelings and impulses linking to artists' 'gestures on canvas' and the arts 'profoundly influence both our theory and our practice' (Byrne, 1995: 235).

CONCLUSION

The people at Black Mountain didn't come up with the specific disciplines of the arts therapies, nor with their techniques, or direct, therapeutic aims for the arts. However, the kinds of questions being asked, and the kinds of work being undertaken, threw up relevant possibilities in their experimentation. The arts therapies are born within this same spirit of challenge and unrest with a status quo, of cultural, political and artistic experimentation and enquiry.

The illustration of the 'First Happening' event of 1952 is *in the spirit* of the arts therapies. In relating some of the story of Albers and Black Mountain, and by highlighting the way ideas and processes were being exchanged between disciplines, certain concerns can be seen. These concerns and connections show the ways the arts therapies were in the air. It was not by chance that the arts therapies formed, but by the coming together of different developments in different fields. It happened in many places at around the same time. The time for the connections and the creation of the arts therapies was right.

9 'Everything is ripe'

INTRODUCTION: MANY PLACES

In many places practices such as artists working in hospitals, teachers using the arts with children, or occupational therapists and psychiatrists using arts activities within their work were developing during the early and middle twentieth century. This had occurred for many years in many different countries, from the Bellevue Hospital in Jamaica (Hickling, 1989) to India (Jones, 1996).

Though the wide extent of such practice was new, some of the basic ideas, such as the presence of the arts in asylums, was not. As has been shown earlier, there was a tradition of art studios and performance spaces for music and theatre. Ticehurst Asylum, for example, founded in eighteenth-century England, and 'favoured with the aristocracy', had fortnightly concerts with as many as thirty-six patients taking part. An 'excellent theatre with scenery' was constructed there for the use of patients in an environment 'to restore health to diseased minds' (Souall, 1981: 207; Jones, 1996: 47). Charenton, an asylum outside Paris, held theatre productions involving patients. Coulmier, director of the asylum, was involved in creating them between 1879 and 1811, along with De Sade, who wrote some of the productions whilst an inmate there (Jones, 1996: 47). Italian psychiatric hospitals at Aversa, Naples and Palermo, all built around this time, have theatres.

Arts activities became much more common in such settings by the mid-twentieth century. Fryrear and Fleshman have said that much of this activity was 'caretaking' rather than therapy, and say that this kind of attitude and situation prevailed until well into the 1940s in many countries. The idea here is that the *groundwork* for the arts therapies lay in such arenas of activity. One example is the arts and crafts movement that was often linked to hospital occupational therapy taking place after the First World War in parts of Europe and the USA, though this was largely recreational (Fryrear and Fleshman, 1981: 14). Van de Wall, in 1936, for example, illustrates this attitude well, as music is placed alongside fresh air and flowers:

The hospitalised patients should enjoy music as a cultural and social interest and occupation that is entirely divorced in their minds from concepts of illness. The sheer contact with efficient and sensible musicians and with an art that, like fresh air, sunshine and flowers, introduces in the ward elements of joyful cultural and social living, has value in improving the quality of his [*sic*] life and pervades it with ideas, feelings and events which are part of normal social life at its best.

(Van de Wall and Liepmann, 1936: 8)

Alongside the development of therapeutic work with clients in hospitals, arts work became more common in schools, educational units for pupils with learning disabilities and other clinical settings such as day centres for adults with learning disabilities. People such as Naumburg and Cane (Junge and Asawa, 1994) founded early thinking and practice in these areas. They were both involved in the innovative Walden School in New York City in the early twentieth century. Naumburg forged links between the discoveries of psychoanalysis and education. This work included an emphasis on emotional development within education, and a part of this involved the encouragement of creativity and spontaneity in the classroom. Cane began teaching art at Walden around 1920, where she developed ways of working that aimed to free children from stereotyped copying, drawing and painting. These methods included using movement and sound, techniques based in free scribbling and 'had as their goal loosening defences, evoking a type of free association, and tapping into fantasies and the unconscious' (Junge and Asawa, 1994: 15).

This was not a static situation, where arts practices from outside health and education were shipped in. The therapeutic and special educational settings began to affect the way the arts were seen and practised – the responses, needs and situations of the clients in the institutions or hospitals began to show particular facets and capacities of the arts. This was noticed by the practitioners, and began to affect the direction and application of the arts. By this I mean that practitioners began to notice that the arts seemed to have an effect on the way people behaved, related to themselves and others, their emotional conditions and the ways they could express themselves. The practitioners facilitating these arts activities were also coming into contact with ideas and approaches in therapy practised within such settings, and began to see new potentials in the arts that would connect to therapeutic potentials for the people they worked with. Crucially, the nature and level of the work began to change, as I will show.

CONFERENCE FOR THE SOCIETY FOR MUSIC THERAPY AND REMEDIAL MUSIC, 1960

Individuals began to be aware of each other's practice and discoveries, small groups developed and these began to be connected with other such groupings.

Eventually this led to the formation of associations of arts therapists (Jones, 1996). In the 1950s and '60s, especially, we see an increasing number of conferences, summer schools and opportunities for people to gather. From these connections training and professional associations grew. Here is an illustration from an opening speech and paper from such an event in London in 1960.

The Society for Music Therapy and Remedial Music One-Day Conference on Music Therapy, London on 30 April 1960

OPENING ADDRESS

Professor A.V. Judges, Head of the Department of Education, King's College

We are here amongst professional educationalists, and perhaps with some sense of mission, inasmuch as educationalists, even those who have to do with learning problems among the abnormal and unsophisticated and retarded, are only too prone to think that people grow and mature almost entirely under intellectual stimulus, and that progress will submit to test only by verbal analysis. Well, of course this is an outmoded view. It goes back to the time when inspectors of education measured growth by literacy and literacy by intellectual learning achieved, whether in the D stream or A stream, by young people sitting bolt upright in trance-like rigidity on knife-board benches and with their hands clasped before them. We are now discovering once more, and very slowly indeed, that ease and strength in making progress, and also in finding one's personal role depend quite as much on emotional involvement, and on muscular exercise and co-ordination and in all kinds of felt experience – all of these taking place on any but an intellectual plane.

At this Conference, we study especially the parts played by music and rhythm. I have mentioned the broader field of experience, because in a sense we are only specialists representing one stream in a current of new ideas which also embrace new practices in the use of dramatic action and role-playing, and free movement too and painting and modelling, all of which have accepted remedial uses as well as more orthodox parts to play . . . thus the therapeutic uses of painting and drawing are growing more important.

One wonders how far these parallel experiments with the therapy of self-expression have a bearing on one's own interests to-day. Sometimes the life of the expressionist artist in the ward is short. Diagnosis is easier, treatment is nowadays more confident. There is more affection (at least in some asylums), more opportunities for restoring courage and uplifting broken spirits. And there are new drugs for some cases (whether permanently effective I don't know) which seem to produce miracle cures. For art teachers, paradoxically enough, perhaps the most disheartening incident in the curative regime is the sequel to one of these quick recoveries after drugs. Gone suddenly are the brilliancy, the love of contrasting colour, the abandon, the acrobatic draughtsmanship. And the same artist now smugly presents prim and conventional little pencil drawings of houses and gardens – no longer the serpents and rearing dragons and wild horses. This apparent collapse of artistic activity is a sign for discharge, and for the relatives to come and take the cured patient back to normality!

(Judges, 1960: 1–2)

MUSIC THERAPY IN ENGLAND

Miss Nora Gruhn, Music Therapist, Warlingham Park, Cane Hill and Netherne hospitals

It was in 1947 that the Council for Music in Hospitals was formed to provide monthly concerts of high quality music in mental hospitals. This work has continued most successfully until today; many professional musicians give concerts in hospitals all over the country.

It was from America that the first financial help came to employ musicians to work part time in mental hospitals. From that initial encouragement emerged the Association for Music Therapy in Hospitals. Another more recently formed society is the Society for Music Therapy and Remedial Music who have sponsored this conference today.

The exciting thing about the position in this country is the challenge offered by so much pioneering work ahead. There is still some disagreement about methods especially on the type of training a musician or music therapist should receive. Some doctors consider medical knowledge unnecessary, and would like to employ a musician without any other training. Others would like their nurses who have an interest in music to take a special course of training for this work. Personally I favour a three year course at one of the Music Colleges with a further six months' training at a hospital giving lectures and practical work which would lead to a professional status of music therapist. Without some medical knowledge the musician must work blind to any therapeutic goal, and this, to my mind seems undesirable.

. . .

The word music therapist is used so loosely that naturally it is very unpopular with doctors. Therapy comes from a Greek word meaning treatment to cure or alleviate disease. As the only persons authorised to do this are the doctors it follows that a therapy should be limited, first of all, to a prescription given by a doctor. Where a musician is not working under the direction of a doctor the work would seem to me to be only recreational.

Whether in this country we shall ever have music therapists conforming to these ideals is very uncertain at present. The future of music therapy lies in scientific research aimed at results which will convert the sceptics, and act as a basis on which to build new techniques.

(Gruhn, 1960: 4–5)

The timing of these speeches is interesting – made in the middle of the period described above, when those involved in the arts therapies in some countries were forming into associations, individuals were developing techniques, ways of working, concepts and trainings. Judges shows himself aware of the time he is speaking: of being part of what he calls 'one stream in a current of new ideas' relating to 'new practices in the use of dramatic action and role-playing, and free movement too and painting and modelling'.

The development of the arts therapies over time can be usefully divided into three phases within health services and provision. The first phase is the presence of artistic activities in health and education settings as recreation or occupation. The second is that the arts become seen and acknowledged as having some beneficial effects, but that this is offered as an adjunct, addition or subordinate activity to the major means of 'treatment' or therapeutic activity. The third is the gradual establishment of the arts therapies as independent therapeutic modalities capable of engendering change in their own right (Jones, 1996; Bunt, 1997). In these speeches we can see illustrated some of these stages reflected within the words of the speakers. Before we look at this, to help us see these processes at work, I want to parallel it with another account of the development of the arts therapies in the UK in the early 1960s.

One of the key pioneers of the arts therapies, Sue Jennings, describes events that were happening at the same time as the Music Therapy Conference but in another part of London and in nearby St Albans:

> The Remedial Drama Group I started with Gordon Wiseman in the early 1960s. I was doing remedial drama at a special school in St Albans before the Remedial Drama Centre opened and at St George's Hospital, a psychiatric centre there, and also at the Marlborough Centre, as an instructor explicitly to do drama. There was an interest in 'doing drama with special needs'. I was also employed by the London School of Occupational Therapy to teach OT students. I also worked at a special nursery in St Albans.
>
> Drama and music were seen as ways of enabling children to do things that otherwise they couldn't have done. Quite a lot of work we were doing was helping maturation to happen . . . Maturation steps were gained and retrieved through drama; steps that hadn't been there, or had been lost through institutionalisation, for example . . . because play reading and drama activities were seen as 'a good thing' in the 1930s and 1940s, it was therefore easier for the likes of us to take it a stage further in the 1950s and 1960s . . . Everything was ripe. Art therapy started as remedial art. St Albans College of Art had a first course in remedial art before it became art therapy. We called our thing remedial drama and it was almost as if one had to make an enormous step to call something therapy. But it was about 1970 that the step from remedial drama to dramatherapy was made.
>
> (Jennings in Jones, 1996: 90–1)

In these accounts we can see different areas being drawn into contact – education, psychiatry, therapy, the arts. The Music Therapy Conference includes educators, artists and therapists as its anticipated audience. Jennings talks of a life busy innovating in education and special education for children with learning difficulties, whilst also working in mental health wards in hospitals alongside practice with occupational therapists. You can feel in the accounts that relations between fields such as the arts, therapy and education were growing out of their different contexts and coming into contact with each other – as artists, educationalists, therapists met and as pupils and patients made connections between different parts of their experiences in schools or in hospitals. You can also feel the early 'sense of mission' as the first speaker says, as these areas were being brought into a creative connection. It's not as if these people knew exactly what they would find. They were often following a mixture of intuition, exploratory zeal and pursuing what they noticed was happening as they used the arts or were involved in therapeutic activities in such settings.

The use of language is interesting. The time-bound descriptions of 'the abnormal and unsophisticated and retarded' in the first speech are an indicator of the shift made from the era at the start of the arts therapies, and are clearly different from contemporary understandings of difference and disability. However, the language is also useful to consider the process I described earlier, as the arts therapies emerge from rehabilitation or as being only an adjunct to therapy. Both Jennings and Judges refer to the shift from 'remedial' work to 'therapy'. It's worth looking at these terms as they occur in many accounts of the historical development of the arts therapies (Jones, 1996; Bunt, 1997). Judges talks of the idea of 'remedial uses' of the arts, initially, and this is followed by a shift in the next sentence saying that 'the therapeutic uses of painting and drawing are growing more important'. Similarly, Jennings talks of the hesitancy to make an 'enormous step' to call what was happening therapy rather than a 'remedial' art. It's almost as if we can see the step being tried out during the opening address as Judges, interestingly and significantly, shifts in one sentence from 'remedial' to try out this interesting phrase: 'growing more therapeutic'. The arts therapies were making this step with Judges at that time, becoming clearer about what it was they could offer, moving from an adjunct to a mode of therapy in their own right. Gruhn goes on to speculate what would happen if music therapy could develop (beneath the sceptical gaze and prescriptions of doctors, 'the sceptics').

Gilroy and Lee, in their review of the histories of art therapy and music therapy, draw attention to attitudes towards the nature of these changes in the period of the 1940s and 1950s. They, too, comment on the tradition of arts as occupational activity, but also on the use of art or music as 'inherently healing' processes (Gilroy and Lee, 1995: 2). They refer to traditions such as those developed by Hill, where patients made images in a studio-based environment (Hill, 1945; 1951), or the use of pre-composed or improvised music within work with children by Nordoff and Robbins (1971), focusing on work with a piano and percussion. They also include Alvin's work using a range of instruments and looking at the structure and elements of music within a therapeutic relationship (Alvin, 1965).

As mentioned earlier, such discoveries were occurring in many places. A parallel process occurred in Japan, for example. Okazaki-Sakaue (2003) notes that music therapy began to be practised in the 1950s and '60s with people from different professions coming into contact such as psychiatrist Dr Matsui, psychologist Dr Yamamatsu, and Dr Murai, who was both a musician and psychiatrist. He notes the importance of Alvin, who visited Tokyo in the 1960s, and whose work was translated by Sakurabayashi. Interestingly, making connections between King's College, London in 1960 and Japan in the same decade, the London Conference speeches by Judges and Gruhn were followed by one made by Alvin, who was also presenting at the Conference. The translation of Nordoff-Robbins into Japanese, occurring in 1972, is also seen as a significant factor in the development of music therapy there. This follows the pattern we've been identifying and that has been common in many countries. In the 1970s and '80s self-taught individuals came into contact with trained arts therapists, who had often studied abroad. 'These individuals began practising in institutions such as welfare centres, nursing homes, rehabilitation facilities and hospitals. They also formed several music therapy study groups, some of which later became local associations' (Okazaki-Sakaue, 2003: 1). Two associations were formed – the Clinical Music Therapy Association and the Bio-Music Association, joining together in 1995 to become the Japanese Federation for Music Therapy (JFMT).

These examples involve the 'step' that the 1960 Music Therapy Conference speech by Judges alludes to, and is illustrated in its move from the use of the terms 'remedial activity' to 'therapy'. There has been a crucial change in the arts therapies from the arts as being seen to be 'useful' in a therapeutic or care context, but needing the context of another more accepted form of treatment or therapy – such as drug treatment or psychiatry – to be effective or safe. The art form looked at in this way can still be used in only recreation or diagnosis, or in evoking material that will be worked with by one of the accepted modes of 'treatment'. In 1950, for example, in his book *Drama Therapy* Solomon can still write that drama can be used with a therapeutic *intent* only if connected to another form of treatment: 'This therapeutic intent, however, cannot be accomplished by the use of drama alone, but drama used in conjunction with the technique of psychiatry and psychoanalysis in a group psychotherapy setting' (Solomon, 1950: 247).

This attitude did not die out overnight. Many would still recognise it, especially in countries where the arts therapies have not been recognised formally by the national or major providers of healthcare. As late as 1989, art therapist Edwards, working in a large hospital for clients with mental health problems in England, can write about the expectations in his setting that art therapy is either concerned with diagnosis only, or with recreation:

> The issue of professional autonomy and recognition so often discussed by art therapists was one it was necessary to grapple with shortly after taking up my post. At that time the art therapy service was managed by the head occupational therapist and there appeared to be little immediate prospect of any change in this arrangement. Still more disheartening was the realisation that art therapy was widely regarded as an essentially diversional activity, with the art therapy hut being seen as a place to send patients en masse in order to keep them occupied.
>
> (Edwards, 1989: 169–70)

TRANSITIONS

Edwards, however, notes that he achieved a shift, both out of the occupational therapy department and in perceptions of the nature and function of art therapy. This he sees as a position where art therapy was regarded as a 'valid way of working with people in need', and as a 'therapeutic intervention' in its own right (Edwards, 1989: 168, 172).

Judges's speech also shows another link to the era of fascination with 'psychotic' art that is seen as qualitatively different, exotic and fascinating:

> For art teachers, paradoxically enough, perhaps the most disheartening incident in the curative regime is the sequel to one of these quick recoveries after drugs. Gone suddenly are the brilliancy, the love of contrasting colour, the abandon, the acrobatic draughtsmanship.

Here is the idea of a 'special' art, and that the quality of expressions can be clearly identified as illustrative of psychiatric illness. The notion of health is paralleled with pictures of 'smugly presented prim and conventional little pencil drawings of houses and gardens'. There's no doubt there that the speaker prefers what is referred to as the serpents, rearing dragons and wild horses. He is almost nostalgic that an 'apparent collapse of artistic activity is a sign for discharge, and for the relatives to come and take the cured patient back to normality'. A part of this may be linked to the extreme expressions that can accompany certain conditions, but we can also see his response as linking to the attitudes and movements of which the Prinzhorn collection is one of the most recognised examples: the interest in the artistic expression of 'the insane' as 'outsider art' – separated off and identifiable. Many, as we will see, would now challenge such ideas and comments.

In this part of the speech, again, we can see a transition. Judges is clearly acknowledging the importance of artistic expression of the clients, and the validity of the experience of their mental illness and artistic products. However, this idea is still linked to a romanticised picture of art by people with mental health problems – of the 'insane' as outsider against the 'smug' world of 'the normal'. There has yet to be the shift which sees any person as capable of artistic expression, and that the art in art therapy is, in itself, neither more nor less special than any other utterance, not set apart for 'special people'.

Edwards has looked at the history of such ideas and attitudes towards art and mental illness (Edwards, 1989: 79). He cites examples from the display of the art of people in asylums, such as those shown in Hogarth's depictions of Bedlam. He links such attitudes to being 'diverted by the shocking spectacle of lunacy – an acceptable form of recreation at the time' (1989: 78). One scene, for example, shows an open cell with an inmate drawing a moon, a ship and a geometrical shape on the asylum wall. It's a tradition rooted more in nineteenth- and early twentieth-century attitudes as described by Edwards when non-professional work by 'the mentally ill' tended to be of interest for its curiosity value – 'hospitals assembled little museums for fee-paying visitors' (Edwards, 1989: 80). This is in sharp contrast with viewing art as a part of healing, and artistic expression as a way to achieve health. Schaverien draws attention to contemporary UK art therapy attitudes where the notion that particular forms of artistic expression can automatically be linked with psychotic states is dismissed as too simplistic: that 'imagery can be thought of as pathological. This can never be the case. The crudest versions of such assessments make assumptions regarding the type of imagery: for example, a client may be assumed to be psychotic because there are many disjointed elements in the picture, or a hat on the head may be considered evidence of a castration anxiety. Clearly such assumptions lack subtlety and an under-standing of the complexity of the ways in which pictures come to be made' (Schaverien, 1992: 3). Schaverien illustrates here some of the shifts in attitude and practice that the music therapy speech illustrates in transition. The way 'the step' has been made for art therapists such as herself is clearly illustrated. The image in not simply diagnostic for others to work with, nor is the art process only a recreational or occupational one. Here, demonstrated by her comments, is an illustration of the ways in which image production, and its relationship to therapy, is now more fully understood, more fully realised for the client as a way of engaging with change. It reflects a related but substantially different way of looking at arts processes and their relationship to change. The movement from 'remedial' to 'therapy', in transit in 1960, has been made.

Schaverien describes a key aspect of the changes:

> This is because the art therapist takes account of the picture in relation to the artist. Thus they assess the whole person in relation to the pictures, and in relation to the art therapist. The juxtaposition of certain colours, shapes or images does not indicate disturbance in any finite way. A pic-ture which is peppered with detached eyes or ears does not *tell* us that the

patient is paranoid but it might indicate this as a possibility to be borne in mind in relation to other aspects of the person. There are no rules governing interpretation of pictures.

(Schaverien, 1992: 3)

Here is the final shift illustrated. The attention is on art therapy as the primary means of therapy, not as an assistant to other methods. The image is not seen as an interesting curiosity. Nor is it looked at by her as a diagnostic indication of a condition to be handed over to other professionals to be cured by treatment through psychiatry or drugs, after which the client's artistic capacity will vanish or lose its potency or relevance. The image, client and art therapist are seen within a process that Schaverien clearly elucidates. The image is part of a therapeutic relationship. Its function and complexity is acknowledged and worked with, the process is one that can result in therapeutic change for the client. Here are illustrated some of the key themes in current understandings of the arts therapies. It is echoed, for example, by the definition of art therapy established by the British Association of Art Therapists in 1989:

> The focus of art therapy is the image, and the process involves a transaction between the creator (the patient), the artefact and the therapist. As in all therapy, bringing unconscious feelings to a conscious level and thereafter exploring them holds true for art therapy, but here the richness of artistic symbol and metaphor illustrate the process . . . the expression and condensation of unconscious feelings that art making engenders are at the heart of art therapy.
>
> (Standing Committee of Arts Therapies Professions, 1989: 5)

As we saw in Part II, this is in parallel with many contemporary definitions of change and outcome: the American Art Therapy Association stresses the therapeutic use of art making, within a professional relationship, involving creating art and reflecting on the art products and processes. It says that this process will result in outcomes for clients such as increased awareness of self and others; being able to cope with symptoms, stress and traumatic experiences; enhancing cognitive abilities; and enjoying the life-affirming pleasures of making art.

In both of these UK and US definitions the three-way relationship between therapist, client and artistic expression, products and processes is identified as central to efficacy. The UK Association of Professional Music Therapists looks at the nature of change in a similar way. They say that music therapy:

> provides a framework for the building of a mutual relationship between client and therapist through which the music therapist will communicate with the client finding a musical idiom . . . [that] enables change to occur,

both in the condition of the client and in the form the therapy takes. By using skilled and creative musicianship . . . the therapist seeks to establish an interaction – a shared musical experience – leading to the pursuit of therapeutic goals.

(SCATP, 1989: 6)

I think these accounts can be summarised in the following way:

- The arts therapies can be a primary therapeutic modality and not only occupational or recreational
- Both definitions acknowledge clearly that specific changes in the client's condition are expected outcomes of the intervention
- Whilst they can have relationships with other therapeutic modalities, the arts therapies are distinct therapies in their own right, with their own working practices and theory

The nature of change is able to be described, and is centred around two areas in these definitions:

- The artistic process, through areas such as image or sound, as a means of communication, containment and process within therapy
- The triangular relationship between client, art form and therapist as central to change

What is important about this is that it illustrates that the arts therapies have reached a position where they can be offered to clients as therapies in their own right, and can articulate what processes and potential outcomes they work with. Key aspects of this will be defined later in Chapter 17, on the core processes of the arts therapies.

CONCLUSION

We've seen, then, the ways in which the ground was ready for the arts therapies to grow. Black Mountain College showed some of the ways in which the climate for the arts therapies was forming. There were many other places and occasions in the twentieth century when people, ideas and practices came together. In the words of Sue Jennings, 'Everything was ripe' (Jennings in Jones, 1996). The opening speeches from the Conference for the Society for Music Therapy and Remedial Music in 1960 illustrate the kind of transitions which occurred when the arts therapies were moving from being supportive, recreational and occupational, to seeing themselves, and being seen, as a primary mode of therapy. As Waller has described, 'in any discipline, ideas have been in circulation for some time, but at certain points in history they get taken up, spread and a new discipline develops (Waller, 1998: 77). I said earlier, the 1960 speeches represent many other meetings in the 1950s and '60s in countries such as the Netherlands, the USA and the UK, when the arts therapies were emerging in their own right. By including the illustration from Japan, we can see that such processes have been at work in different countries at other times. I've also shown how thinking and ways of working became ever more articulate, and the position of the arts therapies more consolidated, by comparing this 1960 speech with later definitions, made at a national level in the UK as part of the process of state registration of the arts therapies.

10 Art and science: the rise of the medical model and the shadow of logic

INTRODUCTION: OPPOSITES ATTRACTING?

As we have seen earlier in Part III, and as numerous texts on the arts therapies have pointed out, the twentieth century saw a dramatic increase in the presence of the arts in organisations or institutions which were involved in healthcare in various countries. This is followed by an increase in the arts as a mode of intervention in the recovery and maintenance of health, or in the treatment of ill-health. In parallel with this, Bourne and Ekstrand (1985) describe the emergence of nineteenth- and twentieth-century psychology as marking a shift: 'Before the nineteenth century our curiosity about ourselves was largely speculative, yielding few conclusions that all could agree on' (1985: 14). They note the emergence of what is described as 'scientific psychology', as scholars trained in medicine and allied sciences developed an approach: 'In place of speculation came evidence based on observation . . . The scientific method offered a means for a real breakthrough in our understanding of human behaviour' (1985: 14).

Some arts therapists, as we will see, question this simple division between 'speculation' and 'science' and assumptions about 'evidence' and 'scientific method'. A number of arts therapists point to tension or difficulty which often reflect the relationship between arts practised in what some see as a science-based environment. British art therapist Edwards (1989), for example, has written of art and science in relation to the question of efficacy:

> When considering the problem of developing an appropriate methodology for evaluating art therapy it is necessary to acknowledge that while art therapists in general feel more comfortable with ideas and influences drawn from the humanities, it is within a world very largely dominated by science that we must live and work. It is from science that traditional forms of psychiatric treatment draw their authority and power, and it is with these forms of treatment and the ideology that accompanies them that art therapists must find ways of co-existing.
>
> (Edwards, 1989: 173)

Brazilian music therapists, note, similarly:

> In a scientific context there are some resistances related to new informa-
> tion, the attachment to the accepted structures. Indeed there is not always
> an understanding about the resources and the nature of this profession
> that explores, once more and in an innovative way, musical-sonorous
> elements.
>
> (Smith, 2003: 2; Music Therapy in Brazil website)

KINDS OF DIALOGUE

There are different responses within the arts therapies to this issue. One
approach involves the arts therapies entering into dialogue with traditional
modes of medical provision and care and their frameworks of understanding and accounting for change as described by Bourne and Ekstrand. This,
in itself, involves challenge, innovation and experimentation. Many speak
of a mutual challenge involved in this assimilation. On the one hand
aspects of the health systems and users are challenged by the presence of
the arts therapies. Some speak of changes in the systems, ideas and understandings at work within existing health provision as they respond to the
presence of the arts therapies. On the other hand the arts therapies are
challenged to find languages, ways of working and concepts which speak
to, and can learn from, existing modes of working. Areas include the way
the arts therapies connect to the general provision of services for clients,
how arts therapists communicate and work within multidisciplinary teams
and the evaluation of client change in relation to existing systems and
procedures.

Others acknowledge difficulties and resistance from the main providers of
traditional health services. Many excellent lines of communication between
the arts therapies and other disciplines exist, and the field abounds with
conferences that bear witness to the development of commonalities in understanding between major health service providers and the arts therapies. However, the relationship between the arts therapies and the existing models and
practices of healthcare has been, and still is, a complex one. In some countries
there are established arts therapies professions, recognition of qualifications
and practices; in others this is not the case, and the relationship between
the arts therapies and general health provision can be marked by tension or
exclusion. Killick (Killick and Greenwood, 1995), for example, an art
therapist, notes that she encountered 'considerable ambiguity in the attitudes
of colleagues towards the purpose of schizophrenic patients' involvement in
art therapy . . . the prevailing belief within the medical model culture of the
hospital appeared to be that psychotherapeutic work with psychotic patients
was at best ineffective, and at worst dangerous' (Killick and Greenwood,
1995: 103–4).

This is echoed in the introduction to one of the most comprehensive collections of research in music therapy and art therapy. Gilroy and Lee discuss whether research that 'asks "What is the effect of this specific kind of art therapy/music therapy intervention with this particular client group?" can be conducted through the standardised procedures of experimental psychology and the medical model. It is usually orientated towards a sceptical audience' (Gilroy and Lee, 1995: 8).

It could be said that such scepticism or concern about efficacy, or even safety, is bound to be the case with any emergent or developing discipline. However, I think this is too general a stance to take. Whatever the state of integration, assimilation or provision, it is interesting to look at what is *particular* about people's experiences of the developing relationship, or struggle, between existing systems of health provision and the arts therapies. I especially want to pay attention to some of the earlier comments about the challenge of the meeting between areas often seen, within the mainstream provision for health services, as unconnected – arts and healthcare. What is the relationship? Is the presence of the arts therapies in clinics, hospitals and schools as oppositional, or as radical, as some would suggest?

Skaife (1995) and Wald (1999), for example, have both discussed the arts therapies in terms of their political nature as 'radical and subversive' (Wald, 1999: 11), and claim that their inherent potential is to challenge the status quo rather than to induce conformity. This contrasts with the more conciliatory position of music therapist Pavlicevic. She sees the relationship in terms of, 'A rich tradition . . . [that] exists in allied fields – such as psychiatry, psychology, psychotherapy, neurology, musical aesthetics and musical analysis – and music therapists need to be confident about crossing the great divides, building bridges and venturing into the unfamiliar' (Pavlicevic, 1995: 64). I want to make two points about this. One is that there are systems of health at work, in both Western and in non-Western cultures, that do not rely on the medical model referred to by Bourne and Ekstrand or Gilroy and Lee. A number of authors refer to 'the increasingly plural nature of healthcare' (Budd and Sharma, 1994: 2). Other modes and ways of working were, and are, operating alongside the medical model. These include areas such as private practice or alternative health practices or education.

Writers such as anthropologist Douglas have said, 'The United States and the United Kingdom are two industrial nations which have inherited and share the same medical system' (Douglas, 1994: 35). She says that industrial society tends to draw individuals out of their primordial contexts of loyalty and support and 'strands them' in illness, isolating them in a system that looks at separation rather than connection (Douglas, 1994: 40). She typifies this separateness as one in which medicine is split off from religion, psychic troubles from bodily ones and different parts of the body split off to different specialists.

I want to parallel this with Halley (1988), who says that there are certain characteristics that often occur in the practice of art in the period between the Second World War and the late twentieth century. He links creative movements in the 'industrialised world' as a response to people feeling stripped of their vitality, spirituality and emotionality – art is here a response to alienation, to what he calls a mechanised, repressed bourgeois world:

> The post war period attributed to modernism a vanguard, heroic role, not in the political sense, but in the sense that it claimed that art was capable of reuniting humans with some lost essence and that art was able, as well, to release hidden, heretofore unaccomplished potentialities in the human being.
>
> (Halley, 1988 quoted in Harrison and Wood, 1992: 1074)

He places this in the context of a further trend in the arts in areas such as the mass media and advertising. This change reflects the 'post-industrial concerns' of manipulating what exists rather than creating new forms: 'wilderness is bracketed by law, while tribal and folk modes of social organization have been almost completely assimilated (there remains only the difficult question of the unconscious)' (Halley in Harrison and Wood, 1992: 173).

He cites as of central concern those areas referred to by Foucault in his description of contemporary culture as 'a place in which the technologies of surveillance, normalisation, and categorisation have ever broadening control over social life' (Halley in Harrison and Wood, 1992: 1074). He urges the need for artists to engage with, and counteract this regimentation. The points made by Douglas, Halley and Foucault about culture, health and the arts are extremely relevant for arts therapists and clients in arts therapy, as they are for other artists.

Many arts therapists would find this notion sympathetic: of the arts being modes of expression and creation that are set against regimentation. They would, similarly, echo Douglas's concerns about the isolation and separation of the client into segments to be treated. There is a need to find expression through the arts that is not to do with conformity and imitation of a norm, but to find a voice that is individual. In addition, the arts therapies are very much about enabling connection and relationship: between client and therapist and art form, and in groups, the development of relationships between people. Many arts therapists would cite integration as key to their practice: treating the client as a whole, rather than separating off feeling from physical illness, one part of the body, or sick part, from another. Many arts therapists do not mention these areas as problematic. However, tensions are cited by some arts therapists working in the context of institutions, and institutionalised attitudes, and they can be experienced by therapists and clients as oppressive in the ways that Douglas, Halley and Foucault describe.

A part of this process can be seen in terms of the different 'worlds' that the arts therapist connects with. These are both where the potential of the arts therapies lies, in bringing connection between art making and healing contexts, but also where tensions can exist. Peters, in writing about sharing responsibility for patient care, has pointed to the potential for tension between different professions in areas such as referral, treatment plans and collaboration regarding 'discourse about health . . . [and] different languages in healthcare' (Peters, 1994: 189). Reason echoes this: 'Clinicians from different disciplines clash because while they may agree about what the patient needs, they interpret those needs through different frameworks [with] . . . different assumptions about what an intervention may do' (Reason, 1991). Peters points to the importance of a client-centred approach. This involves analysing working practices, the discussion of theory and practice, resource allocation, referral procedures, and, crucially, the understanding of different clinical models and languages to encourage positive interdisciplinary practice and inter-professional work in healthcare and the ideal in the client's interest of 'congruence, trust, respect' (Peters, 1994: 179).

McNiff talks about the importance of what he calls 'artistic knowing and creative experimentation' in response to the preponderance, as he sees it, of areas such as the analysis of numerical data and behavioural science research in some institutional contexts. He says, 'I do not in any way oppose science. I am suggesting a partnership identifying areas of common concern with "scientific research" distinguishing creative objects and processes that require new ways of understanding' (McNiff, 1998: 13).

SHADOW OF LOGIC?

Warner has spoken of a continuing, deep and unexamined commitment to an idea of *reason* as distinct from the *imagination* that 'may set up in itself a false opposition between the methods the mind uses to gain and apply knowledge' (Warner, 1996: 14). She recalls a conversation with Edmund White concerning the need for multiple systems of enquiry into meaning, many-faceted analyses and representations on consciousness and creation to 'enrich the languages by which we know ourselves and the world, expand syntax and give us more to grow in – a broader vocabulary' (Warner, 1996: 16).

It's interesting to think of the period of the early development of the arts therapies and how unusual it must have been for psychiatric hospitals that used drugs as a primary mode of treatment to also have a room where patients painted, made music or danced. Are these incompatible, or are they an example of the multifaceted analysis spoken of by Warner and White? Are the arts a revolutionary challenge to concepts such as the medical model? Are they having the radical energy drawn from them by producing a language which speaks to the 'medical' but which teaches the arts to lie? Is radical energy being made to talk numbers and become part of the world of bureaucratic isolates which Douglas speaks of? Is the individual who dances in the DMT studio being forced through an act of seemingly individual expression, but is actually being subverted to 'provide a corrective experience that helps a person behave in a more socially appropriate, adequate and adaptive way' (Bourne and Ekstrand, 1985: 455)? I would argue that the answer to all these questions is 'no', as we will see. However, they illustrate the tensions and difficulties described earlier. But what can the relationship be between the arts therapies and art and healthcare systems?

Johnson, in my view rightly, sums this up in the following way: 'Neither . . . trying to clone ourselves as psychiatrists or analysts, nor seeking our culture's shadow side of the tribal shaman, seem satisfactory . . . then what are we to do?' (Johnson, 1999: 115). He looks to a vision of arts therapist 'as embodying both science and soul, logic and magic' (Johnson, 1999: 115). For me, it is in this way that the arts therapies need not be seen as either art or science. The arts therapies are a product of a link made in a divide present in cultural concepts and practices. They are a sign of a vital connection between areas often seen as divided. They should not be split by their birth being between art and science parents whose artist and scientist families often can seem suspicious of each other. Some, such as Gregory and Garner, look towards a similar mutuality: 'Art therapy, as its name implies, is a combination of art and science' (Gregory and Garner, 2000: 1). Young says that art therapy has grown up in the 'shadow of the medical model' (Young, 1995); others have said that, as a discipline, 'art therapy has uniquely combined art and science providing a model for the interaction between two disciplines often viewed as separate' (Gregory and Garner, 2000: 1).

Pavlicevic expresses a need I would echo: to obtain a 'clear understanding of what it is that makes our work unique, different from *and* similar to that of other allied professions' (Pavlicevic, 1995: 64). Langham says that it is import- ant not to put a frame around the profession of art therapy, or 'to rigidly define its position in relation to either the art or the medical establishments. It is in a fluid and radical position between the two' (Lanham, 1989: 21).

Both Johnson and Young use the term 'shadow' in describing the relationship between the arts therapies and medical contexts. I think one of the processes reflected in their use of this term can be linked to Jung's representation of the shadow: 'The shadow as we know, usually presents a fundamental contrast to the conscious personality. This contrast is the pre- requisite for the difference of potential from which psychic energy arises. Without it the necessary tension would be lacking' (Jung, 1955, par 707, 1997: 168). The connection of these two areas, Jung argues, brings about full potential: 'the resolution of opposites is always an "energic process"' (Jung, 1955, par 705, 1997: 166). Perhaps we could argue that in the current development of the arts therapies a meeting is occurring between areas often split into opposites – art and science. This is part of the tension often experienced by arts therapists, and by clients in some settings in relation to issues such as medical model practice. It is important to see this potential split as expressing an opportunity. This is to retain the aspect of arts practice that, for whatever reasons, involves the aspects of creativity that are seen to be allied with questioning, with innovation. Looked at in relation to Jung's ideas of potential, the necessary creativity and imprecision of improvisation and the arts offers an energetic challenge within settings that can often be experienced as at odds with these qualities. It is in encountering this contrast and in looking for balance that the arts therapies are radical.

CONCLUSION: REVOLUTION OR COLLUSION?

At a conference on computers, creativity and cognition (1999), Ferran asserted that creativity was one of the most used words of the late twentieth century. This was seen as symptomatic of an era of intense and rapid transition, fuelled by 'accelerating technological changes, inventions and discoveries', alongside the

> Introduction of new methods and processes drawn from a comprehension and understanding of the shifting nature of creativity itself . . . Key features from the observation of current trends include a widespread [global] shift towards interdisciplinarity; an associated recognition of the importance of sustaining new forms of creativity . . . open ended research and development . . . the need for recognition that the next generation/s may regard binary approaches now current (such as the division of students into arts orientated and science orientated disciplines) may be broken down by the introduction of interdisciplinary opportunities . . . [to] break down conventional disciplinary boundaries and divisions . . . the dissolution of hitherto accepted norms and modes of perception and categorisation.
>
> (Ferran, 1999: 34)

It is in this that the radicalism of the arts therapies should be seen – that a mutual change can occur, one that involves discovering more about the *other*, the breaking down of distinctions and oppositions where appropriate, and the creation of dialogues, and respect where there is diversity. Crucial to this is an understanding of 'what works' for clients. The complexity of this understanding will be a thread through subsequent chapters, focused on especially in Chapter 16 on evidence and efficacy. However, I want to gain inspiration from a video artist talking about survival, evolution and extinction, about the avant-garde and the mainstream. Torres talks about the challenges of video art to mainstream art, about how, in cultural, political and economic spheres, 'stasis' is a 'guarantee of death'. She describes change, by contrast, as a 'by-product of curiosity, the desire for knowledge and a clear indication of creative vitality' (Torres, 1996: 209).

For the arts therapies the art of the possible is the project still being realised – of the curiosity and vitality of understanding itself as it comes into contact with clients in different settings and different clinical situations. In acknowledging and drawing energy from the apparently oppositional worlds of art and science the arts therapies are still developing, discovering: the changes in healthcare they offer to clients are the by-product of curiosity. The creative energy represented by the early connections, the hopes of Gruhn, for example, is still present in the pioneering curiosities and discoveries in arts therapies clinical work and theory. The nature of these findings and discoveries form the backbone of the rest of this book.

Part IV
Agents of transformation: arts, therapy, play

Louise Bourgeois's I DO, I UNDO, I REDO (1999) installed in the inaugural exhibition of the Tate Modern at Turbine Hall in 2000. Collection of the Artist, courtesy Cheim & Read, New York. Photo: Marcus Leith © Tate, London.

The patient is no longer dependent upon his dreams or on his doctors' knowledge; instead by painting himself he gives shape to himself. For what he paints are active fantasies – that which is active is within himself.

C.G. Jung in 'The Practice of Psychotherapy' (1931: 106)

11 The arts in the arts therapies

INTRODUCTION: ARTS AND THERAPY

Is being involved in the arts as necessary to humans as eating, sleeping or sex? Some have argued that creativity is as essential to living, to well-being and to healthy fulfilment as these activities. An absence of creativity in general, or through its particular expression in the arts, they assert, will result in ill-health.

As we saw in the last chapter, the arts therapies ask questions about our need for, or use of, the arts in ways that connect to these ideas. Is there a relationship between the arts and health? Can they add to the quality of life? Is there a difference between generally participating in the arts, and using the arts *as* therapy in terms of maintaining health or dealing with difficulties? Is there a danger that allying the arts to medicine destroys the heart of art making? The arts therapies have evolved particular ways of answering these questions about the arts. This chapter will explore these answers, as well as the ways in which the arts feature within the application of the arts therapies.

Some have criticised the arts therapies for merely using the art form as an extension of verbal therapeutic process. They say the image or dance becomes an adjunct, subordinate to words. Seen in this way, art therapy can be psychotherapy with pictures as a 'helping hand', or dramatherapy can be brief therapy that contains some role-playing. The art form is an addition to the main activity, which is seen to be the verbal therapy. Those criticising this position see it as a waste of the full potential of the arts therapies. There may be some practice where this subordination occurs; however, within most arts therapy practice this is not the case. Most would argue that in arts therapy the two areas – arts and therapy – are intertwined and each *changes* the other. Arts therapies are not two disciplines joined for convenience; the term can be seen to mark a discovery of mutuality and of unique potential, as the last chapter proposed.

One thing we can be sure of is that in the arts therapies clients and therapists alike are engaged in an art form within the therapy session. Even if the client and therapist are not directly painting or moving within a single session, the opportunity for *potential* expression is implied and available – it is a constant. Beyond this basic assumption, though, matters become more complex. These complexities relate to the variety of art forms and ideas within the arts therapies. Firstly, I want to identify some questions that will help explore this diversity.

The art form normally varies according to the different arts therapy. Does the particular arts modality, drama, for example, or dance, make a difference to the experience of the client and therapist? Does it make any difference to the client if they have access to only one art form or to a variety of art forms within the therapy? As we saw in Chapter 7, some specific approaches, for example that of expressive arts therapy, have argued for the value of the client and therapist having access to all forms of the arts within the therapy. Some, as we saw earlier, have pointed out that in a number of cultures divisions between areas such as music or dance do not exist, and that the division of the arts therapies into single expressive areas does not relate to some clients' experiences, or to some cultures' norms.

Many have argued for the value of working within a single art form in the arts therapies. In current practice, and in the development of professions in most countries, the arts therapies have separated out the art forms as we saw in Part II. Even within the individual art form there are various special-ised or specific ways of working or techniques. In exploring material in art therapy or dance movement therapy, for example, the therapist and client may normally engage in a particular aspect of the individual art form. In art therapy a client might engage in painting, clay work or collage, for example. Does it make any difference to a client whether they use clay or collage in art therapy, objects to depict a story, or perform a script in dramatherapy, or whether they play an instrument, or listen to a recording in music therapy? This chapter will look at the arts therapies from the perspective of the arts and will look at these questions to try to understand the arts element within the arts therapies.

STARTING OUT

Most arts therapists attempt to identify what the best routes to engaging in an art form within the therapy can be for clients. This happens in different ways. Some therapists will try to work in a relatively non-directive way, allowing the client to discover materials within the therapy space. For example, an art therapist might invite a client to choose materials present within the art therapy room. A music therapist, similarly, might invite the client to work with instruments available in the room, and to follow the lead of the client's choice of instrument and way of working. Once the client makes a start, the therapist will attempt to be sensitive to the creative direction the client takes, as they discover ways of expressing themselves using the art form, or as they encounter creative frustrations. All arts therapy work within this approach, though, is rooted in the idea that the client discovers his or her own relationship to the art form. There would be no formal attempt to train or teach the client in the art form or expression. The basic assumption echoes that made by McFee and Degge:

> Art is a principal means of communicating ideas and emotional meanings from one person to another, from one group to another, from one generation to another. When people have new experiences, they symbolise the experiences in an art form; they observe their art and then obtain new insights about their experiences.
>
> (McFee and Degge, 1977: 272)

A client's movements and the physical interaction between therapist and client, for example, can also be seen in this way. As Callaghan says, 'People's bodies and ways of moving express individual, family and cultural movement patterns, which are manifestations of the individual, family and cultural psyche' (Callaghan, 1996: 256). Here, the emphasis is upon clients creating spontaneous movement that emphasises feelings expressed in, and through, the body. This can occur through the way individuals express themselves in dance movement; the way clients physically interact with each other and with the therapist.

Some arts therapists offer a more structured introduction to the art form, helping clients to become familiar with using the media to express themselves. This is normally through a process of 'warm-up', whereby simple activities begin to provide access to the art form. This might be an invitation to make marks, or the therapist might offer a short series of exercises developing the client's ability to play a role.

Music therapist Pavlicevic describes the issue of directive compared to non-directive approaches in the development of what she calls the 'musical space' in relation to her practice in South Africa between 1991 and 1994. She locates her choice of approach partly in political tensions that existed at the time: 'It must be remembered that these groups took place in South Africa during a very fraught political climate in which no-one was protected from the tensions dominating the country. For many these groups were an opportunity to "forget about our problems" ' (Pavlicevic, 1995: 363). She records two comments made by clients in the initial stages of the group:

> We need you to play with us so that you can provide the structure for the improvisation, because once you provide it we know that we can just relax and play inside it . . .
>
> Playing with you means that I am guided into new directions which I would not otherwise find on my own.
>
> (Pavlicevic, 1995: 363)

Pavlicevic also talks about the musical silence that often marks the beginning of music therapy work, along with the initial improvisation with music that is made by a group. She says that key questions at this stage include how the improvisation begins, how the musical space is defined, formed and controlled: 'is it offered, grasped, taken?' (Pavlicevic, 1995: 362). The basic assumption is that the nature of the formation of this space consists of the relationships between participants and their initial experience of improvisation, their relationship to any instruments used, and their relationships with the therapist and each other. These elements are seen to contain the initial dynamics of the group, as well as expressing or connecting to personal issues for individual clients. She gives as an example an individual making the first sound, an 'opening solo': for example, this might be very loud, full, complex and busy. Here other players might begin to feel superfluous, asking whether there is any space for them, any need. Can they make a relevant contribution? She says that such initial periods move the group towards areas such as feeling cohesive fairly quickly, or forming feelings of uncertainty and unpredictability. Hence a soundscape is seen to express the relationships and issues within the forming group.

The dilemma for Pavlicevic is how to work with client requests or comments such as those quoted above: 'by providing a musical structure within which the group improvises, rather than allowing for the space to unfold, I could be imposing and limiting the possibilities of musical spontaneity' (Pavlicevic, 1995: 363). She says that she sometimes works directly by offering structure, and at other times works in a more non-directive way by seeing how the group engage with the musical space without her providing a direction. Some of her thinking about this important choice is present in her comment on the decision she made in this instance. She cites the political tensions, the general feelings of lack of safety, as well as the material from clients quoted earlier as relevant to her choice. In addition, the groups were relatively brief, normally six two-hour weekly sessions. She made the decision that her role was 'to provide a facilitating environment within which people could be enabled to play as fully and freely as possible', and that providing a musical structure 'could be seen as enabling the group to get on with playing'. So, in this instance, Pavlicevic shows us her thinking in deciding how to enable the group to 'create and claim space' in order to 'play'. It is based on a number of factors including her perception of wider social issues and experiences of group members, especially concerning tension and safety, the length of the group and the nature of the clients and their comments (Pavlicevic, 1995: 363).

So, the entry into the arts space is a dynamic one, reflecting processes such as the relationship between therapist and client, or between clients in a group context. The initial relationship with the opportunities the arts space offers is seen as a communication between therapist and client. The decisions made at this time by the therapist, concerning issues such as being directive or non-directive in their approach, are a part of this encounter with initial meanings found in the therapy.

Some arts therapists, then, might introduce or suggest an activity or way of working which would aim to support the process of the therapeutic work.

This is normally following the goal of assisting the client's exploration of personal material in the therapy. This idea is that the arts experience is connected to the client's engagement with emotional material, problematic issues or areas of potential development. Any suggestion about the use of the art form made by the therapist within such an approach is informed by their perception of the psychological or emotional needs of the client, or by an attempt to assist the process of the therapy. The therapist mostly tries to follow the client's direction and needs. A music therapist, for example, says that she works without the notion of a conductor or director in the process; she never, for example, gives a beat to begin with: 'We usually begin with a complete silence . . . before the first sound is heard; then anyone can begin as they like' (Alvin, 1975: 14).

THERAPEUTIC IMPROVISATION

These examples also highlight one of the key ideas about the nature of the arts within much arts therapies practice. The route into the art form and expression is one that is based in improvisation. It would be unusual for an art therapist to give 'lessons' to the client in life drawing, for the music therapist to teach scales and fingering, the dance therapist to teach a dance form, or for the dramatherapist to give direct training in a style of acting. This echoes some contemporary attitudes towards improvisation in the arts. For example, musician Tang-Chun Li, in 'Who or What is Making the Music: Music Creation in a Machine Age', defines the act of composing by improvisation as, 'To externalise the ideas and constructs of the mind, or mental maps, by performing some operations on some type(s) of sonic medium' (Li, 1999: 57). This improvisation can draw upon more formal forms such as harmonic series, chromatic scales, or can use a squeaking door, or sequencers: the 'roaring of speeding cars on a highway during a quiet night' (Li, 1999: 57).

Here the emphasis is upon the immediacy of creation, and of the individual's drawing on materials, processes and participation to express or to communicate rather than to use the art form according to a prescribed tradition. Li's attitude towards creation and improvisation is similar to that in the arts process in the arts therapies. There can be an element of instruction, but this is usually done indirectly, as a background or support to the client's encounter with the open space of the arts therapy, or the encounter with the arts therapy triangle of client–therapist–art form, as described in Chapters 3 and 17.

The issue of whether someone is 'good at' the art form often enters into the client's initial encounter with the arts therapy. Art therapist Lanham describes this common occurrence:

> I frequently find myself saying to clients in art therapy words such as 'It doesn't matter if you can't draw'. In doing this I am attempting to help them move beyond some of the stereotyped views of art and artists held

by our society, in particular the commonly held view by adults that if you are not 'good at art' then it is best not to try it.

(Lanham, 1989: 18)

For many clients the initial move to engagement with the art form is not so free. Labels encountered in life, such as 'not good at art', 'tone deaf', 'playing is for children' or 'shy', are present, especially on first contemplating or engaging in the arts therapy space. This attitude is rooted in the division present in many societies between artists and non-artists: this disenfranchises people from feeling they have the capacity to use or express themselves through the arts. Looked at in this way, a part of the arts therapists' role is to assist the client in dealing with the barriers that society places around access to using the arts as makers rather than consumers, and dealing with labels such as 'not good at art' or 'not an artist'. Lanham says that, 'We all know that these are not labels that need to be adhered to' (Lanham, 1989: 18).

This does not mean to say that skill or proficiency in expression, or aesthetic considerations do not enter into the therapy. There is a difference between a belief that everyone can express themselves through the arts, and saying that the language or form does not matter. The difference is that in the arts therapies the client can engage in a relationship with the art form and process whereby they discover, challenge themselves, and develop this relationship within the space and with the therapist, rather than being taught a prescribed notion of how to express and what to express. Skaife shows the way that choices over colour or form, over aesthetic considerations, are not seen in terms of learning or education about an art form, but rather as a part of the personal process within the therapy:

The process of deciding whether to put red there or not in a picture, of taking the risk of losing the picture by restructuring the whole piece, creating a dull piece of work because of avoiding feeling, giving up on something because of feeling no good at it, all these things can be experienced and mastered with the aim of making an exciting piece of art work. Development of an aesthetic sense is part of the endeavour, without this there are no boundaries and so no precision.

(Skaife, 2000: 115)

Here Skaife neatly shows parallels between the ways in which someone's relationship with creating in an arts therapy session can be seen as part of a personal process, rather than simply as a matter of skill. Within the therapy space the significance is often less on whether someone has a training in an art form and more on the ways in which the 'dullness' or aesthetic 'risk' take on meaning as part of the process in the therapy, as a part of the client's feelings and relationships.

In some situations, some arts therapists might work with the client to develop a greater proficiency in an aspect of the art form. This is not, though, to do with the therapist teaching the client a form of arts process, or language, according to a set notion of necessary music skills for music therapy, or dance movement language for dance movement therapy, for example. The client might wish, or need, to hone their capacity to use the medium in order to find the precision of expression they wish to engage with in expressing or exploring an aspect of their lives. The client might, alternatively, arrive at a greater dexterity, or develop the capacity to express themselves more effectively through their continuous use of the art form. Byrne has undertaken research in this area, and his conclusion was that competence emerged during the client's course of art therapy 'despite art therapists' refusal to "teach" them how to make pictures' (Byrne, 1995: 236). He considered areas such as the development of a vocabulary of images, the use of materials, and the capacity of the work to hold and communicate meaning for the client. In some circumstances, as we will see, the development of the client's capacity to use the art form, or the level and the nature of his or her engagement might form a part of the process of change in the therapy. Some arts therapists might offer therapy in a way that focuses on a particular aspect of their expressive form. For example, a dramatherapist might offer a role-play based group, or an art therapist might offer a series of sessions using group painting. Here the clients might elect to attend this session, deciding for themselves that the form might be of interest or use. However, improvisation, rather than taught expressive methods or forms, remains at the core of all these approaches.

In the early stages of therapy, then, the arts therapist attempts to identify with the client what the best routes to using an art form within the therapy can be for them. This concerns the form or language to be used, as well as the approach to establishing a relationship between the client, the therapist and the arts therapy space.

CREATION OF AN ARTISTIC SPACE

There should, though, be no assumption that 'improvisational' means careless or lacking in involvement. The relationship between arts processes, client and therapist in arts therapy is not casual, passive or incidental. It is not that of a listener to piped music in a supermarket, or of a passive encounter with images on a roadside advertising hoarding. The arts therapies encourage and depend on an intense engagement with an art form, with an intention that this will be a key factor in change within the client's life. The client's experience of the arts aspect of the arts therapy over the time of the therapy might vary enormously: from boredom, to rejection or a lack of inspiration, through to deep absorption. The client is not forced into this kind of engagement; the therapist does not coerce. However, the process, when seen as a whole, aims at an intimate, powerful meeting between the client's life and the art form and process. The ways in which the arts offer specific routes to awareness and communication are made available to assist the client in their attempts to change.

Artistic processes can occur in many different ways – some can happen within, and as a part of, everyday living. Others can occur in extremely disruptive conditions, whether physical or emotional. For instance, graffiti art can be produced in the middle of urban noise with the constant threat of interruption, owing to the illegal nature of the situation the work is being created in. Youths, for example, might be stopped by passers-by, or by police. Other art has been created in situations of intense deprivation and disruption, in concentration camps or in internment, for example. Within many cultures, though, the creation of art, or engagement with artistic activity, is often set aside in a special place.

As we've already seen, some arts therapists have drawn inspiration from children's play, viewing it as a part of, or allied to, art making. This will be considered in more depth in Chapter 13. Whilst some forms of play happen alongside other, everyday activities, a number of analyses of play have pointed out that 'deep' or concentrated play can normally only occur in circumstances or situations which have specific qualities. Arts therapists attempt to create a space within the therapy room which is, in many ways, similar to that appropriate for deep play (see The Player Client opposite). One of the best discussions of this is by Wood (2000) in her description of the art therapy studio. She stresses its role as a container, as a place which encourages absorption, and where play and mess can be tolerated. This provision of a space, whether in art, drama, music or dance, attempts to assist creativity: to maintain a fine balance between not seeming too controlled or contrived, whilst creating a consistent place where opportunities for spontaneity can occur. In some ways this might seem a paradox – a deliberately created place and time for spontaneity to occur! This, though, is something that the therapist tries to enable – a deliberate space for spontaneity. This spontaneity refers to artistic expression within the session, but is also central to the opportunities for therapeutic change which are crucial to the client's use of the arts therapy.

The practicalities of enabling this space to occur are not, however, based in a romantic notion of the artist in their ivory tower. They are as relevant to work done in a factory, a playgroup or an artist's studio. The key factor concerns a necessary *protection*, given that in this creative space intimate, private material may emerge, enhancing the need for boundaries of privacy. Simply put, the conditions allow the artwork to emerge, they are suitable for the arts work to take place, and are safe for the client to create arts expressions that concern the issues they are bringing to therapy.

There are basic assumptions regarding the nature of the requirements of space that are common across the arts therapies (see The Creative Space opposite).

The common denominators here, as mentioned above, are akin to those for deep play. The focus is on consistency, on privacy and being free from disruption to art making. In most circumstances regularity of time concerns a

The player client

Most arts therapists would have sympathy for Jung's view that:

> All the works of man have their origin in creative imagination. What right then, have we to disparage fantasy? [It is] closely bound up with the tap-root of human and animal instinct. It has a surprising way of always coming out right in the end. The creative activity of imagination frees man from his bondage to the 'nothing but' and raises him to the status of one who plays. As Schiller says, man is completely human only when he is at play.
> My aim is to bring about a psychic state in which my patient begins to experiment with his own nature – a state of fluidity, change, and growth where nothing is eternally fixed and hopelessly petrified.
>
> (Jung, 1997: 91)

Here Jung is talking of the basic aims of therapy. Many arts therapists, no matter what framework of change they bring to their work, would agree that the arts therapist attempts to create a space where the client can be at play, and that this is seen to create a playful state – where, as Jung says, the client can experience themselves as capable of change and growth.

The creative space

The space needs to:

have the clear boundaries of regular availability

have clear boundaries of relationship – that the therapist maintains a regular presence and responds in a consistent but flexible way

remain uninterrupted by other activities, or others not part of the activity

be private, not overlooked by casual passers-by or be overheard

provide access to necessary materials

be adequate to the task – not too small or large (e.g. a space which is too small might hinder dance work, a space which is too large might lead the client to feel overwhelmed and unable to concentrate)

---

consistent slot each week. However, for some forms of arts therapy, such as art therapy's open studio, this is slightly different. In this situation an open art room is accessible for most of the day and an art therapist is in the space, available should the client wish to engage with them. These 'basics' are experienced in different ways, though. Therapists and clients bring different expectations and associations. A number of practitioners write about how people's experiences of space and creativity will affect the way they come into and use the arts therapy room. People used to creating in groups or large spaces may feel locked in by an individual therapy room – may find it a 'restrictive, physical space' (McFee and Degge, 1977: 360). Issues concerning the use of shared space, privacy often surface. For example, clients who have been raised in 'structured . . . environments' with 'don't touch' attitudes towards the things around them, compared to those who were 'allowed to open and shut, crawl through, handle and feel the surfaces of the things around them', may bring different assumptions and engagements to the arts therapy space (McFee and Degge, 1977: 264).

CASE EXAMPLES

Here are two contrasting examples of the ways arts therapists and clients create a space for the arts to take place in a therapeutic context:

Creating a space: dramatherapy

In his account of individual dramatherapy over five sessions, Mitchell says that his initial concerns are whether a therapeutic alliance can be developed and 'to introduce slowly dramatherapy procedures' (Mitchell, 1996: 73). He tells the client that he sees work as collaboration between them, and that he will be introducing some of the ways of working. This gives the client an opportunity to see whether these ways of working are appropriate.

In the first session the client is invited into two different areas of the room – one is for reflection, the other marked by a cushion or chair that the client selects and sits in. The therapist asks them to say how they feel and to close their eyes and concentrate on their feelings. The client moves back from the chair and talks about the experience.

In the second session Mitchell introduces an activity, asking the client to create a 'life map'. This involves drawing important incidents from their life on a large piece of paper: 'I ask the clients to tell their story in the third person; this offers both a form of containment for potentially emotive material and subtly introduces the first steps towards dramatic distance.'

He then reflects on this with the client, and attempts to identify a story, image or theme. He notes that in some situations this will emerge immediately; with other clients the week between sessions will be used by them to think and to locate an image or story. In the third session Mitchell introduces a story structure to explore the image or story dramatically. For example, the client may be invited to play a role from the story: 'I ask the client to pick one of the characters from their story. What quality of personality does this character have? . . . I ask the client to imagine how their character might sit in the character seat. The client becomes a director and directs me as their actor, into a sculpt of their character.'

The client is also asked to play characters briefly for short moments. Mitchell tells the client that he is not teaching them to act: 'I am not too interested in the outward presentation of any character, but much more interested in helping the client experience the dynamic of a character from inside.'

He describes this stage as the client learning the process of the work – only once the form is known, and the alliance between therapist and client has developed, will the client begin to introduce characters which 'challenge the psychic status quo'.

From here Mitchell interviews the character, and the work may develop into other characters, the client interviewing the character, or into improvisations with two characters interacting.

(Mitchell, 1996: 74–6)

Creating a space: art therapy

An art therapist describes how a client, John, arrives for the first time in an art therapy session. He comes in, sits down, asks a question 'where is Mr T?' and sits down with his coat on. He looks over to a box with toys in, moves over and takes out cars, commenting to the art therapist about the toys.

The therapist notes his play, the way he moves the cars, keeps hold of some, and pushes others away. As he plays he asks about painting. The therapist asks if he wants to do some; he replies he's not sure. He then takes up the therapist's umbrella, putting it over his own and the therapist's head and leaves it on the floor, comes over to a table and asks 'Shall we do some painting?'

The therapist sees the playing with objects as a testing of the space and herself, before John feels safe enough to begin work with art materials. She sees it as his seeing if the act of painting could be contained.

He puts on protective clothing and then pushes paint out of tubes onto a palette. The therapist physically helps him when he has difficulty squeezing paint out, and the client paints a circle on a piece of paper. He dips his paint in white, then black and paints the circle saying 'It's all black'. He tries the same process again, and says 'Oh No that's all wrong' and that he will have to throw it away. The client folds the paper carefully, and asks the therapist where the bin is. He goes on to make a cracker out of folded paper and asks the therapist to pull it with him.

The therapist, in her reflection, sees a possible meaning in this: the client trying to mix together two different aspects of his life without success. The mess made him worried and anxious, which perhaps mirrored his inner experience. This is not reflected back to the client, however; rather it is the therapist attempting to note her own responses and ideas.

'The most important issue is that the picture surface has a "voice" of its own and gradually a dialogue builds up through which both patient and therapist communicate.'

(Case and Dalley, 1992: 185)

In the first example, the therapist is following the themes that emerge during the work, but provides activities to enable the client to create access to the art form within the therapy. He simultaneously suggests developments that assist the potential of the activities to reflect personal material and exploration.

In the second example, the therapist does not direct the client into activity – rather she observes, providing physical assistance if the client requests. She notes her own responses and ideas. The notion is that the client is initiating a series of relationships, testing the space to create and explore in, and to see how they can relate to the therapist. The assumption by the therapist is that the space, the materials used, the things made and their own responses all provide an 'open space'. The client's activities and responses are all held as potentially meaningful, and as having an opportunity for expressing personal material. The therapist attempts to find her own meaning through her own responses, feelings, observations and ideas.

In Mitchell's way of working a structure is used to introduce the client into the art form. This involves a combination of fixed forms – the use of the space within the room, the request to select material such as a story or image. Here he is creating opportunities for the client to explore the art form, with expression through drama, as well as to begin the relationship with Mitchell as therapist. The emphasis is on following the client's selection of images, themes and expressions within the structure.

In both cases the client is seen to be progressing towards their own creative expression. Their explorations are seen to hold significance of which the clients might not be consciously aware. The therapist does not provide meaning, or tell the client what meanings are potentially within the work. The direction and feelings which the client finds are seen as significant, and provide opportunities for meaning to emerge in itself within the potential space of the arts therapy.

One of the fears for clients can be that the arts expression might be harmful rather than helpful, the improvisation and spontaneity being experienced as a lack of control or holding. Here two clients talk about this:

Client account

Gloria: Some of the role play had an adverse effect rather than clarifying. Instead of coming out feeling I'd resolved something I came out feeling halfway through an issue – perhaps it was more deeply embedded: it took a number of sessions to dismiss, something had resurfaced . . . Some issues are still deeply embedded.

Jenny: I can't put myself back together and everything feels floating and in bits and that stayed like that for a while so I felt on my guard . . . I don't know how to handle it when I come home. He was good at getting it out but no good at telling me how to put it back. Perhaps finish a bit sooner and talk about what we'd done, and leave a bit more time at the end to stick myself together, pick up the pieces.

(Casson, 2001: 24–5).

The fears expressed here are clearly sometimes experienced by clients, and echo some concerns about the nature of the arts expressions in the arts therapies being uncontrolled or uncontrollable. In part, such comments may be expressions of anxiety concerning the expression and containment of complex, held-in feelings or issues. However, they also emphasise the importance of appropriate containment within the arts therapies space. The dramatherapist, Casson, responds to these comments by ensuring a section of time for 're-integration', de-roling, closure and preparing to leave the arts therapy space (Casson, 2001: 24–5).

FORMS FOR FEELING: IMPROVISATION AND CULTURE

As we saw earlier in this chapter, the value of improvisation or the spontaneous has been a theme in many art forms in many cultures for many years. However, it is important to note that the particular values attached to improvisatory form at the heart of much use of the arts in the arts therapies are only one way of making.

Within different cultures, eras or groups, other approaches to the arts are seen to be valid. Amongst these is the idea that the arts are solely or primarily the territory of trained artists. Artists are seen as people who have formal training, who may have access to specific, specialised techniques. They may be recognised by having a professional or ritual title, or their work may be given recognition through formal display or through payment. Another notion, often linked to the role of artist, is that of 'talent': some may view participation in the arts as being of value only to those who are seen as specially talented or gifted. Some ways of defining art may have very specific requirements that an art form needs to have before it is recognised as valid. For example, someone might feel that acting needs a level of skill and expertise in depicting a character in a sustained and convincing way or that an artistic expression must have spiritual inspiration to be valid. Others may consider that work with clay might need to have particular qualities such as the creation of pottery with evenness of texture and proportion, or a musical instrument will need to be mastered in order to comply with ideas of the production of harmony, melody or rhythm. This may also manifest itself in issues to do with cultural difference. People's expectations of the arts are linked to their cultural identity or background. Factors in this might concern age – the expectations of different generations on art or music, for example; of race – the different traditions in expression; or of religion – certain forms may be acceptable or not acceptable according to religious belief. Picton (1996) has described this complexity of expectations and ideas about art making and art products:

> By the 1960s when the countries of West Africa gained their independence, a survey of visual arts would have included fine art and design

departments at universities, self taught sign painters, masked performers, potters, weavers, dyers and sculptors in various media. In Nigeria there was a reaction against the kind of genre subject matter encouraged in art colleges at that time, in favour of a return to the traditions inherited from the past as a legacy of forms with which to represent a variety of identities, all Nigerian. In due course these developments would lead to the formation of artistic 'schools' based upon local design forms, the diversity nevertheless continuing to celebrate a Nigerian identity. The particular ritual and decorative needs of Christianity and Islam have also proved significant as sources of subject matter and patronage. In the 1960s, too, 'summer schools' were started at which anyone with or without formal education could practice art.

(Picton, 1996: 345)

In describing the situation in Nigeria, he stresses the importance of acknowledging the vigour and diversity concerning notions of what art is, who can make art, how it is used, and how these changing opinions are linked to political and social forces. All of these socio-political factors will have an impact on the client and therapist's encounters in arts therapy practice. Within a group there may be different views on spontaneous expression compared to rehearsed products or crafted form, for example, or there may be different expectations or associations regarding what form of expressions an art form can take.

These feelings may affect the way someone participates. If, for example, their expectation is that an art form can only be produced through training, this might restrict their capacity to engage with the arts therapies' cultural norm of 'spontaneous' arts work, where the emphasis is more on the arts as a reflection of personal material than on highly crafted and finished work.

Some clients may feel frustrated because their capacity to maintain character or express themselves through an instrument are frustrated by their unfamiliarity with the modes of expression possible within the art form. Arts therapists might work with the feelings this arouses, but also might assist the client in deepening their participation with the art form's modes through their exploration and usage of media or processes.

Others would see such differences between people's cultural ideas about the arts, and their different levels of experience, as part of the potential within the therapeutic encounter. These are openings to learn about differences, and to see such areas as reflecting other issues to do with diversity and difference in their lives and experience. Many authors connect art forms and culture in this way. Different cultural attitudes towards the body, and an individual's experience of their own body are connected, for example:

By looking at dance we can see enacted on a broad scale, and in a codified fashion, socially constructed and historically specific attitudes towards the body in general, toward specific social groups' usage of the body in particular, and about the relationships among various marked bodies, as well as social attitudes toward the use of space and time.

(Desmond, 1998: 154)

Dance, for Desmond, is linked to the way an individual's 'use' of their body contains and communicates a wealth of experiences: of who they are, how they have become this person, and how they relate to their own cultural experiences and those of the people around them. Dance is a way of embodying and exploring, of creating, recreating and relating to these cultural experiences. The arts form and process within the arts therapy becomes a place to explore differences and similarities between clients, between therapist and client, and the client's own opinions, thoughts and experiences about their relationship to their own culture and to others' cultures.

Movement psychotherapist Callaghan sees the arts therapies as having particular value in this area. Such differences are to be shared, and are a potential for mutual adaptation. She gives, as an example, different attitudes to space and touch, adding that 'the arts are inherently radical and encourage creative exploration. These factors help individual movement psychotherapists to resolve conflicts between traditional models and . . . new approaches' (Callaghan, 1996: 262).

The arts therapy space can become one that reflects and encounters the artistic approaches of all its participants. This reflection, though, occurs within a framework that is rooted in the assumption that the art processes and work are 'radical', to use Callaghan's word, and will be centred on exploration and improvisation. So, any cultural form used will need to be open to dialogue with the idea that it can act as a vehicle for personal change. As we have seen, expression in the arts therapies is based in improvisation. However, in working with clients from backgrounds or with experiences which do not reflect these norms, arts therapists traditionally set up dialogue by creating opportunities for the client to work within expressive forms which reflect their cultural identity. It is normal, though, for these to be adapted within the arts therapy session. Music therapist Amir, for example, describes her work from the perspective of her own and her clients' cultural experiences of traditional song: 'In my music therapy practice in Israel, singing Israeli folksongs often serves as a very important and dominant element. Very often the song repertoire chosen in my music therapy groups represented personal, usually unresolved issues concerning interpersonal relationships, death, bereavement, grief, ageing, past history, present and future' (Amir, 1998: 217). A client, Rina, brings a traditional folk song, 'Rakefet' or Cyclamen, to the music therapy group. This was a song she sang to her deceased daughter: 'I asked Rina to recite the song as if it were a poem, while the group hummed the melody and swayed together. I also asked her to close her eyes, imagine her daughter as she recited the song, and dedicate the song to her daughter.' This becomes a part of a process of exploring Rina's depression, sleeplessness and grief. The therapist describes it in this way: 'Rina, together with the group mourned her daughter. While reciting the song she had a very powerful insight: the cyclamen became her daughter.' This is seen to mark the beginning of Rina's being able to 'start the mourning process and to begin to separate from her daughter' (Amir, 1998: 227).

As we shall see, dance movement therapists work with dance forms their clients bring, but then introduce an improvisatory or exploratory element. Arts therapists work with cultural references and ways of making rooted in the client's previous experience. However, these are used within a framework of change, and where the images made are seen as personal material. A dramatherapist, for example, might use a script or text from a client's own cultural background, but might use this with the client for improvisation and personal exploration.

THE ART FORM AND THE TRIANGLE

In some arts therapies the materials or expressive media are easily seen to be available, and so the client's initial response to them does not need a significant amount of direction or advice from the arts therapist, for example in the art therapy open studio, where materials are in an allocated room, or in play therapy, or forms of music therapy where a variety of instruments are present in a room. Here the emphasis can be on the client responding to the opportunities, stimuli or challenge of three things: the materials or expressive forms; the creative and therapeutic opportunity presented by the space; and by the potential relationship with the therapist:

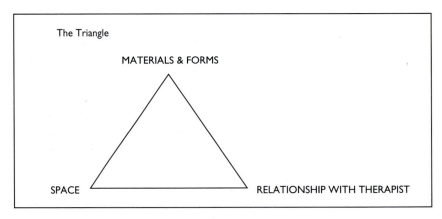

The Triangle

MATERIALS & FORMS

SPACE

RELATIONSHIP WITH THERAPIST

The stress is on the client's responses to these three areas. As we've seen, *the client's response to the arts opportunity for expression and the developing relationship with the therapist reflects the concerns or issues they are bringing to the arts therapy.*

The relationships between the three are seen as opportunities to begin to use the therapy. Therapists often understand the way the client uses these opportunities as having various degrees of conscious awareness. By this I mean that in some situations clients may be very aware of what troubles them, or why they have come to therapy, and deliberately try to use the arts materials, space and relationship to communicate and explore these areas. In others the clients may not have such conscious awareness, and express them unconsciously through their responses and participation.

Lawes, for example, had been in individual ongoing music therapy. He talks about his experience as a client, exploring unresolved issues concerning his mother's death from a brain tumour many years earlier. He describes the original situation in his life as offering no real understanding, or holding, of the impact on him and his family of her illness and death. An image forms in his mind and this is shared with his music therapist: of 'a boy sitting silently in extreme cold, darkness and desolation' (Lawes, 2001: 24). He talks about how his signs of depression and rage resulted in his being told that he was 'difficult'. He describes how he began to experience the music therapy as an opportunity 'to try to find some music to articulate and hold this experience together' (Lawes, 2001: 24).

He says that he feels his therapy had been heading towards a particular point for three years 'and now it was time to see whether the boy could find any music to articulate this scene beyond words' (Lawes, 2001: 24).

Client account

At the piano, I knew that I had to become this boy fully and let his hands play the notes. The first letting-go was the most disturbing and frightening experience in music that I have ever had. I found myself playing incoherent discords with no sense of meaning or energy; it felt as if I were dying and completely disintegrating. Then something began to happen as the boy started to play the music which articulated what he was seeing. I suddenly knew that he was only a few months old, which is why he could not speak. In my imagination I was able to see my dead mother and respond to her. I felt that I was able to remain human, to experience and articulate my tender and compassionate feelings. This profound experience in music gave me evidence that I could not doubt . . . It was my first completely improvised music, and was an experience of 'therapy in music' in the most healing and transformational sense for me.

The music itself had a kind of repeating heartbeat motif involving two notes of a minor chord with a wide spaced two-part chorale above . . . Around the sounds, the music articulated sheer silence. There were several versions over two or three days, and then I seemed to have done enough. An image came to mind of a deep-sea pipe on the ocean floor that had come apart years before, but had finally been rejoined by this boy who could not speak. Being able to look at my dead mother meant finally being able to separate from her.

(Lawes, 2001: 24–5)

Lawes is familiar with music and musical form, and this affects the way he is able to articulate his experience as a client. The process of the music therapy has enabled him to gain insight into the direction and focus of the work. He has decided on the area he wishes to explore, and goes into the music with an intention to look at issues concerning his dead mother. Beyond this, though, the form that the music making takes is unplanned. The experience is framed by the client as one that allowed him not to plan or compose, but to allow spontaneous improvisation to occur. This is seen as a 'letting-go' in relation to the letting-go he had to endure as a boy on the death of his mother. This allows feelings, images and musical form to combine in retrieving or evoking an experience, and in working through his contemporary distress that was held in the image of the silent boy. As described in Chapter 4, the experience of the client here uses the qualities of music to evoke hidden memories, to express and contain material that cannot be put into words, and to revive experiences in the present of the therapy session. He decided on the area that would be the focus of his therapy, but the form and process lie in the spontaneous use of music within the therapeutic relationship. This evocation into the present of the therapy session through musical form enables unresolved, silenced material to be expressed and communicated. The importance of the therapist is described by the client as 'she sat with the boy who could not speak' (Lawes, 2001: 26), and provided the space and opportunity to work with the material. Lawes says that insight or understanding alone would not have been adequate for him. He stresses the importance of the 'aesthetic/emotional nature of the music' in allowing him to have an experience that was encountered through the senses, and was highly emotional. His feeling was that the music and emotion came together from his unconscious during the spontaneous improvisation, and that this was a crucial factor in his work in the therapy.

For other clients, though, the importance is in the ways in which the triangle is used to express things which they either cannot use words to talk about, or of which they are not consciously aware. Someone might not be able to focus with Lawes's precision on what troubles them. Some clients, for example those with severe learning disabilities, may not use verbal language at all to communicate. Here the triangle provides a way into the beginning of non-verbal expression and exploration. The arts forms and processes are seen as a special language, which allows the material to be discovered or for issues to emerge in ways that need to be oblique. One way of understanding the creation of images, patterns, relationships within and through the art form is that they can allow censored material to emerge. They can also create a sense of safety for the client to play, or allow a distancing which gives the client permission to express material which they would not be able to name directly. Art therapist Rust gives an example of this in her description of practice with women with eating disorders:

Therapist comment

As she begins to paint she interacts and plays with physical materials in an activity using her body. As she makes images she is faced with a range of experiences. Sometimes the art object appears as a raw intensifying of what she feels . . . [for example in] . . . a woman depicting a binge scene. With the help of this image she can bring these feelings into the here and now of the session and begin to reflect on what happens that is so frightening.

At other times the art object may contain a very powerful sense of meaning which cannot yet be linked to anything she understands. A simple colour or shape may make her weep, and through feeling like this she gropes her way to a fuller understanding of the issues.

(Rust in Sandle, 1998: 163)

Here is a description of a similar process of discovery from the point of view of a client working with integrative arts psychotherapist, James.

Client comment

'I arrived at my session with a familiar feeling of wanting to talk but not feeling able to articulate my words. I felt full of feeling, confused, churned up. Fortunately for me I was surrounded by a choice of expressive media. I chose paints. This I could do in silence. As I painted tears began to flow and I felt more confused, more anxious and yet purposeful even though I had no idea what I was painting or how it would turn out.'

She describes staring down at her painting, and feeling irritated that she could not 'make sense' of it. James encourages her to stay with the image. Together they look at it from 'as many different angles as possible'. Eventually the client says she is surprised. 'An image of what looked to me like a detached breast with its nipple pointing towards a foetus emerged. I was adamant that the baby must not drink from the breast. It was bad, a false breast. I cut it out of the picture, having found my voice at last.'

(James, 1998: 20–1)

The idea here is that the client finds his or her own way into the material and that this lack of conscious intention in relation to the art form allows such opportunities to be maximised. Whilst the art form is crucial to this, the triangle always needs to be kept in mind to try to fully see the meaning and effect of the work.

Meaning and effect

- Does the way the client responds to the materials and expressive possibilities say something to the therapist?
- Does the way the client responds to the materials and expressive possibilities say something about the way they feel about the space?
- Do they reflect some of the issues the client brings to therapy? Or, put another way, is either of these areas being used as a way for the client to begin to bring their concerns to the therapy?
- Do the feelings evoked in the therapist by the client's use of the therapy and their response to the art form provide any insight into what the client is bringing to the therapy?

These questions are often present within the therapy concerning the making or expression of arts work. They might inform the way the experience is understood or talked about. The temptation is often to look at the image, dance movement pattern, role-play in terms of its *content* primarily – and to use this as the main focus of seeing what is happening in the therapy. However, by bearing in mind the idea of a triangle of concerns that relate to the art form in the arts therapy, a fuller picture can be seen to emerge. These areas will be considered in more depth in Chapters 14 and 15 concerning the client–therapist relationship.

EXPERIENCE OF THE CLIENT AND MEANING

A number of practitioners and theorists have referred to the notion that the arts are a way of 'making meaning' – of discovering and communicating. As the therapy space and the relationships are engaged in, as the client begins their work, the area of how the arts enable meaning to emerge for the client is often seen as central to arts therapy practice.

Warner talks of a constant human drive to make visible the invisible. She traces this through art making, 'the desire to make unperceived objects of fear and fantasy stand before one's eyes as if they were real' (Warner, 1996: 11). She illustrates this from history. For example, after the creation of the magic lantern one of its first uses was to project onto a wall the image of a soul burning in purgatory. The 'most exciting optical instrument' of the day was 'immediately used to make visible something that of its very nature cannot be seen and does not exist in visible form' (Warner, 1996: 12).

Warner focuses on the human capacity to conjure up pictures in our heads. Whilst we are standing in a supermarket queue, pictures can form in the mind of memories, fantasies, hopes or daydreams; some seen by the eyes of the body, and some not. She concludes, 'Consciousness is a picture palace, among other things; and one that is filled with phantasms' (Warner, 1996: 12).

How do such images have meaning for their creators? The artistic creations within arts therapy sessions can, similarly, be seen as a kind of 'picture palace' of the clients' making. The ways in which meaning emerges from the image making, music making, enactment or movement are seen as an important aspect of the clients' experience of the therapy.

Music therapist Aldridge talks about the way in which the artistic product, or the process of making, acquires meaning in terms of empiricism: *knowledge* being gained through *experience*. This is seen as the heart of what the arts therapies offer the client in terms of their experience of themselves and their lives. Aldridge uses this way of considering meaning to say that knowledge comes through the senses and that this is linked to 'cognitive perception':

> This cognitive perception is a process of organization where meaning is imposed upon what is heard. In this way a seemingly meaningless ground of sound is given meaning. To perceive, then, is to give meaning to what is heard, an act of identity. However, the non-sensory process of cognition is transparent, or rather, silent, and appears as if hearing were solely a sensory experience.
>
> (Aldridge, 1996: 25)

Within the arts therapies it's possible to say that there is a useful tension between arts making and discussion, reflection or analysis. Some such as Skaife have described this tension as a potential for 'radical therapeutic possibilities' (2000: 115).

The question raised by some therapists is whether the experience itself is enough: whether the artistic and therapeutic experience in the art form needs to be verbalised in order for meaning to emerge. As music therapist Pavlicevic puts it:

> When working with verbal clients, is it through verbalising the musical, non-verbal act that both the therapist and client give the experience meaning – and possibly prevent it from slipping away or disappearing? Were we to leave the musical experience to speak for itself would it remain unconscious, un-recovered, unaccessed by the client?
>
> (Pavlicevic, 1997: 10)

Do words detract from the experience? Or do they put coherency and a certain kind of cognition upon experiences that do not happily fit into words?

Nordoff and Robbins have said of music therapy that 'the therapists make no effort to establish a relationship with the child other than on the basis of musical expression and musical activity' (Nordoff and Robbins, 1977: 189). In contrast to this, John says that:

Music is half the management process: conscious assimilation needs words in order that the unconscious material can be managed and thought about. This process of music being literally a medium through which unconscious material can bypass repression and become conscious in words form[s] the basis of music psychotherapy.

(John, 1992: 12)

Simpson, in his study of using words in music therapy, concludes that the use of verbal language within music therapy has a variety of different functions and purposes. These comments, I think, are relevant across the arts therapies. The purpose and use of words varies enormously depending on the client group or on the individual client – for some clients verbal language will not have meaning, for example. Simpson's analysis of the work of several therapists and their relationship to verbal language looked at the ways words could both facilitate and hinder the process. Words could hinder by being used to avoid engagement, to dilute the arts experience, or to remain cognitive as a defence against spontaneous or emotional engagement. Alternatively, words could help in putting clients at ease, creating opportunities for insight for both client and therapist, and to give feedback and enhance the experience (Simpson, 2000: 87).

He concludes that 'music itself is the transforming locus of the therapy. Within the therapeutic frame, words can be considered as wrapping around the music as a secondary "skin" of interaction' (Simpson, 2000: 86). I'm not entirely happy with this image of words as a containing skin, though. His study indicates, as described above, the many roles verbal language can have within the arts therapies, but for me the relationship is one that involves a flow – and not a distinct difference as the image of a containing skin suggests. I don't see words as necessarily so separate from the art form – one can move into another, images can contain words that need to be spoken, words can contain images that need to be enacted, sounds can move into words and vice versa. One of the therapists in Simpson's study acknowledged a part of this when they said: 'The therapist can hear the tonal range, rhythmic characteristics and flow of the client's words, and in this way begin to enter the music that underlies them' (Simpson, 2000: 88).

The therapist needs to be able to respond to the client, and to be as sensitive as possible regarding when words seem a defence and an avoidance, or when they are an aid and an integral part of an arts therapy process. Many arts therapists would find sympathy in the advice written by Jung to 'Mr O'. The quotation below is from one of a series of letters to Mr O, who Jung is advising about the use of what he calls 'the active imagination'. He's talking about a dream that Mr O has described: a quantity of yellow substance has grown under the hand of the dreamer. Attempts to wash it down the drain fail because the drain is blocked. Jung's advice is to work with the image – to start with the yellow mass:

Jung and the yellow mass

Contemplate it and carefully observe how the picture begins to unfold or to change. Don't try to make it into something, just do nothing but observe what its spontaneous changes are. Any mental picture you contemplate in this way will sooner or later change through a spontaneous association that causes a slight alteration in the picture. You must carefully avoid impatient jumping from one subject to another. Hold fast to the one image you have chosen and wait until it changes by itself. Note all these changes and eventually step into the picture yourself, and if it is a speaking figure at all then say what you have to say to that figure and listen to what he or she has to say.

(Jung, 1997: 164)

In a later letter (1997: 165) he talks about the importance of stepping into the picture with what he calls ordinary human reactions and emotions. He says that not only will Mr O analyse his unconscious, but that he will give his unconscious a chance to analyse him – and thereby begin to create a unity of unconscious and conscious, and the route to 'individuation'.

Interpretation, or the emergence of meaning through interaction, is often seen as something that can engender change. This occurs through insight and the mediation of artistic expressions made within the relationship between client, art form and therapist. A connection made with suppressed images, for example, can be seen to vitalise the client's conscious life. The importance here is the idea that expressions through the arts, such as images or movements, can be 'carriers' and hold potentially useful meanings. In addition, arts expressions and forms can allow distance, or an added perspective. Interpretation is one way to use the urge to make the 'invisible visible' that Warner talked of. Consciousness can mediate meaning from arts expressions made within the therapeutic relationship. The particular relations between the unconscious and interpretation in the arts therapies will be looked at further in the next chapter. More generally, we can say that, looked at in this way, the arts become a way of *making meaning* – of discovering and communicating meaning in a dynamic process of change within the arts therapies. Music therapist Pavlicevic sums up issues around meaning in the arts therapies in a succinct and illuminating way. She says that 'the act of embodying, or of making the thought "flesh", be it through music, sculpture, art or words, prevents it from being suppressed, repressed, or disappearing altogether. However, the nature of this embodiment may give the thought a different emphasis, a different dynamism and a different colour' (1997: 10).

EXPRESSIVE FORMS OF THE ARTS

So far we've looked at the way that the client and therapist begin to engage with the arts therapy language and process, the ways in which a client might enter into expression, or begin their use of the medium, and the way in which meaning can emerge. Do the different art forms in the arts therapies make any difference to the client within these processes? Does the choice of dance movement compared to music make any difference? Does this influence the direction or effect of the therapy? I want to contrast some examples to look at this.

As we saw in Part II, the different arts therapies mostly use specific areas of artistic expression and process. Gale and Matthews, in a collaborative project involving an art therapist, dramatherapist and music therapist, for example, noted areas that were parallel or similar. They also recorded areas of language, session structure, ways of relating to clients and the use of physical objects that were different (Gale and Matthews, 1998: 182–3). But what exactly are these parallels and differences, and do they make any difference to the client? I want to briefly look at the arts processes in the arts therapies as a way into exploring this area. I will look at all the arts therapies, but will focus on dramatherapy and music therapy in slightly more depth, as examples.

In my experience of working with students and trained arts therapists within the different disciplines over the past twenty years, there are three responses arts therapists often make in relation to participating in each other's arts in workshops. One is suspicion that the other art forms are anxiety-provoking, that it's 'not their language', they feel de-skilled and unable to express themselves as they would do in their 'own' art form and they are reluctant to engage. The second is that in response to potential difference they say, 'but we do that too' or 'that's no different from when we . . .'. The third, and the one of which this book is, I hope, a part, is interest in the others' forms and practices, as a way forward for mutual discovery about the arts and change in therapy.

In the way they have evolved to date, the individual arts therapies have both things in common and elements of difference. The next section looks at the way in which some aspects of the arts forms emphasise, or foreground, some processes, experiences and kinds of language over others in the client's participation.

Dramatherapists, for example, use all aspects of the spectrum of dramatic expression. This varies from early movement relationships through to staged enactments where roles are played in front of an audience. The main ways of working include role and improvisation; work with objects, story and movement.

More specifically, role-play and improvisation might be used to explore material brought by the client. In some contexts this might be a deliberate re-creation of a life situation. Other situations might be more oblique: for example, creating an improvisation with imaginary characters in a fantasy situation. In a role-play based on a life situation the client might cast members of a group, or the group and therapist, to play people from their lives outside the therapy. The client might play himself or herself – so a difficult encounter might be played out in the group. The idea is that this piece of life is brought into the session, and can then be looked at afresh by the client with the support of group members. Emotions can be re-experienced, but can be worked with, reflected on in the space of the therapy.

Movement or physical theatre is seen to develop the client's ability to express themselves bodily. Here the emphasis is more on non-verbal expression than in role-play-based activity. Words might hinder some clients, so the experience of working non-verbally might permit expression and exploration. Words, for example, might encourage censorship or defensiveness. Work that focuses on the body might allow material expression through a change of emphasis or a different kind of permission that can be given when verbal language is not the main means of communication. Clients may play themselves directly, or may take on other characters or identities. This might mean playing people from their own, or other group members' lives, or they might play fantasy characters. This work might include masks, costume and scenery.

The dramatherapist can stay outside the activity, acting as a facilitator for the process as a whole, or making suggestions as to the way the work might develop, suggesting techniques, or asking questions as the work develops. Some dramatherapists might take on roles during the work, playing a part within the action.

Drama in dramatherapy, then, emphasises physical work – the client often uses their body either through improvisation or role, movement or physical play. Dramatherapy foregrounds the therapeutic potentials of identity transformation through taking on the roles of others, fantasy characters or gives opportunities for the client to play themselves in a different time or space. In group dramatherapy a client also engages with others who have transformed their identities – for example, in a role-play where a number of people have taken on roles. The client can leave their usual identity with its attendant ways of behaving, and try out new ways to relate, or respond, to people or events. Dramatherapy foregrounds the client's opportunity to 'try not being themselves'. In addition, other people may depict the client. Others in the dramatherapy group, or in some situations the therapist, may play the client – the client can look at him- or herself. This might occur though someone playing them, through role-play, or video playback. This foregrounds the reflective capacity of the client's being outside their normal self and looking at their own life. This reflexivity and transformation is different from art therapy and music therapy, where the therapy does not emphasise pretending bodily to become someone else, or playing a role, or the client's seeing someone else playing themselves, for example.

Dramatherapy backgrounds areas of experience such as the idea of physiological change due to sound, or the use of objects made through painting, or use of clay to express feelings and the relationship with the therapist. It backgrounds the use of instruments to create improvisation and communication between therapist and client, or between clients, and the use of the client listening to recorded music as a primary agent of therapeutic change.

In music therapy, the experience of music might vary from direct involvement in improvisation to the client and therapist listening to recorded music. A client might listen to music produced by the therapist, or work might consist of the client lying on a bed which makes use of the vibrations caused by musical sound. The Nordoff–Robbins (1977) approach, for example, involves the client in making music. The therapist can make music with the client, encouraging them to improvise with musical instruments. Practitioners such as Darnley Smith (1996) have pointed to the importance of twentieth-century music developments in relation to music therapy's use of the art form in such situations. She points out a wide range of harmonic and tonal sounds which neither provide a formal resolution nor have a sense of recognisable form. She says this has contributed to the musical space in music therapy, which can allow sounds not crafted into compositions, and which she characterises as 'raw' and 'spontaneous' (Darnley-Smith, 1996: 2).

In some work the therapist participates in the creation of music. The therapist may sing with the patient, or play with them on an instrument such as the piano. This approach does not necessarily involve interpretation in the psychoanalytic sense. The creativity of improvising music, the relationship developing between therapist and client, are seen as the therapy. In this way of working the therapist tries to match the mood or feel of the client's music. Bunt describes how, working in this way with children:

> behaviour can . . . be answered by the therapist in a way that partially imitates but also extends that communication, so as to indicate an understanding of what the child was attempting to express. For example, a child may play a drum at a quick tempo which is taken by the therapist to indicate a feeling of excitement: the therapist then plays the drum (or responds via another modality such as the voice) at a similar tempo but also loudly. Turn taking between the child and therapist may then ensue.
>
> (Bunt, 1997: 255–6)

Rhythm is also used – this is seen as a communication. Especially interesting to music therapy is the notion of *personal rhythm*. Rhythm is seen as something which expresses the self, but which also can be important in communication between people. Circadian rhythms such as sleep and temperature or of breathing and pulse are considered in this way: 'It is rhythm that provides the ground of being, and a rhythm of which being is generally unaware. Rhythm is the matrix of identity' (Aldridge, 1996: 29).

Alvin writes that 'Drums or percussive instruments can speak to one another and express unlimited kinds of feeling through rhythm, tone and intensity' (Alvin, 1975: 16). Areas such as volume, tempo, phrasing, responsiveness, and the musical relationship are paid attention to.

Music foregrounds non-verbal communication through sound – the use of instruments or the use of the voice singing but not using words. This might help those for whom the cognitive use of words, the conscious awareness that words might bring, is not appropriate. They can find expression using sound: 'Music can sometimes effect communication with a completely withdrawn patient when other methods have failed' (Gruhn, 1960: 4). Music foregrounds hearing. Though other senses such as seeing are present, hearing is the sense most appealed to. People who do not or cannot use words or sight easily, or at all, might find expression or communication particularly effective through this mode. The use of instruments allows parallel playing or singing. The use of rhythm creates opportunities for feelings or relationships to be established in particular ways.

The effect of music on physiological and psychological states has been looked at in terms of the effects of sound. Here the emphasis is on the physiological effects or benefits for the client. Music helping recall in coma patients is one example of this way of looking at change (Andsell, 1995). Rider (1987) has undertaken research on the effects of music on the body's immune system and the reduction of pain and stress. Vibro-acoustic work, which focuses on areas such as the use of low-frequency pulsed tones through adapted beds, is also an aspect of this area of music therapy.

Music can also foreground cultural experiences of song, evoking memories and associations, group processes and engagement in singing. Music can emphasise the ways in which objects can be used to form and hold relationships. In contrast to art therapy where the object is painted or made and in dramatherapy where the object may be reminiscent of toys, in music therapy the object produces sound. Music does not involve the creation of objects through mark making or manipulation in the same way as art therapy. The focus is more on the use of objects to produce sound, or relationship, through making music, or being handled and passed, compared to the use of objects in relation to image making in art therapy.

Music backgrounds the creation of fictive states. Much music therapy stays in the here and now of the playing, rather than moving explicitly into fantasy states involving taking on other identities. Aspects of the client's identity might be foregrounded, or experimented with in creating sound, rhythm or lyrics, but they do not normally consciously play a character, or another client, for sustained periods of time. Music backgrounds the use of the body in the way dramatherapy or dance movement therapy might seek to express identities or the development of themes through playing roles and creating stories.

Art therapy often foregrounds the creation of static images, the creation of objects which can be kept beyond the session in which they are created; the made thing is kept over a period of time. Art therapy emphasises engagement with materials such as paper or clay which are used to reflect personal material and to create images. The direct expressive potentials of the body of the client are not used as frequently as in dance movement therapy or dramatherapy, where the client could be engaged in physical movement, or mime, or expressing a role physically through the way they move their body.

Art foregrounds the client's staying within their identity. The focus is on what they have made; they do not normally enter into different identities through role-playing. When looked at within a model which focuses on transference, a part of this is that the client may take on different aspects of themselves within the interaction. They may, for example, feel like a child, a parent, a rival within the therapy, but within this they normally stay within their own identity. There is no formal shift into taking on an identity by role-playing and pretending to be themselves at age 7, or taking on the movement qualities of their mother in order to depict her. Similarly, the therapist would not actively take on a role, as in dramatherapy, where the therapist might play a role in the client's imaginary world, or in dance movement therapy where the therapist might touch or enter into physical engagement and movement work with the client.

Art foregrounds the creation of a private creative space – there is often a period of time when the client engages in solitary creative activity – drawing or painting, for example. The therapist is present, others may be present – but the emphasis is upon private space and engagement. The exception to this is group painting, or work created in dialogue with a therapist. However, with these exceptions art therapy creates opportunities for privacy in work in ways which are not often paralleled in the other arts therapies. There work is more usually actively witnessed by the therapist, or made in front of, or with others – for example, the creation of sound and music, movement or enactment. One of the few areas that are parallel is the use of approaches related to world technique in play or dramatherapy, where a sand tray or objects may be used by clients to play privately. Wood describes 'reverie' as an aspect of these kinds of space:

> Art-making involves reverie and this can be totally absorbing . . . Studios throughout the centuries have contributed to the environmental circumstances that make this possible . . . The life difficulties experienced by many clients are extreme yet the availability of a studio can add to their capacity to face what they feel. This is because the actual making of art can engender a sense of thoughtful absorption and this can make it possible to reflect upon what is felt and then possibly even to see the feelings in the artwork. This is uniquely a part of what art therapy can provide.
>
> (Wood, 2000: 42–3)

Art emphasises the role of images as mediating between self and experience – the potential of a made, physical image to reflect, transform and mediate.

Dance movement therapy foregrounds the physical development of relationships through dance and movement as a cultural form that allows participation and connection to a person's culture. Movement prioritises the body as communicator, and foregrounds areas such as non-verbal communication and signals made by the body. It foregrounds the ways in which discomfort, distress or illness are reflected through the body and the ways in which movement can both reflect and release. The way the body and movement connect to identity is central to DMT. Client experiences emphasise this relationship between the body and identity, and the way in which movement reflects and allows change in this. It involves ways of working that stress how the body can experience release, transformation and new ways of experiencing the self and relationships with others through movement. It also uses the potentials of dance and movement as ways of expressing, exploring and transforming relationships

Dance movement therapy uses the physiological effects of movement on the body. The notion of bodily development is drawn on, and the way in which an individual grows and develops through their body. There are stages in the way someone relates to their body, and to others through their body. Developmental stages can be worked with to assist development that has not occurred, or which has been blocked.

These, then, are brief summaries to give a flavour of the ways in which the art forms can be seen to highlight certain processes or aspects of expression. Obviously these are very general statements, and each client and therapist's experiences will differ. However, I have attempted to provide some sense of the ways in which the arts therapies may differ for those involved. Part V discusses these areas in more depth.

DOES THE ART FORM MATTER?

It's possible to see in these brief outlines areas that are parallel and that are different in terms of the ways in which the client might experience the art form and process within the arts therapy. Having reviewed the different modes and ways of expressing it's important for us to ask: does the expressive form matter? Does it make any difference to the client? If there are differences what are they?

The creation of an image in art therapy through painting, compared to a story enacted in dramatherapy, is experientially very different. The expression and encounter with the arts medium of the client varies considerably if looked at in this way. I think it is possible to say that, within the variety of practices that have been developed, clear differences can be identified between the languages and processes at work within the different disciplines. There is little extant art therapy work, for example, which consists of the client's role as primarily audience to the art therapist's painting or, in the case of the dramatherapist or dance movement therapist, the client's experience as primarily witness to the acting or dance of a therapist. However, one approach within music therapy involves the therapist playing an instrument whilst clients witness – their role is to be involved by listening, not making directly. As an example, this primacy of witnessing the therapist illustrates the way in which the use of one arts language and process can create a difference in the client–therapist relationship. Other contrasts do exist – for example, as described above, some dance movement therapists become directly and bodily involved in moving with clients, whilst art therapists may engage in painting artwork with their client, but here the difference between the art forms has an effect on the relationship. The engagement in touch, body work and movement is substantially different from mark making with the paper and instruments as an expression and embodiment of the process and relationship. These examples illustrate that there are some differences of method, tradition and experience for the client.

So, can we say, for example, that the client's *experience* in music therapy is substantially different from that of the client in art therapy? The answer is yes and no. The arts forms discussed have shown the ways in which the different arts processes and languages within the arts therapies have both commonalities and differences. The ways the art form affects the relationship between client and therapist also has commonalities and differences. We have seen that the arts therapies argue that they foreground the healing possibilities within the arts and within the potentials of relationship, expression, communication and reflection that the arts engender. For the client the different arts therapies do offer different languages and opportunities. I would argue, though, that the above descriptions illustrate that, even though the arts languages and processes within the arts therapies differ in some areas, it is possible to identify common processes which are at the core of change within the arts therapies. The above consideration of arts languages and processes has shown that there are differences, but I will argue that there are processes that can be identified across the arts therapies that create a common link. These will be described in Chapter 17.

CONCLUSION

The arts therapies, then, utilise the potentials of the arts for healing. Within the diversity of languages and processes they foreground spontaneous or improvisational expression. On the one hand the engagement with arts processes and products can allow for a different experience for clients. Patterns, way of behaving can be reproduced but in a way and in an arts therapy space where reflection might be possible, where re-working the experience is possible, and where the client can attempt new ways – a re-learning. The arts processes and languages allow access to material or issues through images, dramatic process or music, for example, within the therapeutic relationship. These are different from the original experience, and yet can create or re-create aspects of the original experience. They are enriched containers or coded expressions. The difference is that the client can give themselves different permissions. They enter a playful relationship with the experience because it is fictive and because they express it through artistic means. In addition it is created or re-created within the boundaries of the therapeutic space and the therapeutic relationship.

Hence things can be practised or worked with in comparative safety, or with other permissions. The arts therapies also draw on the potentials of arts forms as experiences involving creativity, different kinds of qualities and opportunities for expression and relationship. They might, for example, use sound as a way of assisting or enriching communication for someone, or the potentials of image making to create connection between two people. Entering into the arts form within a safe space and within a therapeutic relationship allows aspects of the client's ways of relating to be experienced differently, or the client can experience themselves differently. This might, for example, be true as a client with autism experiences communication with and relationship to another through paint, compared to words and eye-contact which are experienced as impossible routes to contact. A number of arts therapists have stressed the importance of such participatory experiences of the arts in the arts therapies. It is this act of participation that can engender change through its experiencing rather than reflecting or describing alone: 'Through such a group there is the possibility of rediscovering *experienced* culture, not just receiving a passive and often processed observation' (Jennings, 1983: 49).

All arts forms and expressions occur in a space that defines the way the art medium is experienced by the client. We have seen how this occurs within a creative therapy space and within a triangle between client, therapist and art form. A key link within this concerns the ways in which the arts relate to notions of the unconscious within the therapeutic relationship. The next chapter will explore this important aspect of the way the arts and therapy relate.

12 The sensuous encounter: the arts therapies and the unconscious

INTRODUCTION: THE UNCONSCIOUS – DEFINITIONS AND ENCOUNTERS

As he was falling asleep one night, André Breton heard his first automatic sentence. The sentence was 'There is a man cut in two by the window.' He called it an automatic sentence because it came, he said, from nowhere, 'like a knock on the windowpane of consciousness'. With it came a faint visual image – of a man with a window around his middle. Later, in 1919, he produced a book called *Les Champs Magnétique*. The first section was called 'The Unsilvered Mirror'. This title – a mirror that can be seen through – seems to talk of staring through into a world beyond the surface, suggestive of looking beyond the everyday experience of visible reality, into an area present, but normally unseen. Some have seen this as an image of encountering the unconscious.

In the 1930s, artist André Masson scattered sand, spread glue and paint to create images quickly – trying to minimise the censorship he felt his conscious mind subjected his creativity to. He was deliberately trying to reach into parts of his mind he was not actively aware of. Others who worked around him likened this kind of practice to awake dreaming: to an act which tried to revolutionise people's ideas and experience of reality by unleashing the power of a domain inside the self which was known as the unconscious (Conley, 2001: 105).

Artists and analysts alike have tried to encounter, describe and understand the function and uses of the unconscious. Claims have been made for it as a major 'discovery', affecting many facets of living, from the arts to advertising to politics. Some of these claims maintain that engaging with unconscious material is vital in therapeutic change. Counter-claims have been made that the existence of the unconscious is an unprovable proposition: a hypothetical construct which has no basis in fact.

The idea of the unconscious has been central to some areas of the arts therapies: their thinking and their methodology. This chapter will explore the notion of the unconscious in relation to the arts therapies and to their concepts of change. Can we, for example, say that there is any proof that the act

Ariadne's thread

This work was produced by Masson in the 1930s. It was one of a series of images produced by him through automatic drawing. The notion of automatic writing and drawing was to find a way to create the optimum state for material from the unconscious to emerge. It was akin to creating a dreaming state whilst being still awake. Ariadne is not guiding Theseus through the maze but seems to be embracing him. The labyrinth motif has been noted as a metaphor for the unconscious. This painting was bought by psychoanalyst Lacan in 1939. Lacan was in a relationship with the sister of Masson's wife. I mention this because it gives some sense of the connected worlds of analytic thinking and avant-garde art. As this chapter shows, this dialogue was an important one in the mutual development of both fields – of the arts and psychoanalysis.

André Masson's ARIADNE'S THREAD. Copyright © ADAGP, Paris and DACS, London 2004.

of painting can achieve a relationship to the unconscious of a person diagnosed as schizophrenic? If this relationship can exist, can it bring about positive change? Can we say that sound has any connection with unconscious processes? Is there any evidence to tell us whether working with the enactment of a 'forgotten' or suppressed traumatic experience can bring about recovery for someone who has been tortured?

For some arts therapists all these questions revolve around the relationship between the unconscious, therapeutic processes, arts activities and the bringing about of positive change or development. At the heart of these connections is an assumption which is central to a significant number of arts therapy approaches. This is that there exists an aspect of the self which can be described as 'the unconscious', that connects with certain illnesses or problems which cause distress or dysfunction.

This assertion is followed by another: that there are ways of engaging with the unconscious which can bring about change or healing. Art making and arts products within the therapeutic process are seen to relate to the unconscious in ways that are fundamental to the recovery of health, or the improvement or maintenance of well-being. What are these ways? How do arts therapists see the unconscious? Does it exist? In the encounter between arts therapist and client how can the unconscious feature?

Not all forms of arts therapies work with the unconscious, or with a model of identity which acknowledges the existence of the unconscious. As described in Chapter 4, for example, some forms of music therapy concentrate their attention on the physiological changes brought about in clients when they are in contact with music. This way of working looks at the role of vibration and tonality in effecting change, for example (Wigram, 1993). Other arts therapy practice works within other therapeutic paradigms such as the cognitive or developmental. These will be looked at in Chapters 14 and 15.

However, a significant proportion of work is centred within a psycho-dynamic approach in which the notion of the unconscious features. Karkou's research (1999a; 1999b) into the main theoretical influences within the UK arts therapies indicated the prevalence of the work of Winnicott, psycho-analytic theory, object relations theory and the work of Jung and Klein. The extent of this varies within the different disciplines; for example the influence of the analytic school is more prevalent within UK art therapy than drama-therapy (Valente and Fontana, 1993). This chapter looks at the ways in which arts therapies practice relates to unconscious material, and the ways in which arts therapists understand the complex relationship between the therapeutic process, art making and creativity in relation to the unconscious.

ANALYTIC PERSPECTIVE

Towards the end of his career Freud described the unconscious in this way:

> The oldest and best meaning of the word 'unconscious' is the descriptive one; we call a psychical process unconscious whose existence we are obliged to assume – for some such reason as that we infer from its effects – but of which we know nothing. In that case we have the same relation to it as we have to a psychical process in another person, except that it is in fact one of our own . . . we call a process unconscious if we are obliged

to assume that it is being activated *at the moment*, though *at the moment* we know nothing about it.

(Freud, 1964/1973: 102)

This quotation is typical of what often happens when the unconscious is described or discussed. An attempt is made to try to define something that is, by its supposed nature, elusive and hard to determine by words, by cognitive thinking and concepts. We 'know nothing', Freud says, for example, yet we must 'assume' that it is there. A number of themes arise from this definition which all relate to this *elusiveness*. They are central to the relationship between the unconscious and the arts therapies. The self is seen as divided: Freud's description is of a psychic existence which is at the same time both a part of us, and yet unknown. He uses terms to describe the unconscious that create a seeming paradox: it is both of us, and yet it is as if it is *not* us. We know of its existence and yet do not know directly of its existence: at the same time 'we know nothing' and yet we *must*, we are 'obliged' to assume that it exists. This 'must' is because unconscious forces are at work, and are manifested – they have 'effects'. Yet we cannot see the origin, the unconscious, directly. We can infer only from signs, effects, that it exists and is active.

The theme of the unconscious as an *area*, a *region* is also here; Freud goes on to describe it as 'a mental *province* rather than a quality of what is mental' (Freud, 1964/1973: 104). These different areas are given names, attributes and relationships with each other: ego, superego, unconscious and id. Part of psychical illness is seen to occur when the relationship between the different regions of the mind becomes problematic. The act of analysis is one whereby the ego's field of vision is widened; it can appropriate that which is buried in the unconscious: 'It is a work of culture not unlike the draining of the Zuider Zee' (Freud, 1964/1973: 112). Here the theme of a region or geography is continued – the image is one to which I will return – of the therapeutic act being likened to an act of transforming the landscape; of uncovering, making something invisible. The bed of the sea – made into land that can be seen and used, the Zuider Zee bed drained and made visible.

Some see anxiety as central to this process. We are seen as organisms who structure our lives defensively to avoid anxiety. Anxiety is

not only a painful bodily sensation, but [it] can interrupt thoughts and intentions leading to disorganisation of moment to moment behaviour. When extreme, anxiety can lead to feelings of disintegration and threaten the sense of being a whole person. All psychodynamic viewpoints share the notion that our central identity, whether we call it ego or self, has to be constantly defended against anxiety in order to limit disruption and maintain a sense of unity.

(Thomas, 1996: 284)

These defence mechanisms such as repression, denial and projection are seen as part of our normal psychological mechanisms, but they are largely unconscious, we are not consciously aware of them. Traditional Freudianism draws a 'metaphorical "horizontal" divide between consciousness and that which is pushed down into the unconscious' (Thomas, 1996: 312).

Others within the analytic tradition have emphasised different aspects of the unconscious. Winnicott, for example, has argued that in some situations in infancy the 'true self' has to be hidden deep in the unconscious, and protected by a conscious compliant version of the individual called the 'false self' (Winnicott, 1986). Jung critiqued the idea of a unitary 'self', and the unconscious is seen by him as a part of this questioning: 'the so-called unity of the self is an illusion . . . We like to think we are one, but we are not, most decidedly not . . . I hold that our personal unconscious, as well as the collective unconscious, consists of an indefinite, because unknown, number of complexes or fragmentary personalities' (Jung, 1935: 81).

Some have challenged Freudian views of the unconscious as too negative. Storr (1972), for example, says that because Freud's initial work was with hysterics, this tainted his view of the unconscious and explains why it is mainly a repository of 'unacceptable' material. This view has been contrasted with the role of the unconscious in creativity where it can be seen as playing a role in inspiration and motivation for making. Again, as we shall see, this way of critiquing Freud is relevant to the ways many arts therapists understand and relate to the idea of the unconscious.

Jung, in *Archetypes and the Collective Unconscious*, refers to the unconscious in relation to a client, Miss X:

> Long experience has taught me not to know anything in advance and not to know better, but to let the unconscious take precedence. Our instincts have ridden so infinitely many times, unharmed, over the problems that arise at this stage of life that we may be sure the transformation processes which make the transition possible have long been prepared in the unconscious and are only waiting to be released.
>
> (Jung, 1959: 100)

Here themes of connections between instinct and the unconscious have a different relationship from the qualities that Freud attributed to the unconscious. Stress is placed on the notion of an *innate wisdom* based on experience, and that the unconscious is a place where material is stored which can be accessed to support an individual during crisis.

Within this framework the 'collective unconscious' can be expressed through contact with archetypes. These are present in the expressions and the power of phenomena such as dreams and myths. As art therapist Schaverien says, the idea is that archetypes do not take on form, but are 'the underlying element which influences the choice of a certain image at a particular time' (Schaverien, 1992: 21). The reasons for the activation of certain archetypes at a specific time for individuals vary. Schaverien notes that Jung, based on his own experience and that of his patients, considered that making pictures was a useful method of accessing the healing potential of the unconscious. He encouraged some of his patients to paint 'in order to escape the censor of the conscious mind' (Schaverien, 1992: 21).

ARTISTS AND THE UNCONSCIOUS

Though the idea of the unconscious had existed before Freud began his work, the influence of his *specific* ideas has permeated the field of therapy and Western culture as a whole. It's tempting to say that ideas of and about the unconscious have come to the arts therapies only through the field of psycho-analysis and psychotherapy. However, we *can* say that though analysis has exerted an important influence on the arts therapies' relationship to the unconscious, there are other elements to consider.

The first point to make in relation to this is that the idea of the unconscious was extant in the arts prior to the work of analysts such as Freud and Jung. This heritage is something which the arts therapies reflect through their relationship to artistic expression and traditions.

Another element concerns the arts in a 'post-Freudian' world. Numerous artists, writers, musicians and dramatists have described and shown how Freud's ideas of the unconscious in particular have impacted on their work. These concepts have been influential in the ways in which artists have related to their media, their process and the relationship between themselves and their art making. The responses made by artists in different fields – from painters to dramatists – to the ideas of analysts such as Freud or Jung have developed into independent discoveries and findings about the unconscious.

Sometimes these initial responses by artists were based on general ideas, or even misunderstandings, rather than on actual reading of Freudian or other analytic texts. These 'mistakes', however, have sometimes created interesting and valuable contributions to our perceptions of the unconscious. They reflect their creator's discoveries, the initial Freudian idea, or the mistaken notion of what Freud was saying, for example, serving as a starting point or prompt for the development or expression of a different idea.

This can be seen in one of the chief groupings of artists in dialogue with ideas about the unconscious – the Surrealists. Many artists in this group were 'influenced' by Freud's ideas of the unconscious: in their theories, the forms their creative products took, and in the actual process of creation. They deliberately attempted to revolutionise their ways of working. For example, as described earlier, artists such as Masson tried to reduce conscious control in their writing and drawing. Not only did they record and use images from dreams, but also they tried to create a dreamlike state in the techniques they developed to make art or to write. This was in order to reflect the unconscious arena of the undirected and uncensored. Their concern was often with the idea of the unconscious as a source of 'unbound' energy, relatively free from censorship (Mundy, 2001: 12 ref.; Breton, 1972).

The Freudian notion of the mechanics of the psyche was often used as a way of framing their goals or mission. Artists echo his concerns in the titles and content of their images, Max Ernst's *Oedipus Rex* for example, or the dream collages of *Rêve d'une petit fille qui voulut entrer au carmel*. Films such as *Un chien andalou* (1929) and *L'Age d'or* (1930) or Dali's contribution to Hitchcock's *Spellbound*, work with ideas of dreamlike unconscious associ-ation as a way of moving through the film, rather than using a logical narra-tive. Surrealist manifesto and journal material often features analytic ideas and considerations alongside artists' writings. The *Erotika* review published in Czechoslovakia, for example, featured work on Freud alongside texts by artists Aragon and Breton (Mundy, 2001: 239). Breton talks of the emergence of poetry as involving material struggling for expression in its journey from the unconscious as it encounters censoring: 'What I have wanted to do above all is to show the precautions and the ruses which desire, in search of its object, employs as it manoeuvres in preconscious waters, and, once this object is discovered, the means (so far stupefying) it uses to reveal it through consciousness' (Breton, 1987: 24–5).

The Surrealists, whilst influenced by analytic ideas concerning repression, condensation and the work of dreams, did not merely accept these ideas uncritically. On the one hand their practice and artistic products created new dimensions to the cultural work of exploring and reflecting the unconscious – an additional route to that of psychoanalysis. Also, many artists rejected the goal of a cure, along with ideas of normality contained within the field (Mundy, 2001: 27). One of the appeals of their ideas of the unconscious is connected to their cultural and political goals. Their work was inspired by a determination to revolutionise on a political, artistic and personal level. The 'freed imagination' was a stated goal – the restraints of culture or politics were to be torn away. The liberation of the unconscious and its arena of the unrepressed and uncensored was a part of this vision. One of their stated goals was to challenge the rational Cartesian world view, to liberate desires, feelings and impulses buried in the unconscious and to bring them to be incorporated into the accepted 'allowed' reality.

Freud was in written communication with some of those involved in the arts in the twentieth century, though he often expressed bafflement about their practice. For example, he wrote to André Breton in 1932 that he had received many testimonies from Breton and other Surrealists that they were interested in his research. He went on to add that he was not clear what Surrealism was, nor what it wanted: 'Perhaps I am not destined to understand it, I who am so distant from art' (in Mundy, 2001: 75). Others from the analytic movement, such as Lacan, were close to Surrealist circles. Harrison and Wood, for example, point to analyst Lacan's role in 'mediating' the Freudian theory of the unconscious 'through his pre-war involvement with the Surrealist group to produce an account of the human individual which considerably privileged

'La Rue Surréalisme'

All arts forms were involved in this work. At the 1938 Exposition Internationale du Surréalisme the event took the form of several different environments, each trying to challenge the limits of everyday normality, normal social and moral codes. The 'Rue Surréalisme', for example, contained a massive grotto. One thousand and two hundred stuffed coal sacks were suspended from the ceiling, the undulating floor was covered with dead leaves, there was a pool, a brazier burning coals, immense beds and there was a soundtrack of laughter recorded at an asylum. On the opening night dancer Hélène Varel performed an 'unconsummated act' which included wailing, gyrating, wrestling with a live rooster on some of the beds, along with partial nudity and a torn costume. Here we can see the ways in which all the arts are present within the Surrealist event, the emphasis on a sensual engagement with the unconscious and an attempt to challenge the norms of the everyday 'conscious' world by unleashing their version of the unconscious.

the act of looking: few ideas have proved more fruitful for later representations of human subjectivity than his "mirror phase" ' (1992: 552). Lacan, for example, published some of his work in the Surrealist journal *Minotaure*. We can see some of the common language, images and concerns shared by the Surrealists and Lacan – the relationship between identity, mirror, the conscious and unconscious – in the work of Masson which opened this chapter (Lacan, 1969). The idea Harrison and Wood suggest is that Lacan's engagement with the Surrealists had an effect on his influential ideas concerning identity, image recognition and the infant's relationship to looking at her- or himself in a mirror (Harrison and Wood, 1992: 552, 609).

Lomas sums up the mutual incomprehension between Freud and Breton as not being to do with Surrealism's misunderstanding of Freud's work, but in its 'imperative to change the world'. For the Surrealists, he argues 'it was a matter of knowing not only how our dreams are shaped by the remote past, but also how they might be realised concretely in the future' (Lomas, 2001: 76). Others have cited desire and sensuality as a key difference. Though the ideas attracted artists, they are said to have drawn back from the methods and ultimate goals of analysis. Whilst psychoanalysis recognises desire and the senses within the clients' world, it prefers to see 'its own practices as unmarked by desire, as if they were entirely governed by rationality' (Le Brun in Mundy, 2001: 308). In contrast the Surrealists believed that only an approach which was sensual, which engaged with the senses, could come to terms with the unconscious.

In this way, the arts have developed their own history of responses to the unconscious and to Freudian or analytic ideas. Artists such as Bourgeois have made their own discoveries following on from initial ideas by analysts such as Freud and Klein about the unconscious. Artists' research and findings

Louise Bourgeois, 'I Do, I Undo, I Redo'

These three towers, called 'I Do', 'I Undo' and 'I Redo', are made from steel, marble, fabric and mixed media, and were created between 1999 and 2000. They stand between nine and fourteen metres high and were constructed of spiralling staircases and stairwells. Commentators, and Bourgeois herself, have drawn attention to the influence of analyst Klein's ideas within the work. The spiralling forms have been described by her as: 'the spiral is the study of the self' (Bourgeois in Warner, 2000: 18). The texts and images accompanying the towers, or built into the towers, deliberately create a dialogue with Kleinian ideas. For example, text written by Bourgeois relating to the 'I Do' tower contains, 'I am the good mother. I am generous and caring – the giver, the Provider. It is the "I Love You" no matter what' (Bourgeois, in Warner, 2000: 32).

She writes of the 'Undo' tower:

> The UNDO is the unravelling. The torment that things are not right and the anxiety of not knowing what to do. There can be total destruction in the attempt to find an answer, and there can be terrific violence that descends into depression ... It is the return of the repressed ... I smash things, relations are broken. I am the bad mother. It is the disappearance of the love object. The guilt leads to a deep despair and passivity.
>
> (Bourgeois, in Warner, 2000: 32)

In the 'Redo' a solution is found communicated in the text by notions of confidence, activity, reparation and reconciliation, 'There is hope and love again' (Bourgeois, 2000: 32).

The viewer enters into or walks around the towers, meeting huge angled mirrors, chairs and staircases enclosed in metal. Sculptures of a mother embracing a baby, of a distracted mother with milk spouting from a breast and a mother connected to a floating baby by an umbilical cord are contained within bell jars in the body of each tower.

Bourgeois's art takes place in a culture that has appropriated the work of Klein and Freud. She shows this in the language of her work, her images and the process she creates for the viewer. These include, for example, Freudian and Kleinian ideas of object relations: of the mother as an early object of intense projections and splitting. In both Kleinian writing and in Bourgeois's sculptures we can see, on the one hand, an idealised image of the 'perfect' mother whom we seek for and unconsciously reinstate in other relationships, and an equivalent image of the 'bad' frustrating mother, whom we defend ourselves against. A goal of psychoanalysis within this approach can concern a reintegration of this split: idealised and despised, good and bad. However, Bourgeois's work is not a mere reproduction of analytic ideas about the unconscious. The personal iconography of towers, spirals, huge angled mirrors and encounter brings her own discoveries, her own world and her creativity to connect with and confront Klein's ideas. She offers us her *own* artistic experiences and discoveries in a way that invites participation and active response.

Louise Bourgeois's I DO, I UNDO, I REDO (1999) installed in the inaugural exhibition of the Tate Modern at Turbine Hall in 2000. Collection of the Artist, courtesy Cheim & Read, New York. Photo: Marcus Leith © Tate, London.

concerning the 'unconscious' are as valid to our consideration of the arts therapies as the developments of thinking and practice in the fields of therapy and psychology.

Music therapists Alvin (1975), Darnley-Smith (1996) and Tyler (2000) acknowledge the importance of twentieth-century work, such as the above, on the language and form of the arts therapies. Alvin comments, 'Contemporary composers of the avant-garde act as explorers in a world of sounds and often provide us with strange experiences' (Alvin, 1975: 104–5).

Darnley-Smith notes, in particular, that the possibilities of improvisation in music therapy have been influenced by the developments of twentieth-century musical movements. Particularly important have been those that have emphasised the potentials of atonality and free work, that do not require logical development, resolution or crafted composition, that are, rather, 'raw and spontaneous' (Darnley-Smith, 1996: 2). Tyler, writing about the development of music therapy, draws a direct correlation between contemporary forms of musical improvisation, and the way this opened up possibilities in accessing unconscious material. She speaks of the far-reaching changes in music, 'the progression from the harmonic language of Wagner and Richard Strauss, to the atonality of Berg, Webern . . . the music of Messiaen, Boulez, Stockhausen . . . and especially Cage' (Tyler, 2000: 385). These new forms and ways of working, improvising atonally, of self-expression are 'the musical equivalent of free association' (Tyler, 2000: 385).

So, the arts therapies' relationship to the unconscious is not just with the ideas Freud first articulated in the field of psychoanalysis. They also relate to developments in the arts, the way in which the arts have created and modified the notion of the unconscious as well. This relationship includes the modes of expression and languages used within the arts therapies. Put another way, the practice and methods of movements such as the Surrealists or musical work emphasising atonality or improvisation have influenced the artistic processes and languages within the arts therapies sessions.

Also, importantly, in their emphasis on the sensual encounter through the physical relationship with paint, clay, touch or sound, the arts therapies reflect the points made above about the discoveries and emphases in some twentieth-century arts movements on the physical *sensual encounter* with the unconscious. This involves working in a way that is not rooted in verbal language alone, but in the *physical senses* engaged in the arts. The point here is that the arts therapies offer an *additional aspect* of contact through the relationship between physical, sensual acts such as dance movement or sculpture and the therapeutic encounter with unconscious material. The next sections consider these particular ways of encounter and the arts therapies in more detail.

THE DYNAMIC UNCONSCIOUS

The unconscious can be seen as linked to the ways each individual makes sense of the external world. The individual represents this external reality symbolically, inside, creating what Thomas calls 'psychic realities and ultimately our selfhood' (Thomas, 1996: 282). Within the differing frameworks which have developed in the analytic tradition, some have observed that all share a sense of 'a self that is potentially divided' (Thomas, 1996: 315). As mentioned, this is seen to have emerged from the Freudian model of the self, with its ideas of conflicts centring on subdued desires repressed into the unconscious: of conflict being subdued to try to create a sense of unity. In the analytic approach focusing on object relations, for example, there is particular concern with internal conflicts and of fragmentation, of tension between identities introjected during childhood.

As we have seen, within this approach consciousness is seen as partial, a filtered version of what we know and have experienced. As Thomas says, 'Much that is meaningful and most that is motivating is hidden in the unconscious . . . consciousness, rational thought and agency are largely subjugated to the main driving force – the dynamic determining unconscious' (Thomas, 1996: 283). According to psychoanalytic thinking human behaviour is largely determined by

> primitive motives which originate in the unconscious, and remain so deeply buried that we have no access to them, although we can gain partial access with the help of psychoanalysis. Because the unconscious is thought of as the source of motivation, it is called the dynamic unconscious. Unconscious motives are frequently in conflict with conscious thoughts and intentions.

It is this dynamic unconscious which is 'in control most of the time, playing out a drama in which the narrative is beyond awareness and the enactments are beyond conscious control of the experiencing subject' (Thomas, 1996: 286).

At heart most arts therapy work which frames its practice and theory in terms of an unconscious would echo these notions: of the unconscious as something which cannot be fully appropriated by verbal interpretation, or located at an original source. For example, the following ideas of both dramatherapist Grainger and music therapist Aldridge share these concepts. The arts therapies' engagement with the unconscious is seen as dynamic, linking art making, the relationship with the therapist or with others, as a route to *uncover* and *communicate*; to create contact where there is disconnection and to allow healing to occur with material which is buried or split off. The notion, though, is not that the unconscious is fully appropriated. Rather, it is that material which has been located there is creating difficulty, and that this can be reflected or encountered through the medium of image, movement or sound, and the relationships between therapist and client or between clients within the therapy space. These contacts can reflect and effect, can establish communication and change.

How does this occur? Why it is seen to be effective? How do different ways of framing and understanding the unconscious connect this to change? These questions relate to the ways in which arts therapists view the unconscious, and to their understanding and practice of how they work with clients.

HOW DO THE ARTS THERAPIES SEE THE UNCONSCIOUS?

Various theories of the unconscious are represented within the arts therapies. Though some elements are common within the arts therapies' consideration of the unconscious, differences in emphasis do occur. Dramatherapist Grainger, for example, says that because arts therapists use the imagination for sharing personal experience, 'welcoming other people into what would otherwise remain private worlds, the creative therapies regard it [the unconscious] as an active presence rather than the simple projection of something inside people' (Grainger, 1999: 14). He links this with a Jungian model of 'psychic reality'. As the individual unconscious is differentiated from the collective reservoir of unconscious psychic life, the artistic imagination assumes the role of 'intermediary between persons and the source of their person-hood' (Grainger, 1999: 14).

In contrast, Aldridge (1996) refers to Bateson's theories of the unconscious and learning. Aldridge, in his consideration of consciousness and music therapy, says that in our relationships with others we exchange information about unconscious processes all the time. He allies art with this: 'art is a form of behaviour which perfects the communication about how to handle unconscious material. In addition it has the ability to express the fact that we are dealing with the interface between unconscious and conscious material' (Aldridge, 1996: 97). He describes how Bateson's theory of the unconscious is centred on learning and habituation. As habits form, 'knowledge sinks down to less conscious and more archaic levels' (Aldridge, 1996: 98). This knowledge often contains painful matters that we do not want to look at, but also things with which we are familiar. The 'economics' of the mental system are seen to sink generalities of the relationship, which remain permanently true, into the unconscious, keeping conscious 'the pragmatics of particular instances' (Aldridge, 1996: 98).

The relationship between music therapy and the unconscious here is seen in terms of *economy*. The conscious mind cannot be aware of every detail, but habit formation 'has its price in terms of accessibility' (Aldridge, 1996: 98). It is difficult to change or examine all material consciously – such central processes are difficult to express verbally or consciously. However, Aldridge argues, they can be expressed artistically and musically: 'the skill of the artist, or rather the demonstration of his or her skill, becomes a message about those parts of the unconscious, but not a message from the unconscious. Our challenge then is to provide a vehicle for the expression and articulation of that which is hidden' (Aldridge, 1996: 98).

As this demonstrates, arts therapists do not have a uniform view of the unconscious, but hold a variety of positions – this, in turn, will affect the experience of the client. By comparing these two views on the arts therapies' relationship to the unconscious, we can see that, though some aspects are common to both of these arts therapists, there are also differences in orientation. This will impact both on the practice of the therapist and the experience of the client. Grainger, influenced by Jungian ideas of the unconscious, sees the arts therapy space creating access to collective aspects of the unconscious which are needed but not directly connected; a part of the process of healing or developing identity. For Aldridge, the arts therapy space connects with a way of seeing the unconscious as a part of a recreation, of access to material which has been experienced or learned, but is not easily accessible.

ARTS THERAPIES PRACTICE AND THE UNCONSCIOUS

Within the arts therapies, there are specific, particular connections between unconscious material and change. The connections form some of the particular qualities which the arts therapies offer within therapy. These develop from the ways in which the arts are seen by some as a particular kind of 'messenger' between the conscious and unconscious. The next section will look at these areas in relation to the unconscious:

- The process of art making and the created product, and the perspective offered by arts processes and products
- The arts therapies and the non-verbal
- The nature of the emotional experience of the client within the arts therapies
- The dynamic relationship with the therapist
- The play space

A PARTICULAR MESSENGER: UNCLOAKING, EXCAVATION AND THE UNCONSCIOUS

The arts therapies are seen to offer specific qualities in their relationship with the unconscious. There are a number of different elements within the way people see this. Some emphasise the ways in which the arts element of the process offers particular opportunities to the client. Carter (1992) and Howat (1992) argue that music can create a bridge between the ego, the temporal or the outer, and the psyche or inner world: that musical language directly expresses the archetypal, the unconscious. Hitchcock (1987) has pointed out that Jung considered that music should be a part of every analysis, commenting on how music reached deep, archetypal material. Sobey (1992) goes further, and argues that music is a 'short cut' to the unconscious, that it moves through defences and touches us deeply and suddenly. Others echo this idea of immediacy and the ways in which arts processes can assist in working through defences in an accelerated and helpful way: Aiello, for example, talks about how music communicates unconsciously with the power and speed of a lightning flash (Aiello, 1994).

Case and Dalley say that it is the presence of the art form that 'creates the complexity and essentially the uniqueness of art therapy, and the intensity of the relationship is fundamental to the art therapy process' (Case and Dalley, 1992: 52). They see the art in art therapy as a process of spontaneous imagery *released from* the unconscious. This notion can be said to be true of all the arts therapies. They, as the music therapists did, parallel it to the process of free association and dream analysis used by Freud: giving access to unconscious chains of association and the 'unconscious determinants of communication' (Case and Dalley, 1992: 52). However, they contrast art therapy to processes such as free association, as a painting or sculpture is *concrete* and can take on a life of its own. An object is made and remains present, unlike in verbal free association or the analysis of a dream.

Birtchnell (1984), similarly, draws an analogy between arts processes in the arts therapies and dreaming. He relates this to Freud's idea of the processes of censorship that occur within the individual. This censoring controls what we allow ourselves to be aware of, and there exists an 'interplay between the pressing forward of suppressed emotions and the pushing back of the censor' (Birtchnell, 1984: 33). Material suppressed to the unconscious is expressed owing to the 'slackening off' of the censoring – these are played out in fantasy, and the dreams camouflage this material through ambiguous images, changing identities.

The creation of artistic products within the arts therapies is seen not simply to allow access to material related to the unconscious. As Schaverien says of art therapy:

> When a picture is made in therapy it may 'uncloak' an image of which the artist was previously unconscious. Once such an image is pictured it is 'out there' rather than internal; it can be seen and this effects a change in the unconscious state, in the artist, to a more conscious one. As a result of this, even without verbal interpretation, a transformation begins to take place in the inner world of the artist.
>
> (Schaverien, 1992: 7)

Schaverien identifies a crucial aspect of the arts therapies' relationship to the unconscious. The notion here is of a move from being 'cloaked' to 'uncloaked'. The being 'seen', as the image emerges, is part of being 'out there' rather than being held internally. Even *without* interpretation this creation of the artistic product is a therapeutic act purely by its creation within the therapeutic space. The idea is that the creation of the art is accompanied by an effect on the 'internal world', as internally held material is moved into the external world and is experienced by the client and therapist.

Another aspect of this externalisation of internally held matter through a shared product is described in terms of *ambiguity*. Ambiguity can occur, says Birtchnell, in telling or writing a story, play or poem about someone who feels as you do, or who is given permissions that you do not give yourself. In art therapy there is 'more scope for ambiguity, since you can represent yourself as an animal or even an object' (Birtchnell, 1984: 35). Unlike dreams, the art therapy painting or object can be presented physically for others to witness. The creation of images which partially express or represent latent or suppressed material can allow their more complete integration into the personality: 'allowing and owning the less acceptable aspects of oneself means that less energy is spent on denying their existence' (Birtchnell, 1984: 39).

In these ways, the process of art making and the products created are seen to offer specific qualities in their relationship with the unconscious. Here, then, arts therapists argue that the experience of arts work in therapy can be one of 'uncloaking' material relating to the unconscious. In some cases the creation of the artwork, whether dance or painting, is one of 'lightning' – of a particular speed or directness, due to the reduction of conscious censoring which can be a part of creativity. They speak of a particular intensity that accompanies the experience of expression and encounter through the art form. If the artistic process within the therapy results in a product such as a painting, photograph, recorded music, script or video of dance, it is something that has a concrete, maintained presence – unlike a dream or a verbal association. The ambiguity of the artistic representations and their physical presence in front of others or the therapist can also offer opportunities for integration.

ARTS PROCESS AND NON-VERBAL EXPERIENCE

Thomas has compared the 'psychodynamic' approach to other psychological perspectives and concludes that there is more emphasis on the pre-verbal and non-verbal modes of communication. She gives examples of this – concerning the emotions, early forms of thinking, and persistence and survival into adulthood of infantile and highly charged forms of internal representation. She argues that any consideration of the impact of society on individuals has to take account of the fact that:

> by the time language arrives, most of the influential events have already happened and most of the structure of the mind is already laid down. Language will elaborate experience but, according to many psychodynamic theorists, language, in particular for the purpose of relating to others, is an impoverished medium whose precision in factual domains fails to make up for the loss of more primitive kinds of communication.
>
> (Thomas, 1996: 291)

The importance is less on words but on the emotional charge they carry, and on the way they are used, 'ways which tap into more primitive and unconscious processes' (Thomas, 1996: 291). She later adds that some feelings and images often seem to be 'beyond or apart from language' (Thomas,

1996: 294). There are individual variations in the experience of the inadequacy of language, feelings or images that cannot be expressed in words, and these may reflect material that *pre-dates* language. For example, difficulties in speaking about a feeling or experience may be a defence against a painful memory. Sometimes this will be a manifestation of an unconscious process (such as a defence), but it may also be because the material is not easily connected to words.

However, the arts therapies, through the non-verbal aspects of their practice, can offer clients the capacity to work in ways that are 'beyond verbal language'. The capacity to work through embodiment, movement and dance, music, or through clay, paint or video can offer a medium and an arena where work can take place without words, and without the kinds of mapping or thinking related to verbal language. Experiences which were non-verbal can be reflected more easily, and a means can be created to engage with them where verbal language might hinder or render the contact or work impossible.

Shapero, for example, in discussing the 'musical mind' considers areas such as the 'mechanism' of tonal memory and composition, talking about how a great deal of what is heard becomes 'submerged in the unconscious' (Shapero in Ghiselin, 1952: 50). Within this process sounds or rhythms are linked with experiences. He describes what he calls the 'creative unconscious' which renders music 'more than an acoustical series of tones'; what is heard becomes submerged in the unconscious where it is 'compounded with emotional experiences' (1952: 50). For maker of music and listener alike, emotions are evoked through this connection. The author and listener are not consciously aware of the connections, however, but the psyche holds such connections unconsciously, and feelings are evoked by them without conscious connection. McDougal (1989), Jones (1996: 164) and Wood (1998) have discussed the ways in which the body can hold memories and experiences which are not easily described or encountered through words and through cognitive processes, and which can best be accessed and explored through the non-verbal means of movement or physically based drama or art work.

You will see from the comment opposite that the therapist attempts to mirror the client's expressions. In the description of the session she assumes that these expressions are concerned with rage and grief. The client, because of the nature of their disability, is not able to verbally confirm or deny this connection. However, the therapeutic space serves to allow him to use voice, music and movement to create expression.

The therapist's assumption is that the client is finding a way to contact and express feelings which had been repressed, and which had not been able to find a form or route. James says that her therapeutic approach was that 'the client [could] understand, if not consciously then at least unconsciously. If he was willing to allow me, I just wanted to feel, to sense, to intuit my way into his internal landscape' (James, 1998: 24). This could be seen as an intrusion; however, the therapist acknowledges this and tries to act in a way which is as sensitive as possible. The work here relies on the idea that the art form and the

Therapist comment

Arts therapist James describes her work with a client with learning disabilities. The man had, in a short period of time, lost both parents and he had moved into residential care as a consequence. He is described as withdrawn, depressed, refusing contact and had lost weight. After a number of weeks where a relationship is built, both with the language of the arts therapy, and with herself as therapist, she describes a session as follows:

'He began to make quite loud and free sounds with movement. I joined him using the same pitch, the same intonation and attuning to the emotions I could hear in his voice. In response the sounds grew and he began to make bigger and bigger noises until eventually he roared with feeling, he shouted loudly, and banged the drum hard with his hands, the ground hard with his feet. His frustration, rage and anguish were apparent . . . I too banged a drum alongside and joined his stamping affirmatively.'

(James, 1998: 24)

relationship with the therapist enable a communication to occur. The internal world finds external expression. Relief is in the expression and connection that the art form permits within the safety of the therapeutic space and relationship. There may be a cathartic or releasing element that the art form facilitates – the internally held-in feelings are vented. The expression and containment may give some relief to feelings that have been suppressed and therefore held on to. This holding and suppression is seen to cause part of the client's distress. The client's internal world is seen to be reflected in the work. Words would not have been an option in this situation, and the arts therapies are seen to offer a way of enabling the feelings repressed into the unconscious to be made accessible. By accessing the unconscious world through its reflection in the art forms of movement, music and vocalisation some relief of the client's difficulties is seen to be achieved. Reflecting on the practice, James says that the quality of contact between client and therapist can 'deepen profoundly' when relationships are made without words, and that a depth and range of human experience can be encountered through music, movement and touch (James, 1998: 22).

Here, then, is an example of how the artistic medium and the relationship with the therapist, whether in improvisation, movement, drawing or music, can enable the expression and exploration of material that might not be verbally engaged with by the client. The space and language of the arts therapy session can allow such possibilities. Particular sets of emotions can enter the therapeutic encounter as the client is involved in the anticipation, making and aftermath of creative work, expression or creation.

Some, however, have argued that it is necessary for words to be used to help assimilate such experiences into the conscious mind. Others argue that there is no need to reflect or analyse the experience. Still others would argue that the dichotomy between thinking, reflecting and cognition versus emotion, sensation and intuition is a false one. Courtney, for example, talks about *knowing with the body* (Courtney, 1988). Still others would argue that there is a simultaneity of emotion and reflection, or that any separation between the two is not useful. Landy (1993), for example, talks lucidly about the goal of a balance within the therapeutic encounter. This is not an 'either-or' situation – it is not that arts therapies do not encompass verbal language or cognition. It is rather that there are *aspects* of the client's experience or identity which can be accessed through the arts element of the therapy, and which can be encountered because they are not primarily mediated by cognition. In addition, for some clients who are not verbal, and for whom verbal psychotherapy would not be possible, the arts expression can enable therapeutic encounters with material related to unconscious processes or content to occur. Some clients with learning difficulties might be included within this area, for example (Dubowski, 1984). Also, for some clients for whom verbal language encourages too cognitive a response, where always adopting an intellectual analysis of their lives can become a defence, the artistic means of encounter can provide a way of working which enables a freer, less cognitive experience.

The arts therapies, then, in these ways enable particular kinds of access to experiences to occur, allowing encounters and explorations within the therapy which are evoked and held by the artistic medium and the relationship with the therapist.

EMOTIONAL ENCOUNTER

Wiser *et al.* (1996), in researching psychodynamic therapy, consider the emotional state of the client within the therapy space. They draw conclusions which seem to indicate that when clients are in 'emotional states' within the therapy, 'deeper and perhaps more enduring shifts occur for them' (Wiser *et al.*, 1996: 125). They say that this may be due to the client's cognition, which can be more susceptible to change owing to the heightened emotional state. The state can bring suppressed or repressed 'historical' material into the present within the session, and issues can be more effectively addressed and integrated.

They say there is mounting evidence that 'facilitating clients' *affective* or emotional experience of their issues can lead to positive shifts for them . . . a move away from "talking about" their affective experience, to an in-the-moment "experiencing of" affecting experience is critical' (Wiser *et al.*, 1996: 125). They advocate a range of therapeutic experiences that facilitate in-the-moment emotional experiencing. These include attention to bodily cues such as clenching fists, tapping feet and concentration on the 'here and now' physical feelings of the client. The arts therapies can be said to have specific ways of operating with such notions of in-the-moment experiences by means of their opportunities for artistic expression and activity that enhance or offer particular routes to such emotional states.

Examples of this include the ways in which a re-enactment of an experience through drama can re-create strong feelings which are experienced physically in the bodily encounter of a role-play. Here a client might work in a group which re-creates a scene from someone's life. The physical and imaginary *recreation* often leads to strong feelings. These are enhanced by the physical replaying and embodiment of the problematic situation. Repressed feelings that would not be allowed expression in everyday living can be expressed in the safety of the re-enactment in the dramatherapy space. Similarly, in dance movement therapy the embodied exploration can activate and enable the connection and working through of feelings rooted in bodily experience in a powerful way. This encourages and contains strong emotions within the therapy session.

The capacity of art forms and ways of working to combine both the allowing of strong emotions and containment of those emotions in a form of artistic expression is related to the above ideas of the importance of emotional encounter within therapy. Oatley's brief summary of the nature of change in the relationship between the conscious and unconscious within a Freudian therapy offers an interesting perspective on this idea. He says that, for Freud:

> therapy was the tracing of associations to their intersections and proper terminals, so that a sense of what the original and undisguised feelings and desires were might emerge. By readmitting them to consciousness, they would again become the person's own: the person's self rather than a symptom of not-self . . . to gather up those more troublesome aspects of the self, the disowned parts – mistakes, lapses, symptoms, until these too can be admitted to the space of mind: owned, admitted to consciousness, so that people might know themselves.
>
> (Oatley, 1984: 42–3)

Seen from this perspective some argue that the arts therapies draw on the particular capacity of the arts to reflect, contain and transform material relating to the unconscious. When powerful, previously repressed material is allowed to emerge through the expression of the art form, it can be admitted to consciousness in the way Oatley describes. They argue that there are particular qualities which arts forms offer which are different from purely verbal therapy.

Grainger, for example, relates the arts therapies to Freud's notion of the role of the unconscious in a way that highlights a particular capacity of the arts within the therapy. He cites Freud's idea that vital psychological adjustments which involve the acceptance of 'powerful realities' are struggled with at an unconscious level until they can be brought into some bearable relationship with conscious awareness. Grainger asserts that this 're-adjustment' is something which the 'arts therapy environment' tries to allow and contain: 'to allow because of art's ability to contain powerful and disruptive feelings in a way that disarms the urge to deny their presence' (Grainger, 1999: 131).

He goes on to discuss the relationship between arts therapy processes and rites of passage as an example of this. He cites authors who draw 'attention to the creative chaos at the rite's centre by means of which an existing psychosocial context is effectively destroyed so that a new and as yet unknown world of personal and social experience may come into being' (Grainger, 1999: 131).

Various arts therapists have described and analysed this aspect of artistic or cultural form and expression. This basically says that art forms function in ways that enables expression, but do so in a way that both *encourages* and *holds* the expression of strong, repressed material. The following is from an art therapy session. Therapist McClelland is working in a small group who 'came together to explore and share difficult, emotionally charged experiences' (McClelland *et al.*, 1993: 116). In an early session one of the group members, Ann, has drawn graphic images of her experience of rape and violence. Another member, Pat, comments on Ann's work that:

Client comment

Ann did not seem to be drawing from her head. She sketched and moved over the paper in a way that did not seem pre-planned. This was a real breakthrough for me, as I believed that no one could draw without planning it first. I decided to have a go. I shut off my head and just went with how I felt . . . I did not know what I would draw, but I found myself drawing a door . . . After the door, I drew a tiny figure [me] and a large figure [the father]. I noticed that I had drawn his hands very large and claw like. I felt physically sick but carried on drawing. I began to hurt from the hands and scribbled them out very firmly. I actually felt the hands doing things to me that I hate. At the top of the paper, I drew two large figures of almost equal size. I was very, very careful to get them the same size. It was to represent me and him, and the equality I feel I am now looking for.

(McClelland *et al.*, 1993: 119)

The commentary on this, written collaboratively, is that Pat had switched from a focus on the verbal and auditory, to movement and the production of imagery. This is accompanied by strong feelings that are described as re-accessing the actual physical pain and hurt of the original assault. At the same time, though, Pat has created an image and is relating as both creator and witness to the painting. McClelland notes the intensity of Pat's gaze and encourages her in the act of looking. In reflection Pat says that she had never before been able to articulate her feelings, her experience and her awareness (McClelland *et al.*, 1993: 121).

The argument is that the art form and the relationship with the arts therapist in an encounter such as this acts as a particular form of container which allows a particularly powerful way to both evoke and contain. If the ideas of Wiser *et al.* are accepted, then the presence of strong feeling in this way, combining expression and containment, can powerfully add to the efficacy of the way the client utilises the therapy space.

DYNAMIC RELATIONSHIP

There is a dynamic relationship between the arts therapies and the unconscious – it is not just about making the unconscious known. Schaverien has described the inadequacy of the situation in art therapy, for example, where this dynamic aspect within the process is not addressed sufficiently in this way: 'The picture may then be reduced to a mode of description of a state, or an illustration of the transference' (Schaverien, 1992: 7). She refers to a crucial part of this dynamic as concerning 'the central role of the picture as a vessel within which transformation may take place and this involves the picture as an object of transference' (Schaverien, 1992: 7).

This can be said to be as true for the dance movement, enactment or music created by the client. Case and Dalley indicate some of the elements of this process:

> Art therapy involves using images to facilitate the unfolding and understanding of psychic processes. It is not so much a matter of art making the unconscious, or to widen and strengthen the ego, as of providing a setting in which healing can occur and connections with previously repressed, split off and lost aspects of the self can be re-established.
>
> (Case and Dalley, 1992: 54)

Schaverien refers to Jung's separation of the production of art or images for therapeutic purposes and the pictures created as 'art'. She draws attention to the former's parallel with Jung's idea of the active imagination. Active imagination 'is an active production of inward images' (Jacobi, 1942: 163 in Schaverien, 1992: 81). The individual is encouraged to move to their unconscious and watch and observe the contents to integrate them with consciousness. However, she notes, importantly, that 'a picture is not a mental image; it is a picture. A picture has certain ways of interesting, influencing and affecting the people who view it' (Schaverien, 1992: 82).

The expression makes a dynamic connection between inner and outer. The internally held material is expressed; in addition the expression and the made artefact affects the inner world, the unconscious. All these elements, the made product, the making process, the relationship with others and with the therapist are part of this dynamic. Material is expressed, brought into the arena of the therapeutic space and the relationship between the client and therapist. All elements interact together.

The dynamic relationship

The following is a summary of the complex process involved in the 'dynamic relationship'.
    The client:

- projects internal material into the *form* of the art, whether music, dance or painting, and into the *process of making* the art.
- experiences *the made object or expression* in a way which reflects internal material.
- experiences the *relationship with others*, if the work is in a group, in ways that can also reflect internal material.
- experiences the *relationship with the therapist* present and involved in the creation in ways that also reflect unconscious processes.

PLAY SPACE AND THE UNCONSCIOUS

Creativity has been understood in a number of ways. Hayes (1994), for example, places it within the framework of being able to produce new ideas or approaches: 'one of the most important mainstays of a technological culture' (Hayes, 1994: 159). In a review of definitions of creativity she notes that creativity involves escaping from conventional modes of thought or assumptions, linking this to novel styles of thought or originality in problem solving. She goes on to consider this within attitudes to thinking and representation, comparing Hudson's identification of two different cognitive styles: convergent and divergent thinking. Based on a study of schoolboys and their approaches to academic work, convergent thinking tended to focus tightly on particular problems and seeking answers within existing frameworks, divergent thinking ranged widely in searching solutions, venturing outside usual frameworks.

Reflecting or accessing unconscious material in the arts therapies space allows it to come into contact with the creativity of the client, and the opportunities offered within the creative work with the therapist. This material may previously have been held hidden or suppressed. By being allowed into the artistic opportunities within the therapy, the material can be opened up to creative possibilities. Imagery or expression can be played with, explored, extended or developed and re-framed. The client can be involved with the creative act of movement, painting or drama, or engaged in working with the creativity of another or others, whether this is the group or the therapist. This allows held unconscious material to be open to creative 'divergent' opportunities and possibilities.

Jung's building games

In *Memories, Dreams, Reflections* Jung discusses the emergence of his thinking in ways which involve the arts and their relationship to the unconscious. He talks explicitly about the importance of a childhood memory. This concerned his playing 'passionately' with building blocks, mud and mortar. This is accompanied by strong feelings: 'I distinctly recalled how I had built little houses and castles, using bottles to form the sides of gates and vaults . . . These structures had fascinated me for a long time. To my astonishment, this memory was accompanied by a good deal of emotion' (Jung, 1961: 197).

He draws a conclusion, that the small boy is still around and has the creative life that the older Jung lacked. So, he begins to collect suitable stones and to play 'childish games', building cottages, a castle, a village. The mature analyst spends time playing, with breaks to see his clients and to have meals. During the activity he says his thoughts began to clear and he discovers an 'inner certainty' that the playing and building was helping him discover what he calls his 'own myth'.

The building game is accompanied by streams of fantasies that he writes down. He goes on to describe how his work, thinking and own healing grew out of the creation of such stone structures; internal images and fantasies are expressed in them: 'had I left those images hidden in the emotions, I might have been torn to pieces by them . . . I learned how helpful it can be, from the therapeutic point of view, to find the particular images which lie behind emotions' (Jung, 1961: 201).

A key part of this is that in the arts therapies something can be represented and *yet it is not that thing*. Birtchnell points out that a picture of a person or a thing is not the same as the person or thing, and yet *carries* some of their characteristics (Birtchnell, 1984: 41). It represents a 'half-way stage' – the client can shout at, or accuse, the representative image or enacted representation of a person in a manner that would be difficult to do face-to-face. This combination of distance and encounter is a part of the way the *playful space* of the arts therapies permits particular opportunities for unconscious material to be encountered and worked with. This will be considered in greater depth in Chapters 13 and 17.

The arts therapies can be seen, then, as a way to reflect, encounter and transform unconscious material that is part of a problematic situation for the client. The nature of the arts experience and relationships within the arts therapies is seen to offer specific opportunities to the client. The arts products and process alike are seen to be a way to reflect and transform unconscious material. Importantly, though, the process is not just to do with the creation of opportunities for access. The process of expression and the process of creativity along with contact with others, or the therapist, are seen as crucial to the process of change.

From this develop questions concerning meaning. Can we say, for example, that there is a specific artistic language of the unconscious that can be understood? The next section will focus on the way in which meaning emerges in the arts therapies encounter with the unconscious.

A DICTIONARY OF THE UNCONSCIOUS?

Can there be a language of the unconscious? Can images, movements or sounds which seem to reflect the unconscious *be* translated? Can there be a lexicon of the artistic expressions of clients? Can there be any conclusions drawn about their state of mind from the way someone makes an image about their state of mind? Can one person's expression be linked to a general set of expressions from which general conclusions have been drawn? If, for example, a client makes a specific set of expressions musically, expresses themselves through movement, character or specific ways of drawing themselves, can we make conclusions about dysfunction through diagnostic readings of internal problems in the unconscious? This has been a concern for some arts therapists.

Opinion varies. As we've seen, some would question the basic ideas that this connection assumes, for example, the existence of an internal world, the unconscious or a cartography of the self which divides identity into inner and outer in this way. Such questions relate to the ways in which arts therapists and clients can understand the expressions made or created within a session. The existence or formulation of a kind of lexicon, some argue, could contribute to the therapeutic work by assisting the understanding of the communications processes at work within an activity. Diagnostic possibilities in the arts therapies have been linked to such expressions, and the capacity to 'read' them, for example. Therapist, therapeutic organisation and client could draw conclusions about a client's state of mind owing to assumptions about movements, images or other artistic expressions made by clients. This is based in the gathering and analysis of previous experiences and expressions made by clients.

McNiff states that it is the 'diagnostic approaches' to art therapy which have shown the most consistent 'tendency to analyze visual data' (McNiff, 1998: 92). His critique of this body of work is that 'visual phenomena are reduced to principles of largely unrelated psychological theories. The art diagnosticians identify visual phenomena but quickly transfer them to verbal constructs' (McNiff, 1998: 92). Some have criticised models of the arts therapies involving such diagnostic work as inherently problematic. Dramatherapist Milioni argues, for example, that 'psychodynamic approaches . . . have been criticised for an abuse of power, when the therapist positions him/herself as "expert" in the therapeutic encounter . . . [which] makes it hard for the client to resist the expert discourse or version of truth . . . the therapist hijacks their story' (Milioni, 2001: 11).

An often expressed idea linked to this criticism is that it is impossible to accurately read one person's expressions in the light of others. Each expression is seen as a unique amalgam of specific life experiences – so that meaning can only be drawn from the specific image and that this can only be found from, or with, the individual client.

Arts therapists such as Schaverien often use the metaphor of *diving, digging* and *excavation* when referring to artistic expression and the unconscious. Their descriptions and analysis create an endeavour where therapist and client *together* are engaged in the task of uncovering, or allowing the expression of buried, covered or layered material. The expression made within the relationship between client and therapist and through art making is seen as one that is akin to archaeology – digging, allowing something to emerge from the 'depths'. What does this metaphor reveal? Can it be trusted or justified? Is it valid or effective? Is it a structure placed upon individuals and on therapy, rather than something that is actually present?

As described earlier, arts therapists have different positions on processes such as the use of verbal reflection and intervention within their work with clients. Some forms of music therapy, for example, create a deliberate connection between reflection and exploration, seeking to link material reflecting the unconscious with verbal communication (Priestley, 1995; John, 1992). Others emphasise the centrality of musical form within the therapeutic encounter (Andsell, 1995) without the need for verbal exploration. Within approaches emphasising verbal intervention, interpretation can be an important aspect of the way in which meaning emerges from the therapeutic encounter.

Writing about the historian's relationship to documents or descriptions of the past, Lacapra describes the act of interpretation as creative, as 'a performing art' (Lacapra, 1983: 62). He comments that art is 'never entirely free . . . the belief in pure interpretation is itself a bid for absolute transcendence that denies both the finite nature of understanding and the need to confront critically what Freud described as "transference"' (Lacapra, 1983: 63). He goes on to describe historical texts as a network of resistances, and advocates the recognition of interpretation as a dialogue, 'a good reader is also an attentive listener' (Lacapra, 1983: 64).

Harris talks about some facts contesting and contradicting the frame of reference of the reader. The centrality of these ideas is that 'a notion of vision, or gazing, or looking, or seeing, as an essentially neutral activity is untenable . . . vision . . . is necessarily subject to social and ideological values and interests' (Harris, 2001: 151). Notions of pure form, a culturally universal vision, are dismissed as ways of avoiding the importance of understanding vision in the *specific context* of its relationship to socially and politically specific institutions or situations.

Lacapra emphasises the importance of an interest in what does not fit a model or fixed framework for understanding, saying that 'an openness to what one does not expect to hear from the past may even help to transform the very questions one poses to the past . . . the seeming anomaly should be seen as having a special value . . . for it constrains one to doubt overly reductive interpretations and excessively "economical" shortcuts from understanding to action' (Lacapra, 1983: 64). Though he's talking about historical texts, I think this approach is useful when considering the idea of interpretation in the arts therapies. He talks about the value of the *anomaly* from the *general*. This way of thinking recognises that systems of scientific categorisation might be, at one extreme, inappropriate for the anomalous psyche and for the analysis of artistic expressions: human nature is not best served by such a notion. Human nature's complexity is not best served in terms of psychotherapy by an approach that categorises in this way. Each individual must be given his or her specific acknowledgement. There are some areas that might usefully be seen in the context of a set of assumptions, but the individual experience of that may be more complex. The individual's difference may alter the framework applied, and categories or frameworks should be in constant evolution. Each client can affect the development of any framework – the framework can affect the client. It is a *dialogue* not a monologue – as Lacapra calls it, a 'dialogical relationship' (1983: 64). This way of looking at texts, whether they are historical or the expressions in an arts therapy session, is one that is important to the arts therapies.

Arts therapists such as Maclagan, for example, echo some of these concerns. He calls imagination, dream and fantasy 'slippery concepts' (Maclagan, 1989: 35). He points out that oppositions between outside and inside, real and imaginary, literal and metaphorical are 'neither necessary nor inevitable: they are, rather, the consequences of a complex set of assumptions about the nature of imagery, and about how "figures" should translate the invisible into visible terms' (Maclagan, 1989: 35). He argues that often a fixed range of concepts is used as a baseline which images can be read from, or reduced to. He says the danger is that this is reductive and conservative.

In the following Maclagan talks about art therapy, but it could be said to be true of all the arts therapies: the art therapist, 'standing . . . between the therapeutic need to connect and to articulate, and a creative involvement with imagery that is immediate and inarticulate, is bound to have to deal with this tension between the programmatic and the unaccountable' (Maclagan, 1989: 36). He says that the structures of meaning that regulate the 'traffic' between 'inside and outside' and that effectively license certain forms of expression whilst disqualifying others, have 'real human consequences; we have an ethical responsibility to re-examine them'.

Maclagan develops this to discuss what he calls a tension in art therapy: 'while the idea of an objective science concerned with the quantifiable aspects of phenomena develops, so the more elusive and qualitative aspects of experience come to be assigned to a private and subjective realm' (Maclagan, 1989: 37). He goes on to say that the pathologising of certain forms of imagery, or the 'imposition with the full weight of diagnostic authority', of what he says is an interpretative straitjacket, are 'the authoritarian effects of a model of imagination that is inherently conservative' (Maclagan, 1989: 39). So, deviation from a 'figurative norm' by clients in a psychiatric setting is seen as indicative of disorder, of non-figurative work as being indicative of a withdrawal from reality, or as a refusal to signify in a proper way.

Music has also been seen by some as particularly difficult to 'read' or interpret. Authors such as Walker (1990: 4) make the point that the sounds of music are 'vague' as symbols. It is hard, for example, to isolate a musical sound that is always obviously 'heroic' or 'cowardly'. There is a difficulty in identifying musical elements and showing they represent non-musical objects: 'musical symbolism is not a simple matter of matching each symbolised object with a different sound so as to form a sort of universal lexicon of musical symbols' (Walker, 1990: 5). He goes on to add that whereas in art shapes can be made to resemble everyday objects familiar to the observer, and words have more or less fixed meanings, some musical forms can imitate (e.g. a birdcall or a barking dog), but normally musical art operates differently from literal reproduction. A composer might choose a sound to represent something, and, by musical convention, that sound may acquire particular evocative or representational powers within a particular context or milieu, but this cannot be guaranteed. He says that the translation of specific musical imagery from one culture to another is impossible. Composers create their own language, and an audience may listen and understand, but musical communication occurs 'despite the relatively abstract constructions in sound' (Walker, 1990: 9).

Pavlicevic asks whether it is essential to use words to make the music therapy process full, or, 'were we to leave the musical experience to speak for itself, would it remain unconscious, un-recovered, unaccessed by the client? Could it be limiting a client who was fully verbal – or would it enhance the experience? Might the act of speaking detract from the power of the experience itself?' (Pavlicevic, 1997: 10). Aiello (1994), speaking about conscious and unconscious reactions to music, says that the response of listeners is dependent on the training or natural psychological inclination of each individual. Some, she argues, rationalise and make conscious their responses to the music, for example. For others the 'mental tensions' are experienced mainly as a feeling or affect rather than as conscious cognition.

Some arts therapists have written about interpretation *within* the art form, that the therapist, for example, uses music or mark making or movement to make an interpretation of the material which reflects unconscious content or processes (Odell, 1989).

Pavlicevic (1997: 164) asks whether, if the therapist interprets only through music, the musical act can come to a 'full conscious meaning' for the client? Sometimes clients 'know' something has happened without being able or needing to verbalise it. This knowing is musical in nature, part of the process of making and communicating through music. She asks whether this kind of knowing which is contained within musical expression marks a shift from unconscious to conscious life. Are words needed to 'explicate' it? Behind this lies a question – how to find a 'language' that fully embraces the complexity of the experience: 'In music therapy, this language needs to do justice to the interactive complexities, to the musical inter-dynamic, and to the unconscious meaning of any feature of these aspects of the therapeutic event, as well as to the whole event' (Pavlicevic, 1997: 164–5).

She, like many other arts therapists, views interpretation as something which *can* rather than *must* be used, saying that it is important to guard against interpretation being made just because of theoretical leanings (Pavlicevic, 1997: 165). It can become a creative act, at best involving client and therapist together looking at bringing meaning out of the therapeutic experience. It is important to ask whether verbal interpretation is a reassurance – the therapist needing to assert or to feel that they 'know what is going on', or is a part of the process of counter-transference. This creative mutuality is at the heart of the digging metaphors referred to at the start of this section. The following case example illustrates this.

Schaverien, in discussing client Harry's process in art therapy, rightly speaks of the creation of an image by him – she says that at the time of the emergence of the image *there were no words* for. She says *the image itself* is 'eloquent', and was born from a need to articulate a feeling state, but that the client could not verbalise. He was able 'to split off and so externalise a state which is likely to have been previously unconscious' (Schaverien, 1992: 227). She adds that no words could be found by the client, as words could not match the depth which the image touched in 'the artist' as viewer of his own creation. Over weeks, and around the production of further images, the original image became familiar, less surprising and Schaverien notes that its content was acknowledged and eventually assimilated – though, she notes, this took several years.

Birtchnell says that the arts product or work is 'put together' in the first place 'in order to accommodate a number of conflicting themes and, in the finished product, these are ingeniously interlocked' (Birtchnell, 1984: 37). Part of the 'job' of the arts therapist is to 'move in' and disentangle the aesthetic creation to 'get back to the underlying turmoil' (Birtchnell, 1984: 37): 'I see my role as a therapist in assisting the subject to bring . . . conflicts nearer the surface' (Birtchnell, 1984: 41).

Bunt (1997) talks about the ideas of Stern (1985) in relation to the unconscious and meaning. He emphasises Stern's idea that communication concerns 'affect attunement' (Bunt, 1997: 255). Two communicators are trying to understand each other's emotional state, and once this has occurred then communication is able to happen in several modalities. This could be said to be a part of the way the relationship between arts therapist and client can form – the attunement of trying to understand followed by different layers of communication within the arts therapy session. This sums up key elements of what both Birtchnell and Schaverien describe – the ways in which the relationship within the session, between client, art making and product, and therapist, allows complexities of communication and relationship to become meaningful. These allow conscious and unconscious to connect in particular ways – to become, in Schaverien's sense of the word, eloquent.

CONCLUSION

In arts therapy practice operating within a framework that acknowledges the unconscious, the relationship between *internal* and *external* is at the core of change. The basic notion is that the client's internal unconscious world, containing repressed material, becomes connected with the arts products, the materials used, and the processes within the session. This can involve the making of music, images, enactments or dance, the relationship with the therapist, and with other clients, if the therapy involves a group. The arts therapies' engagement with the unconscious is seen as dynamic: linking art making, the process of the relationship with the therapist or with others, as a route to uncover, to create contact where there is disconnection, and to allow healing to occur with material that is buried or split off.

Some arts therapists, as we have seen, when discussing clinical practice, use topographic imagery. This relationship is one where the unconscious is seen as a domain, a repository or as a resource. The arts therapist and client together engage in an act of archaeology within the therapy – the excavation can lead to the emergence of material through image, movement, enactment or sound. The relationship between therapist and client is also seen to be reflective of patterns, issues, internally held aspects of identity and relationships from outside the session through transference. The presence of making and the made artefact or product is also seen as an important aspect of reflecting and working with unconscious material.

The therapist and client work with meaning and how the emergent meaning alters the client. For some clients the change from holding something within to finding expression in an artistic form is a key aspect of therapeutic change. Another aspect is seen to be the relationship with the therapist as this develops – the client 'working through' issues. Another facet is the act of intervention from the therapist – through interpretation or engagement with the clients' work. The arts therapy space is seen as an opportunity for access, expression, exploration and change. The arts form and product is a means of contact, becoming both a container and transformative agent.

This is the way the unconscious is viewed, and seen as an agent of change. The unconscious is seen by most arts therapists in ways that reflect both the analytic and the artistic traditions: revolutions in the way the psyche and self are seen. Some work reflects ideas of the unconscious as a place which is the origin of inspiration and creativity. The processes of making can be connected to the unconscious as a way of assisting healing or reparative processes. The unconscious here is a source of creativity, and of reflecting ways in which therapist and client can work together to achieve an integration of splits or difficulties. For others the unconscious is a place of suppressed memories, experiences or unacceptable aspects of identity. The arts therapies enable a particular relationship to occur, where the artistic process within a therapeutic framework and relationship enhances and provides particular forms of reflection and communication with the material which is seen as buried or suppressed. Once expression and communication are made then the potentials of the therapeutic space and encounter can be connected to the buried or cut-off material. Robbins describes the process in this way:

> All too often ... the psychological implications of one's art are unconscious or dissociated from self-expression. In art therapy, on the other hand, we are constantly working to make aesthetic expression a complement to self-expression in one's relationship with others. In that process, the art therapist works with an individual's character defences and slowly helps him to digest emotionally the full impact of the symbolic communications.
>
> (Robbins, 1987: 23)

The emphasis is upon the potentials that the arts therapies bring to their contact and dialogue with the unconscious. The unconscious is encountered through the physical expression and artistic processes within the arts therapies. They evoke and enable the encounter of material in particular ways.

The relationship is not one-way – it is not only that the unconscious material is given expression and that consciousness enables change. There is a dialectical, alive relationship that is established between expression and engagement in the arts therapy space and the clients' unconscious. The unconscious is not closed; it is seen to be a living, changing element, brought into dialogue through the unique opportunities the arts therapies make possible. It must be remembered, as the start of this chapter acknowledged, that though ideas connecting the arts, the unconscious and change are important in the arts therapies, not all practice is connected to these concepts. The therapy space, the relationship between the arts, the arts therapist and the client are seen very differently by some arts therapists with different orientations.

How, then, does the therapeutic orientation of the arts therapy practice affect the opportunities for the client? Case and Dalley say that the various perspectives concerning orientation will 'place different emphases in terms of understanding this art process' (1992: 53). They contrast, for example, those emphasising the healing qualities of the arts form with more psychoanalytically influenced art therapists. Is this the case? Are there such differences for clients? The next chapter will look further at this relationship.

13 Playing, development and change

INTRODUCTION: DEFINITIONS AND THEORIES OF PLAY

One morning, during breaktime, schoolchildren were at play whilst work was being undertaken on an adjacent building. A man working on the lights of this building fell to his death during this break. The incident occurred only a few feet away from where a dozen children were playing.

By chance, a project happened to be in progress at the school. This involved recording and analysing the ways the children played. The recordings, based on three- to six-year-olds, began to show patterns and themes in the play. For months afterwards the children's play reflected the incident. Children played falling and jumping, referring to falling on their head, asking questions such as 'Where's the body? We have to go to hospital and take the body', giving instructions such as, 'Fall like that man'. In their play they used details of the accident such as bleeding eyes, nose and mouth, wearing hard hats and hospital. A variety of dangerous situations concerning falling and death were created. A cat was shot dead and fell out of a tree, for example, and a group of boys re-played an incident for many months in which one of them fell and died, was taken to hospital and examined with stethoscopes (Brown *et al.*, 1971: 29).

What have such observations to do with the arts therapies? How can such playing be connected to the therapeutic potentials of the arts? Developments in understanding play, made through observations such as this, have contributed to the arts therapies in many ways. The last chapter emphasised how notions of the unconscious have been influential in considering why the arts therapies are effective. Another important influence in the historical emergence of the arts therapies, and in their ways of working, has been children's play. This chapter will explore how radical shifts in understandings of play have been important to theories of change in the arts therapies, and in developing ways of working practically.

It's no coincidence that a number of key figures involved in creating the early connections between the arts and therapy worked with children. Some have argued that their inspiration for seeing how the arts and therapy could connect lay in their observations and experiences of the way healing occurred for children in and through their play. Peter Slade, for example, who first used the term dramatherapy in the 1930s, says:

> I wasn't happy at school. We would go up into the Downs and dance and improvise. We'd improvise about the masters we hated. The stage, the formal stage was never enough for me . . . looking at children gave me the feeling that . . . children had a drama of their own . . . You're allowed to be like a child again and you can spit out what you want.
>
> (Slade in Jones, 1996: 83–4)

He has said that his own experiences of playing, combined with his work in schools with play and drama, enabled him to begin to realise the therapeutic possibilities of the arts. He began to see the potentials of play and drama to reflect, contain and transform experiences for those involved (Slade, 1995). As we will see, such insights into play occurred in many places, and from different perspectives. In the Netherlands, for example, Wils (1973) produced his influential book *Bij wijze van spelen* (By Means of Playing), which was formative in the development of thinking and practice of the arts as a potential for therapy in that country.

Some arts therapists have proposed that play and creativity in the arts have many common properties. The area of play, especially in relationship to object play, is seen as the origin of creativity. Arts therapists such as Malchiodi argue that inherent in playing, and in creating through the arts, are potentials for healing. It is as if children, within their play, spontaneously deal with a number of difficulties they are encountering. Some arts therapists argue that the arts therapies can draw parallels between these inherent potentials for dealing with difficulty that play can enable, and creative processes within arts therapies sessions. Malchiodi, for example, says that 'in clinical work with children, art and play have always been closely intertwined . . . [sharing] . . . a common bond through their natural appeal to children and their healing qualities of creativity, spontaneous expression, make-believe, and non-threatening, developmentally appropriate communication' (Malchiodi, 1999a: 22). Blatner and Blatner refer to the connections between play and the therapeutic space in psychodrama as 'a fluid dimension', where reality becomes more malleable and hence safer, enabling 'creative risk taking' (Blatner and Blatner, 1988: 78). As this chapter will show, looked at in this way, the arts therapist is creating a space and an opportunity for this *playful state* to emerge. Within this they are using their relationship with the client to try to encourage and support inherent healing processes within playing and the arts to be realised to their fullest potential.

Other ways of looking at play within the arts therapies concern the notion that play enables development and maturation. This claim builds on the work of analysts, psychologists, educationalists and play specialists who argue that play is vital to children's psychological, emotional and social development. Here the arts therapy space becomes a place for problems with stages of development to be worked with. This might involve using arts processes and the relationship with the arts therapist to assist a client with an aspect of their emotional, psychological or social development. Other work aims to revisit stages of development that are problematic, and to renegotiate or re-work them. Here the language of the arts is seen to reflect the possibilities that play offers, or the relationship with the therapist is seen as one that can support or work through the developmental process. This chapter will look at examples of such a developmental perspective on play and the arts therapies.

Questions arise from these ideas and possibilities: what is play? Is play something that ends at the close of childhood? Are ideas about the healing aspects of play grounded in evidence? How do such areas relate to the arts therapies? This chapter will explore these questions in order to examine how play and the arts therapies relate to each other.

What is play?

Baker has said that there are probably as many approaches to understanding play as there are psychologists, zoologists and philosophers (1981). Psychologists, psychoanalysts, biologists, anthropologists, economists and educationalists have all re-examined play in ways that have completely changed our perceptions of what play is, and how it relates to living. The arts therapies have been influenced by a number of these, particularly ideas and discoveries concerning play and psychological development, and psychoanalytic theories of play.

In many situations children are seen to play spontaneously, that is, they will often provide their own impetus and involvement in play without the encouragement of adults. Many researchers and practitioners comment on the satisfaction and absorption that play often seems to provide. Courtney describes this very well: 'Play is something that all children want and need to do: their motivation is so strong that, at home, they can often be so absorbed in their play that they forget to come for meals' (Courtney, 1988: 59).

Activities and processes described as 'play' vary enormously, and change as the individual develops and grows. These include movement: from a baby playing with their own toes to crawling to throwing, catching, running; sound making; talking; games; fantasy activities and playing with objects. Processes often described as 'play' also vary enormously from imitative play, where the focus is on copying and repeating, through to areas such as constructive play and pretend play, where the emphasis is upon combining objects and materials or creating make-believe situations (Andersen-Warren and Grainger, 2000: 52–3). The understanding of how and why play occurs varies widely. The past century has seen enormous changes in the way play is understood. Rather than being seen as incidental, it is now considered to be central to areas such as maturation, and a child's understanding of him or herself and the world they encounter. It is understood as an arena reflecting emotional and psychological concerns, where a child's play is a means of expressing feelings, dealing with difficulties and assimilating experiences. Many, such as psychoanalyst Winnicott, have connected play to the arts; as Case and Dalley say, 'cultural experience begins with creative living first manifested in play' (1992: 88). Such changes have enabled the area of play to have an important role in the emergence and development of the arts therapies.

Play does not happen in a sealed vacuum, and its languages and processes are not the same for all people. A number of factors can affect play. Research has shown that play can vary between different cultures, for example. Some researchers have looked at the effects of cultural and socio-economic factors on the different ways in which play occurs. Some look at the parallels in play and play processes between cultures. Others look at the ways in which specific processes are inhibited due to socio-economic or cultural factors. Researchers have said, for example, that when children are seen as an 'economic asset' and work, then play is reduced. The effects of negative attitudes from adults have also been studied, for example, in play in Gussii childhood in Kenya (Levine and Levine, 1963). Bowlby has commented that in some institutional settings play may be limited as individual activity might be seen as a nuisance, or toys may be lacking, or positive encouraging attention is absent (Bowlby, 1985: 64).

Some authors have pointed to research indicating the negative impact on play of changes in urban life and the way children have access to opportunities for playing. Factors such as parental fear of children's safety from dangers of traffic and violent crime (Rosenbaum, 1993) are cited. Others indicate that children from minority ethnic groups may be inhibited from playing outside the home by fears of racial harassment (Robb, 2001: 23). Robb also points to cultural changes in areas such as mass media. The impact of computers and television, for example, means there is less social interaction in children's play. However, some have indicated that this area of playing still impacts on emotional development. Gunter says that computer games may have a positive effect on dealing with emotional and behavioural problems and in developing cognitive skills (Gunter, 1998).

These perspectives all show how play is important to both a child's or client's internal world, and within the context in which they live their lives. Many theories of play have emphasised play within the child's life situation rather than focusing primarily on the internal processes of the child. Vygotsky's (1967) theories, for example, concern the ways in which play relates to social and emotional needs. Play, he proposes, frees the child from the immediate constraints of a situation by creating a mental arena. Play often involves the creation of an imaginary situation. This is seen as part of the child's developing a social framework. The child develops internal mental representations of how objects, for example, can be manipulated. Internal mental structures are constructed and developed from the child's use of signs. Speech becomes a powerful factor in controlling and using objects as tools and in developing understanding. Playing involves the child's creating a commentary or inner monologue about what is happening. This becomes a kind of inner speech that allows the child to monitor what he or she is doing, and forms the basis of communication. These factors combine to create a mental framework for the child in the formation of their imagination, and in relating to and understanding the world they are within.

These, then, are some of the ways in which views on play have radically changed. How are these relevant to the arts therapies?

The arts therapies and play

A central idea within the arts therapies is that play and the arts have important parallels. As we saw, some of the early pioneers held this opinion. From one point of view early play develops into creativity and art making, from another playing and art-making share many processes. As we will see, the discoveries made in each area can help us see how and why change happens more clearly. Case and Dalley, for example, have commented on how people working with play and therapy, such as Winnicott, have given names to concepts 'of importance to art therapy' (1992: 88): these include the child's first use of symbol, the idea of the transitional object, the importance of fantasy and of play's relationship to cultural experience. This section shows how some of the discoveries and ways of working in areas such as psychoanalysis, play therapy and in developmental work with play relate to the arts therapies. It then goes on to look more directly at areas in arts therapies practice.

Within psychoanalysis practitioners such as Klein (1932) and Anna Freud (1965) used spontaneous play in a way that is analogous to free association. One of the key notions here is of play involving an expression of underlying psychological conflicts and complexes. This tradition can be seen in play therapist Axline's work with her client 'Dibs'. Here is a sample of the play Dibs engaged in:

Therapist's account

Dibs buried three toy soldiers in the sand. 'This makes them unhappy,' he said. 'They cannot see. They cannot hear. They cannot breathe,' he explained. 'Dibs dig them out of there,' he ordered himself . . . He held out one toward me. 'This is Papa,' he said identifying it.

'Oh? That one is Papa, is it?' I remarked casually.

'Yes,' he replied. He stood it on the floor in front of him, shut his fist, knocked it over, stood it up, knocked it over with his fist. He repeated this several times. Then he looked at me. 'Four more minutes left?' he asked.

(Axline, 1964: 67)

This is a moment from a long process of therapeutic work. Over time, Axline and Dibs have created a space where Dibs can play within the safe boundaries of a therapeutic space and a therapeutic relationship. Axline accompanies him in his playing. As the excerpt illustrates, Dibs can play in front of her, and can comment, discuss and think about his play with her. The idea here is that play is a natural *language* for the child, and that the *process* of playing within the space that they have created can hold therapeutic opportunities for Dibs. The language of play can enable Dibs to express, explore and work with themes and situations that are problematic. Things that might be hard to discuss with words alone can be reflected and expressed indirectly through the play images of soldiers, sand and breathing. It can also provide images that may help Dibs feel and understand things about his life. For example, the play with soldiers and sand may help by enabling him to create aspects of his relationship with his father. The presence of the play space, the relationship with Axline and the available fantasy images help him to see things about himself and his father. In addition, he can communicate these things to someone else who is accompanying him in his playing. Hayes sums up an aspect of this approach to play in his analysis of Axline's therapeutic work with Dibs, saying that the child's behaviour as he plays, 'not only allowed the therapist to gain insight into the child's problems, but also allowed the child to express the hidden anger and distress which he could not express at home' (Hayes, 1994: 745).

The relationship of play to maturation has been important within the arts therapies. Play is seen as a key factor in human development in a variety of areas: cognitive, intellectual and social maturation. Piaget (1962), for example, argued that children pass through stages of cognitive development – sensorimotor, pre-operational, concrete operational and formal operational stages. The types of play engaged in are different during these cognitive stages. For example, in the sensorimotor stage the child engages in mastery play. This is seen to allow the child to gain control of its environment, learning to control muscles and actions. In the pre-operational stage the child is more likely to engage in symbolic play involving fantasy and make-believe: this is seen to reflect the developmental issues the child is engaged with – creating an understanding of their world. Sheridan sums up this developmental approach to play succinctly:

> Each aspect of development is intricately linked and if one aspect is hampered or neglected in some way a child will fail to reach her full potential . . . Play is as important for a child's developmental needs as good nutrition, warmth and protection. It provides opportunities to improve gross and fine motor skills and maintain physical health. It helps to develop imagination and creativity, provides a context in which to practise social skills, acts as an outlet for emotional expression and provides opportunities to understand value systems.
>
> (Sheridan, 1999: 6)

A number of approaches to understanding and working with such notions of development are used within the arts therapies. The idea of normative development is one that has created debate and challenge, though. Some, for example, have challenged the idea that underlies some of the developmental models described above. They criticise the notion of stages that are used to define 'normal' progression, and advocate the idea of different routes through development that reflect difference and idiosyncrasy. Art therapist Burt, for example, has criticised traditional notions of development from a feminist perspective (Burt, 1997). However, a number of arts therapists have created approaches rooted in understandings of play and the arts from a developmental point of view.

Read Johnson (1998) has noted the influence of aspects of Piaget's work on arts therapists' practice, for example. He particularly identifies the application of Piaget's ideas of accommodation and assimilation in interpersonal relationships. Baker echoes this in summarising aspects of play relating to the child's negotiating a relationship between themselves and the world they encounter:

> around the age of four co-operative play emerges clearly, and we notice children in . . . corresponding long periods of time in play . . . these children are deliberately playing at life. In group or co-operative play, children often consciously play out events they have witnessed or heard in order to master the puzzling or frightening new experiences, and subsequently learn how to come to terms with them, to cope with new sensations, new ideas, new people and things . . .
>
> (Baker, 1981: 223)

This aspect of play – of children accommodating and assimilating the connections of things they see or are involved in – relates to the play described at the opening of this chapter. In replaying the accident, or in playing with themes relating to their encounter with the event, the children were trying to deal with what had happened by re-encountering it through play. In their games they worked with each other and with shared images and processes. Similarly, as we saw, the play of Dibs with Axline showed the child discovering connections between the soldiers and sand and his father. Malchiodi describes this process within art therapy with an eight-year-old boy on a pedriatric burns unit. He continually repeated a drawing of his house where he was burnt in a fire:

> My interaction with the boy during his hospitalization involved helping him develop themes of safety through play and resolution of his fears about being in his house for fear of being burned again. Repetitions of art or play are an important part of the curative process of medical art therapy, in that it allows the child to gain a symbolic power over the trauma through repeating an image and with the therapist's help, eventually mastering the traumatic event.
>
> (Malchiodi, 1999a: 179)

Garvey (1984) has described the importance of children forming relationships and communicating key aspects of their experience. She refers to research in play undertaken by Gottman and Parkhurst (1977). Their study considered the ways in which play developed within friendships. One strand was described by them as 'shared deviance', which involved planning naughty or forbidden actions. One, for example, involved a plot to poison the mother of one of the children by hiding pretend lethal beans in food she was cooking. The Mother was not poisoned, but Gottman and Parkhurst see this activity in terms of consolidating intimacy. Garvey adds that such fantasy play creates 'shared understandings and mutually constructed history of their play and life together [this] permits the communicative work of play to move beyond the essential organisational negotiations into the exploration of both personal images and feelings and new experiences they want to share and extend' (Garvey, 1984: 172).

This emphasis on the creation of fantasy images that have a capacity to hold personal meaning and relationship is important in thinking about the processes at work within the arts therapies. There is an analogy here between the image work of the children and the creation of imagery within some arts therapy work. Murphy, for example, has said that the arts and play have the spontaneous externalisation of images in common; these 'enable children to face anxiety-provoking situations metaphorically' (Murphy, 2001: 5). She says that children often move from what she calls 'one medium to another', in relation to image making, from art to play. In reality, I think that many arts therapists from different disciplines would see play and the arts as closely interrelated in this area, as we will see.

These crucial processes do not finish when the child becomes an adult. Many argue that play is not something that is confined to children and childhood. Indeed, the presence of play as an active force within the arts therapies with all groups and individuals supports this notion:

> The classic authors in developmental psychology . . . Piaget or Freud, portray early fantasy and early pretend play as something that is immature and will be outgrown. Piaget describes this narcissistic self absorption in unrealistic fantasies and he talks about pretend play as a form of associative thinking that will eventually disappear as the child becomes more objective. But if you look at children with autism and see how restricted their imagination is, you are forced to the conclusion that imagination is probably something that we can't do without, and not something that we need to overcome.
>
> (Harris, 2001: 2)

This led Harris to explore the idea of continuities from children's pretend play into adulthood. The arts therapies, as we will see, use play in work with adults as well as with children, and offer a rationale for one way of considering the need for a continuity of play outside childhood.

In what ways, then, do the arts therapies specifically relate to play and playing? The next sections look at key areas in detail: the playful space; playfulness, the play shift and a developmental perspective. Here we will see how play and the arts therapies relate, not only in terms of theory, but also in the way practice is undertaken.

THE PLAY SPACE

The creation of a play space involves an area that is both set apart yet connected to the everyday life of the client. As described by theorists referred to earlier in this chapter, this space has specific rules and ways of being. Within the arts therapies Winnicott's notion of the transitional object and the related idea of potential space have been important. Winnicott (1974) described play as a 'potential space', essential for the infant to establish relationships between their inner world and outer experience. This space is one in which a negotiation between an individual's identity and the surrounding world takes place. Read Johnson (1999) has said that the concept of 'transitional space' permeates the literature of the arts therapies. He says, however, that Winnicott did not make use of the term transitional space, and that his phrase 'potential space' focused on the interpersonal interaction. For arts therapists, Read Johnson argues, the main use of this concept has concerned the *spatial* aspects of its meaning: 'The notion of transitional space provides an excellent description of the environment that is re-created in the creative arts therapy session: that is, an aesthetic, imaginal, metaphoric space in which inside and outside, self and other, are mixed' (Read Johnson, 1999: 146). It is part of creating and negotiating meaning and relationship: 'The areas of communication, the manipulation, mastery and coming to terms with reality and the notion of testing and assimilating which typifies the state of playing are all relevant to the way play manifests itself in therapy' (Jones, 1996: 173).

This space within the arts therapies often echoes Griffing's (1983) four areas of preparation for play: a distinct time; a safe space; appropriate materials; and preparatory activities. Axline, to return briefly to her work with Dibs, defines the therapy space in a way that brings together play space and therapeutic space, also indicating the importance of time and safety. Dibs initiates a discussion of the boundaries by taking the card Axline puts on the therapy room door to ask people not to enter:

Therapist's account

Suddenly he pulled his feet out of the sand, stood up, jumped out of the sandbox, and opened the playroom door. He reached up, took the card out of the holder, came back into the room, closed the door, thrust the card at me.
  'What is therapy?' he asked me.

I was astonished. 'Therapy?' I said, 'Well, let me think for a minute.' Why had he asked this question, I wondered. What explanation would make a sensible reply?

'I would say that it means a chance to come here and play and talk just about any way you want to,' I said. 'It's a time when you can be the way you want to be. A time you can use any way you want to use it. A time when you can be you.' That was the best explanation I could come up with then. He took the card out of my hand. He turned it to the other side.

'I know what this means,' he said. "Do not disturb" means everybody please let them alone. Don't bother them . . . Just let them both be. This side means they are being. And this side says you let them both be!'

(Axline, 1964: 105)

A part of this interaction shows us what Dibs seems to be saying about the space, that they are 'let . . . alone' and that he is 'being' with himself and Axline. It's also interesting to see how Axline answers his question about the definition of therapy by starting three of her four sentences with 'time'. This might be seen as an unconscious reflection on her part of the importance of this aspect of boundaries and the creation of a safe space: time. She also stresses the importance of Dibs's being able to do what he wants, that he decides on the direction and content of the sessions. It's also interesting to note the emotional content of this moment – that Dibs, in a way, hands her astonishment. She hands back an explanation and answers his question. It's a moment both inside and outside the playing. He moves out of the play of the sandbox and the playroom, asking her to answer why he's there. She replies in a way that confirms the boundaries around his freedom to play. She doesn't tell him what to do, or ask him why he's interested, but confirms the space in ways that relate to the kinds of preparation talked of by Griffing: time, a safe space, appropriate materials and preparatory activities such as the notice assuring privacy. The kind of unpredictability, astonishment within Dibs's and Axline's interaction, is a part of the potential of this play space. So, in a way, Dibs is giving her the feelings he experiences of this as a place for anything to happen, to astonish. It also demonstrates to them both that the space is related to the world around them, but it is set apart from that world. Both things are true: the opening of the door, and the bringing in of the sign that says 'No entry', for me, symbolises this duality.

The capacity of engaging in this astonishment lies alongside other factors in Smitskamp's analysis of the task of the arts therapist in relation to the play space and the creative process:

He must create an environment for the patients in which they can begin to experiment for themselves – however small and primitive those experiments may be at first.

This demands a great deal of knowledge and experience of the therapist in the area of activity . . . It demands insight and [the] capability in the creation of play and play situations. It also demands the skill to actively follow, to wait, to let things happen; active in the sense of making things possible and being curious about the way a patient is going to express himself . . .

(Smitskamp, 1989: 36)

Read Johnson has allied the play space with the arts therapy space; each is 'an interpersonal field in an imaginary realm, consciously set off from the real world by the participants' (Read Johnson, 1981: 21). Many have also spoken of the importance of play's role in mastering the separation and relationship between fantasy and reality, of play from life and the capacity to consider the relationship between specific experiences and generalisation, the capacity to conceptualise and make abstractions.

This is not play occurring spontaneously; rather, paradoxically, it is the creation of a deliberate space for spontaneous play to occur in: 'play processes are a part of a deliberate therapeutic programme for working with the client' (Jones, 1996: 181). An additional difference is that the arts therapist will be present with the client throughout the process; the individual is not playing freely on their own. The play also has a goal: for the therapist and client to create play together in order to express, explore and work towards resolution of any issues brought into the therapy space.

PLAYING AND PLAYFULNESS

The Investigacao em Musicoterapia, Center for Training and Research in Music Therapy, which has been involved in work with the Department of Music Therapy at the Centro Regional de Salud Mental (University Psychiatric Hospital) of Rosario, Argentina, says that in music therapy each 'unconscious sound identity' of the therapist and of the client communicates with the other. It describes the relationship like this:

Where they meet in the music, there exists a transitional area of musical forms, which cannot be attributed clearly to the one or the other, but which at the same time will be experienced by both partners as their own. The therapist has the task to help develop such forms, so that the client will be able to experience his own sound identity and the emerging deep unconscious material, without having to fear the burden of his responsibility for those forms.

(Centre for Training and Research in Music Therapy, ADIMU website)

The arts therapies can be seen to create a framework – one that encourages such playfulness. This involves the creation of a 'play space' within the arts therapy session as discussed in the last section. Here the client in the arts therapies can be said to have a playful relationship with reality, without the same 'burden of responsibility' as in the rest of their life. The playful state can be summarised as one that is seen to reflect aspects of the client's experience, but in such a way that they can relate to the experience differently from the way they would outside the therapy.

Bourne and Ekstrand (1985: 237–8) examine the importance of creativity in relation to this idea. Some of the uses they see in creativity being stimulated include: looking beyond what seem to be accepted boundaries, or a shift in perspective on a problem, for example. Creativity can also enable what they call a 'shift in mode' – if verbal thinking doesn't help, then the exploration through making images might be of use. Another example they describe as creative 'reasoning by analogy', where a way of dealing with something from one aspect of someone's life is applied to the current problem brought to therapy. Duggan and Grainger frame this in terms of the idea of 'as if':

> 'As if' is the determining condition for, and the primary purpose of, every transitional object. Toys, plays, symphonies; wedding rings, academic hoods, membership certificates; stages, arenas, acting areas of every kind, formal or improvised – all are objects of and for transition. 'As if' is the experimental gambit in which an appreciation of the reality of otherness – difference from myself – depends. Its importance in the development of individual people cannot be overestimated.
>
> (Duggan and Grainger, 1997: 16)

Bolton talks about an awareness within playfulness that is interesting in relation to the arts therapies. He argues that play is not just about being lost or absorbed in the experience, that at the same time the player is aware of the relationship between their playing, themselves and the world outside the play. He describes a *dual perspective*, an active identification with the imaginary creation and what he calls a 'heightened awareness' of their own identification: 'So, far from escaping from life, the quality of life is momentarily intensified because he is knowing what he thinks as he thinks it, seeing what he says as he says it and evaluating what he does as he does it' (Bolton, 1981: 183).

Bolton argues that reflection concurrent with identification leads to this heightened awareness and the potential for someone to learn about themselves and their experience. Play, then, can be seen to offer opportunities to do with entering into an intensified state. Playfulness refers to the ways in which a client can enter a state that has a special relationship with space, everyday rules and boundaries. This state permits spontaneity and creativity, frequently connected to playing. It is characterised by a more flexible, creative attitude towards events, consequences and held ideas. This enables the client to adopt a playful, experimenting attitude towards themselves and their life experiences.

Smitskamp sums this up as follows: 'Play and "pretend" situations often provide a great degree of structural security. In these situations feelings can be experienced extremely genuinely and intensively. The realisation that he was "just playing", however, gives the patient the protection necessary to permit himself these feelings' (Smitskamp, 1989: 35).

THE PLAY SHIFT

As we've seen, play can be characterised by specific activities and by particular types of relationships between individuals. In 'Play Behaviour in Higher Primates: A Review' (1969) Loizos defines the function of play for primates. She says it is a behaviour that borrows or adopts patterns that appear in other contexts within the primate's life. In their usual place within the primates' activities these 'patterns' appear to have immediate and obvious ends and goals. However, she states that: 'When these patterns appear in play they seem to be divorced from their original motivation and are qualitatively distinct from the same patterns appearing in their originally motivated contexts' (Loizos, 1969: 228–9). Here then a shift in *meaning* is seen to occur – I have called this the 'play shift'. This means that whilst many of the ways of behaving or doing things are seen to happen in play, their intention is different. So aggressive behaviour patterns may be shown, but they do not have the same intent as when they are displayed outside play. A child might play games that contain experiences from life relating to aggression or anger, but the emotions and situations would not be experienced by the child in the same way as they would be in their lives outside the play. Piaget (1962) echoes this when he says that in play the individual's interest is transferred from the goal to the activity itself – to the enjoyment of the pleasure of play.

Watson-Gegeo and Boggs's observation of play in a Hawaiian neighbourhood includes a description of two children. In a fictive play the children were witnessed competing, contradicting, challenging and insulting one another. They argue that this was play reflecting scenes they had witnessed of parents challenging and accusing each other. They note that parents became involved in the play: 'parents modelled and elicited playful contradictions with the children and encouraged their attempts. Children used the contradicting routine in their disputes' (Watson-Gegeo and Boggs, 1977: 67).

Garvey describes this process in relation to research into primary school children from Fiji:

> In one sequence the following shows a stepwise escalation of the content of the prior message–
>
> *A:* I can lift up this whole school.
> *B:* I can lift up our whole family. I bet you can't lift up that with one finger.
> *A:* I can lift up the whole world with one finger.
> *B:* Well, I can lift up the universe.

Since the children were pretending to have a quarrel, their communication and behaviour [were] more highly stylised than most non-play confrontations. The regularity of the patterning of exchange sequences reported in these studies, however, shows that the participants understood the underlying structure of verbal conflict. That competence can be used to enact a conflict within the pretend frame or in a more seriously motivated confrontation.

(Garvey, 1984: 150–1)

Schechner parallels the workshop experience with play. He argues that the workshop is a way of playing around with reality, a means of examining behaviour by 're-ordering, exaggerating, fragmenting, recombining and adumbrating it'. The workshop is a protected time and space where 'intergroup relationships may thrive without being threatened by intergroup aggression' (Schechener, 1988: 103–4).

Garvey (1977) has argued that play is typified by what he calls non-literal behaviours. These are behaviours that are pretended. Though they have many of the characteristics of behaviours out of play, they are not the same thing. Authors such as Bateson (1955) and Cohen (1969) have described a part of the way this functions as 'metacommunication'. The idea is that a part of play involves an awareness and communication that the activities are not the same as in real life, that they are exploratory and safe. So someone can *play* angry: they have many of the characteristics that they would have if they were really angry, but at the same time, they give indicators that this is *play*, not 'for real'.

The notion of a play shift in the arts therapies is related to these ideas. In play as described by Loizos and Piaget elements of real life are *retained* but they are subjected to *different motivations* – enjoyment, exploration, assimilation. 'The play shift involves reality being taken into the play space and treated in a way that encourages experimentation and digestion' (Jones, 1996: 177).

UK dramatherapist McAlister talks of a client, L, in a forensic setting. Initially they work within the sessions using story, object play and improvisation. However, the therapist notes of L: 'he could not reflect on it at all' (1999: 107). Work continues over a number of months. The client becomes increasingly interested in objects such as boxes and shells. L had previously commented that the hospital at times felt like a container. This led into work around what aspects of himself the client felt needed to be contained by the hospital and the therapy, and what parts wanted to be free:

Therapist's account

He was able to use objects to represent these things, the most significant being a small plastic dinosaur which he placed inside a box, fastened the lid and placed . . . underneath a table. This led him to begin talking for the first time about his violence when ill . . . Following this, L began using fences and boundaries to contain the dinosaur so that it was out in the open yet still contained. Again these were themes that were returned to at later stages, as he continued to use various fierce animals to create stories about family groupings, zoos and captivity and reasons for his aggression. His capacity to make links between himself and session material gradually became much stronger. Eventually he was able to state 'I am the angry lion. That's me. I'm an angry man.'

(McAlister, 1999: 108)

She says that this area of symbolic play with objects allowed L to express and explore parts of himself symbolically. This work allows the kind of playful state described above in which the client was able to look at and 'to reveal areas of his psychopathology, i.e. his dangerousness'. As he explores and uses the space more deeply and as trust develops, 'often difficult and painful feelings surface'. Playful activity takes on meaning and the playful state allows the client to express and explore things he would not usually permit himself to do:

For example, in one session we passed a ball and L began bouncing it hard. This developed into work expressing sounds and words as we bounced the ball back and forth, and L expressed a lot of anger in the exercise. Later he said the phrases he had used were the things he should have said to his abusers.

(McAlister, 1999: 109)

Here the initial work seems to provide the client with the opportunity to play without creating overt connections to his life situation – the 'protection' described earlier, enabling L to permit himself to express and engage. He may also be seeing if the therapy space and his relationship with the therapist can be trusted. Once this safety has been established L seems to begin to work more deeply and to begin to allow areas of expression to enter into the play space that McAlister says he has not previously allowed to occur. In addition L permits the spontaneity and creativity, described earlier as often connected to playing, to explore his feelings and situation. The play with objects such as the dinosaur, or with the ball, reflect aspects of the client's experience. However, this is different from how he would express himself outside the therapy. L adopts a playful, experimenting attitude towards himself and his life experience. In the dinosaur work, for example, he allows himself to explore issues of his experiences and needs in relation to anger, aggression and containment. In the work with the ball he allows the spontaneous play to become suggestive of previous experiences and begins to say things within the play space and the therapeutic relationship that he could not say outside the therapy. The 'play shift' can be seen in the way that aggressive and violent aspects of the client's experience are brought into the playful space. They can be reproduced, but are away from their original context. They do not have the same intent as when they were encountered outside the dramatherapy, and can therefore be expressed and experienced differently. They can, therefore, be explored in a more distanced way, the client can 'look' at himself within the space and the relationship with the therapist. In this way, for L, the 'play space' becomes an area that is both set apart yet connected to his everyday life. McAlister describes the positive changes in the client concerning his being able to communicate, to make connections, to manage his condition more effectively: 'his capacity to make links between himself and the drama, reflect on our relationship and his capacity for insight' (McAlister, 1999: 110).

PLAY AND DEVELOPMENT

Arts therapists such as Aldridge do not see a developmental approach consisting of the notion of a series of stages that all children must pass through in areas such as cognition, emotion or relationship. They work with the idea that developmental stages can help them to see differences in individuals. This can guide the therapist in considering where issues may lie for individuals, and in looking at where work on development might assist the client in areas that are forming a difficulty. Maturation models of children used in areas such as assessment are criticised in that they have difficulty taking into account variability and individual differences. Each child needs to be seen in terms of the way they relate to these areas as individuals:

> Children select and transform what is meaningful for them from the context within which they find themselves. What is selected and transformed is in part in accordance with their cognitive abilities, yet these abilities are not separate from other related developmental processes. Each child may differ in his or her development. Furthermore, children not only take from the environment; they too give out signals that modify their environment. Infants give clues to their mothers about how they expect them to react. Improvised creative music therapy, with its emphasis on activity within a dynamic personal relationship, may play a role in encouraging development particularly when it focuses on communicative abilities.
>
> (Aldridge *et al.*, 1995: 190).

Here the child is not seen as a passive recipient of messages or norms concerning relationship and communication. They are seen as active within a relationship that forms. Each individual is seen as such, rather than as a child who should be performing in certain ways at certain times. An issue is framed in terms of development: if an area needs to be engaged with, this is seen as a challenge rather than a feature indicating some disfunction or disorder set against a generalised norm. So, for example, Aldridge sees work with children with learning disabilities as 'music therapy' aiming to help 'developmentally challenged children progress towards a richer communicative life' (Aldridge *et al.*, 1995: 190). The situation of the client is seen in terms of interrelated areas rather than as a disfunction owned by the child and defined by the professional. He sees delay as the potential consequence of a variety of factors – physical, mental or social. So, for example, issues might arise from experiences of rejection when standards or expectations associated with chronological age are not met. The relationship between a child and their social environment is recognised. A child's situation is considered in terms of the ways in which communication differences can result in frustrations over developmental tasks and challenges in areas such as being loved, stimulated and educated. Aldridge *et al.* say: 'Our therapeutic task is to respond to abilities and potentials so that those limitations themselves are minimised. If both environment and individual are important for developmental change, the therapist provides, albeit temporarily, an environment in which individual change can occur (Aldridge *et al.*, 1995: 190).

The idea is that music can assist developmental change. Their study used a structure to look at a variety of areas of the child's communication to see if changes were occurring as a result of coming to music therapy. The therapists saw these areas as giving information on developmental change. These included the relationship between child and music therapist, and the state of musical communication: whether the relationship manifested total obliviousness, or some response or mutuality in playing music, for example. Musical communication included looking at the child's use of instruments and vocal activity along with body movement. These are seen by them to be interrelated: 'musical dialogue in the music therapy relationship seems to bring about an improvement in the ability to form and maintain personal social relationships in other contexts' (Aldridge *et al.*, 1995: 203).

They emphasise that they did not use music to try to manipulate children so that particular goals in communication, or their use of an instrument, were met. They are interested in what, if any, developmental changes took place within the opportunities offered to the child by the presence of both musical instruments and the therapists. Here is an example of how they understand this approach:

> the active playing of a drum demands that the child listen to the therapist who in turn is listening to and playing for him or her. This act entails the physical co-ordination of a musical intention within the context of a relationship. We would argue that this unity of the cognitive, gestural, emotional and relational is the strength of active music therapy for developmentally challenged children.
>
> (Aldridge *et al.*, 1995: 203)

CONCLUSION

This chapter has shown how processes such as the play shift and the creation of a play space are central to ideas of change in the arts therapies. As we also saw, Harris challenges the idea that playing is only important for children. He argues against the idea that pretend play and fantasy is something character- istic of young children and that by adulthood it has mostly disappeared. He argues that this is wrong: 'Human beings have a gift for fantasy which shows itself at a very early age and then continues to make all sorts of contributions to our intellectual and emotional life throughout the lifespan' (Harris, 2001: 1). It is also seen by him to be important in comprehension. He says that when an adult listens to a narrative, they build a mind's eye mental image or model of the situation or events. It's the mental model that remains, not the words. This he argues is allied to the play space and pretend play in children as 'a time and place that is removed from their current situation' (2001: 1). As we have seen, this is akin to the function of the transitional space described by Winnicott. At the heart of his proposition is an 'interweave':

> No longer are we either introvert or extrovert. We experience life in that area of transitional phenomena, in the exciting interweave of subjectivity and objective observation, and in an area that is intermediate between the inner reality of the individual and the shared reality of the world that is external to individuals.
>
> (Winnicott, 1974: 75)

This idea sums up much of what is important to therapeutic change in the arts therapies. The arts therapy space and the arts therapist enable clients to inhabit a space between internal and external, where playfulness can be brought into contact with areas of difficulty or that are in need of develop- ment. Cattanach describes this space as a kind of gap: 'It is in this gap between art and life, in a sort of timeless space, that we can experiment with ways of being which can help and heal both individual and group' (Cattanach, 1992: 3).

This is the arena of the play space and the play shift which is used by all clients in the arts therapies.

Part V

Client–therapist relationship: paradigms, dialogues and discoveries

What the uncertainty of thoughts does have in common with the uncertainty of particles is that the difficulty is not just a practical one, but a systematic limitation which cannot even in theory be circumvented. It is patently not resolved by the efforts of psychologists or psychoanalysts ... the whole possibility of saying or thinking anything about the world, even the most apparently objective, abstract aspects of it studied by the natural sciences, depends upon human observation, and is subject to the limitations which the human mind imposes, the uncertainty in our thinking is also fundamental to the nature of the world.

Michael Frayn, Postscript to his play Copenhagen (1998: 101)

14 Client and arts therapist: dialogues and diversity

INTRODUCTION

The nature of the relationship between therapist and client within the arts therapies varies enormously. Here are some brief vignettes to illustrate this, sometimes bewildering, diversity:

> A client, Jason, is improvising and playing roles based on Shakespeare's King Lear. Themes emerge on father-and-son relationships.
>
> The client sits in a chair playing himself at a younger age, he then moves to another chair playing the part of his own stepfather, speaking as him, saying critical, negative things about Jason. The therapist later sits in the same chair, playing the stepfather, repeating these words back to Jason.
>
> (Mitchell, 1996: 80)

> A woman's daughter has died, and she is in a long period of grief. She paints on an easel, an image of the interior of a church, a body in a coffin and a figure in a black cloak leaning against the coffin. The therapist sits in the room and is largely silent, the client says that the image is of her daughter in the coffin, and herself in the cloak, grieving. She goes for lunch and the image is left on the easel. The therapist makes no interpretation, but the client, upon returning after her break, with a sense of real shock, suddenly says that she realises that the picture is not what it had seemed. She now sees the painting as showing herself in the coffin, and the cloaked figure is her own mother.
>
> (Schaverien, 1992: 109)

> A group of five women enter a room; they listen for thirty minutes to a tape that has been created by the therapist, consisting of recorded music of Daniel Kobialka's 'Timeless Lullaby' with an added pulse of low-frequency tone of 44Hz. The therapist accompanies them to and from the room, and five minutes after the session their heartbeat and blood pressure are taken.
>
> (Wigram, 1993: 181–2)

A client imitates the movements of a therapist; both are standing opposite each other. The therapist swings his/her arms in arc-like circles from the shoulder, a series of movement patterns follow – initially the therapist moves only peripheral parts of the body, then creates movements which involve the trunk, head and arms in co-ordination. The client follows and mirrors the therapist's movements.

(Higgins, 1993: 150)

Here are therapists who play the roles of people from their clients' lives, who produce movement patterns whilst their clients imitate them, who create tapes of music to play whilst clients listen, and who sit quietly whilst clients paint, and then hear what they have to say before and after lunch. The differences are mirrored in clients' experiences as they play roles based on a seventeenth-century text, improvise dance or imitate movement, paint images and listen to music.

Questions arise from this diversity of contact between therapist and client. Are there areas of *homogeneity* in the arts therapies? Can any useful observations be made about the relationship between therapist and client across the disciplines because of these differences? This chapter will examine this diversity, and try to identify whether there are any commonalities within the arts therapies in terms of the way client and therapist relate.

Other questions are connected to this. Do the arts therapies have anything original to say about the client–therapist relationship? Do they merely reproduce the relationships present within the existing major schools of therapy such as the cognitive or analytic? In short, have they come up with anything new? This chapter will consider these questions.

CLIENT–THERAPIST TRANSACTION

Budd and Sharma have said that the 'healing bond' relies on the assumption that the healer or therapist has something to offer which can make a difference. This can involve a 'remedy', or providing the conditions and resources for the client to heal themselves. They assert that healers are not passive; they have views about the client's condition, the nature of the healing process, what kind of outcome may be expected and what the limitations of the process might be (Budd and Sharma, 1994: 17, 102). Budd and Sharma also rightly acknowledge that the process of healing relies on both parties. The client and the therapist are in a 'transaction' together, the client playing an active role in whether change occurs.

This framework is an interesting one to use to explore the nature of the relationship between client and therapist in the arts therapies. A transaction occurs – involving opinions, opportunities and limitations, choices, actions and exchanges. Arts therapists such as Hogan (1997) have explored aspects of this interaction concerning the social construction of illness. So how do these areas relate to the arts therapies? How do arts therapists act? What part does the client play? How do arts therapists view the conditions their clients bring to the therapy? What role does their relationship play within the outcomes and limitations of the arts therapies? How adaptable are the arts therapies? How responsive are they to the individual therapist and client?

The notion of *context* underlies all these questions. Increasingly, the arts therapies have found themselves practised in an enormous range of settings and within a mix of cultures and contexts. The next chapters will consider practice relating to client and therapist encounters in relation to Turkey, Israel, the US and the UK, for example. Is there a way of working with the relationship that is appropriate across these different cultures? Is the relationship between therapist and client the same in Turkey as it is in South Africa? Is the relationship between an adolescent client and their therapist in the Bronx the same as that between an elderly client and their therapist in Taiwan? Here a host of other questions regarding difference and similarity arise – concerning race, culture, gender, class, age and sexuality. Of course, these are questions that every form of health practice needs to address. However, in the arts therapies there are particular complexities, concerning culture and context – areas such as the art form and artistic expression. As we have seen, cultural attitudes towards the arts play an important part in forming the nature of the contact between arts therapist and client. This chapter will explore these themes within arts therapies practice.

As already noted, the arts therapies have evolved a great diversity in the ways in which the client–therapist relationship can be created. An important element in this diversity of relationships is in response to the wide variety of clients who make use of the arts therapies. As Part II showed, the arts therapies work diversely with, for example, clients with learning difficulties, as well as with clients with schizophrenia; they work with families, groups or with individuals. This, then, can be seen as a transaction: the ways the arts therapies have developed *in response* to the demands and needs of clients. The next section will begin to examine a key aspect of this transaction: the different roles within the therapeutic relationship.

ROLES OF THE ARTS THERAPIST

The arts therapist combines different roles within the transaction between client and therapist. This can be said of any therapist, but for the arts therapist there is a unique combination of traditions and roles. I will argue that this mixture creates an innovative relationship between therapist and client.

As pointed out above, arts therapists practise within a wide range of therapeutic approaches. These all affect the ways in which the therapist conducts himself or herself, the way in which they understand the difficulties and potentials which bring the client to therapy, and the way they relate to clients. The arts therapist has evolved from artist, therapist and arts teacher – this is a historical reality as shown in Chapters 8, 9 and 10. In her extensive history of the development of art therapy Waller says, for example, 'art therapy had seemed to emerge as a segment both of art teaching and also of psychoanalysis' (Waller, 1991: 73). For the practising therapist, I would argue, this 'role history' is present in their everyday relationship with their clients. The presence of the therapist and their relationship with their clients contains these different roles. The relationship between these roles is a dynamic one. It varies within different frameworks of practice, and it varies during the life of any therapeutic contact, from within a single session to the whole extent or time of the therapy. This dynamic provides a way of understanding the special opportunities that the arts therapies offer the client in their ways of working. I am going to use it to explore the client–therapist relationship in the arts therapies.

This chapter along with the next will explore this role triad: therapist, artist and teacher. They will look at each of the roles, but also at the ways in which the *sum* of the triad is more than its *parts*. Specifically this chapter will look at the 'therapist' element of the arts therapist's identity and will consider this aspect of their role. It will also look at the ways in which the different therapeutic models arts therapists relate to, affects their thinking and practice, as well as the experience of the client. The next chapter will look at the 'artist' and 'teacher' aspects of the therapist's identity and the ways in which these aspects of the arts therapist's role function together.

THERAPIST AND CLIENT

The task of the arts therapist is to provide an opportunity for change to occur for the client. Most would recognise Clarkson's definition of the therapist as someone who 'can only point the way, facilitate the journey, but in the end cannot do it for the client. The client has to do it for himself' (Clarkson, 2002: 283). The way in which this happens varies widely across the different arts therapies.

Looked at historically, by the late twentieth century the arts therapies had developed as independent disciplines, as described earlier. However, they emerged in dialogue with a variety of therapeutic frameworks, as we have seen in many of the clinical examples so far. Often the arts therapies have allied themselves, or become related, to specific schools of therapy, which have developed alongside the arts therapies. Sometimes, as Part II showed, the very titles of the arts therapies indicate this. Art therapy, in particular, reflects alliances through a variety of names. As well as 'art therapy', other alternatives are used such as 'analytic art therapy' or 'art psychotherapy', for example. These reflect the allegiance between art therapy and the practice of analysis or psychotherapy respectively. Other theorists have argued for what they call a more 'independent' way of thinking – that the arts therapies have their own framework concerning change and the client–therapist relationship. This way of thinking tends to reduce allegiances with other schools of therapy, and look towards ways of understanding the nature of change in the arts therapy as unique. This approach tends to try not to use other frameworks to help describe or understand the way the therapy is effective.

This chapter will look at these different frameworks in terms of the therapist and client. It will consider some of the main influences from the field of therapy on the relationship between therapist and client including the analytic, cognitive behavioural, developmental and humanistic traditions. In addition, it will look at what is different or unique about the client–therapist relationship in the arts therapies.

The following gives a very brief summary of the main relevant features of the paradigms or schools of therapy which have been most involved in dialogue with the arts therapies.

Within the *analytic framework* the emphasis is upon the nature of the client–therapist relationship and the way in which the client makes use of this within the therapy. Conceptual ideas such as transference and counter-transference, projection and introjection are used within this approach to make sense of how therapeutic change occurs. The therapist encourages the client to use the relationship between them within the therapy, and the therapist may make use of strategies such as interpretation.

Within the *cognitive behavioural approach* the therapist and client work together in an alliance. The therapist enables the client to formulate therapeutic goals and together they work to achieve those ends. The therapist encourages the client to reflect and discuss the ways in which they can achieve changes in the way they function and relate, looking to set manageable goals and then to review the process of change as it develops.

The *humanistic* therapist emphasises the 'in the moment' experience of the relationship between therapist and client. The therapist will draw the client's attention to difficulties or issues that arise within this, and emphasise the creation of empathy and genuineness. Stress is placed on the idea that there is an innate drive towards growth within each human being and that the therapist aims to enable this: 'the human organism is . . . active, not passive. For instance, inhibition of certain behaviours is not merely absence of these behaviours . . . an active holding in. If the inhibition is lifted, what was being held in does not then passively emerge. Rather the person actively, eagerly brings it forth' (in Perls *et al.*, 1951/89: 22 quoted in Clarkson, 1994).

> The *developmental* perspective sees the client's position in terms of a block or halt in development. Assessment looks at the client in relation to a developmental sequence, and attempts to identify where the difficulty or halt has occurred. This is followed by the developmental process being revisited within the therapy in order to renegotiate the stage, or stoppage, with the therapist as companion or guide (Read Johnson, 1982). Drama and play therapist Cattanach summarises the approach in relation to developmental psychology which uses 'the concept of living in time as a way to understand human development. Their exploration is of life stages and the mechanisms and processes of human development. Individual theorists put forward developmental schemes which emphasise a variety of aspects of the self' (Cattanach 1994: 31).

These differences matter, as they affect the way the client is understood, and the way in which they work within the therapy space and with the therapy methods.

Where there is choice, the client might select a particular therapeutic approach. Where referral is the procedure then the question of how best any paradigm will suit the needs and demands of the client must be a feature in considering the selection of a framework. However, as I will show, the arts therapies have not simply taken the approaches described above, and transferred them wholesale into their theory and practice. Their relationship is more complex than that, as the next section will show.

ARTS THERAPY RELATIONSHIPS: DIALOGUE AND DISCOVERY

I will argue that two main things have occurred. One is that the arts therapies have evolved in *dialogue* with other models of therapeutic relationship, and also with other disciplines such as teaching, or arts practice. The second is that the arts therapies have made *unique discoveries* about the relationship between client and therapist.

There are numerous examples of the way dialogue has occurred between the arts therapies and other therapies. Bunt, for example, points out that there was a tradition in the US during the 1960s and 1970s of music therapists developing a view of music therapy as a form of behavioural science (Bunt, 1997: 256). Here music therapy developed a dialogue with behavioural therapy. The root of the idea is that certain activities can be encouraged and reinforced by rewarding the client, so that action and reward are associated. Listening to music was evaluated as a reward, for example. Studies looked at music's role in the reduction of aggressive, stereotyped behaviour, or in the development of concentration or reading skills.

The next sections form a detailed *sample* of the dialogue between the arts therapies and two different therapeutic frameworks. They show how music therapy, as an example, finds a variety of ways in which the relationship between client and therapist feature in therapeutic change.

ARTS THERAPISTS AND CLIENTS

Dialogue with analytic psychotherapy

The first example is from music therapist Rogers's practice (1993). Her work is within a large mental health unit attended by children, adolescents and adults. Rogers's description of the 'paradigm' she works within emphasises many of the areas described earlier as being connected to an analytic frame-work, in terms of the interaction between therapist and client. The practice focused on 'the symbolic use of material by sexually abused clients' (Rogers, 1993: 203). The description of her work is especially useful in that it stressed the importance for clients themselves to determine the factors that contrib-uted to change. This included weekly written feedback from the clients during the course of the therapy, as well as in retrospect, approximately six months after the close of the therapy.

Client A: aims of the music therapy

Rogers sees music therapy as allowing the non-verbal expression of emotions: this is equated with the sessions' providing a non-threatening medium for her clients. This is, in turn, seen to assist in the exploration of 'underlying issues' in a safe environment (Rogers, 1993: 206). Goals for the clients are related to the immense difficulties in examining emotional pain associated with abuse. She highlights music therapy's use for the clients by seeing it in relation to concepts of resistance, denial and low self-esteem. These are characteristics of the difficulties brought by clients to the therapy. Music therapy is seen as a 'highly effective means of dealing' with these phenomena (Rogers, 1993: 206).

Client A: method and the client–therapist relationship

The method used in the therapy is free musical improvisation. The rationale for the choice of this approach within music therapy is that 'clinical impro-visation within the therapeutic environment allows the inner emotional world of the client to be examined and acknowledged' (Rogers, 1993: 206). This is seen as a way in which the therapist 'examines the relationship between herself and the client'. Rogers defines the central agents of change as the client–therapist relationship and the music (1993: 206).

The therapist's role is stated by Rogers as being to understand, reflect and interpret – either musically or verbally – therapeutic issues that have particu-lar relevance for the client. She sees sound in terms of forming a relationship of 'dialogue' between therapist and client. Areas such as the pattern of shared music, or verbal and musical dialogue, are seen in relation to the client expressing the 'pain of their inner emotional world' through musical improvisation. The improvisations serve to externalise emotions that are then discussed with the client. For some clients, who she says may have no conscious recollection of the abuse, the boundaries of the therapeutic relationship can provide safety to express and make memories conscious. Once emotions have been communicated, links between behaviour and feelings may be explored. The role of the therapist is defined in this situation as chiefly being to listen, observe, think and respond.

Emphasis is placed upon the therapist's needing to use boundaries, and to encourage 'symbolic roles for the instruments' (Rogers, 1993: 207). Instruments are seen as ways for the client to create direct experience of working with emotions through projection. One client, for example, connects a conga drum with a father, the xylophone as the mother, and himself as a beater to be used on either instrument (Rogers, 1993: 211). Rogers says that some clinical improvisations can relate to specific situations: for example, the client's feelings during an interaction with a family member. Here, the client plays music herself and directs the therapist's improvisation on a second instrument. The therapist's improvisations are said to represent a member of the client's family, whilst the client plays herself. Musical expression in the sessions can also be non-directed with free-form, non-specific improvisation characterised by Rogers as a 'mess' or confusion of sounds.

The contractual boundaries of the therapy – areas such as the room, regular time and duration, the provision of the same choice of instruments and the protection from intrusions – are seen as crucial. They are symbolically linked to the psyche of the client, and the progress of the therapy. The way the music therapist is experienced by the client, and the therapist's experience of the client, are seen as important aspects of the therapy. The therapist can touch the client, and the sharing of instruments is seen as a 'very intimate form of communication'. This, again, is symbolically linked to the client's previous and current experiences of space, the body and protection, respect or invasion.

The uses of instruments and space, as well as the relationship with the therapist, can express the pain that is encountered within the sessions. This is seen in terms of 'regression' and the encountering of defence mechanisms. For example, a client placing musical instruments round himself is seen as forming a protective barrier. Arising from this, Rogers works with the client to explore issues such as the 'danger of getting too close'. Rogers talks about how, over time, trust develops and this 'musical barrier' is moved. Issues of transference and counter-transference are referred to, and the client's relationship to the therapist is understood to reflect relationships outside the therapy, concerning the client's experience of abuse. The relationship to Rogers is seen as a transferential one – the client unconsciously bringing other relationships to their contact with the therapist in a symbolic expression. The relationship with the therapist is expressed through the use of space and instruments, and is presented by Rogers as both an expression of the distress, but also as the means to its resolution. As the case example below will show, the therapist sees the client's use of instruments and changes in the use of space in the light of a reparative relationship. For example, she creates, with the client, an opportunity for change to occur through play with the instruments; gradually they cease to be a barrier, and are used to communicate within a trusting relationship.

Here the music therapist attempts to balance making responses to issues as they arise with giving directions. Rogers, for example, can introduce an activity such as the use of instruments to represent and indicate family members and relationships.

Case example analysis

> ### Case example: Client A
>
> An adult – Client A – had an initial diagnosis of depression and an eating disorder. She had been repeatedly abused by a member of her family. It's also noted that she displayed some paralysis of movement when awake and used a wheelchair, but could move the affected area when asleep. Rogers describes how, in the initial stages of the therapy, A denies that there is any problem, saying that her only issue is with her weight, and that if this were dealt with, the depression would stop.
>
> The client initially creates an improvised rhythm on musical instruments. The therapist responds to these rhythms – she tries a 'musical overture' that is rejected, but A is described as being able to tolerate the therapist's presence when she uses modal improvisation. This response by the therapist is seen by Rogers in terms of 'holding' and 'supporting' the client's initial rhythms on an instrument. The understanding of this interaction is that the sounds are expressions of unconscious material and A's relationship with the therapist. When, for example, the sounds from the therapist are rejected, this is seen as symbolic of the client's relationship to the therapist. In turn, this reflects issues about contact and A's resistance to the therapeutic space. The instruments and the sounds are used to create a dialogue, and a more trusting relationship develops through the dialogue.
>
> Rogers sees A begin to use the therapy to explore her inner emotional world – using music which is described as chaotic and angry through syncopated rhythms and drums. The therapist reflects this development – working by also creating music atonally and with dissonance – this is seen by Rogers as 'chaos' and 'mess'.
>
> Here again, sounds and relationships are seen to represent internally held feelings and experiences. The music, and the relationship it is part of, is seen to function as a way for A to express these things. Once expressed, the material becomes available to be worked with. The chaos and mess that has been held by the client is expressed, and can now be examined and worked with. The therapist creates sound to reflect, amplify and respond to the music A makes.

A often puts beaters inside musical instruments such as the piano within the session. This is seen as having a preoccupation, and as an analogy with taking material into her body. In addition she is described as stroking the surface in a 'highly sensual way whilst gazing in a provocative manner at the therapist' (Rogers, 1993: 212). In this way A's inner reality is linked to the manipulation of the materials. As Rogers explores this with her, A relates this to her feelings about her abuser, subsequently verbalising the abuse.

The use of certain instruments – the piano, a large gong, large conga drums – is used by A to drown out the therapist's sounds, or to make a 'rage of sound' (Rogers, 1993: 213), and to control the nature of the musical relationship. This is seen as a reflection of A's feeling of lack of control in her world, and that the need for control was focused on her eating and anorexia. This is also seen as a reflection of the initial relationship with the abuser, whose home she still lived in. In turn, her sexuality and physical form is also linked with her eating disorder and abuse. She verbally expressed ambivalence within the session – still wanting to receive 'love' from the abuser. Preoccupations with chaos, mess and musical instruments as 'containers' are seen as symbolic ways to express the situation. 'The nature of improvisation is that it finds ways to ask clients questions about their inner emotional world or about the abuse . . . rather than leaving the onus on the client to "tell"' (Rogers, 1993: 215).

Here the therapist and client use the music therapy as a way of exploring how behaviour, thinking and feeling within the sessions are influenced by the unconscious. Through dialogue, the playing of rhythms or patterns, Rogers is a witness to the client's expressions. She also responds, inviting differences of interaction: for example, offering melody at the start of the therapy. The therapist acts to encourage the client to use the sessions to reflect life experiences, by direct representation, or through free-form improvisation. The relationship with the therapist evolves through the playing and symbolic use of instruments. As the implicit material is made explicit through the music, it can be worked with. The therapist, through listening, responding and interpreting, enables the client to express and resolve the issues they bring. This is framed, in part, by the notion of a reparative relationship: the establishment of trust following on from mistrust and denial. The therapist makes reflections and interpretations enabling the client to engage with cut-off, or repressed, material. The client is enabled to see the ways in which the music making and the relationship with the therapist reflect such material. She can then consider the situation, and explore new possibilities.

Read Johnson (1998) has summarised what he has described as a psychodynamic model of the arts therapies as containing three main components: *projection, transformation* and *internalisation*. In *projection* aspects of the self are expressed in artistic products and processes. *Transformation* is the process through which personal material formed in artistic expression is 'altered, worked through or mediated' (Read Johnson, 1998: 85). He acknowledges a debate within the arts therapies as to whether this transformative element is one that occurs 'naturally' as the result of the arts medium, or is dependent on the therapist's intervention. *Internalisation* concerns the way in which the transformed material is 'reintegrated' into the client's psychological state.

Aspects of these three processes can be seen in the case example of Client A. Central to this approach, then, are the ways in which music processes and products engage with material related to the client's unconscious. The emphasis in Read Johnson's account is on the created product. Many would argue that, as shown in the situation with Client A, the relationship between therapist, client and created product is an important aspect of the dialogue. This focuses on the ways in which the arts products and processes are part of the *relationship* with the therapist. In the work with Client A, for example, this concerns how the relationship is affected by the use of sound, rhythm and melody. The therapist is directly involved through the art form – playing, improvising, repeating and touching the musical instruments which the client has used.

A psychoanalytic framework: critiques and limitations

> Our internal worlds and our psychic realities are our selves. Selfhood is deeply influenced by other people. Much of the self is seen as constituted from internal representations of other people and relationships – whole people, aspects of people and . . . the ways they relate to us, and to each other.
>
> (Stevens, 1996: 285)

Some have criticised this way of viewing the self, as being too rooted in a particular way of dealing with identity and client problems, and this limits its usefulness. Holland, for example, has said that Freud and Freudian thought are readily identified as products of late nineteenth-century European society: 'a period in which family life was relatively autonomous and thus of considerable importance in psychic development. With the decline of the nuclear family's autonomy in our own, very different late-twentieth-century society, however, the continuing relevance of orthodox psychoanalysis is far less readily apparent' (Holland, 1988: 405). In relation to transcultural counselling, D'Ardenne and Mahtani (1989) describe transference as the attitudes and feelings placed by the client on to the counsellor or therapist. There is an additional dimension – clients who have had a lifetime of cultural and racial prejudice will bring the scars of these experiences to the relationship.

Interpretation is used in the case example, but a number of authors have pointed out the importance of the therapist's making sure that the meaning emerges from the client. Rogers uses music as an interpretation, her sounds, rhythms and responses are articulated interventions, offering invitations to meaning. The therapist, within this framework, can make suggestions as interventions. However, this needs to be done with sensitivity and an awareness of power issues in the client–therapist relationship, and the differences of cultural awareness and language as discussed by D'Ardenne and Mahtani (1989).

It's not as if all practitioners within an analytic framework will directly connect with the approach taken here by Rogers – as within the analytic field itself there are a diversity of emphases and approaches such as Jungian, Kleinian or Lacanian. Jung, for example, speaks of the goals of psychotherapy as involving the therapist being guided by the patient's own irrationalities. He says that 'we must follow nature as a guide, and what the doctor then does is less a question of treatment than of developing the creative possibilities latent in the patient himself' (Jung, 1931: 88).

A number of arts therapists have pointed out that it is important that the arts aspect of the process is not seen only as a way of realising analytic processes within the therapy. Skaife, for example, has pointed to the danger of a tendency in 'art therapy groups run along group analytic lines' (Skaife, 2000: 116) for the artwork to be regarded primarily as a reflection of the group process, of the relationships in the group. She says it is important for the aesthetic aspects of making art, which parallel the interactions between self and the world, for example, to be paid attention to in the conversation between arts and therapy. In Rogers's work we can see an illustration of this approach: how the arts form is an integral part of the dialogue.

The next case example illustrates another of the dialogues, this time with a developmental approach to therapy.

Dialogue with a developmental approach to therapy

Sophie: method and the client–therapist relationship

Aldridge (1996) describes his approach as being related to music therapy as developed by Nordoff Robbins. This is typified as the therapist's being in the role of encourager: to encourage the client to improvise using percussion and tuned percussive instruments; to sing with the patient; and to encourage the client to play with the therapist at the piano (Aldridge, 1996: 9). He specifies that there is *no attempt* to interpret the music psychotherapeutically. The vehicle for therapy is the development of a musical relationship between therapist and client within the creativity of improvisation.

Sophie: aims of the music therapy

The case example below is from work with children referred to by Aldridge as being 'developmentally delayed'. In describing the issues brought to therapy Aldridge frames the children's situation in developmental terms. The concerns for the child, Sophie, in the case example relate to the acquisition of speech and meaningful communication. Music therapy is seen as a way of encouraging children without language, or who are experiencing a developmental delay, to communicate. Such developmental delay can be seen in terms of emotional conflict, the experience of rejection or behavioural disturbance. Aldridge focuses upon the area that relates to the client's situation or context, and on communication: 'Our therapeutic task is to respond to abilities and potentials so that those limitations themselves are minimised. If both environment and the individual are important for developmental change, the therapist provides, albeit temporarily, an environment in which individual change can occur' (Aldridge, 1996: 245). He sees this as an 'ecological' way of understanding the child. This places the client in a *context*, in terms of relationship, identifying the difficulty in terms of interaction with others, and the development of communication. This is at 'the heart' of the music therapy's approach: when referring to development he is 'speaking about the ability to communicate either non-verbally or verbally' (Aldridge, 1996: 268).

The focus in this framework is upon the ways in which communication is dependent upon motor activities and responses. These are seen as ways of also indicating that a child is developing. Communication is seen to be dependent upon 'doing' and this, in conjunction with relating to another person, is central to the working hypothesis.

Aldridge sees the locus of music therapy here as being a non-verbal therapy that enables the establishment of a communicative relationship before 'complexities of lexical', or verbal, meaning are necessary (Aldridge, 1996: 248). The emphasis is seen to be on the development of the inherent *potentials* of the client rather than on 'known pathologies'. He draws a clear boundary with a behavioural approach which would have set specific goals for developmental change, as this would not have aimed to elicit potential in the same way, and would have detracted from the client and therapist's making music together.

The music therapy aims to 'foster' this potential, creating opportunities for the development of purposive co-ordinated change in a context of time and relationship. Aldridge uses the term 'dialogue' and sees the importance of the therapeutic relationship as a 'joint activity'. He sees the therapist and client in parity. The therapist and client alike have joint responsibility – both in creating improvisations and for continuing them.

Case example – Sophie

Aldridge saw Sophie in individual sessions over a three-month period. She was part of a group also receiving treatment, all of whom were between 4 and 6.5 years old with a developmental age of 1.5 to 3.5 years, with no previous experience of music therapy.

The framework involved an initial assessment based on psychological and functional criteria, and used the Nordoff–Robbins and Griffiths scales. These can be seen as framing ideas within the therapy, as they inform the criteria chosen to understand therapeutic change. The Griffiths scale, for example, is based on the observation of small children, and concerns itself with gaining insight into areas of learning. The idea is to provide 'a profile of capabilities from which the child might respond' (Aldridge, 1996: 255). It looks at areas such as locomotor development – whether the child pushes with feet, lifts their head, kicks vigorously or can catch a ball. Other areas include 'personal–social criteria' – whether the child responds to being held, makes anticipatory movements, plays with others, whether they can make vocalisations other than crying, searches for sound visually, or appears to listen to music.

In Nordoff–Robbins, the other scale used, one assessment area is described as 'Child–Therapist Relationship in Musical Activity'. This sees the work totally in terms of observable actions, such as participation in activities, mutuality in the expressive mobility of the music, whether there are 'assertive co-activity and signs of awareness' (Aldridge, 1996: 252–3). Another area 'Musical Comunicativeness', sees therapy in terms of levels of communicativeness described as a series of criteria – such as commitment, enthusiasm, musical competence, attentive responsiveness and evoked responses in musical form (Aldridge, 1996: 254). Again the emphasis is upon physical observation – of the client's use of instruments, vocal expression or body movement.

The notion here is of a developmental process. Initially the therapist assesses the relationship between *therapist* and *client*: whether, for example, there seems to be total obliviousness, limited response, or a stability and mutuality of playing music together. Another frame uses the notion of no communicative response, active participation or 'intelligent musical commitment' (Aldridge, 1996: 259). During the music therapy the relationship is seen and developed through the musical activity. In Nordoff–Robbins a correlation is drawn between the personality development of a child and the character and consistency of the musical communicativeness they show (Nordoff and Robbins, 1977: 193 in Aldridge, 1996: 259).

In the case history of Sophie, this framework is reflected in the way Aldridge conducts and reports the therapy. She is introduced in terms of physical and social development. She is reported as much-wanted by her mother. Sophie could sit at four months, but did not develop crawling and pulling up to stand, though there seemed to be no organic cause. She could hear but not use speech; she played alone. The first session is reported in terms of Sophie's relationships – she clings to her mother, and is physically carried into the room by a co-therapist, remaining on the co-therapist's arm during the session. She seems to show signs of anxiety, whimpers and plays a small bell and chime bar so quietly Aldridge can hardly hear them.

The therapeutic process is described in terms of a variety of developmental changes. So, for example, Aldridge comments that Sophie by the fourth session enters the room alone. She initially goes to a piano and plays single unrelated notes; she sits in the co-therapist's lap and plays drum and cymbal. Aldridge plays on the piano at the same time as Sophie improvises. Her notes are 'accidentally met by the therapist . . . [she] was very insecure in the musical pauses and immediately retreated from rhythmical impulses' (Aldridge, 1996: 266). She goes on to play more often 'in relationship to the music' (Aldridge, 1996: 266), using both hands in drumming in parallel and in alternation. She is described as being more 'sure in the therapeutic relationship', and makes more 'effort' to play. She is described as becoming happy, expectant and playing with more security.

In the eighth session Aldridge describes a 'significant change' concerning her being constantly active, her musical playing being more recognisable. Sophie accompanies him, decides between loud and soft, repeats musical motifs, and she can focus without being distracted. Aldridge is described as supporting her accidental changes in the music into becoming part of a 'musical whole'; Sophie 'worked hard' to maintain the musical relationship. By the final session she is described as having the capacity to use many developed, musical improvisational possibilities.

Through processes of internal monitoring, using the scales described earlier, and through feedback from Sophie's mother, change is noted in terms of factors such as listening, or hand-and-eye co-ordination. Other observable areas are used, such as playing with others, independent activity and independence in communication, Sophie's capacity to relate to toys, and her initiative in establishing communication, or movement and locomotion: 'That Sophie could show both sadness and happiness was considered to be important for her mother. That she could also cuddle was a significant milestone in the emotional relationship of child and mother' (Aldridge, 1996: 268).

Case example analysis

Aldridge frames this therapeutic change as connecting to music therapy's capacity to facilitate development, and to enhance it for those whose development is impaired. Other arts therapists (Cattanach, 1994; Ferrara, 1991) have described how, as Ferrara says in the context of art therapy,

> Art can be a vehicle for development and a reflection of a child's cognitive and emotional growth. Art also may provide the opportunity for growth in intellectual, social and aesthetic areas. As an expressive communicative channel, art may embrace creativity, self-expression and manipulation of the environment. Therefore art contributes to overall development by providing the conduit for responding to experience and expressing the change that occurs at every developmental stage.
>
> (Ferrara, 1991: 44)

Ferrara points out that art can 'reconstruct' elements of personality attenuated by developmental processes, quoting Williams and Wood's view of art as an opportunity for 'new learning where a gap has existed. It is a means for venturing into the next, new steps' (Williams and Wood, 1977: vii).

Aldridge and Ferrara both relate their practice to literature which refers to human development in a framework of areas such as non-verbal communication, gesture and emotional expression and in cognitive development (Merlin, 1993; Alibali and Goldin-Meadow, 1993). Here cognitive, gestural, emotional and relational development are brought together. The therapist and client relationship is seen as valuable as it involves playing together, the therapist and child together developing new possibilities. For Aldridge, the musical relationship is seen as a 'domain' – a 'zone'. The emphasis is on creativity, listening and playing in this area. The therapist responds to the child, the child to the therapist: this is a 'mutual realm'. Through contact with the therapist and music, the child becomes open to variety, and variety leads to development.

The relationship created through making music together enables action along with developmental and cognitive change. The emphasis is on music as being non-verbal and not language-dependent. This is seen as especially important for clients such as Sophie – developmentally delayed infants. The underlying concept within this paradigm is neatly summed up by art therapist Ferrara when she refers to the 'dynamic interdependence of physical growth, intellectual and emotional development, and creativity' (Ferrara, 1991: 50). The therapist and client work together to identify problems in terms of a developmental framework. They go on to use the connections which the artistic process has with opportunities to negotiate, renegotiate or achieve the developmental work which has not yet occurred, but which is needed.

Developmental approach: critiques and limitations

Some arts therapists have pointed out the importance of issues concerning race and culture in terms of developmental assumptions. If, for example, the therapist and client are from different cultural or racial backgrounds, with different models or assumptions of development, this can result in problems within the therapy. Importance is placed on the therapist and client being conscious of power relations, of majority–minority issues in relation to culture, and to difference, as well as the way in which artistic expression and products relate to such areas.

Barber and Campbell (1999) in their discussion of 'colour and identity' raise issues that concern difference and power: 'The art therapy process allows images of the self to be created and recreated in as many ways as is necessary for the person to tell her story of who she is and how she comes to be how she is' (Barber and Campbell, 1999: 31). This is relevant to developmental thinking. They advocate the 'narrative' and 'co-construction' mode of therapy. They mention, in particular, the notion of the way in which meaning needs to be constructed in dialogue – not something held by the therapist alone. In, for example, a mixed race art therapy group 'the images and dialogues which are created allow for the generation of new and multiple meanings of being black, or white, or brown' (Barber and Campbell, 1999: 34). They go on to echo some of the areas described by Cattanach and Read Johnson as concerning the developmental approach to self, development and time: 'there is not one truth but rather multiple meanings born of subjective, lived experiences. This is very important to the image-making process in mixed groups, for in any one image a person can convey experiences of self across time and space, both internal and external' (Barber and Campbell, 1999: 34). Here there is no such thing as an 'objective viewpoint'; people are not studied or understood in terms of object and subject 'uncontaminated' by the viewer's viewpoint, or the context in which the work takes place: 'As black female leaders of an art therapy group, therefore, the fact of our blackness will colour how we understand or speak about what happens in the group' (Barber and Campbell, 1999: 34).

Clarkson has pointed out that ideas and experiences of identity and relationship differ between cultures:

> Some cultures don't have the notion of an individualised separate 'self' at all. They think that 'self' is an absurdity – as if it makes any sense to say that a person can be separate from others – or from the rest of the universe . . . The importance of the group or family system in many cultures as the matrix for learning, resolving conflicts and facilitating healing is sadly contrasted with the individualistic (if exclusive) Western conception of the individual as separate from their culture, their family, their ancestral roots, their ongoing living communities, their one-ness with the fabric of their living spaces and with all of nature.
>
> (Clarkson, 2002a: 218)

She notes the importance of being open to other paradigms of 'human-beingness' (Clarkson, 2002a: 218). Here the dialogues and mutuality dis-cussed in this chapter – concerning the culture, beliefs, expressions, artistic traditions and views of the world – are relevant to the ideas of 'development' and 'self' brought into the arts therapy space.

Such views emphasise the necessary attention needed to foreground the individual client's experience in relation to approaching therapy from a developmental perspective. They highlight the need to constantly acknow-ledge the complexities of areas such as power and difference. They bear testimony to the importance of dialogue rather than prescription within the arts therapy space, and in the relationship between arts therapist and client.

Dialogue with different therapeutic paradigms compared

The two case illustrations above demonstrate the nature of the true dialogue that can occur between the arts therapies and other therapeutic paradigms. In each we can see the way that, though the work is informed by analytic or developmental therapy, the relationship between client and therapist reflects a unique way of working which brings together the arts therapy with another therapeutic paradigm. We can see that the art form and arts process affect the nature of the relationship. This is illustrated by the ways of working actively with music making, the benefits of musical communication and expression, together with the way creativity features in the exploration and resolution of the client's needs.

Both of these case studies, though working in dialogue with different therapeutic paradigms, have much in common. The two pieces of work illustrated use musical improvisation, both emphasise a developing relationship between client and therapist, both therapists use participation with the client, both play instruments with the client, both use the notion of dialogue, both use music as a communication of relationship, and as an indicator of change. Both argue for the particular potency for the client of the non-verbal aspects of the therapy. Neither sets fixed targets for change, but attempts to follow the client's potential and lead (Aldridge, 1996: 268).

The goals have differences, however, and the nature of the material encountered also has differences. For Aldridge, the arts therapy space is an opportunity for the development of capacities that will be reflected in the client's ability to communicate in relationships outside the session. Change in the client's capacity to develop musical dialogue is seen to 'bring about improvement in the ability to form and maintain personal, social relationships in other contexts' (Aldridge, 1996: 269). The therapist's responsibility to the client is to assess the developmental issue, and then to frame the ways in which the music and the support of the therapist can most effectively follow the child's developmental needs. The client experiences the therapist as a support and they play music together, improvising and creating a musical dialogue. For Rogers, the therapeutic space reflects and impacts on aspects of the client's internal world, the musical instruments, the relationship between client and therapist; all become symbolic of the world held within the client. The client–therapist relationship becomes an arena for expressing and renegotiating the content and form of this internal world.

I deliberately chose the same art form – music therapy – to illustrate the ways in which the client–therapist relationship can *vary considerably* within the same modality. Though, as the above two cases illustrate, some aspects of the work are common, the basic assumptions and language used to understand change are quite different. It's fair to say that the differences that these two illustrations demonstrate can be equally illustrated in the other arts therapies.

WHY THE DIVERSITY?

Clarkson, in reviewing research on the therapeutic relationship in psychoanalysis, counselling psychology and psychoanalysis, asks a series of questions relevant to the array of approaches within the arts therapies. These are: why are there so many different approaches? Why does the *relationship* between therapist and client appear to be more important in assessing the effectiveness of psychotherapy than any of these different approaches? Are the approaches talking about the therapeutic relationship, but from 'different universes of discourse or focusing on different aspects of it?' (Clarkson, 1998: 75).

Her work involves identifying the variables, and then analysing them in terms of commonalities and contrasts. The five kinds of relationship she identifies within her research are: the working alliance; the transference–counter-transference relationship; the developmentally needed or reparative relationship; the person-to-person or real relationship; and the transpersonal relationship (Clarkson, 1998: 84). Her hypothesis is that these kinds of relationship are present in most approaches to therapy. She concludes that this functions as 'a unifying and inclusive framework which allows for the co-existence of multiple perspectives on the therapeutic relationship as well as developments in any one approach' (Clarkson, 1998: 91). She goes on to ally this with a postmodern approach, which attempts to give validity to different methodologies.

A fair question to ask is whether the clients are best served by the ways of relating chosen by the therapist. Could Client A, for example, be better served by the way of relating chosen by Aldridge than that chosen by Rogers, or Sophie by Rogers's approach to music therapy? I think that in these two cases the clients and the approach taken seem to reflect the client's needs. The two clients have been referred with different presenting issues – as described earlier – Sophie's concerning developmental issues which create problems in relating, Client A with depression, eating disorders and a history of abuse. Referral seems to reflect the areas of need and growth for the client. Each therapist works within the paradigm used by the service the client is referred to. The client Rogers sees is within a psychodynamically orientated service; Aldridge's work takes place in a setting that aims to work developmentally. Client A's work enables her to recover memory and work with relationship issues. For Sophie the language and developmental possibilities made available within the music seem to fit her needs appropriately. Here is an illustration of the kinds of commonalities and contrasts of which Clarkson speaks. We've seen in the two examples that there are differences, but these seem to meet the needs of the clients. Such variety and diversity is necessary to reflect the complexities of the situations clients bring to the potentials of the arts therapy space and relationship.

AN ARTS THERAPIES APPROACH VERSUS APPROACHES RELATED TO OTHER DISCIPLINES

Some arts therapists, such as Milioni (2001), have been critical of arts therapists working within specific paradigms. She echoes Clarkson, emphasising the importance of exploring 'meaning for the client' rather than what she calls, 'theory-prescribed imposition of meaning by the dramatherapist' (Milioni, 2001: 15). Though I would argue that none of the work described in this chapter falls into such a category, it is important to take note of such a criticism. The danger is that the paradigm can affect the capacity of the therapist and client to work mutually. It might stop the therapist seeing clearly, colouring their experience so that they fit the client's experience into their paradigm, rather than trying to see what is occurring as clearly as possible, and to recognise the individuality of the contact between therapist and client.

Some, though, are critical of the stance we have looked at in this chapter, of arts therapists allying themselves with paradigms seen to be 'outside' the arts therapies. Many arts therapists would argue that whilst their work has a dialogue with other disciplines their practice is rooted in the specific theory and methods of the arts therapies. Though the history of the arts therapies gives an indication of growing in dialogue, or in parallel, with other disciplines, they see their practice as having a distinct identity and way of working that is not based in the therapeutic framework of other approaches. Often these approaches see themselves as strongly allied with the art form or arts processes within the arts therapies. Case material in the next chapter will explore the client–therapist relationship from other perspectives, to develop our understanding of the range of ideas and approaches within the arts therapies.

15 Client and arts therapist: traditions and discoveries

INTRODUCTION

The last chapter looked at the relationship between the client and therapist in the arts therapies by focusing on the frameworks and traditions of therapy. This chapter looks at the role of the arts therapist in different ways, in order to try to see more fully what an arts therapist is and does. It will explore, for example, the ways that the arts therapist brings the function and role of the artist to the therapeutic encounter. It's worth noting that many trainings throughout the world emphasise that, prior to entry, the arts therapist must have a qualification, or extensive experience, in an art form, and also that the trainings themselves include a substantial amount of experiential work in the art form. Once qualified, professional organisations often require that the therapist continues to engage in their art form as an artist. Looked at in one way, this contrasts with the statement often made by arts therapists to clients, and often written about in arts therapies literature, that the client need not have prior experience in the art form to benefit from the arts therapy. It might be possible to say that this creates a divide between the trained, artistically literate arts therapist, and the client who may never have painted or danced before. This might be seen to create tensions or difficulties in the relationship, where the therapist becomes strongly identified by the client with the expertise and mastery of the arts arena of the therapy. As we shall see, though these issues *can* be present, the reality is often more complex than this.

ROLE OF THE ARTS THERAPIST: THERAPIST AND CLIENT, ARTIST AND ARTIST TOGETHER

How is the 'artist' role of the arts therapist present in the therapy? A part of the answer to this might link the therapist to the arts through the therapy space and the materials in the session. For many clients the therapist becomes allied with the artistic space: the art room, studio or dance space, or to the materials they bring – musical instruments, clay, mask or prop. Here, the arts therapist becomes someone who offers access to the arts. They are, whether they are participating actively in using the art form themselves in therapy sessions with a client or not, someone who is linked to creativity. The therapist, by offering materials such as paint, may be seen by the client as an artist. At its most basic, this will be because they offer the opportunity to use an art form, and there is the expectation that they will be present whilst the client is engaged with artistic media and processes. In some circumstances they may sit in a room where artistic materials are available, though they themselves do not directly engage in active art – the materials and the space being latent to the desires, blocks or resistances of the client. In others, they may actively work with the client by creating art themselves – their dancing or music making being an integral element of the therapy.

As we have seen, a music therapist may play the piano whilst the client listens, and an art therapist might engage in drawing on a sheet of paper at the same time as the client. As we saw at the start of the last chapter, a dramatherapist might take on an active role within a client's enactment, or a dance movement therapist might engage in improvised dance with a client. Here the therapist's experience, skills and language as an artist are brought into their active use of the art form within the work. This is seen to function in a number of ways. First the therapist, by using the art form, can enable the arts to become a part of the therapy: for example, the therapist playing the piano. This might be seen to encourage the client to enter into the art form. It might also be a way for the client to develop a role: playing or dancing with the therapist. Here they can begin to accompany the therapist as a way of participating; this can then be developed to enable them to discover more independence, or to find their own language.

The therapist might also choose to make an intervention or interpretation, a response in movement or in role. Here they use the language of the art form to connect with the client's contribution. For example, as we saw in the last chapter, if the client makes a rhythm with a drum the therapist might use an instrument to reply or echo the sound. A dance movement therapist using movement, or gesture, might make a similar intervention as seen in the example that started the last chapter. Skewes says that the music therapist is creative in 'both their music making and in their therapy': 'Musically, it is essential for the therapist to be creatively present, responding in the moment to the musical material of participants, enhancing what is being heard or playing something that opens up the possibilities of the art form' (Skewes, 2002: 51). She might play to assist the client, to help 'knit together' strands of music, or to use 'their creative sense to determine where the music leads and what journey it may take' (2002: 51), or in responding and using words in relation to the music. Skewes emphasises the role of intuition, the need for the music therapist to be 'musically intuitive regarding the aesthetic sound of the group . . . playing when they think their music will assist the group . . . and judging how subtle or direct the form should be' (2002: 51).

Here the therapist is using their art form in communication with clients. In addition, they are attempting to connect with the client's world through the art form, using the music language of the client. The manifest content – the therapist's gesture, sound or words spoken in role – might be an important part of their response. However, the fact that the therapist is participating *at all* might have an equally important role to play. The therapist's engaging in the art form might be experienced by the client as a recognition of their inner world, or of their experiences expressed through the art form: they might feel seen, heard or responded to. The therapist's participation might evoke role connections for the client – of parent, playmate, rival: these may be positive or negative – but all are a point of contact. This evocation can bring past problematic relationships into the therapy room, and can enable them to be worked with through the mutual participation in the art form, as client and therapist dance or make music.

Some have spoken against the therapist's active involvement as participating artist in the art form within the therapy. They argue that the experience might be overwhelming for the client, that the therapist may be unconsciously displaying their own counter-transference in an unhelpful way by taking part. Skaife (1995) has pointed out some of the complexities in these areas:

> If the art therapist encourages verbalisation is she directing the client away from expression through the artwork? If the art therapist only talks and does not paint what sort of unconscious message is she giving? If she paints, how does she model authentic expression of deep feeling without shifting the attention in the therapy onto herself? How does the art therapist balance the need for a reality-based attitude towards the practical aspects of art-making, with the more reflective attitude required in response to verbal communication?
>
> (Skaife, 1995: 7)

She does not point to an obvious answer, but indicates the need to engage with these issues and the tensions of the therapist's involvement and role within the arts therapy.

Whatever ways the therapist participates in the therapy, she or he is using the part of their identity that is an artist within the session. Their knowledge of the art form will have an effect upon their experience of the client: their knowledge of the body and how it is used in movement or drama; their knowledge of the potentialities of the arts medium; how voice is used; how clay can be responded to; the way drawing or sound can be used. All these will be a part of the way they see the client and the relationships within the sessions.

For example, their knowledge of clay may be used in seeing how the client responds to their work. The way the client manipulates the clay will be a source of the development of relationship. Similarly, the way a client uses their body in dance will be a part of the way a dance movement therapist relates to the client. In this the therapist is using their knowledge of and familiarity with the arts form and its possibilities. They will not only draw upon their own creative experience, but also their knowledge of cultural traditions and the accounts of artistic practices which others have made.

So, for example, the way the client takes up role, uses their voice and body will be responded to by the therapist as an artist with knowledge of the way character portrayals can develop, or with traditions of movement to draw upon. This knowledge of the art form feeds their interactions and responses to the client.

Similarly, an element of the therapist's function is to enable the artist within the client to come to the fore. This, in part, concerns the therapist's enabling the client to engage with arts media and processes, but the matter is more complex. As the client brings their life into relation with the therapeutic space, and as their creativity is expressed and developed within the sessions, so their capacity to relate creatively to the life problems they are encountering within the sessions is enhanced.

This does not mean that it is always necessary for the client to be creative within the session, only that the potential is there. Nor is it the case that the client is on an evolving path of increasing creativity or artistic competence. This is not usually a goal of the arts therapist. Rather, it is that the space can be an opportunity for this element of the client, the artist, to come to the fore. The client may, at various times, feel unable to use the space, feel uncreative, antagonistic toward the art form or therapist – but the *potential* is there. Clients often express feelings of being blocked or uncreative in their lives, and the expressions and feelings of being able to be creative or expressive may enable the client to feel empowered. A client may have issues relating to feeling incapable, unacknowledged or unseen, for example. The fact of *making* may enable the client to experience themselves differently, as someone capable of having effect, or of being recognised or witnessed. The creative process may also allow the client to permit feelings and memories concerning these aspects of themselves, and their lives, to be reflected in their experience of themselves as artists within the sessions.

It is important that the arts therapist continue to function as an artist. Otherwise they may try to realise their own needs or issues about creative expression through the client – to live vicariously through the client's artistic process. Gilroy (1989), in her research into art therapy practitioners, reports that therapists who were still actively engaged in their own art making found in it refreshment, self-affirmation, self-discovery and insight.

The therapist also may experience blocks, periods of turmoil: lacking inspiration within their work. This is important to look at in terms of the 'artist' part of their role in relation to their own creativity. It may also be a part of the transferential and counter-transferential process. The therapist's experiences of their own creativity and identity may be linked to the client's work within the therapy space. Hence the 'artist' and 'therapist' elements of the arts therapist work together to create meaning out of such experiences.

THERAPIST AND CLIENT: TEACHER AND PUPIL

Another part of the way in which the arts therapist and client encounter each other relates to the teacher–pupil relationship. This involves the ways in which the therapist engages with the client's use of the therapeutic space. Some would, rightly, argue that most therapists do not directly 'educate' clients on how to use a therapy session. This varies according to the model of therapy, however. The client's experience of the therapist within a cognitive behavioural framework will be different from that of one within an analytic orientation, as we have seen. The extent of the role of 'teacher' present within the therapy may vary according to the model within which the work takes place.

Some clients may arrive at the sessions with either the skills or capacity to use the art form. However, as mentioned earlier, it is understood in all the arts therapies that a client need not be conversant with an art form in order to use the arts therapies. Indeed, some have commented that if a client is a trained actor, or dancer, for example, they may need to find a different way of relating to the art form, as their training can form a barrier to spontaneously exploring personal material. The trained methods may be focused on performing, for example, rather than making personal connections and connecting with life experiences. In some situations, though, if the client is fluent in the art form, then the aspect of the therapy involving assisting the client to work within the expressive forms may be minimised. The therapist might make suggestions for new ways of working, for example, should this assist a direction of the work. If the client was constantly using clay to the exclusion of all other media, the therapist working within an analytic framework might explore the unconscious reasons why the client continues to use this form, or their avoidance of new areas of expression. In contrast, the arts therapist working in a brief cognitive therapy framework might review how different expressive forms would best suit the work to be done with the client, and negotiate the way of working accordingly.

For other clients who feel they have little experience of the art form, an aspect of the work might involve the therapist's helping the client to discover the arts therapies' expressive forms and the therapeutic possibilities within this. A psychotherapist working with verbal language alone does not normally create introductory exercises in which the client might use words, making suggestions about exploring different ways of using their voice or talking, for example. However, in many societies the relationship that clients have with art forms is different from their relationship with the spoken word. There are differences within different cultures and sub-groups. So, for example, in some societies song and movement is more generally prevalent as a participatory activity than in others. Some have argued that in many Western cultures participating in art making is more a part of children's lives than of adults' (Slade, 1995). As we considered earlier, many adults may be consumers of the arts, but not active participants. Some have brought attention to the way in which access or participation in the arts is a power issue. Some sectors of society are seen to have been provided with more access as consumers or participants to the arts, others have not, and this is seen as a part of a wider issue of disenfranchisement or disempowerment. People with disabilities, or groups and individuals from ethnic groups not of a majority culture, are seen as being cut off from consuming and expressing their identity through the arts (Pickard, 1989). Some would see the offering of opportunities for expression and for creativity as a crucial part of the arts therapies. As discussed in Chapter 7, this is different from the arts activities that are deliberately giving opportunities to redress political imbalance to access in the arts. However, this may be an important element within arts therapists' practice. The need is to recognise that some individuals and groups will be alienated from artistic expression. This is a part of the dynamics between therapist and client that may be at work within the sessions.

This dynamic might manifest itself in the ways in which a client feels unfamiliar with the art form. It might manifest itself in the way a client associates the arts experience in the arts therapy with the last time such activities were engaged with by them. This might, for example, have been as a child – so the art experience may be seen variously as an opportunity to be free as a child, or be dismissed as 'childish'. Memories and associations from that time might also accompany it. The artistic space can be accompanied by memories and feelings from this time: this might be conscious or unconscious. Similarly, feelings and responses accompanying issues such as disenfranchisement may also come into the session. If, for example, the client experiences being silenced or sidelined by a mainstream culture, this may enter into the process of the therapy. If the therapist is not familiar with the cultural forms or background of the client this might repeat the process of disenfranchisement and disempowerment.

As touched on earlier, there are a number of power-related issues potentially present in the 'teacher–pupil' element of the therapeutic relationship. Many therapists see it as crucial that they are aware of the potential power structure: the therapist is the one who may 'own' the rules and means of the art form. They become the experts, the client the novice. For some forms of therapy, for example in brief therapy, the potential exploration of this aspect of the relationship would be minimised; the focus is on the creation of an alliance, and for the client to develop their own relationship with expression. In other ways of working, such as those influenced by an analytic approach, this aspect of the relationship would be made visible, interpreted and explored.

In her review of music therapist practitioners in the US, Skewes found a diversity of practice reflecting these issues. She concludes that the level of structure and direction used by therapists varied in accordance with the philosophical stance and the clientele they worked with. She says that:

> those clinicians who worked with verbal clients, or maintained a transpersonal philosophy, were more likely to assume a non-directive

leadership role, allowing the group to find its own meaning and follow its own volition. Specialists with a focus on interpretation were more likely to desire a verbal consolidation of what had occurred musically, in order to facilitate cognitive insight and behavioural change.

(Skewes, 2002: 54)

It could be argued that for many arts therapists the teacher role is often more to the fore than that of the artist. When artists work, they normally engage directly in their arts practice. For arts therapists their primary role is often to witness, support or be in the presence of someone else creating.

This can lead to frustrations, or envy, feelings that need to be reflected on by the therapist. Wood talks very practically about an experience, not untypical, of a first encounter with a client. She notes that some clients in art therapy may never directly use art. Wood says that, upon first meeting, clients may understand that talking to someone might help, but often wonder, 'why I might suggest them using art materials'. She goes on to acknowledge a teaching element to first encounters:

I think it would be extremely difficult to be non-directive about the art materials, at the very least I think I have to show my clients where the materials are and make it clear to them that they can use whatever they want. Also at some point early on I indicate that if the materials they feel inclined to use are not there in the room then between us we can do our best to improvise and bring additional materials from outside to future sessions.

(Wood, 1990: 8)

Most arts therapists do not see themselves as teachers in the sense of being directive and instructional – it is rather how, as Wood puts it, to 'introduce the possibility of art work appropriately' (Wood, 1990: 11).

At the start of many arts therapies sessions issues such as confidence, familiarity and skill can be at the fore of the sessions. Some have questioned the nature of statements, looked at earlier, saying that the client need not 'be good at' art:

In a sense this admonition tells them that art making is not what is important, but 'telling something' through using art – in other words a conceptual idea – or finding something out that is hidden in the art work. We are certainly not inviting them to use a therapeutic tool in which it is possible to really engage with their feelings.

(Skaife, 2000: 119)

Skaife advocates addressing the issue as the first therapeutic step. Here the arts therapist reassures the client that they are involved in aesthetic decisions all the time, such as the choice of their clothes, their history of involvement with the arts. She stresses the importance of making good art materials available, along with an appropriate space (Skaife, 2000: 131).

In a sense then, the therapist and client are teacher and pupil together, with elements of the role being held by each, and the configuration of the roles changing over the period of the therapy, even within one therapy session. However, the arts therapist is substantially different from an arts teacher. The above material seeks only to draw out an *aspect* of the identity of the arts therapist. This involves the function of enabling the client to enter into the therapeutic opportunities and language of an arts therapy session. The main role of the therapist is not to teach, but to see how the client relates to the space and process, and to try to enable the maximum opportunities for arts therapy to occur. As we have seen, the specific way this can happen varies according to the approach of the therapy – but the primacy of this therapeutic function is a constant.

CULTURE AND CONTEXT

Authors such as Bondi and Burman (2001) have challenged the terminology and concepts used within the health services to define health and ill-health, and the relationship between practitioner and user. They argue that notions of mental health, for example, are 'saturated with pathology'. What is 'normal' or acceptable 'mental health' is unspecified, shrouded in 'mystery and assumption' (Bondi and Berman, 2001: 7). Such terminology, they argue, betrays the contemporary predominance of a medical model in ways of thinking about well-being and distress, and is accompanied by cultural, historical issues that frame the encounter.

What are the implications of these ideas for the arts therapies? This book has acknowledged that contact between therapist and client is accompanied by sets of assumptions. We have seen the attempts by both client and therapist to work across the divide of role and responsibility, within the complexities of communication, experience, privilege, knowledge and power. All of these factors need to be considered, not only in the light of the therapeutic process, but also in terms of creativity and artistic expression. Bondi and Berman help us to see the complexity of each of these areas in defining and encountering the roles of therapist and client.

There is a difference between skill, knowledge and power, for example, but these areas often become confused. Some argue that, at the heart of the medical system, lies an inbuilt process which disempowers the patient. The healer has power, knowledge, skills and is active; the patient does not know, is unwell, is disempowered and passive. Sharma argues there is an inherent contradiction:

> at the heart of modern medical practice – that between an ethic
> which declares that the patient's needs and interests must always be the

physician's priority, and the professional insistence that practice is based on a specific form of knowledge (increasingly technical and scientific) which can only be acquired through training, and is therefore inaccessible to the patient.

(Sharma, 1994: 85)

Sharma goes on to say that there can be a tendency for patients who seek collaboration, or to discuss outcome where 'medical opinion' does not admit uncertainty, to be labelled as 'problematic'. Here informed consent, choice and the ways in which roles are seen and carried out, as well as the nature of participation in healing, are key issues.

These matters are certainly central for the client–therapist relationship within the arts therapies. Some would argue that whilst knowledge and training are crucial, they do not necessarily lead to the disenfranchisement of the client. This is reflected in areas such as the development of collaborative research. Others are of the opinion that the arts therapies encourage the patient to be active, that the participatory act is experienced in such a way that the client is empowered. Some review their practice to examine issues of power which manifest themselves in counter-therapeutic ways. However, some would argue that issues around power are inevitable, but can provide a useful feature to explore within the therapeutic relationship. The models of therapy will approach this differently – the cognitive approach stressing the need to establish collaboration and alliance, the analytic exploring issues through transference and counter-transference, for example.

Douglas places similar issues in an intercultural context. She considers health in the context of collaboration and rejection, notions of illness or disease affording powerful weapons for 'self interested blaming and excluding' in any society (Douglas, 1994: 33). She says that communities always involve judgement and persuasion: 'the fragile human body is the political touchstone, and blame is the justification for exclusion'. She asks questions across cultures:

> If the Punjabi patient has a sinking heart, what does he expect his community to do about it? If the Lele with pneumonia suffers from crossed-over ribs, what can be done to uncross them? In either case what was the cause of the ailment? Who is to blame? The patient? Or the doctor? Or the mother-in-law?
>
> (Douglas, 1994: 33)

Her argument is that to encounter such situations it is necessary to know what she calls the whole scenario: 'To describe diagnoses as if they were museum items is of no interest. We need a holistic context. According to what kind of blaming is going on, the role of the therapist will be differently constructed: to avert the finger of blame, to point it or attract it' (Douglas, 1994: 33). She says that the more highly organised the society, the more intense the accusing and blame. She says that the experience of ill-health in industrialised societies, for example, involves the tendency to draw individuals out of their normal context. The ties of loyalty and support can become removed and individuals are stranded as what she calls 'isolates' (Douglas, 1994: 40).

Helman (1994: 280) has said that when therapist and client come from similar backgrounds they are more likely to share assumptions about the origin, nature and treatment of psychological disorders. However, if this is not the case then clients

> may have to *learn* this world view gradually, acquiring with each session a further understanding of the concepts, symbols and vocabulary that comprise it. This can be seen as a form of 'acculturation', whereby they acquire a new mythic world couched, for example, in terms of the Freudian, Jungian, Kleinian or Laingian models.
>
> (Helman, 1994: 280)

Here the criticism is that the patient must accommodate the world view of the therapist.

Clarkson and Nippoda have echoed these perceptions in a way that can help understand how the arts therapies can address these matters. They say that each therapeutic relationship occurs within the idiom and atmosphere, the climate and background of the cultures which 'impinge on it' (Clarkson and Nippoda, 1998: 96). They define cultures as structures of feeling and list these relating to gender, religion, organisation, profession, sexual orientation, class, nationality, country of origin, and parts of the country of ancestral origin.

They note the variety of attitudes towards therapy relating to areas such as class and ethnicity. These factors can lead to attitudes such as 'it [being] experienced as a stigma to benefit from therapy services' (Clarkson and Nippoda, 1998: 97). They also acknowledge that many more people in the world rely on 'symbolic healing or culturally traditional approaches to personal development than on West European models' (Clarkson and Nippoda, 1998: 97).

It's important to acknowledge the different traditions and assumptions which the arts therapist and client bring to the therapeutic relationship in the light of these ideas. Skaife (2000) usefully considers issues relating to this issue of acculturation, and the potential power of the arts therapist in relation to the client's work. She points out how important it is for the arts therapist to keep in touch with the creative, artist aspect of their identity in relating to clients. If the therapist only comments on the content of the work, for example, this may encourage the client or the 'artist/patient' as Skaife says, to focus too much on the 'message'. If the therapist only comments on the process which the client is engaged in when making, this may ignore aspects of the content which the client might wish the therapist to be aware of. Similarly, if, in a group, the therapist confines comment to the group process, the clients are likely to involve themselves less and less in the art. It's as if the client reflects the aspect of the role identity and framework brought by the therapist. The need is for a balance between these different aspects of identity and relationship.

Authors such as Klineberg (1987) note the importance of the facilitator's trying to learn as much as they can about the cultural background of the client. However, Fernando (1991) has shown that such knowledge is not necessarily effective. Authors such as Nadirshaw indicate the importance of factors such as being able to read the expression of emotions in different cultures, the necessity of the therapist aiming to work through their own racist attitudes, beliefs and prejudices, along with the different influences of culture on goals and tasks (Nadirshaw, 1992: 260).

Case and Dalley speak of art therapy in a way that acknowledges this importance:

> It is ... the process of image-making and how the final product is received within the bounds of a therapeutic situation that forms the basis of the art therapeutic process. It is here that the orientation of the therapist is of most importance in terms of how she receives and works with images produced.
>
> (1992: 53)

Callaghan (1996) places this issue right at the heart of the client–therapist relationship in her account of dance movement therapy with individuals and groups who are refugees from Africa, Europe the Middle East, South America and South West Asia. She puts movement psychotherapy, and her own role and practice as a dance movement therapist, within a framework defined by European and North American ideas and her own, 'multi-cultural, predominantly western experience' (1996: 250). She identifies the complex connection of issues regarding status, cultural practices, language and notions of relationship in such work. Callaghan stresses the need for these areas to be very much a part of the therapeutic relationship in a way which encourages 'mutual dialogue' (1996: 250). She uses the concept of culture in an interesting way. Callaghan places not only the identity and role of the client in relation to general issues concerning acculturation, for example to social structures or religious beliefs – but also sees the traumatic experience of the client in terms of culture. She says she works within an acknowledge-ment of both ethnicity and also the 'cultures inherent in torture, such as the cultures of politics, trauma and refugeedom' (1996: 250).

She argues that the same elements of movement are used by all human beings: space, touch, rhythm, weight, eye-contact and gesture. However, it is the way these are used, and their meaning, that varies between individuals and cultures. The therapist–client encounter becomes a site where ethnic background and differences concerning areas such as touch, space and feelings can be acknowledged. The therapist, for example, if she or he is a member of the 'host' society, 'partakes in a dialogue of mutual adaptation, and helps survivors explore how they can maintain their culture while adapting to the new one' (1996: 260). Within differences of culture a therapeutic relationship based on the body can be developed. If this can acknowledge aspects of each individual's 'body culture', then 'the meaning of the body and movement in the person's individual and cultural experience' can be explored (1996: 260). The movement element of therapy, she argues, is an activity associated in many cultures with celebration, art and sport and is 'acceptable', whereas therapy and sharing feelings with strangers, sitting and talking might be uncomfortable, unfamiliar and alien. By focusing on movement that is culturally relevant, this can help build trust and the 'unfolding' of the client's experiences. She points out an illustration of this in her work with clients who have been tortured. An Iranian client 'stretched his thigh backwards, drawing an analogy to the ways camels were tied up in Iran to prevent them from running away – this enables him to develop into his own movements about being restricted and moving to avoid mines' (1996: 258).

The argument here is that, through the language and process of the artistic expression within the therapy, the client and therapist can find a way to develop dialogue concerning difference. The client's experience of an art form within their own culture can begin to be worked with by the therapist as a way of validating the client, of engaging with their language and culture, and to try to begin to create a mutuality of expression. Implicit in what she is saying is that this can begin to assist the client to make use of the space to find a way to address their needs. This doesn't fully acknowledge some of the issues regarding status or power and issues regarding cultures within which the notion of therapy is alien. However, it acknowledges the importance and the potentials of the artist within both client and therapist to attempt to create mutuality or dialogue through the art form and process.

The arts have been seen as often linked to creative ways of attempting to solve or sort such differences, problems or barriers (Liebmann, 1996; Jones, 1996). Throughout this book the theme of the possibilities created by the contact between therapy and the arts is described in different ways. In this particular context we have seen the ways in which the presence of the artist and the therapist roles together can produce new combinations and possibilities. For me, it is this that is radical, that allows exploration and new approaches to respond to the emerging needs of clients in many situations. As Callaghan's dance movement work illustrates, this can help to meet the challenges of new social or political needs.

ARTS THERAPIST AND CLIENT: DIFFERENCES BETWEEN THE ARTS THERAPIES

Are there significant differences for client and therapist between the different arts therapies? There *are* many parallels between the different art forms, as described in this and the previous chapter. These include some of the basic assumptions concerning the ways the arts can contribute to developmental processes, or the notions of change ascribed to psychodynamic work as described earlier by Read Johnson. All these assume parallel processes at work between client and therapist.

There are, as we saw in Chapter 11, differences that are brought to the client–therapist relationship based upon the different art forms, and the ways in which each arts therapy has evolved. The following material gives some brief examples of how these differences can affect the client–therapist relationship.

Some dance movement therapists, for example, become directly and bodily involved in moving with clients, whilst art therapists may engage in painting or making art with their client. Here a difference between the art forms has an effect on the relationship. The dance therapist and client may engage in touch, bodywork and physical movement: this is substantially different from art therapist and client mark making with paper and paint.

Another area that can illustrate such differences is in the taking on of *role* in the client–therapist relationship. A dance movement therapist or dramatherapist might physicalise, or embody, their relationship with the client. They might dance and move with the client taking on a pretended identity, or embodying a particular kind of relationship towards the client. Dramatherapist Landy, for example, takes on the role of a mouse in order to express his perception of the role dynamics between a client and himself (Landy, 1993). As the example at the beginning of the last chapter showed, a dramatherapist might also actively take on and enact the role of a fictional person from a story, or actively play a role from the client's life. They might speak and maintain this role in enacted fictional representations that are created in the therapy room. This would not generally be the case for an art or music therapist, though they might *symbolically hold* roles for the client, as seen in the example of Rogers with Client A described earlier in Chapter 14. The art or music therapist would not try to reproduce important roles or people in the client's world through imitation of movement, representation of speech, or by formally taking on a pretended role over a sustained period of time. Whilst dramatherapists have techniques to enable clients to safely enter into and leave roles, this is not the case in art or music therapy. This is an indicator of the difference in the area of enacted or embodied role between the arts therapies and how this impacts on the client–therapist relationship.

Some people argue that the different modes – of art, drama, music or dance – do not matter, that the key process at work within the arts therapies is one of creativity. But, as we have seen, though there are, indeed, important commonalities, the different experiences of the art forms can be crucial to what can be offered to the client. Whilst there may be parallels, the different media and ways of creating mark a difference of method, tradition and experience which can affect the way the client and therapist relate.

CONCLUSION

At the start of the last chapter I talked about the client and the therapist being in a 'transaction' together: the client playing an active role in whether change occurs. We've seen that in the arts therapies one of the key factors in the therapeutic relationship is that the client is invited to be actively creative with an artistic medium. This is central to the ways the client plays an active role in the way change occurs. The engagement with the art form, whether music, drama, art or dance, creates opportunities for specific processes, relationships and products to be brought into the therapeutic relationship and space. We have seen some of these opportunities illustrated and analysed: the therapist and client who move or paint together, creating artefacts such as a series of drum beats or a painting; the therapist who plays music to the client or who transforms themselves into a parent or an animal. These rules, artistic traditions and languages affect the way the arts therapist behaves, and impact on the way a client experiences the therapeutic relationship.

The last chapter also showed how the arts therapies have developed in response to other forms of therapy. We've seen how verbal language is only *one* way to articulate and create a relationship between therapist and client. The arts therapies offer a wide range of routes to discover and create contact between therapist and client. If this relationship is seen as the heart of therapy, then the processes of creativity, learning and change that the arts therapies unite, provide a unique combination of languages. There are opportunities within the therapeutic relationship – a mutual discovery in the ways in which the artist within both therapist and client emerges. This chapter has shown that such combinations of art form and creativity in the therapeutic space creates unique possibilities for change.

As we've seen, then, the arts therapist and client together can inhabit a range of roles and paradigms within the arts therapy space. We've seen how the arts therapies can be involved in a dialogue with other therapeutic paradigms, particular ways of working, and opportunities for the client. We've also seen how the relationship involves specific qualities of the artist within both the client and therapist. In addition, this chapter has illustrated how the process of mutual learning and discovery between client and therapist is a central feature in the healing and growth of the client.

Running through much of this work is the notion that there are particular, innovative qualities within the arts therapies that are offered to the client. The next chapters look at how the effectiveness of these qualities is examined, and how best to describe the unique opportunities for the client and therapist to work together.

16 Efficacy: what works in the art gallery? What works in the clinic?

INTRODUCTION: DOES IT WORK?

For any client entering therapy, or for any organisation, parent or guardian considering the provision of arts therapies, the issue of efficacy is bound to surface. Do the arts therapies work? How do you know? What are the goals of the therapy? What will the outcome be? For the arts therapist also, the same questions are asked, but usually from a different angle.

The future survival and existence of the arts therapies depends on the answers to such questions. Increasingly, in a number of countries and health-care systems, the definition and proof of clinical efficacy are primary issues affecting provision, patient choice and funding. How clients, therapists and organisations evaluate the outcomes of the arts therapies is becoming espe-cially important. If clients, or organisations funding health services, are not satisfied that change is occurring in a way they understand, or at a pace they find satisfactory, then the arts therapies will dwindle into abandonment as viable options in client care. In the UK, for example, Parry, in her description of evidence-based practice, cites the National Health Service's explicit commitment:

> to drive policy, make commissioning decisions and allocate resources on the basis of research evidence on what is clinically effective and cost-effective. This includes assessing evidence of need for a service or an intervention (basically defined in terms of people's capacity to benefit) and the measurable health gain for a given investment of revenue.
>
> (Parry, 2000: 61)

In 1973 the developmental psychologist Gardner, in his writing about the arts and human development, said:

> Whilst it would be most promising to find that the arts can aid in the cure of psychological diseases, evidence on the question is most limited. Certainly the causal connection is in doubt: there is no way of

determining whether an aesthetic breakthrough is a symptom or a cause
of psychological development.

(Gardner, 1973: 346)

His view is that 'impairment' due to conditions such as psychosis, regression
or senility results in the destruction of the capacity to communicate through
art and that they 'impair the artistic process' (1973: 346). Reviewing the
situation over three decades later, can we challenge this assumption? Is there
any proof of the efficacy of the arts therapies in 'aiding' or in 'cure'?

There are different aspects of the therapeutic encounter that concern
efficacy. These processes are common to all arts therapy practice, but their
contexts vary from everyday procedures through to specialised research.
These contexts include any initial assessment, forming of aims and evaluation
of work with clients undertaken as part of everyday arts therapy practice.
Efficacy also embraces specific research-based projects where more formal
procedures involve specialised monitoring, evaluating and communication
through thesis or publication. Authors have pointed to issues regarding the
value of what is discovered within all of these processes, such as the difference
between looking at outcome research compared to looking at the process of
change (Wiser *et al.*, 1996: 102), or the validity of a particular way of looking
at change and outcome. These different areas of efficacy are all related, and
will be explored in this chapter.

For example, a client comes out of one of a series of dramatherapy
sessions feeling that something has changed, but that they can't put whatever
is happening into words: they are wondering whether to continue with the
therapy. At this moment, they are making a choice based on their experience
of therapy and their opinion about efficacy. A department of mental health,
in conjunction with a university research department, undertakes research on
the outcomes of dance movement therapy based on systematic analysis of
video material of therapy sessions between client and therapist. Their
research may have funding implications for the future of the provision of the
arts therapy in the unit. Part of the research concerns whether and how such
outcomes can be reproduced elsewhere by other practitioners and clients.
Clearly the needs and approaches for client and therapist are related but
different in these two examples.

For the client in the first example, questions around efficacy might include:
how to make sense of what is occurring, whether the time, money and effort is
having any of the effects they wanted when they went to therapy, or whether
there are any unexpected effects they wish to pursue further. The dramatherapist in the first situation might be concerned with how to assist the client
in gaining a perspective on what is occurring in the therapy, to review the
progress of the work, and to empower them to make choices about the direction and provision of their therapy. Issues about the meaning of their feelings
around continuing or finishing may be explored. This could involve areas
such as whether this reflects any patterns in their lives concerning attachment,

for example. The work might explore whether the desire to terminate is based in unconscious resistance to areas surfacing within the therapy, or in a sense of readiness to move on.

For a client in the second example, some of the issues might be similar and contribute to the mutual discoveries between therapist, client and departments about how effective the therapy is. For the therapist, similar concerns are present regarding the progress of the client. In addition, the evaluation of how effective the therapy has been gives an understanding that will contribute to others within the field, and to the continuity of the work at the setting. Any insights into how change has happened will also assist in looking at whether, and how, the specific practice is developing, and in finding a language to help reflect upon and communicate the processes and effects of the arts therapy.

The common aspect, in both of these examples and in every piece of work that takes place, from private therapy session to more formal research, is that the area of efficacy plays a crucial role in *all* arts therapies practice. Some would see a continuum existing between the informal and formal procedures in everyday clinical practice and formal clinical research projects. However, all aspects of effectiveness relate to each other. For example, any discovery and research into whether, and how, the arts therapies work fuels the experience of every practitioner and client. This can happen, for example, by helping to identify whether specific techniques are effective for particular difficulties or conditions brought to therapy. Taylor (1998) usefully defines research in a way that embraces these concerns:

> The term 'research' refers not only to quantitative, scientific regimes, but . . . also encompasses a wide range of methods and depths of analysis. It could range from a short interview to an experimental set-up in a laboratory. Analyses might involve the use of text transcription, percentages or sophisticated statistical interpretation. Whatever the method and depth of analysis adopted, the important thing to remember at all times is the appropriateness of [the] strategy used.
>
> (Taylor, 1998: 204)

Looked at in this way, enquiry into efficacy helps inform the creation of a dialogue, or language, between therapist and client about the progress and outcome of their work. As we will see, new research and evidence continues to inform this dialogue further. There are groups and individuals looking at practice in this way in a number of different countries. From the Centro de Investigación y Tratamiento del Área Corporal (CITAC: Centre for Research and Treatment of the Body Area) and the ADIM programme, Asistencia, Desarrollo en Investigación en Musicoterapia (Assistance, Development and Research in Music Therapy) in Uruguay (Hugo, 2002), to the collaborative work with clinical settings undertaken by the Institute for Music Therapy at the University of Witten Herdecke in Germany. Recorded research in the arts therapies spans an extremely broad range of client contexts. This extends from music therapy with clients living with HIV and AIDS (Lee, 1995) to art therapy with children on the autistic spectrum (Evans and Dubowski, 2001); from dance movement with refugees and asylum seekers (Callaghan, 1996) to dramatherapy with clients with psychosis (Casson, 2001).

WHAT WORKS IN THE ART GALLERY? WHAT WORKS IN THE CLINIC?

How can we understand efficacy? Much writing about how to look at change in the arts therapies features a consideration of the relationship between the arts and the sciences (Byrne, 1995; Erkkila, 1997). At times this relationship is one of mutuality, at others of extreme difference, and still others one of tension. Sometimes all three of these qualities can be present at the same time! Can the arts and sciences both be used to help understand efficacy in the arts therapies? Some would argue that ways of looking at what works, what is effective in the arts and ways of looking in the sciences have no common ground. If I try to judge whether an artist or artwork is being effective, do I use very different processes than if I try to establish whether a behavioural therapy process has helped in making a difference in a client's life? Are the contexts of theatre or art gallery and clinic so different that 'what works' in each can't find a mutual connection? Or can the arts therapies draw on discoveries and processes from each area?

In the arts, efficacy often concerns itself with aesthetic questions of debate and the idea that there is not necessarily a *correct* answer to whether an artwork is 'effective'. What is meant by efficacy in the arts within some societies, or sections of societies, and in different eras has been governed by strict orthodoxy. At other times, though, and for many artists and arts movements described in this book, the nature of how and whether work is effective is the subject of constant debate, argument and re-evaluation. The effectiveness of the arts is an extremely volatile and mutable subject. At any one time there can be a number of conflicting variations on what is valuable, what 'works' as art. In addition the situation of the postmodern centres around a diversity of meaning: 'Something has changed, and the Faustian, Promethean (perhaps Oedipal) period of production and consumption gives way to the "proteinic" era of networks, to the narcissistic and protean era of connections, contact, continuity, feedback and generalised interface that goes with the universe of communication' (Baudrillard, 1983: 126). Different individuals or groups, different makers, participants and consumers or audiences involved in the arts can all have different views on efficacy in this 'universe of communication'. It is possible to say that the redefinition and constant re-evaluation of efficacy is one of the keys to much contemporary artistic creativity: a time where meaning in the arts is typified by 'profusion and openness, process and struggle' (Cubitt, 1993: 206). I would argue that efficacy is at its most alive when it is *part* of the creative process, a dialogue between all those involved: the makers, participants, audiences and critics. It is brought vitally into every moment and is a crucial part of the experience of all those involved – it engages them in what is happening, affecting their experience of the encounter. It is mutable, debatable; and this fuels the development of the art form and those involved in it.

In areas relating to science and health, concerns about 'what works' have often been to do with observable outcomes, reliability and replicability. Barkham and Mellor-Clark, for example, say that 'a central axiom of the scientific method has been replication' (2000: 129). However, a parallel phenomenon of diversity exists. This too concerns audiences, methods and intense debates about what efficacy means and what evidence is. Who, for example, takes part in deciding what 'effective' means? What are the tools and languages used to try to find out what is happening in the therapy?

Music therapist Aldridge (1996) talks about two very different approaches to 'science'. One concerns the development of precise, fixed procedures 'that yield a stable and fixed empirical content' (1996: 90), such as controlled trial methods. The other depends on 'careful and imaginative life studies' which may lack some of the 'precision of technical instruments' but continue a close relationship with what he calls 'the natural social world of people' (1996: 90).

Are the world of the gallery and the world of the clinic so different that they cannot be reconciled? Music therapist Hoskyns has said, for example, that the 'art/science dichotomy seems to be our biggest hurdle in developing effective research. We fear that we will lose the meaning of the art by evolving strategies for research' (Hoskyns, 1982).

Dramatherapist Milioni (2001) has talked of this issue in terms of a dichotomy between a social constructionist way of working and an empiricist way of approaching change. The social constructionist approach she typifies as relativist, emphasising a reality that is 'elusive, everchanging' (2001: 10). Empiricist research is based in knowledge emphasising ideas of objectivity and value-free judgement. The second position she allies with contemporary attitudes to evidence-based practice and clinical effectiveness, the former with 'freedom and flexibility' (2001: 10–11).

Music therapist Edwards (2002) has looked at Evidence Based Medicine (EBM) in relation to the arts therapies. This is an approach based in the ideas of 'Evidence Based Practice', a framework used within certain sectors of healthcare practice to interpret and present findings for research. She says that 'more and more music therapists in health departments and related clinical posts will be asked to account for their work using this approach to the documentation of clinical effectiveness' and justify practice and posts. This way of looking at therapy is described as being 'positivist' in that there is a set of rules and principles that exist in relation to human behaviour and interactions: 'Scientific research methods in this approach isolate and test specific phenomena with the purpose of increasing predictability and knowledge of causation. It is understood within this frame that laboratory test findings can be generalised to contexts outside the laboratory' (Edwards, 2002: 30). She acknowledges criticisms; for example, that the ideas of EBM can be used by 'cost cutters' and to 'suppress clinical freedom' (Sackett *et al.*, 1996), but says that it is both necessary and possible to respond to EBM in music therapy. The efficacy of arts therapies clinical work may be judged from this standpoint, and Edwards adds that it may be necessary to 'counter challenges to the outcomes we use to justify our posts' (Edwards, 2002: 30).

Evidence here is seen in a series of levels – she refers music therapists to a model she considers useful, that of the Australian National Health and Medical Research Council adoption of the US Preventive Services Task Force levels. This concerns certain kinds of 'evidence', including evidence from a systematic review of all randomised control trials (an analysis of arts therapy literature), from the 'properly designed randomised control trial', and evidence from a case series, either post-test only or pre- and post-test together (Edwards, 2002: 29). Issues in such an approach to clinical research can include the measurement of the effect of phenomena in which the stimuli – e.g. the music within the music therapy – must be consistent for each 'subject' in the 'experiment'.

Edwards points to important differences between medical research and music therapy research. She points out an immediate issue here, in that music therapy does not generally consist of the administration of a consistent stimulus such as three minutes of one sort of music followed by four minutes of another. She also points out that ideas often crucial to medical research, such as the notion of a placebo influence, and trying to isolate placebo phenomena, have not been a concern in music therapy research. In music therapy 'the factors which influence the level of effect achieved may not always be able to be isolated; music therapy as a total package provides the therapeutic outcomes and this, to date, has been the domain of investigation' (Edwards, 2002: 31). Edwards refers to art therapist Gilroy's comments on evidence-based practice as being an arena where the 'only valid knowledge' is based on 'scientific evidence', adding that the use of statistics 'steals the show' with numbers refuting all other arguments (Gilroy, 1996: 57). She adds, echoing many others, that the issue of what *kind* of evidence is considered *valid* is problematic for therapists in demonstrating efficacy (Edwards, 1999).

Edwards advocates respecting difference of approach in this aspect of considering evidence. For example, music therapy involves a number of indeterminate phenomena including music and its effects, as well as the relationship between therapist and client. Edwards also adds that there are context-specific considerations that require attention in music therapy research that may not require attention in medical research. She concludes that music therapy posts funded in relation to EBM will need to create a dialogue with structures such as random control trials: 'Whether we like it or not, the EBM framework has gained wide acceptance and importance . . . nevertheless, familiarity and a facility with the current language (or sometimes jargon) of the practice context can be a starting point for communication' (Edwards, 2002: 33).

The 'mission' is for others to be persuaded of the distinct and important contribution of music therapy, and its ways of working, to therapy services.

The ways in which environmental, social, political and cultural background impact upon these areas is crucial in considering outcome. Practitioners such as art therapist Mauro have pointed out that in many situations 'assessments, interventions and programming of services have been developed to serve the American middle class, hence procuring a "cultural blindness". This is a form of institutional racism' (Mauro, 1998: 135). She goes on to add that culture will affect the way someone perceives changes and psychological factors which influence the way the person 'acts out' their mental illness and responds to treatment, observing that Hispanic families, for example, tend to attribute psychiatric illness to physical deficiencies such as general bodily weakness. Arts therapists have explored issues relating to prejudice and values within the areas of assessment, evaluation and efficacy. Joyce, for example, looks at the ways in which women have been oppressed by medical criteria and diagnosis (Joyce, 1997: 88), while Campbell and Abra Gaga look at women in relation to sexism and racism (1997). They stress the importance of the ideas of social constructivism in the arts therapies. Rather than imposing existing criteria and meaning on the client as object, 'the therapist engages with the client in order to allow the narrative/story to unfold. This is from a position of "not knowing" whereby the client is viewed as "the expert" ' (Campbell and Abra Gaga, 1997: 220).

One of the debates regarding the efficacy of the arts therapies concerns the nature of the evidence on whether something is effective. As we have seen, different positions exist concerning this: some argue for a way of gathering information, or evidence that tries to achieve an objective stance – an empirical approach, for example, using quantitative data that needs to be gathered. Others have argued that this way of gathering information is not valid, especially within a discipline that brings together the complexities of creativity along with the diversity of phenomena that occur between therapist and client or clients within active therapeutic work.

We have also seen how the issue of efficacy is crucial to arts therapies practice. This practice might include processes which aim to empower any client to make decisions based on the progress of their participation in relation to the continuation or termination of therapy. It might also include the arts therapist's working to find a language to communicate to those in departments or organisations making decisions about allocating scarce funding resources to provision, based on whether the arts therapies can be seen to be effective for their clients.

RADICAL RESEARCH?

Tensions are pointed out by a number of practitioners and researchers between what can and cannot be known and expressed or communicated.

Conquergood, for example, in his writing on 'Performance Studies Interventions and Radical Research' (2002), differentiates between 'the dominant way of knowing in the academy . . . of empirical observation and critical analysis from a distanced perspective . . . a view from above the object of inquiry: knowledge that is anchored in paradigm and secured in print', and 'another way of knowing that is grounded in active, intimate, co-experienced, hands-on participation and personal connection' (2002: 146). The first, he argues, has been pre-eminent, 'marching under the banner of science and reason', and having the effect of disqualifying and repressing other ways of knowing, 'such as those rooted in embodied experience, morality and local contingencies' (2002: 146). Haraway has echoed this, contrasting these two different ways from a perspective that is interesting for arts therapists to think about: the 'view from above' being the first and the 'view from a body' being the second (Haraway, 1991: 196). McNiff talks about a 'gap' between what 'can and cannot' be known in a similar way:

> Creative arts therapy is engaged with both aspects of experience, and this clearly distinguishes our practices from disciplines which base themselves on totally predictable outcomes. As an art therapist I recognise the value of science and its research methods; but they can never encapsulate the totality of what I do.
>
> (1998: 31)

He uses the image of flying with one wing, and stresses the need to address arts-based approaches to understanding outcome and change. He says that a particular vision of the world is always linked to any research activity – and that it's important to ask: what view of the world does the approach to understanding outcome represent?

I think such a division between art and science is too stark – the existence of disciplines such as the arts therapies challenge such dichotomies between 'objective' and 'subjective' experience. Some would argue that the identification of the subjective with arts and objective with science is too simplistic. The cultural tensions that these views represent, though, are a part of what the arts therapist inherits in many attitudes towards efficacy. The revolutionary part of the arts therapies' relationship to efficacy is the bringing of these apparently different worlds together as an *opportunity* rather than an *impossibility*.

A number of the approaches described in this chapter try to achieve the task of flying with *both* wings – of bringing together art and science. This is a crucial part of the identity and nature of arts therapy practice, as important in efficacy as elsewhere. It is a unique, complex and challenging task – one to which, as we will see, there are a number of creative and challenging answers.

WHAT ARE THE CONCERNS OF THE ARTS THERAPIES IN RELATION TO EFFICACY?

What *is* evidence for the arts therapies, then? As we have seen, given the many complex processes present in any arts therapy encounter, it is challenging to consider how areas such as description, assessment and outcome can be addressed.

Put at its simplest, in any form of intervention with therapeutic change as an intended outcome, it is important to see what has occurred. This matters for a variety of reasons. These include:

- For the client to gain a sense of whether any change has occurred

- To inform client choice in making any decisions about which therapy may be appropriate for them

- To identify whether specific approaches or methods are particularly useful in intervention in specific circumstances

- For the therapist to try to perceive and understand what is happening – whether, for example, the work is having any effect

- For clients, therapists and organisations to see if there has been any outcome in order to offer the therapy to others

- To know when to stop

- To see what has occurred in order to improve the provision

- In some circumstances, to deal with issues to do with whether one therapy is seen as more 'cost-effective' than another

---

At a more formal level, there are numerous research-orientated projects that attempt to look at areas of change with a greater degree of detailed analysis of the processes at work.

My point is that *all* work, from the questions asked by clients within sessions, to post-doctoral research, are related by the core question of whether and how the arts therapies have effect. These can be seen as part of an investigative project which all participating in the arts therapies are involved in. The next section looks at some of the ways this vital 'project' is taking shape.

Many arts therapists use existing methods based in disciplines such as psychology, or make use of assessment reports made within a multidisciplinary approach by other professionals. For example, those working in education may refer to tests developed by educationalists, those in psychiatry on reports from psychiatrists or psychologists.

Some arts therapists have developed their own strategies and ways of working towards understanding the outcomes of their work by creating a dialogue with other disciplines. This way of working, as we will see, makes use of a model or approach from a discipline such as psychology or education, and adapts it for use within the particular needs and possibilities of an arts therapy. Example 3: Adapting other disciplines which will be looked at in some detail later in this chapter, illustrates this approach.

A collaboration in diagnosis

As discussed earlier, some arts therapists have strong concerns regarding this approach, arguing that art making and meaning is incompatible with such standardised tests and interpretations. Others have developed

---

Work in the arts therapies in diagnosis seeks to identify the situation or condition the client brings to therapy, and to find a reliable way to read this and to describe it usefully, so that it can be used by those involved in providing therapy. A diagnosis might be used to help clarify what is troubling the client, or in considering the route the therapy might take. It might, for example, help differentiate between different kinds of disorder or difficulty.

How does diagnosis relate to outcome? Feder and Feder differentiate between personality assessment and diagnosis:

> Personality assessment purports to identify the persistent characteristic traits that shape an individual's behaviour. Diagnosis ... is designed to identify the emotional and mental disorders that distort an individual's personality
>
> (Feder and Feder, 1998: 261)

Some work such as the Formal Elements Art Therapy Rating Scale (Gantt and Tarbone, 1997) or the Diagnostic Drawing Series (Cohen, 1993) have attempted to achieve a diagnostic scale for art therapy that is tied in with existing, used classification scales: the DSM-III and the DSM-III-R concerning psychiatric symptoms.

Here, for example, in the Formal Elements Art Therapy Rating Scale, clients are asked to draw a person picking an apple from a tree on a 12 in. × 8 in. piece of white paper. Their response is analysed for use of colour, use of space, degree of integration, realism, line quality and developmental level. A manual gives instructions for scoring the picture with details for each category within the analysis. In DDS patients are given twelve different colours of pastel and 18 in. × 24 in. paper, and asked to draw three pictures: a free picture, a tree and a feeling picture. When the drawings are completed, a structured gathering of verbal associations is made. Criteria for analysis include the use of colour, presence of people, pressure, use of space and degree of tilt for the tree.

approaches rooted in the arts tradition and experience: an example of this is Higgins (1993), who has developed a diagnostic approach using movement work.

Many therapists practice in a collaborative fashion with the client on understanding assessment-related work. The Standing Committee on the Arts in Prisons, for example, in talking about assessment reports in prison services says:

> All reports should be prepared with the client's interest to the fore. After a written assessment has been completed it is often useful and empowering to discuss the review with the inmate ... In some cases it may be valuable to ask inmates to provide their own written evaluations of shared work in progress – points gained and recommendations.
>
> (SCAP, 1997: 31)

This assumes the assessment will take the form of a written report, often the main means of communication on such matters within institutions. However, there are also methods and approaches that have developed more clearly as specific to the arts therapies, growing from the languages and processes of art therapy, dramatherapy, music therapy and dance movement therapy. These draw on traditions ranging from the spectogram to the retrospective review of pictures.

The next section will examine some of these approaches to understanding what is happening, what has happened, and what might happen in the arts therapies.

DIFFERENT ASPECTS OF EVIDENCE – VARIETY IN THE ARTS THERAPIES

There are different emphases within the arts therapies in dealing with efficacy. It is not as if there is one approach that dominates the arts therapies as a whole, nor even a single approach within one modality such as art therapy or music therapy. This, in my opinion, would not be desirable. The range of the conditions and situations that clients bring to arts therapy needs to be met as closely as possible by the most appropriate ways of understanding efficacy.

The diversity that we are about to encounter is not a reflection of chaos within the field's attempt to find one strategy, but rather a sign of the diversity of experience, and flexibility of approach and potential in the arts therapies. The other side of this variety is that the client and therapist might become overwhelmed, or confused, in trying to find their direction through the complex routes within this maze of 'efficacy'. The danger is that the diversity of approaches becomes bewildering. The language of worth could become meaningless because of the impossibility of comparing one with another, the choices making it impossible to orientate therapist or client: the language of worth becoming worthless.

A part of this variety concerns the *framework*, or the therapeutic emphasis of the arts therapy. Hence, those practising within a behavioural or analytic framework will draw upon approaches and methods that give them information useful to their approach. As we will see later in this chapter, Case Example 2 draws on projective techniques which give information about the client's relationship with the paintings and the art therapist, whereas Example 3 looks towards behavioural indicators such as eye-contact and gestures.

Another part of this diversity is reflected in the *focus* of the approach taken to evaluate efficacy. This concerns the way of looking, what is used to give information. Some pay attention to the process of interpretation. Image, movement or the relationship between client and therapist are used to look at signs that reveal or express changes in problems, difficulties or underlying disturbances. For others, the changes in the artistic qualities of the clients' process and product – organisation, coherency, particular qualities, changes in expression or process – are seen to parallel changes in life outside sessions. This in turn relates to the *methods* chosen. As we shall see, the methods relate to both the framework and focus of the therapy. The arts therapist tries to identify a method suitable to the needs of the client, the ideology and the way of looking.

Within all these areas the key question for me is how the *meaning* of efficacy emerges as a part of a *dialogue*. This is between therapist, client and, where appropriate, the institutions or organisation they are working within. It concerns how framework, focus and method come together in a way that is meaningful for client and therapist.

LANGUAGE AND OUTCOMES

There has been much debate between arts therapists on the nature and type of research in relation to efficacy. Not all research is directly concerned with the question of the efficacy of the arts therapies. All aspects could be argued to have efficacy as an implicit issue, even if it's not directly related. Some research, for example, is in the area of aesthetic theory or the range of kinds of practice within the field. Even they, though, help within 'the project' in that they assist the field to become clearer about how the arts therapies understand what is involved in the theory of change, or the diversity of practice.

As art therapist Edwards says, though, 'the importance of research in maintaining and developing services cannot be underestimated' (Edwards, 1999: 2). Edwards sees research as essential in learning about, and sharing, clinically relevant knowledge and experience. It ensures clinical account-ability and efficacy in evaluating new developments and in developing the profession. I want, also, to make more explicit the advantages to clients implicit in his comments. For the client one area of benefit is a greater clarity in how the arts therapies are effective in working with specific difficulties or conditions brought to the therapy. In addition, as the arts therapies become clearer about the processes of evaluating efficacy, then the client will benefit by their involvement in more effective ways of looking at change within the therapy.

Edwards goes on to say that there is increasing pressure from a variety of sources to produce research that is 'evidence of clinical effectiveness that is objective, dispassionate, factual and which in order to attain the necessary validity, conforms to the requirements of evidence based practice' (Edwards, 1999: 3). He cites areas of difficulty being: the use of reliable and valid measures; the random allocation of subjects; and whether sufficiently large numbers of 'samples' have been evaluated (Edwards, 1999). He points to the use of Randomised Control Trials (RCT), mentioned earlier, where many clients are involved within a structured testing and are seen to help identify areas such as the comparative benefits of two or more forms of 'treatment'. He says that few arts therapists have access to the resources and institutional support for such research. He indicates some areas of the RCT approach that are problematic, for example that RCTs do not include accounts of how clients feel about the therapy they receive, nor from practitioners about the therapy they have delivered.

He says that the stamp of science in psychotherapy research, with its emphasis on outcome measures, controlled variables, rating scales, internal validity and statistics 'conveys a sense of authority and credibility' (Edwards, 1999: 3). He points out that in the arts therapies subjective experience is crucial and that this may be at odds with such 'scientific' emphasis: 'In my experience, our work is, more often than not, as concerned with feelings, aesthetic sensibilities, moral practices and beliefs as much as it is with objectivity or facts. In practice our work as art therapists embraces both subjective and objective reality' (Edwards, 1999: 3).

This is the issue that underlies much arts therapies research concerning efficacy. The modes of enquiry are seen by many as broader than one that relies on the kinds of language identified by Edwards with 'evidence-based' approaches. As well as such quantitative approaches, the arts therapies have made a strong case for the areas of qualitative research, as well as for new paradigm ways of looking at change and outcome (Payne, 1993). Many also make use of a combination of research approaches.

McNiff, for example, discusses the use of art-based outcomes for art therapy. This involves looking at 'changes in the content of artistic expression, changes in the "quality" of expression, increased spontaneity, greater persistence in the making of art, and fluctuations in the aesthetic satisfaction of both client and therapist' (McNiff, 1998: 203).

Another approach in art therapy concerns evidence based on images. This centres on looking at artwork and ascribing meaning to it – here parallels are assumed between thought patterns, feelings, behaviours and images made.

The creation of images is considered to reflect changes in inner processes, experiences conscious or unconscious and the relationship with the therapist. However, some have made the point that:

> Unconscious defence mechanisms and conscious resistances all operating to shield the conscious from anxiety provoking ideas, tend to make very risky the assumption that a drawing is a direct representation of a patient's concerns or feelings . . . [it is necessary to] go beyond the manifest content . . . peruse it for clues about areas that the patient could not or would not reveal.
>
> (Feder and Feder, 1998: 262)

The role of the therapist here is to act with the client to make suggestions, invitations to explore and connect areas of the painting within the relationship.

All these give some sense of the diversity of ways of approaching understanding and describing change. They raise a common question, however: in the midst of the plethora of phenomena occurring within an arts therapy session, what is *looked* at to give information about change?

OUTCOMES: WHAT IS LOOKED AT?

Many arts therapies' approaches to gathering and understanding evidence are based on the assumption that a focus on clients' products or their process within the session can be understood to provide information to indicate change. The assumption is often made that change in the way the client uses the art form to make images, move, act, or makes music will lead to changes that will transfer to other areas of their life. I have called this aspect of the process the Life–Drama Connection (1996). Some use verbal exploration or reflection as an additional element in looking at what has changed and what has not changed.

Valente and Fontana have rightly said that there are dangers in therapists imposing on clients their own 'interpretations of what it means to be "a psychologically whole person" ' (Valente and Fontana, 1997: 17). They say that in the arts therapies field as a whole there is acceptance that there are a wide range of cues that can be used to monitor client progress and that there can be a wide rage of outcomes. Their research explored how dramatherapists understand the ways clients communicate their notion of improved well-being: a variety of ways to 'answer the question "Is your client getting any better?" ' (Valente and Fontana, 1997: 29). They list broadly the outcomes involved, and consider the following as ways of evaluating change:

Observation of client behaviours

Client self reports

Reports from other professionals

Projective techniques

Clients' use of diagnostic dramatherapy media

Reports by other group members

Kelly's repertory grid

(Valente and Fontana, 1997)

Studies have looked at whether some particular characteristics are mentioned more than others in describing the outcomes of therapy, the changes for clients coming to the arts therapies. A survey identified what was looked for in assessing client progress in dramatherapy. It was intended to highlight the qualities that practitioners felt were 'most amenable to development by dramatherapy'. These were the areas most cited by practitioners:

Self-esteem

Self-awareness

Self-acceptance

Self-confidence

Hope

Communication

Trust

Self–other awareness

Spontaneity

Social interaction

(Valente and Fontana, 1997)

Valente and Fontana comment on the cluster at the top of the list to do with self-esteem, self-awareness, self-acceptance and self-confidence, concluding that there can 'hardly be a more graphic illustration of the power for psycho-logical change of the dramatic experience' (Valente and Fontana, 1997: 26).

Feder and Feder's analysis of music therapy points to a different range of outcomes. These are:

Breaking social isolation

Stimulation of motor and perceptual activity

Development of appropriate mechanics of behaviour control

Reduction of anxiety states

(Feder and Feder, 1998: 319)

Bunt, Burns and Turton in their work with residents of a cancer help centre in Bristol, England looked at the outcomes of a music therapy group which emphasised relaxation and social interaction. The settings' aims were to help residents learn how they themselves could improve the quality of their lives and to influence the outcome of their illness. The programme emphasised the relationship between 'whole mind, body and spirit' (Bunt *et al.*, 2000: 62). Focus groups of residents were used to discuss and evaluate their experience of the music provision at the setting. These evaluative comments included:

The change of mood within the music had a 'knock-on' effect both emotionally and physically (listening)

Early resistance to the listening with more relaxing towards the end

Emotional at times with welling-up of tears and sadness (listening)

Felt fresher after the playing experience

The playing was powerful and releasing

Visually attracted by the different instruments

Felt energised and creative in the playing session, good to participate with others

Playing session was more fun eliciting lots of laughter

Listening experience was lovely and calming, feeling happier and more energised after the playing

(Bunt *et al.*, 2000: 62)

It's interesting to note the less technical language here compared with Valente and Fontana (1997), and Feder and Feder (1998) – indicating, perhaps, the danger of creating different languages of efficacy– one for the therapists or professionals, and another for clients or users.

Valente and Fontana parallel the areas of concern in their research outcomes with Maslow's criteria: emotional openness, perception, spontaneity, self- and self–other acceptance and creativity. The tendency in the music therapy criteria as assessed by Feder and Feder is towards more social and behavioural concerns. The clients working with Bunt, Burns and Turton seem to combine a mixture of enjoyment of the act of playing and listening, of emotional effects and outcomes of listening, and playing, of fun and laughter, of being calm and fresh.

I don't think it's possible to derive conclusions about differences in the effects of music therapy as compared with dramatherapy here, as the studies used different methods to arrive at their inclusion. Nor would I want to make any generalised conclusions about the outcomes of all music or dramatherapy. I include them to show a sample of practitioners and clients looking at efficacy at a particular time, and to emphasise the ways that outcomes are framed by different contexts, by different therapists and clients. As illustrated in the examples, the range reflects the ways in which framework, focus and method vary widely.

The ways in which the arts therapies have approached efficacy have also changed and developed over time. Feder and Feder (1998) have described such a shift in music therapy. In the 1950s and '60s a number of music therapy assessment and diagnostic approaches were rooted in the Freudian notion of projection (Feder and Feder, 1998). They note a subsequent move to a more empirical basis, attempting to establish its value 'in producing measurable physiological or mood changes' (Feder and Feder, 1998). This is seen as a trend towards looking to evidence that was directly observable through behaviour, rather than interpreting, or inferring causation and outcome. They also point out that the orientation of arts therapists' practice is affected by the prevailing trends within their major employers. For example, hospitals treating veterans, the major employer of music therapists in the US following the Second World War, tended to approach change in terms of behaviour modification. This approach was reflected in the way evidence was seen by music therapists in this period, with a growth in behavioural approaches in their evaluation of therapy. Current trends in many countries show the arts therapies responding to issues concerning evidence-based practice (Edwards, 2002; Grainger, 1999). This is especially true for those working within public or state health services. However, the broad issue of evidence and efficacy is one that has concerned the arts therapies for some time, and in ways that are broader than concerns with evidence-based practice alone.

A crucial trend within the development of the arts therapies is the increasing publication of research into how and why they can be useful to participating clients. The growth in practice, which has occurred as the fields have become established in more settings, has been reflected in the amount and range of enquiry into how client and therapist within the arts therapies understand the nature of change (Edwards, 1999; Grainger, 1999; Milioni, 2001). The next section looks at some examples of this diversity. It contains some of the ways in which a variety of answers form the question – does it work?

WAYS OF WORKING: CONSIDERING THE EFFECT OF THE ARTS THERAPIES

A rich and varied culture has emerged, then, concerning understanding and communicating efficacy, whether in the framework, focus or method chosen. This chapter will examine some examples that give a flavour of the diversity of approaches. It will also look at the ways in which dialogues with other disciplines have taken place, as well as some of the new discoveries the arts therapies are making about efficacy.

EXAMPLE 1: CASE STUDY

Writers such as Higgins (1993), Gilroy (1996), Edwards (1999) and Grainger (1999) have examined the case study as an approach to looking at efficacy. Gilroy and Lee have pointed out that the case study can reflect different approaches to understanding outcomes and change. The case study might be based on a descriptive account; it might be part of a collaborative enquiry where clients are involved in describing their experiences as part of the case study (McClelland, 1993). Schaverien has said that a typical art therapy case study is based on the pictures and art objects of the client (Schaverien, 1995). The pattern of the case study often takes the form of: a description of the theoretical underpinning for the approach taken; a description of the setting and the client and any diagnostic material; along with a description of the arts therapy process.

The case study approach has been seen as too subjective to contribute to research, 'too "personal" . . . too untrustworthy, to be considered as reliable evidence of clinical effectiveness' (Edwards, 1999: 6). The problems with the case study approach are in the nature of the account. Edwards points out the 'healthy scepticism' needed when reading some accounts within art therapy and psychotherapy literature. He shows that they have few grounds to be 'objective'. He advocates a 'rigorous . . . creative' approach to case study. This emphasises the way in which the case study can pay attention to the individuality of the client and the difficulties they bring to therapy and how these are communicated through images, words and actions. He says that it engages with what he calls 'the richness, diversity, messiness and complexity of the therapeutic process and lived experience' (Edwards, 1999: 6). Attention has been given to the notion of the 'stories' within clinical work: 'The process of counselling and psychotherapy is one that, in the end, relies on the telling of stories. Stories, about events, recent or long past, in the client's life' (McLeod, 1999: 173). In this way the case study becomes allied to story. The arts therapy session becomes a part of this process where the client's 'narrative' becomes allied to image making, or storytelling, for example. The therapy becomes a way of exploring: 'It is unhelpful to assume the stories these case studies tell are any less truthful than those that depend on purportedly objective telling' (Edwards, 1999: 7). The case study, then, is seen as a form that can embrace the specific situation of the client and adapt to reflect the complexity of communication, the relationship between client, therapist and art form within the session and the client's life. He also says that the case study does not turn 'people' into 'objects', and offers the opportunity to respond to the immediacy of the experience rather than fitting the experience to previously proposed theories or explanations. The case study is also seen to be inclusive and contains the voice of client and therapist.

Hoskyns looks at the effects of a 12-week music therapy group in a UK probation day service centre. The setting worked with women and men over the age of 21 who had repeatedly broken the law, resulting in a number of previous convictions ranging from shoplifting and theft to soliciting. Referrals were from magistrates and Crown Courts, and sentencing involved attendance at the day centre for three months as a condition of a two-year probation order. Clients opted to attend the music therapy group as part of the programme. The aims of the setting's work were to encourage honesty in personal relationships, frank discussion of offending patterns and exploration of related issues. The music therapy aimed to increase clients' self-esteem through creative activity, to increase awareness of choices, and provide a 'playground' to experiment with different approaches, feelings and behaviours. Groups of between three and seven members worked with a therapist and assistant. Various musical instruments from different cultural traditions were made available to clients. The group improvised music: 'the primary focus of the group would be on the non-verbal playground . . . and on helping the clients to play music that was directly expressive of the "self" ' (Hoskyns, 1995: 142). Some verbal discussion was involved.

Based on others' work, and on a pilot study at the City University, London, Hoskyns designed five ratings scales rooted in music therapy experiences and aiming to identify areas that could indicate 'the difference between client behaviour at the beginning and end of a session' (Hoskyns, 1995: 143). These five scales covered areas such as loudness, continuity, resonance of instruments chosen, attention to group task and leadership. Each scale used a simple five-point framework, with a score of 1 being low and 5 being high. She tested the use of the scales in the pilot phase to arrive at parity between different observers. In collaboration with the clients, videotape was used to record sessions, and then a time-sampling approach was taken, sections of videotape were analysed for fixed periods of time within sessions. The scales were used to look at the ways in which clients responded or used the sessions over the period of the therapy. The different scales were used to try to create a picture of the client's use according to fixed reference points and over a period of time to see if any changes occurred. Observers analysing the video-tape were trained in using the scales.

Sample

One client referred to as 'G' is described as a case example within this work. The scores on the scales alter for him within the period of therapy. There is a reduction in his scores on the ratings scales.

Rating scale continuity (music)

(1) No playing (or singing)
(2) Very occasional playing/singing, many breaks
(3) Neither completely continuous nor completely discontinuous playing
(4) Playing tends to be continuous with some breaks
(5) Continuous playing, no breaks

Rating scale loudness (music)

(1) No audible playing/singing
(2) Soft playing, barely audible
(3) Neither completely loud nor completely soft playing
(4) Clearly audible playing at moderate volume
(5) Plays loudly, exceeding general volume of group

The research setting was 'uncontrolled' from an experimental view, and the method does not reveal whether the clients changed expressly because of the music therapy, or whether they would have changed anyway. But, says Hoskyns, the method of looking at change creates a language to consider the ways changes can be observed within the music therapy sessions, and to see whether changes lasted within the therapy. She says that G does show 'a number of observable changes which seemed to be held over the period of music therapy'.

She says that the scales gave her a useful, 'objective assessment of clients' activity–passivity, which was quite close to my case observations . . . Working on the scales and acquiring these results suggests that beneficial outcome in the field of offending is a very complex procedure. Internal change is not necessarily indicated by external behaviours, though certain issues may be very clearly indicated in people's behaviour. For Client G it seems that music therapy was a very engaging process, and he made considerable short-term changes' (Hoskyns, 1995: 149). She says that such external observation can check and confirm more subjective investigations into efficacy. Hoskyns uses the scale to assist her observations and dialogue with her group. She recognises that such qualitative data can only represent a small area of the processes at work and seeks to use this as part of a picture in understanding outcome.

G's case study pays attention to the individuality of the client, it engages with the complexity and diversity of the arts therapy experience and tries to address what Edwards calls the different voices within the therapy: 'case studies usually seek to include, rather than exclude, the "voice", personality and other personal attributes of the therapist/researcher and client' rather than demand that we turn 'subjects (i.e. people) into objects' (Edwards, 1999: 6). Grainger sums up the advantages of case study as the inclusion of a range of data and an attempt to create an overall picture (1999: 84). He says that it is a particularly appropriate way to evaluate outcome as it allows the artistic process to 'speak for itself'. A frame is produced, in which artistic communication is allowed to take place, without the complexities of events or experiences being coded in the same way, 'so that everything may become grist to the scientific mill' (1999: 97). Goss and Rowland in their discussion of evidence-based practice conclude that systematic, detailed case study material, with explicit references to supporting literature, can inform other practitioners and contribute to 'the culture of evaluation in the psychological studies'. They argue that what is 'lost' in numerical precision is compensated for with 'accuracy of representation of the individuals concerned and the vivid, direct insights offered' (Goss and Rowland, 2000: 197).

EXAMPLE 2: ART THERAPY REVIEW OF PICTURES

As detailed earlier in this chapter the methods used to evaluate the process and outcome draw on a variety of forms. In art therapy, Schaverien, for example, has documented the use of a retrospective review of pictures made by the client (Schaverien, 1992; 1995). She makes the point that this is a fundamental difference from other forms of psychotherapy, and from the other arts therapies as 'there is a series of lasting objects created by the patient' (1992: 92). This offers data, but also particular opportunities in evaluating the process and development of the therapy. They are present in the moment of the review, but also 'provide an instant recall of part of the session' (1992: 93). The images are still alive – they reawaken processes seen from the perspective of the present – they recreate the therapy, providing a review of progress.

In the review all pictures made, or pictures from a certain period, are assembled and looked at together and in sequence. This can be self-affirming, to see the work created, but it can also 'reveal connections and links which had been previously unconscious' (Schaverien, 1995: 28).

Harry

In reviewing paintings made over a nine-month period the client had made several pictures a day for a number of days each week. The pace had changed. In the review of pictures some of the following phenomena are noticed:

- During part of the period the pace of production had slowed down. This is reflected on as being a period of regression, relating to 'an early and regressed part of the transference'. Harry staying in the art room, close to the therapist.
- The style of execution changes when Harry begins to relate to others outside the one-to-one relationship with the therapist.
- Pictures become jokey – this is seen as a type of 'adolescence', when images are made to 'impress' peers rather than for the therapist.

Schaverien points out that the retrospective review of pictures has a role for the client in evaluating their process through the therapy, but also notes that the therapist's experience of review is of use to understanding and evaluating the process which has occurred: 'I was surprised to find how much I had previously missed; I thought I had seen these pictures but actually I had only seen a superficial layer. I now began to understand the web that they had woven me into . . . how these pictures with their powerful aesthetic quality had affected the countertransference . . . I had been absorbed into the inner world of the artist in the most subtle manner' (1995: 29).

She says that the images evoked what she calls a reawakening of the counter-transference. This develops into further reflection and understanding of the counter-transference and transference processes as manifested in the pictures, and her response to the retrospective review. A part of this involves insight into collective, as well as personal unconscious material within the pictures and their effects: 'The patient was artist but also viewer, and each of these affected some aspect of the transference and countertransference' (Schaverien, 1995: 31).

The work, reviewed in sequence and in connection with the life history of the client, 'offers unique insights into aspects of the person which may have been previously hidden or unconscious,' (1992: 93) and 'movement in the inner world of the patient' (1992: 99). She parallels changes in the pictures with those taking place in the inner world of the artist/client. She suggests that the combination of the three: viewing made objects such as pictures in the context of sequence; attending to the maker's meanings; and to the art therapist's impressions, can offer insight into the ways the art therapy process effects a 'change in state of the artist/patient' (1992: 102).

The evaluation of the process is undertaken through the therapist and client both reviewing the work as a way of continuing to live with the images. As many art therapists have indicated, images produced in art therapy can offer different significances or meanings at different times. The retrospective review allows the images produced to act as a way of evaluating through the impact of re-encountering the physically present images. The presence of the artefact, Schaverien argues, offers a unique opportunity in evaluation as the reflection is not reliant on memory alone; it is also about how the consideration of the past process is encountered in the here and now of the emotional impact of the image.

Schaverien also illustrates the ways in which the process of seeing the images in sequence, combined with the evaluative perspective of the retrospective review, can be an effective way of enabling therapist and client to understand the nature of change. In discussing a client, Ann, part of whose therapy had produced images associated with being beaten by her father when she was a young child: 'Later when we reviewed the pictures, Ann was more separate from the feelings; they had become familiar and so less loaded with affect. This enabled a freer approach to the associations, and the therapist was able to make comments and interpretations. Links could now be made between these and other pictures and related to her current state' (Schaverien, 1993: 123).

One image of the father, for example, was painted in black; an image from a subsequent session was of a black spider. Schaverien says that in the retrospective Ann connected the two, and client and therapist made links and noticed how they affected them: 'Because some time had elapsed, it was possible to play with possible links and make comments which would have been impossible when the pictures were new ... In the initial stages the pictures evoked very raw and painful feelings, and Ann was "identified" with them' (1992: 123). The review allows for a reflective, evaluative perspective, but at the same time allows an emotional re-encountering with the image. These two combine to produce a unique evaluative process. In describing her approach Schaverien says that her influences are from two different fields – art history and psychoanalysis. The work of the art historian can include writing biographical material of artists making reference to artworks and life history, and the artist may hold a retrospective exhibition of work in a gallery. The other tradition includes analysts who have written about patients who create artwork: she refers to Jung (1959), Klein (1961) and Edinger (1990) as examples.

EXAMPLE 3: ADAPTING OTHER DISCIPLINES

As mentioned earlier, a number of arts therapists have developed an approach to looking at evaluating the outcomes and process of their work through dialogue with other disciplines. In a sense, all the above examples have done this to an extent. However, some arts therapists have adapted specific scales and rating methods, for example from other disciplines. Grainger (1999), for example, did so in his dramatherapy work with people with thought disorders. His practice was based in ideas that people with thought disorders have difficulties in differentiating between 'subject and object, between self-as-participant and self-as-observer', and in telling apart different degrees of involvement and separation. This can be linked to feelings of engulfment and difficulties in relating to others. He aimed to help clarify aspects of the private language of schizoid thinking 'that call forth a response from other people and result in genuine communication' (Grainger, 1999: 50).

He uses an existing test from the field of psychology, the Bannister and Fransella Grid Test of Schizophrenic Thought Disorder (1966). A cross-section of patients attending a psychiatric day hospital were involved in a ten-week dramatherapy group. The aim was to measure 'the effect of this experience on their ability to order their thoughts in a more consistent and effective way than they did before' (Grainger 1999: 50–1). People came to a one-hour group once a week. There were two groups of twenty-four people in total. All were tested three times during the therapy.

The dramatherapy contained activities varying from simple warm-ups, aiming to develop awareness of others, through to exercises practising the ability to predict other people's behaviour and share their feelings. The aimed-for change was an increase in clients' construing as measured in the thought disorder test. The test involves placing a series of eight photographs of both genders in front of clients. The facilitator asks questions about their perceptions of the people in the photographs. So, for example, they are asked who looks kind, and the photographs are ordered in terms of most to least kind. Other emotions include selfish, mean, honest. This was done twice to look at consistency.

Here Grainger connects the processes involved in dramatherapy with a device to evaluate change from another discipline. He identifies a way of evaluating outcome that is consistent with the areas of change appropriate to the needs of the clients, and the aspects of the dramatic processes involved in the dramatherapy work. So, the links between enactment and the use of photographic images in judging the significance of people's facial expressions 'would seem to lead easily enough into the kinds of interpersonal process explored in dramatherapy ... the testing procedures could be seen to be thematically related to the treatment modality' (Granger, 1999: 56).

Jones (1993) and Sanctuary also created a dialogue with another discipline to evaluate efficacy. This work involved dramatherapy and a group of young adolescents with autism. An initial period of assessment identified the appropriate dramatic language to work with. This engaged the group in different types of drama – from role work to mask. From this it was decided that the individuals in the group would most easily relate to working with puppets. The aims were worked out in collaboration between the setting, parents or guardians and the clients. Puppetry would enable clients to become involved with the 'small actors' they created:

> to encourage empathy between the clients and the puppets, I decided on
> the use of glove or hand puppets. Life size or larger than life puppets can

offer potential projections involving being overpowered, I wanted the clients to feel at ease in operating the puppets, so the small size of the glove puppet suited this purpose also.

(Jones, 1993: 50)

The aim was to increase clients' range and frequency of interactions with others through the use of puppets and improvisation. The three individuals spent much of their time withdrawn from contact with others, found it hard to establish contact and would engage in solitary, ritualised patterns of behaviour such as flicking fingers in front of their own eyes for periods of time, with contact with others often typified by occasional slaps or poking. The dramatherapy practice also tried to establish whether the use of the puppets would enable the three individuals to experiment with and use inter-actions in a way that was different from their usual modes of behaviour. Each client made a puppet to represent themselves (see images on p. 175 and 236).

The idea was that the clients might be able to feel both involved and distanced from the puppets. They would identify with the puppet representing themselves, but, at the same time, they would be an audience to the puppet. By being able to look at the puppet, by being an audience to the puppet, the client might feel some distance from this representation of themselves:

we aimed to see whether this relationship meant that behaviour and relationships which proved difficult within actual encounters might be made possible if the clients were audience to representations of them-selves ... [and] ... to see if the work undertaken with the puppets in dramatherapy would have an effect on the clients' relationships outside the group.

(Jones, 1993: 51)

The work looked to see if dramatherapy could help create the opportunity for clients to develop different ways of relating to others. This included seeing if solitary patterns of behaviour, as described above, would change and whether enjoyed contact with others could increase. Videotapes were made with the clients in different situations: after lunch, or at break time, in social situations. From this, psychologist Sanctuary developed a series of evaluative areas. These were based on looking at the ways the clients related to others, and then adapting a series of categories based on Parten's categories developed in his studies of small children (Parten and Sanctuary, in Jones, 1993). These included areas such as 'initiated' contact and 'parallel activity'. A continuum was created from this material, ranging from withdrawn to active and prosocial behaviours and interactions.

The categories were used as a structure to record the way clients interacted during part of a lunch break, for example. The structure was used to time-sample the way clients related for two weeks before the dramatherapy group, during the dramatherapy group, immediately after the groupwork had been

Example of Parten–Sanctuary Scale

CATEGORY: Unoccupied/withdrawn

Staring into space

Playing with own body or hair

Getting up from chair and immediately sitting down

CATEGORY: Responsive

Smiling or laughing in response to another

Answering if addressed

Maintaining eye-contact for over one second

Handing or passing objects in response to another

CATEGORY: Initiated

Addressing other by name

Waving at other

Touching other non-aggressively

Staring conversation

Requesting object

(in Jones, 1993: 52)

---

completed, and with a follow-up two weeks after that. Two people recorded the frequency of clients' behaviours during the time sample.

The group met over eleven weeks. Sessions contained free play with the puppets; structured role-plays using the puppets to simulate lunchtime activities such as practising offering tea to each other; videorecording and viewing playback along with some discussion.

After an initial period, where the puppets were spontaneously used in solitary activity only by the clients, relationships within the sessions developed. For example, one client's puppet fell over and hurt her leg. Another client's puppet immediately offered to bandage the leg and did so. Some change was also noted in some of the categories of activity outside the sessions, during the time-sampled monitoring. This monitoring of change was undertaken by totalling the number of occurrences of each category, and the percentile of the client's time spent and the manner of relating calculated for each period. This was then looked at for each client to see if the observations of kinds of relating developed over the intervention time, and whether changes lasted into the follow-up time. Here is an example of the kinds of calculation used in the evaluation:

Client AC

Category	Prior to therapy	Intervention	Post-intervention	Follow-up
Stereotyped	13.2	6.23	4.17	12.5
Withdrawn	59.29	38.69	34.83	51.2
Solitary	19.4	11.8	26.88	7.7
Responsive	6.19	35.08	28.41	24.25
Initiated	1.88	8.2	4.52	3.65

This was used to compare each client's range and mode of interaction before, during and after the dramatherapy work. As the above table illustrates, when looked at through the categories, change is indicated in terms of the reduction of withdrawn activities, and an increase in responsive and initiated activities occurred. Some of the kinds of potential ways of responding and initiating were introduced to puppet activities. An illustration of this was that, prior to the dramatherapy, clients did not interact with each other. During the sessions puppets were encouraged to have tea together, pouring each other drinks, offering cups to each other. Gradually this was reproduced spontaneously during the lunch break by the clients. The video material helped clients to look at what was happening, and assisted in reflecting on the puppet work.

The work here adapts Parten's method of psychological testing to look at phenomena firmly rooted in dramatherapy. This helps to evaluate how and whether aspects of the clients' ways of relating to each other had changed in any way. The languages of drama, therapy and psychology are brought into relationship with each other: 'In adapting a psychological testing form, linked to the dramatic process of witnessing work with puppets, a mutuality was achieved: one area serving to clarify the other' (Jones, 1993: 54).

McNiff talks about the potential of collaboration for arts therapists: 'we will begin to use research methods from medicine, physics, and the physical sciences to understand the dynamic effects of images on perception, the nervous system, emotions, and consciousness . . . the artistic image . . . its medicinal force therapeutically' (McNiff, 1998: 198). He also says 'we do not have to legitimise ourselves according to another group's values and criteria' (1998: 31). Neither of these examples approach another discipline for validity or legitimacy. The work of Grainger (1999) and Jones (1993) seeks to create a dialogue with expertise from relevant disciplines. I would argue that in doing so they are not admitting that there are no arts therapy tools to achieve their desired understanding of efficacy, but rather they adapt the other discipline to reflect the language and processes of dramatherapy.

KEY THEMES IN EFFICACY

Meaning

The way in which meaning is given or taken from the arts therapy experience is an important part of evaluating efficacy. What has the experience meant for a client – how do the images, products, processes and relationships connect to their lives? Stevens and Wetherell have said that one of the principal distinguishing features of modern Euro-American societies is that the self has 'become a source of meaning and value in itself' (Stevens and Wetherell, 2000: 341).

Milioni (2001) echoes many others in her discussion of meaning by pointing to the inadequacy of trying to place one meaning alone upon an artistic expression within the arts therapy. Images, movements, dramatic activities, musical sounds are simply not reducible to one interpretation made by the therapist, a 'theory-prescribed imposition of meaning by the drama-therapist' (Milioni, 2001: 15). By its very nature, artistic expression within a therapeutic context has multiple meanings. As the example from Schaverien demonstrated, for the client and arts therapist, an image might mean different things at the same time, or at different times. An image produced in a session may signify many things at the same time. This does not mean that the client cannot have a very precise intention, or understanding, of an image on some occasions, and that this precision might be important to the process of the therapy. Rather, it speaks against two important things. The first is the idea that images or expressions made can be given a constant meaning. This point of view argues that it is inappropriate to produce a diagnostic lexicon of interpretations – an 'objective list' based on clients' expressions, such as the Formal Elements in Art Therapy Rating Scale discussed earlier. The second is that the production of complex meaning is central to the arts therapies. Milioni describes this process as involving:

> the focus on the exploration of possibilities arising from the story or metaphor, on the multiplicity of versions/perspectives, on the emphasis on possibilities, not the closing down of meaning according . . . to the therapist's conceptualisation of issues . . . the client, not the therapist, is positioned as the expert . . . the therapist–client relationship becomes collaborative in the generation of meaning. This entails a co-construction, rather than an imposition of meaning and a stance that

represents a move away from pathology, not perpetuating pathologising medical discourses.

(Milioni, 2001: 15)

Conquergood adds to this challenging of 'reductive measurement' or attribution of meaning. He examines the complexity of images given the complexities of multicultural societies, 'a postcolonial world criss-crossed by transnational narratives'. Within diaspora affiliations, the movement and migrations of people, 'transnational circulation of images gets reworked on the ground and redeployed for local, tactical struggles' (Conquergood, 2002: 145). He points out the importance of understanding the complexity of meaning and the way in which it can relate to political oppression. Drawing on work researching the oppositional politics of black musical performance, Conquergood goes on to say that:

> oppressed people everywhere must watch their backs, cover their tracks, suck up feelings, and veil their meanings. The state of emergency under which many people live demands we pay attention to messages that are encoded and encrypted; to indirect, non-verbal and extralinguistic modes of communication where subversive meanings and utopian yearnings can be sheltered and shielded from surveillance.

(Conquergood, 2002: 148)

This theme is continued by music therapist Bunt, quoting Hillman, saying that standard clinical language is 'impoverished', without imagination and not capable of giving good descriptions of phenomena, having become remote, abstract, professional and less and less linked to experience. He goes on to say that new forms of language will emerge. These will meet the uniqueness of the arts therapies (Bunt, 1990: 9). Bunt points out that, in contrast to other areas of research in the arts therapies, meaning is 'more ambiguous', that 'there are no common constructs in artistic expression as in language; it is impossible to use such terms as true and false' (1990: 9).

Challenges

It's important to listen to the voices that question the way in which change is accounted for and understood. Some have argued that the presence of the artistic process and what it represents is inimical, incompatible with the assumptions at the heart of some modes of enquiry. They have asserted that the reduction of artistic expressions to indicators of psychological states not only reduces the complexities of expression unacceptably – but denies the actual nature of the process and expression. Feder and Feder, for example, assert that: 'Therapists tend to overestimate the accuracy of the assessment procedures on which they rely. Many clinicians tend to be impressed, and often overwhelmed, by numbers and complicated formulations that produce the illusion of precision' (Feder and Feder, 1998: 81). They argue that if therapists own that feelings and thought processes are of fallible humans, they 'might use both tests and clinical assessment procedures more realistically' (1998: 81). This way of looking at efficacy argues that the needs of the client are too complex to be pinned down in a way that acknowledged systems identify. In the face of evidence based on physically observable change, where do the more spiritual needs and processes lie? In the face of highly personal accounts of inner processes, where does validity sit?

There is a tension between looking at characteristics or experiences shared by grouping people together, and comparing and contrasting them, and the approach influenced by people such as Maslow that says 'I must approach a person as an individual unique and peculiar, the sole member of his class' (Maslow, 1966: 10). Sharma has said that too much therapeutic and medical practice implies that clients 'can never be equal participants in choices or decisions . . . numerous studies have traced the way in which medical power is established and exercised, some concentrating on the institutional setting in which doctors as a professional group are able to exercise control and exact deference' (Sharma, 1994: 84). This is contrasted with an approach that seeks to inform the patient about choices, that recognises their own experience of their condition, and seeks to work with them to establish their own priorities where 'patients seek an equal and collaborative relationship' (Sharma, 1994: 85).

Clarkson has said that there is no significant objective evidence that any particular theoretical approach or framework is relevant to the successful outcome of what she calls 'Eurocentric psychotherapies' (Clarkson, 2002b: 76). She goes on to add that it is the therapeutic relationship rather than theory, diagnosis or technique that potentates the effects of therapy. She draws on Frank and Frank's survey on the ingredients for healing practices across cultures as:

- The therapeutic relationship
- A culturally congruent narrative
- A dedicated space
- A prescription for some action.

Clarkson advocates that different kinds of relationships are used for different clients. This tends to echo the ways of working with efficacy reviewed in this chapter. The issue is a complex one, as different kinds of needs are present in many situations concerning efficacy. These include those of the client, the therapist and, often, the organisation funding or coordinating the provision of therapy. Arts therapists seem to attempt to find a way of working that relates both to the client's situation and needs and to the demands of an institution or setting. In this work, though, it is important to bear in mind the challenges that have been raised in this section. There can be the temptation within some settings, and within some client–therapist relationships, to need to feel that there can be unquestionable certainty about a particular approach to evaluating efficacy. As this chapter has shown, there are important doubts, questions and ambiguities that are necessarily a part of the therapeutic relationship. Perhaps the most useful thing about such voices, is that they should be with all those looking at efficacy to remind us of the subtlety and complexity of relationships involving therapy and the arts.

Crudeness and possibility

Questions and concerns follow on from these basic points about efficacy and outcomes. As we have seen, then, some have argued that the tools used for the evaluation of efficacy are too crude, too partial to try to account for what happens in an arts therapy process. Others have commented in particular on the difficulty of assessing both the complexities of the therapeutic relationship and the arts process within therapy. Feder and Feder, for example, point out that some arts therapists work with clients for whom areas such as diagnosis are 'irrelevant': 'It is questionable how much value will be derived from a "diagnosis" of a client who has come to therapy in order to cope with the trauma of a messy divorce or the insecurities and fears floating in the wake of domestic violence' (Feder and Feder, 1998: 267). They point out that where, for example, normative tests designed to discover how a patient compares with other patients might be useful for some clients in some contexts, this is by no means the case for all therapeutic situations.

Others have been similarly reluctant to conform to perceived rigidities of 'objective measurement'. Grainger has pointed out that the nature of the therapy itself resists scientific approaches (2000: 3). He says that 'dramatherapy is itself an open-ended, divergent experience, one best evaluated in terms of the uniqueness of what has been produced rather than by the application of a common standard of direction and degree of behavioural change' (Grainger, 1990: 100–1). Rowan says that it is important to be critical of the term 'outcome'. He says that if the outcome of therapy is that someone stops washing their hands thirty times a day, then this is easy to check and follow up. However, if an outcome is that 'someone gets in touch with her real self' (Rowan, 1983: 150), it is much harder to pin this down and measure it. He adds that the search for outcomes is often a search for numbers, and the search for numbers is a search for things to count, and that human beings are not things.

Many arts therapists, though, have pointed out that it is necessary to find a systematic way to understand change, one that looks towards understanding how effects can be acknowledged, or reproduced and communicated to those outside the therapy session. They look for the best possible way to find processes and languages to do this. Males and Males (1982), for example, talk about their understanding of efficacy based on their research into art therapy with people with learning difficulties. They refer to Ulman (2001) and the definition of therapeutic procedures as those designed to assist favourable changes in personality, or in living, that will outlast the session itself. Their work reflected this, focusing on looking at whether the effects of art therapy outlasted the session itself.

Some practitioners would, however, echo the Danish music therapist Mqller when she asks for standardised forms of assessment and evaluation to provide 'more homogenous quality and a greater credibility' as a consolidated form of treatment. She says that 'working in an interdisciplinary team of physio- and occupational therapists, psychologists and pedagogues (who all assess using recognised tests), I feel an urgent need for us to have a standardised form for assessment' (Mqller, in Wigram, 2002: 24). This seems not to be a desire to have something because other therapies have it, but rather recognising a theme that has been present in much of this chapter. This is the need to be able to develop the nature of understanding and communicating efficacy in the arts therapies to clients, funding organisations and other professions.

Much work has been done in the past twenty years, especially, but this area is central to the next phase of the arts therapies and is vital to the future. The need is to continue to develop the diversity of ways of understanding the process and outcomes of the arts therapies; to recognise the complexities of the arts and science connection in the processes and languages; to be as true as possible to what it is that is resulting in change, and identify how best to look at this and to communicate it. The need is to continue to create shoes that fit our feet in this area, rather than to try to fit our feet into others' existing shoes – this might damage the feet, and hinder movement!

It is also vital to continue to create dialogue, and this is at the heart of what Mqller is talking about – the need to acknowledge and represent the *differences* of the arts therapies in relation to other models or approaches to change and efficacy. It is also vital to keep the voice and presence of the artist part of the arts therapist and client in organisations or settings that can often be ill at ease with the ambiguity, idiosyncrasy and mutability of the arts.

Some, such as Bunt, have echoed this, and argued for the kinds of initiatives and dialogues that this chapter has illustrated. Though the danger is that the complexities of artistic process can be reduced to 'almost naïve proportions' in quantifying results, it is possible to bring different strategies and approaches to find a way of converging to increase 'our understanding of the whole picture' (1990: 6). Bunt has said research in the arts therapies offers the opportunity to bring together areas often kept apart in the Cartesian mind/body split 'that still permeates many of the debates within healthcare and our growing research tradition' (Bunt, 1990: 2): the irrational, feeling-centred and bodily versus the clarity of mind and drive for rational order. He adds 'it is surely a sign of good health to blend objective knowledge with subjective feeling' (Bunt, 1990: 4). Edwards echoes this saying that, whilst outside the humanities and social sciences qualitative research continues to be taken less seriously than quantitative research, it is important for the arts therapies to acknowledge that, whilst a quantitative approach has value, that of the qualitative reflects the nature of key aspects of the arts therapies experience: 'by engaging in a more human and co-operative relationship with the "subjects" of our research we might be better placed to understand and give clinical experience meaning' (Edwards, 1999: 4).

He adds that objectivity in the form of scientific research can help understand part of, but not all of, arts therapy processes. It is important that the wildness and elusive qualities of creativity and individuality are not lost within systems that can often seem uncomfortable and antithetical to their presence. However, much has changed or is changing in areas of healthcare provision, and the arts therapies are part of that change. As a number of arts therapists referred to in this chapter have advocated, it is essential to the development and growth of the therapies that dialogue remains open.

The UK Standing Committee on the Arts in Prisons shows how the different strands of work relating to efficacy can meet:

> The preparing of case notes, the development of a diary of philosophical and clinical considerations, the collection of background statistics on inmates using an arts therapy, a written review of service developments, and audio-visual records of products and processes of sessions are all valid forms of data collection. From such record keeping research questions can be raised and answered by subjective and objective appraisal. Findings can then be disseminated . . .
>
> (SCAP, 1997: 33)

CONCLUSION

In her work, *Human Minds: An Exploration* (1992), Donaldson discusses how Western cultures and attitudes have narrowed the way it enables the human mind and the world can interact. She analyses other ways of being and relating that she sees as broader and richer, that 'expand the repertoire' of relationship (1992: 190). As an example, she draws extensively on the experiences and writings of Milner, described by Case and Dalley as 'a figurehead and a person to emulate for many art therapists' (Case and Dalley, 1992: 81). It may seem strange to cite a description of viewing seagulls first published in the 1930s by Milner (under the pseudonym Joanna Field), within a chapter largely dealing with clinical evidence, but I think it's important to do so and to return to the image of flying from page 218..

Donaldson amplifies her concerns about aspects of Western contemporary modes of relating by drawing on Milner's distinction between what she called 'narrow focus attention', and a different way of being. Narrow focus attention selects what serves its immediate interests and ignores the rest.

> One day I was idly watching some gulls as they soared high overhead. I was not interested, for I recognised them as 'just gulls' and vaguely watched first one then another. Then all at once something seemed to have opened. My idle boredom with the familiar became a deep-breathing peace and delight, and my whole attention was gripped by the pattern and rhythm of their flight, their slow sailing which had become a quiet dance.
>
> (Milner, 1986: 71)

Milner likens it to a questing beast keeping its nose close to the trail. What she calls wide attention becomes possible only when these 'questing purposes' cease to be in control, 'to attend to something and yet want nothing from it, these seemed to be the essentials of the second way of perceiving' (1986: 186). Donaldson comments on Milner's experience of herself and the gulls in the following way: 'In brief, what happened was that, quite unexpectedly, she saw the birds in a new way that changed idle boredom into "deep breathing peace and delight" ' (Donaldson, 1992: 239). Donaldson goes on to argue for the importance of the intuitive, for the importance of feeling as a way of perceiving, and for the importance of narrow focused ways of perceiving in addition to this 'wider' perception. The narrowness of expecting what was to be perceived stopped the actual seeing of what was there: 'vivid pictures of what might happen shut me off from perceiving what actually did happen' (Milner, 1986: 186). Donaldson goes on to stress the importance of acknowledging this way of relating, the 'reality of feeling' and experiences that transcend the personal, 'these are facts of the greatest importance for human lives and for the possible development of human societies' (Donaldson, 1992: 244). In the pressure for precise, highly selective ways of looking, and the drawing of conclusions based on these narrow focused notions of evidence and concern, such a plea for the gaps in many aspects of Western attitude so prevalent in much healthcare is an important one to bear in mind.

McNiff (1998) argues that arts therapy outcomes will 'always involve personal assessments of feelings, perceptions, and interpretations of value. Art therapy procedures will probably never be able to meet the strict standards of scientific reliability and this does not have to be perceived as a detriment' (McNiff, 1998: 202). He proposes that there is an increasing realisation that effective therapeutic outcomes are achieved through many approaches that operate outside what he calls 'the realm of conventional medical and psychological treatment'. He goes on to add that 'the creative arts therapies have made significant contributions to this expansion of curative possibilities' (McNiff, 1998: 207).

As the examples in this chapter have shown, though, the ways the arts therapies are responding to the question of efficacy are varied and creative. We have seen how case study, retrospective review of pictures, and the creation of dialogue between arts therapies and other disciplines are all addressing the complex question of how and whether change occurs in the arts therapies. As the disciplines develop further, and as clients and therapists work together to discover more about both the potentials and ways of describing the methods and approaches, the nature and value of change in the arts therapies will become ever more established and articulate. This will not, and should not, happen by the arts therapies using one approach or framework; rather, as Grainger says, 'we need to have several different languages at our command' (1999: 143). This chapter has given a picture of some of the different languages that the arts therapies are using to discover and communicate their efficacy.

17 Conclusion: from the triangular relationship to the active witness: core processes in the arts therapies

INTRODUCTION

An art therapist sits in a room with her client, between them a piece of paper – unused as yet. A dance movement therapist and a client are about to enter an improvised sequence of movements together. In a studio a dramatherapist and group stand in a circle, waiting for a theme to emerge. A client in music therapy begins to try out different instruments, passing them to the therapist. Between therapist, client and art form, in each of these situations, is the tension, the space, for something to happen and for change to occur. As we have seen, this 'potential space' is at the core of the arts therapies.

The opportunities that artistic expression and arts processes create within a therapeutic space and within a therapeutic relationship offer unique possibilities for clients. At the heart of the encounter are the ways in which feeling, creativity and thought combine to explore past, present and future living in the potential between client, therapist and art form. Any description can only be a metaphor for the true process, but this book has tried to show how these forces have come to be understood, and how they can be used. The descriptions and discussions have looked at specific aspects of arts therapy work and form. This chapter tries to summarise the explorations within this book concerning what makes the arts therapies so innovative and so effective. It tries to encapsulate the specific and unique ways in which therapeutic change can occur in the arts therapies. In brief: what is special about the arts therapies? What is it that is especially useful for clients?

It's important to try to find a balance between creating a language that obscures or is over-technical – and a way of describing that is precise enough, that does justice to the processes at work. The following, then, is a series of 'core processes' that tries to be precise, without creating a way of describing how something works which becomes opaque or baffling in its complexity. Nor is the idea of these 'core processes' one that is designed to be prescriptive, with fixed ideas about how they should be applied. Each therapist will use their creativity to relate to how they would be reflected in developing work with clients. Many arts therapists would find Greek dramatherapist Couroucli-Robertson's position a familiar one. Areas of process and practice are common; however, each encounter has an original, fresh creative component: 'Through the years I have developed a personal mode of working which I try to adapt to different clients in order to meet their own individual needs' (Couroucli-Robertson, 1997: 143). The definitions also try to do justice to the things the arts therapies have in common, whilst not denying the differences between art, music, drama and dance movement.

The arts therapies core processes

These processes are:

Artistic projection

The triangular relationship

Perspective and distance

Embodiment

Non-verbal experience

The playful space and the informed player

The participating artist-therapist

The active witness

ARTISTIC PROJECTION

A client creates something in an arts therapy session, or there is the intention or resistance to creating something. Whether art work is being created or not, the act of creation through an art form is always immanent or present. This can involve an image, an enactment, a sound or a movement. The process of creation, and whatever is created within the empty paper sheet or the empty movement space, has a therapeutic importance. This importance arises out of the relationship between the client, their creation and the therapist. One key element of this relationship concerns the way the client connects with the work they produce: what the product becomes to them, and the effect the product has on them.

Authors such as McCully (1987) have paralleled aspects of archaic art and Rorschach inkblot tests in terms of offering what can be called 'projective possibilities'. Wilshire echoes this, in talking about theatre, when he says that people can see themselves reflected in the interactions between characters on stage. He adds that in seeing aspects of oneself reflected a change can occur: 'to come to see oneself is to effect change in oneself in the very act of seeing' (Wilshire, 1982: 5). This 'seeing' is equally true for many art forms and is relevant to understanding one of the processes common to all the arts therapies. This concerns the process of *artistic projection*.

I have described such projection in dramatherapy in the following way:

> The process by which clients project aspects of themselves or their experience into theatrical experience or dramatic materials or into enactment, and thereby externalise inner conflicts. A relationship between the inner state of the client and the external dramatic form is established and developed through action. The dramatic expression enables change through the creation of perspective, along with the opportunity for exploration and insight through the enactment of projected material.
>
> (Jones, 1996: 100)

For classic Freudian or analytic thinking, processes such as projection and projective identification are primarily defensive. Analytic psychotherapist Theilgaard, in *Shakespeare Comes to Broadmoor*, describes this projection in the following terms: 'specific impulses, wishes, aspects of the self are imagined as being located outside the self' (Theilgaard, 1992: 164). She goes on to describe projective identification: 'This process was first described by Klein (1946) as a primitive form of defence mechanism, which enables the individual to project undesirable parts of the self into the object and thereby control it from within' (Theilgaard, 1992: 166). She adds that the projector has the unconscious fantasy that they are getting rid of an unwanted, or endangered, part of the self. Thielgaard talks about the ways in which drama can parallel the process of the Rorschach test. The Rorschach test uses ink-blot shapes as 'a unique vehicle for observing aspects of both perceptual and verbal processes. It illustrates how an individual structures the inkblot, so that we are given an impression of the perceiver's inner world' (1992: 170). She points to the ways in which the stimuli of images and created art forms can offer 'an excellent instrument for projection' (1992: 171). For the arts therapies a vital relationship is created between inner emotional states and external forms and processes in this way.

Projection allied to expression through the arts within the arts therapies operates as a developing, ongoing process. The client projects material into the art form or process. This enables the expression of material and also, crucially, the opportunity for *exploration*. Material that had previously been held unexpressed within the client can be expressed and held by the art form or process. This expression through the arts can be a conscious decision made by a client in order to explore an issue or area, or it can occur in a less direct, or deliberate, way. The client might make a deliberate decision to create an image or a role play or movement sequence relating to a specific issue or aspect of their life. They might, alternatively, be engaged in the creation of images or work without deliberately naming an area or issue: the making of images or movements without a conscious intent or direction. In both situations the client relates to the art processes or products through artistic projection.

This expression can lead to, or allow, exploration. The art form and the relationship within the therapy can encourage the client to work with the material. This exploration can lead to a new awareness, or relationship, to the material brought. This new position can then be integrated into the client's experience of the issue. Dramatherapist Mond, practising in Israel, quotes one of her 12-year-old clients who had been involved in a traumatic road accident, who talks of their experience in a way that illuminates this process of artistic projection: 'Dramatherapy is about touching and playing with objects, drawing and telling stories and making up plays about them. This lets you collect up and get out the frightening feelings from inside you and doing this helps you to be calm' (in Mond, 1994: 184). UK art therapist Levens illuminates the ways in which this process can release, contain and transform in describing her work with clients with eating disorders:

> Art may be seen as an extension of the self and as a psychological double with the property to 'mirror' the self. The art therapist needs to be aware that this reflection is not a static statement of the patients' inner world, but that he or she, unintrusively, may help the patients to use their work as an on-going process, to introduce the concept of time and space and continuity, in which their work can develop and change. In essence, patients for whom there is a lack of stable bodily self may be able to use art therapy, particularly the development of line and form, as an external structure enabling the development of a more stable internal structure.
>
> (Levens, 1990: 283–4)

I would argue that the projection into the object, art form or arts process in the arts therapies need not only concern aspects of the self. Important others or aspects of their life experience, or the client's relationship with the therapist, can also be projected into the image or movement or sound. The processes described by Levens and Mond, and this broader understanding of the way clients can project into art forms, are similar. In this way artistic projection is an ongoing process: one whereby expression is connected to exploration and the development of a new perspective through this expression and exploration.

The presence of the art form and the client's involvement through artistic projection offers specific opportunities within therapy. The use of artistic expression might enable discoveries, or create connections for the client that minimise the cognitive, discursive processes that are often associated with verbal language. This may allow the associative freedom of image creation, or movement, and the particular combinations of feeling and creativity that art processes can facilitate. This process can be seen as one that allows expression and exploration of material, followed by a new relationship to the original issues. The process of introjection allows the client to integrate the exploration back into their experience of themselves or their lives, and to link the discoveries or processes to their sense of who they are and how they live.

Artistic projection offers the client the opportunity for involvement in the issues they bring to therapy, for seeing and exploring material. It is the process that enables the client to become powerfully engaged in the arts products and processes within the therapy. The client can use art, music, drama and movement processes and products within the therapeutic relationship to express and explore personal material or life issues. Artistic projection as a term sums up the particular qualities of painting, role play, musical improvisation or bodily movement to engage, reflect, hold and transform emotional, psychological and communicative experiences for the client within the arts therapies.

THE TRIANGULAR RELATIONSHIP

As I have discussed, many forms of therapy involve the therapist and client talking together. This form of communication and relating is the basis of several elements that are seen to combine to bring about change. Talking is the primary way client and therapist communicate; it forms the main route through which the relationship emerges. The arts therapies profoundly alter this.

In all the accounts of arts therapy given so far, one of the themes which has emerged is the notion of *a triangular relationship*. The therapy is not about the therapist and client alone – the arts process and product have a key role to play within their relationship. Particularly in art therapy, it is this which often is referred to as a 'triangular relationship'. One important way this happens is that an art form enables something different to occur as an arts process or created product enters the therapy room. Some arts therapists, as we have seen, place an emphasis on the presence of the art object or product within therapy. Others assert that this triangularity need not rely on a created product alone; they argue that the arts process itself, of dancing, music, drama or art, creates an element additional to the therapist and client. Either way, the client and therapist's experience of therapy is shifted in crucial ways by the presence of this 'third'.

An object may be created or used within the therapy room and within the therapeutic relationship. In art therapy this can be a made object such as a painting or a sculpture; in dramatherapy objects such as toys or puppets can be; in music an instrument can be used; in dance movement therapy cloth can be moved with, or masks worn. It's not always the client who creates or uses these objects or artefacts. As we have seen, in some forms of the arts therapies the therapist paints, dances, makes music or acts. This involves the therapist's using their creativity through participation in relation to the client, and there is a mutuality in making or using something. Such objects have been emphasised by some arts therapists as a *third element* in the therapeutic relationship. The idea is that this third presence alters the dyad of therapist and client.

This occurs in three main ways. One way, for therapists who work with transference, is that the object alters the transference and counter-transference process. The second is that there is something made or used which can be discussed. The third is that therapist and client can use the object together. Here Evans and Dubowski show one aspect of this triangle, how arts process and materials impact on therapy with children on the autistic spectrum:

> The art materials and art-making processes are an integral part of the art therapy from the beginning of treatment. As such they are one of the most important elements in the art therapy as they provide an indirect focus and shared engagement between therapist and client. By directing social interaction through a focus on art-making activity, a form of relating which children with autism can tolerate, and build up a tolerance for, becomes established.
>
> (Evans and Dubowski, 2001: 100)

Music therapist Levinge summarises her practical understanding of the triangular relationship as follows:

> Whether working with a child or adult, my primary concern is to use music to enable both the patient and me to find a way of being together – that is, to develop a relationship – which makes sense to us both. The three elements involved in this process are myself as therapist, the instruments and the music. The ways in which these are used depends [*sic*] on the nature of the patient's problem.
>
> (Levinge, 1996: 237)

Here the emphasis is on the *process* of music, rather than on an object only, as the third presence. Here the triangularity is created by the involvement of an object *and* by the presence of the arts process. The arts form and arts products allow an additional factor to enter the relationship between therapist and client. The idea is that the arts can provide the client with an opportunity that is *additional* to the focus on the therapist. This allows the client to express personal material into and through the object or creative process, for example.

The creation of the art object or product allows therapist and client to explore material together in a variety of ways. These varied expressions allow different avenues to be explored through artistic forms – until the client finds a way of expression that fits their emotional and psychological needs. Schaverien discusses this from a Jungian perspective, talking about archetypal imagery:

> When archetypal imagery appears in pictures the fire which already exists

may be intensified, or one that apparently did not previously exist sparks into life. These pictures produce an empowered form of relating that draws the artist/patient and the therapist/viewer into a deep transference to the picture itself; and also to each other through the picture. In these pictures, that which usually remains unseen, unstated, even unconscious, between people is evident and cannot completely be denied. The purpose of therapy is to mediate in the divided, inner world of the patient, and the picture offers a means of such mediation.

(Schaverien, 1992: 23)

So, here the presence of the art object and involvement of the art form has a powerful impact on the therapeutic process. The relationship between client and therapist can happen through the object, for example. As discussed earlier, within arts therapies practised within an analytic framework, the creation and presence of an art object such as a painting or clay sculpture, or in music therapy the presence of a musical instrument, is seen to affect the transference process. So, for example, the client might have a transference to a picture they have made, and can make use of the perspective of being able to stand back and observe as a viewer. The client–therapist–object relationship is seen by some art therapists as an arena where what is described as a 'transformation of the transference' can occur. As described earlier, for example, destructive attacks can take place towards and through the object. So the arts therapist role broadens or differs – they can be directly engaged in the transference process or they can, in addition, become a companion in the client's process of analysis in relation to the object created in the therapy. Within this way of viewing the triangular relationship the object changes the function of the therapist: she or he is not the sole object of transferential processes.

The triangular relationship refers to the special relationship that can occur within the arts therapies between client, therapist and the object, arts expression or process. The relationship is one that offers the opportunity for the client to explore material through an agent between themselves and the therapist. It can act in a number of ways. These include the art object becoming a container for emotions, or a way of enabling communication through something rather than directly to the therapist. For some therapists the triangular relationship is seen as a part of communication or the transference and counter-transference relationship. A created object or art form can hold some of the feelings between client and therapist. As such it offers unique properties in mediating and working with the therapeutic process.

PERSPECTIVE AND DISTANCE

Sometimes, when someone is in trouble and comes to therapy they can feel overwhelmed by their problems. It's as if they are completely inhabited by them, it's the foremost thing they're encountering in their life. Maybe they have been living with something for so long it's hard to see any other way of living. Maybe they feel they have no strategy to stop what their experience of themselves is. Perhaps the past feels as if it has happened and it's stuck, fixed, immovable. Others might feel frozen in some way, cut off from their life, themselves or their past. They might deny any connection – they might be experiencing physical pain for which there's no medical reason, but which may be a cut-off expression of buried emotional, or psychological, pain. Perspective or distance can be essential elements within arts therapy work, and can be vital in assisting clients in such situations.

One of the ideas that is common to the arts therapies, and is described in different ways by different practitioners, can be thought of as 'perspective'. Looked at in one way, all therapy can offer perspective if that is seen to mean some time to be apart from the everyday run of life, in a special space and in a relationship with the therapist, or with other clients, that is devoted to exploring and changing. Distance and perspective here, though, means that by working in the arts in therapy it is possible for the client to achieve *a particular state or relationship to themselves and their experiences*. This has been described as 'aesthetic distance' (Landy, 1993).

As we've seen in many case examples within this book, one of the important facets of all the arts therapies involves the way a client becomes engaged in creating, in the art form. This involves both the creative process as the arts expression emerges, or occurs, and the therapeutic relationship between client, art form and therapist. If, for example, I have painted an image, it can both connect deeply with something that has happened to me, or can express or explore an aspect of my sense of who I am. Expression in the arts therapies can involve many different relationships to creating. It can involve a momentary spontaneous movement or a choreographed piece of dance. It can vary from a briefly made mark, through to a painting which is worked on over a long period of time. What most matters is that the client can become creatively and emotionally connected to an expression described earlier as artistic projection. This expression is seen to be related to the reasons the client is coming to therapy.

Dramatherapist Landy has developed the theory of aesthetic distance in the arts therapies. This involves the idea that overdistanced people keep rigid boundaries between self and other; the underdistanced person identifies themselves too readily with others, losing a sense of clear boundary between self and other. The notion of distancing can involve aiming for a balance between the two: a balance between self and other where the boundaries are flexible and change is possible. This point or state is described by Landy as 'aesthetic distance':

> When the individual is at a point midway between two extremes of overdistance and underdistance, he is at aesthetic distance ... At aesthetic distance, the individual achieves a balanced relationship ... he is able to experience a confluence of thought and feeling, to 'see

feelingly', like the blinded Gloucester in *King Lear* . . . one retains a piece of the overdistanced, cognitive observer and a piece of the underdistanced, affective actor.

(Landy, 1986: 100)

It is this state that the arts therapies can offer to the client. Perspective and distance concern:

- the ways in which arts expressions create perspective
- the ways in which arts expressions connect a client's life experience with the material in the session
- the way in which the expression allows new opportunities to achieve a different perspective for the client.

Expression through the art form and process within therapy enables the client to take part in something that is both *of* their lives, but is also *separate* from their lives. To create an image, or a dance, based on their lives is a part, and an extension, of their life. However, the fact that it *is* an expression created in an art form allows the particular qualities that artistic experience brings to be put in contact with the issue or life material.

For a client in the arts therapies the issue of distance or perspective can operate in a variety of ways. For the client who is distanced or separated from their life experiences and feelings this can be a way to increase engagement – the painter rather than the viewer, the actor rather than the audience. For the client who feels overwhelmed, the experience can help to engage with the parts of themselves as viewer, listener and audience and to look at their experience in a more dispassionate way.

The notion of distance means that the client can arrive at an expression that allows them to become maker *and* reader, painter *and* viewer, dancer *and* audience member to their experiences. The artistic experience within a therapeutic framework can assist the client in creating perspective, which can assist them in engaging with their lives, or parts of themselves, in a different way. Philosopher Langer, writing about music, talks of detachment and attachment in a way that summarises a key aspect of this process: 'Music is not self-expression, but formulation and representation of emotions, moods, mental tensions and resolutions – a "logical picture" of sentient, responsive life, a source of insight, not a plea for sympathy.' She adds that when 'psychical distance' has been achieved, the content has been symbolised for us, and what it invites is not emotional response but insight: 'Psychical distance is the experience of apprehending through symbol what was not articulated before' (Langer, 1952: 216, 223).

It is this process which the arts therapies can offer the client. The arts process within the therapeutic relationship can enable the client to discover a needed change. They can discover the ways in which by becoming artist and viewer, actor and audience to their lives they can discover a new relationship to themselves. This changing of roles, this creation of different perspectives, can transform the way they see themselves and their life. The arts enable this process within the therapy owing to the specific demands and possibilities that artistic processes offer.

EMBODIMENT

Embodiment in the arts therapies concerns the ways in which someone's body relates to their identity. The body is also seen as a primary means by which communication occurs between one person and another. This is through gesture, facial expression or voice, for example (Elam, 1991). Embodiment in the arts therapies embraces the ways in which clients communicate both consciously and unconsciously through their body. Sociologists have considered how identity is connected to 'the ways in which the body is presented in social space ... some consider that the self presents selected personae in different situations and arrives at a sense of identity through bodily expression and behaviour in relationship to others' (Jones, 1996: 113).

For many clients 'knowing with the body' is something that is underused or undervalued. For others, for whom verbal language is not the best means of exploration or communication, non-verbal work rooted in physical experience is an important part of the arts therapy process. Courtney, for example, speaks of the importance of knowledge 'gained not through detachment, but through an actual, practical and bodily involvement' (Courtney, 1988: 144).

Issues can be encountered and realised through physical embodiment – expressed and explored through the body. Part of this involves the physical encounter of the active involvement in an arts experience such as dance. The client can combine physical engagement and mental reflection or analysis, connecting the knowledge to be gained through sensory and emotional feeling with the knowledge to be gained by more cognitive perception.

The arts therapies can also focus on aiding the client to inhabit or use their body more effectively. This might concern how clients communicate with others, for example, described by Jennings as individuals who have difficulty 'in using their bodies in positive, effective, creative ways' (Jennings, 1973: 27). Another area concerns the way in which the client takes on a different identity within the arts therapy. In dramatherapy or dance movement therapy, the self may be transformed by taking on a different identity, or encountering forms of expression the client does not normally allow themselves, or that they are not allowed by the strictures and constraints given them by society. This physical transformation can enable insight, new perspectives and release that can result in changes in the client's life outside the exploration in the arts therapy, in the client's life as a whole. This can happen, for example, in creating a character in dramatherapy or exploring the way movement relationships develop in dance movement therapy.

An experience brought to therapy might be only or best expressed through the body. Verbal language might not be able to describe the experience – it

might not yet have words, for example. The work with the b⟨
might be the only way a client can bring the material into t⟨
space. Alternatively, the client might not be able to use verba⟨
therefore physically based work and communication might ⟨
which the therapist and client find a way to communicate usir⟨
of the client. Examples of this might include clients with ⟨.. .⟩
difficulties or clients with Alzheimer's.

Another aspect concerns the exploration of the personal, social and political forces and influences that affect the client's experience of their body. Here
the arts therapy process and space offer the opportunity to explore through
different expressive forms areas such as body image, or emotional traumas
related to the body. Here, for example, the client might create a life-size image
depicting their feelings about their body, or a sculpture of a part or whole of
themselves; they might paint their body, or explore material physically
through movement and sensory work.

Thus embodiment offers a perspective on experience that allows the client
to bring or access material physically, to explore bodily experience through
the body within the therapy space. It enables client and therapist to work
through aspects of the arts that involve embodiment to create an arena for
expression, exploration and change. Some would go so far as to say that
specific aspects of experience can be expressed only through the body – that
words cannot effectively engage in the same way:

> Some theorists would propose that communication through creative art
> forms is the only way of giving expression to the material of primary
> process, and that the use of discursive language must always be restrict-
> ive. Certainly for all of us our bodies and their movement become
> symbols for much of our feeling and our experience of groups is felt in
> the bones more profoundly than it can be described in words.
>
> (Holden, 1990: 270)

NON-VERBAL EXPERIENCE

As we've seen in the descriptions of the core processes so far, the use of an art
form – painting, playing a role, creating music – creates a language that differs
from the spoken word. It offers a different way of encountering the clients'
experiences; it offers a specific way of communicating those experiences. By
'encounter' I mean that an art form depicts experience in a way that differs
from spoken language alone.

For some people words have particular properties – they can, for example,
feel very 'direct'. I find this a strange idea – as an art product can also feel
very direct. I would rather say that the directness is different. By this I mean
that the art form enables a specific kind of 'in the moment experience'
through the creation of artistic, physical engagement in the room with the

herapist. An image or sound or enactment of an experience is different from a verbal description alone.

Aldridge (1996: 268) points to the value of music being 'without the lexical demands of language' as a key factor in communicational improvement. The art form allows the emphasis of communication through rhythm, articulation, sequence, pitch, timbre and physical expression through means such as hand movement and gesture. He points to research indicating that musical dialogue in the music therapy relationship seems to bring about improvement in the ability to form and maintain relationships in other areas of someone's life.

Kristeva has attempted to describe a difference between verbal and what she describes as 'transverbal' communication:

> It seems important to me never to neglect the transverbal dimension in communication, to take into account the visual factor, the plastic aspect of the icon as signifier, which lends itself more readily to playfulness, to invention, to interpretation, than verbal thought, which can have a repressive intellectual weight.
>
> (Kristeva, 1986: 44)

The arts-based engagement between client and therapist can mean that the client becomes an expressive, creative, active partner in treatment. This can affect the relationship: one aspect is described by Sharma as involving the client becoming 'much more active than most orthodox doctors would envis- age or desire. In such a case the term "patient" perhaps requires revision; sick people "suffer" their sickness, but are not "passive" in their suffering' (Sharma, 1994: 101). It allows the client to bring material through image, enactment, movement or sound, not through verbal language alone. This enables opportunities to encompass experiences for which words are not appropriate, or cannot be found by the client. Clients may feel that words disclose in a particular way that they feel uncomfortable with, whereas images or sound contact experiences in a way which allows expression.

McFee and Degge (1977) talk about the difference between *making* involving the arts and *thinking* about something. When people make art they are symbolising their experiences in an art form. They say that the observation of the art enables new insights about their experiences to occur:

> How is this different from just thinking about experiences? It enables people to express what they might not be able to say with words. When people say that they are at a 'loss for words' they may mean that they have had an experience that is so rich in details, in meaning, or in emotional quality that they cannot describe it. If people have learned to use art expressively, the essence of their response can be expressed graphically. They can refer back to their art many times to analyse the ideas and emo- tions they expressed, thus gaining insights into their own development.
>
> (McFee and Degge, 1977: 273)

Murphy (1998) talks of the particular use of visual images in relation to memory and certain kinds of experience relating to childhood sexual abuse:

> The use of visual language could be said to have particular relevance: research shows that traumatic memories are encoded in a 'primitive visually-based memory that records an event as a whole' (Johnson, 1987). Verbalising experiences may present problems because ... the abuse happened at a pre-verbal level of development (Young, 1992) or the child may have been warned by the perpetrator of life-threatening consequences if they speak about the abuse.
>
> (Murphy, 1998: 10)

She argues that art therapy can access material in a way that enables boundaries to be maintained. The properties of art materials, for example, lend themselves to expressing and exploring non-verbal experiences and can facilitate the expression of suppressed feelings. Expression and exploration can be followed by integration: 'the embodied image can contain projected feelings and become a scapegoat which can be preserved, or destroyed without harming anyone' (Murphy, 1998: 11).

Here, the non-verbal nature of aspects of the arts therapy experience is seen to offer particular opportunities to the client. These opportunities relate to areas such as communication, and the client's experiences of themselves and of others that are rooted in image, sound and bodily movement. As Jennings *et al.* (1994) say, 'most psychotherapy and psychoanalysis relies on existing language and especially the language of words; however, it is possible to discover completely new means of communication through intensive work on the body and voice' (Jennings *et al.*, 1994: 105). Such innovative practice can offer opportunities to explore particular kinds of experience that either do not relate to words or are not ready for verbalisation, but which need to be communicated and worked on within the therapeutic relationship.

THE PLAYFUL SPACE AND THE INFORMED PLAYER

As we have seen in Chapter 13, studies of play have highlighted its link to change. They focus on play's capacity to reflect life experiences: to offer opportunities to create states that are *apart from, yet connected to* life outside the play. Research has also shown that, when engaged in play, our ways of relating to events, people and ourselves can change, 'a generalised transfer of a playful attitude or a flexible response set from the play to problem-solving situations. Hence children with play experiences may be more flexible, curious, spontaneous and interested in the task' (Jones, 1996). Secondly, there may be a more specific transfer of novel responses generated by investigation and experimentation in play. Children with play experiences were found to make more use of previous play activities in their responses on separate divergent thinking tasks (Courtney, 1988). They were transferring some of the things they had discovered in play activities to other situations in their lives. The cognitive skill of shifting one's thinking from concrete to abstract during play may be similar to the skill required to generate a variety of novel responses on a divergent thinking task (Johnson, 1976: 69).

As we saw, analyst Winnicott has been influential in the ways that some arts therapists have grown to understand their relationship with clients in terms of the idea of a 'play space'. His ideas are sometimes used as a starting point to explain the arts therapy space, the nature of the contact between therapist, client and art form. His emphasis on the importance and function of play – between baby and mother, for instance – has been linked to some of the discoveries and ways of connecting which have emerged in the arts therapies. He has also said that therapy is 'to do with two people playing' (Winnicott, 1974: 44). Minsky (1996), along with others, draws attention to Winnicott's connecting the child in play with their mother to the patient's relationship to the therapist. Minsky links both to artistic processes: 'Winnicott took the view that play, and the artistic imagination and enjoyment of art, take place in the same psychical space' (Minsky, 1996: 123). This notion is interestingly developed in Winnicott's suggestion that the division into inner and outer reality is inadequate – that there is a third *intermediate state* where phantasy and reality meet. This idea of an intermediate space is an important one for the arts therapies.

Blatner's definition of creativity is one that is useful to consider in relation to the idea of the playful state. He says that creativity refers 'not simply to art or science, but to the activities of everyday life, in relationships, in societal institutions, and in personal and spiritual development' (Blatner, 1997: 152). The therapist and client inhabit a space where artistic expression and arts processes can enhance both client and therapist's creativity. The therapist and client play together – they enter a playful relationship where phenomena associated with play and playfulness can enter the therapy. This allows a *playful relationship* to occur. This is typified by flexibility: an experimental attitude where cause and effect can be considered, without the *actual consequences* that might occur in the client's life outside the therapy space. Cattanach describes this as an arena where it is possible to 'develop new meanings for ourselves uncluttered by the constraints of our own reality' (Cattanach, 1994: 34). In some situations the therapist and client can be seen as 'co-players' – joining in activities together. In others the therapist can *hold* the play space, maintaining boundaries, attention and, in some cases, adopting an interpretative role to enhance the discoveries and insights being made by the client. The relationship tends towards one where the arts therapist combines the perspectives described in Chapters 14 and 15 – of the teacher, artist and therapist elements of the arts therapist. This is brought to the playing role of the therapist within the play space. By this I mean that the arts therapist attempts to be an *informed player* – bringing their knowledge and creativity to the playful space for the benefit of the client.

The creation of a play space in the arts therapies involves the creation of an area set apart and yet related to the everyday world. It has specific rules and ways of being. The client in the arts therapies can be described as having a playful relationship with reality. This does not necessarily refer to a humorous response to real life. Playfulness in the arts therapies concerns the ways in which a client can enter into a state that has a special relationship to time, space and everyday rules and boundaries. This state can involve a heightened degree of spontaneity and creativity frequently associated with playing. This playful relationship with reality is characterised by a more creative, flexible attitude towards events, consequences and held ideas. This enables the client to adopt a playful, experimenting attitude towards themselves and their life experiences.

THE PARTICIPATING ARTIST-THERAPIST

Skaife asks the question: what does the art therapist do whilst the group is painting? She advocates the practice of the art therapist following the aesthetic activity of the clients 'to enter into the painter's experience of the members and to free associate with it – to enter into the painter's experience of making the painting as though one were making it oneself' (Skaife, 2000: 137). She says that in her experience she has found out a great deal about what is going on by working in this way. Art therapist Wadeson describes how a severely depressed man she was working with had become mute after a suicide attempt: 'I found that although a verbal interchange with him was impossible, we were able to communicate non-verbally by making several pictures together. In them I followed his lead, responding with colour, form, or symbol to his graphic ideas as we took turns adding to the picture' (Wadeson, 1980: 42).

This is parallel to the therapist taking on a role in dramatherapy or the therapist playing at the same time as the client in music therapy, or the dance movement therapist engaging in movement.

Callaghan allies the arts with innovation and creativity, saying that the creativity of the art form enhances the potentials of the relationship: 'the arts are inherently radical and encourage creative exploration. These factors can help individual movement psychotherapists to resolve conflicts between traditional models and the new approaches necessary for working with torture survivors and other similar groups' (Callaghan, 1996: 262). She cites as an example of this the fact that movement therapists participate in actively moving with clients, mirroring or taking part in their movement patterns or forms.

She says this mitigates the seemingly disengaged and passive quality of 'Western-style' therapists, which people from other cultures might find alien.

Callaghan (1996) talks about her dance movement work with survivors of torture. In this she talks about her work with a Kurdish man from Turkey and a man from Bangladesh who had virtually no verbal language in common. In a session they 'shuffled despondently from side to side doing Middle Eastern dance-like movements'. Callaghan describes how she shuffles with them. A brief comment from the clients about a feeling of going nowhere is followed by her introducing a slight change in the shuffle, moving into a 'regular, rhythmical side step'.

Callaghan sees her participation in dance with the clients as a crucial factor in the therapeutic process and in working with cultural difference.

The arts therapist can engage in the art form as a way of enhancing the client's experience of therapy, for example by moving with the client, or taking on roles, or playing music. The therapist can engage in an art form with the client as a way of communicating to the client, as seen in the case examples of Sophie and Client A in Chapters 14 and 15. In both situations the therapist, by making music, by creating with a client, formed routes of contact and transformation through active participation.

THE ACTIVE WITNESS

Casson (1997) says that being a witness to theatre 'is a strong stimulus and [is] able to bring into consciousness things we have either not experienced or have avoided or repressed. We may then be confronted with the shock of an encounter with both intrapsychic and interpsychic material that challenges us, facing us with imaginal and real truths' (Casson, 1997: 47). Grainger adds to this, observing that 'objectifying awareness by giving it an independent existence apart from oneself is recognised by creative therapists as inherently therapeutic . . . they locate healing in personal relationship – in other words, in "what is between" self and other. That they value objectified self-expression as a means of making contact with whatever is not the self, bridging the gap of otherness . . . the function of art to stand apart and involve at the same time' (Grainger, 1999: 11). In art therapy Schaverien has talked of a similar dynamic concerning the viewer and artist within the client:

> The picture offers an alternative external presence, it is an object which exists outside of the artist, and yet a part of her or him temporarily inhabits it. A split is made between the part of the person who makes the picture (the artist part) and the part that views the picture (the viewer).
>
> (Schaverien, 1992: 19)

The client is seen as being absorbed in the picture during the making as the 'artist part': then the viewer 'part' comes to the fore and the artist watches whilst the viewer responds. She allies this with the artist-self 'making a transference' to the picture, and the viewer-self being like the therapist 'bringing a more objective response to the picture' (Schaverien, 1992: 19). This aspect of the self looks at meaning and implications, making links. This is seen as contributing to the process of change, a self-analysis occurring, and as a particular way in which transference and counter-transference develop, linked to the witnessing aspect of the client's experience in therapy.

McClean talks about an aspect of this process in art therapy with clients who are dealing with drug dependency. In describing the specific benefits of art therapy she says that 'emotions can take on concrete aspects which are "contained" and held in imagery. This is particularly helpful for drug dependent clients who may feel chaotic or that they lack boundaries. Feelings are physically held up – "mirrored" – to the client through the image' (McClean, 1999: 203).

Witnessing, such as this process described by McClean, is the act of being an audience to oneself or to others, or to created work within the arts therapies. All these aspects can have an equal importance to the client. Within one session the client can be witnessed by other clients, or by the therapist, and in group therapy can be witness to others. Through empathy the therapeutic work done by others can have an effect on the client. This is true in all group therapy – but the engagement in the arts therapies can be different as the client might be actively role-playing someone in another client's life, or may be moving with them in a piece initiated by another client, they might be playing improvisational music or be engaged in group painting when another's mark has an impact on them whilst they are painting elsewhere, or are seeing someone make a mark over their own.

There are a series of possible witnessing interactions:

- A being witnessed by another group member or/and by the therapist
- A witnessing others or the therapist
- Clients witnessing themselves either through video, someone playing them in role or movement or music, or being represented by images or objects
- Clients witnessing arts work created by themselves or others.

Listening in music therapy can be seen to be a part of this process. Aldridge, for example, has written about the therapeutic aspects of listening to others' work in terms of personal–social interaction. He says that 'music therapy seems to have an effect on personal relationship, emphasising the positive benefits of active listening' (Aldridge, 1996: 262). He goes on to look at the possibilities of developmental change being linked to this witnessing. In particular he explores changes in hand–eye coordination and of non-verbal communication in children with learning difficulties, who were developmentally delayed:

The active playing of a drum demands that the child listens to the therapist who in turn is listening to, and playing for, her. This act entails the physical co-ordination of a musical intention within the context of a relationship. We would argue that this unity of the cognitive, gestural, emotional and representational is the strength of active music therapy for developmentally challenged children.

(Aldridge, 1996: 269)

Here, the process of communication is seen, in part, as the development of witnessing between client and therapist. Listening is an act of acknowledging the other, and is seen as an important building block in offering the opportunity for a developmentally delayed child to progress. The music therapy offers the opportunity for the child to experience being witnessed, and for the witness in them – the listener – to emerge. Listening to, and witnessing, others is cited by Skewes as one of the key aspects of music therapy: 'the mechanism of change in the music therapy group involves the creation of an attentive, listening and empathic environment . . . this requires the active listening of group members . . . people become more sensitive in their relationships with others' (Skewes, 2002: 50). Some see the acts of witnessing and being witnessed in a way that is considered as non-judgemental as being inherently therapeutic. Gobey (1996), for example, talks about the exploration of a conflict between boyfriend and girlfriend. A live sculpture is made of the situation. People from the group are placed in positions detailing roles, feelings and attitudes of those in the scene. People in the sculpture, and those watching, do not know whether people's positions represent individuals, or their attitudes and feelings:

Those watching are also unaware of the story or characters, although they will quickly pick up which of the figures are in conflict. They are forced to respond to the concentrated emotions of the image and interpret it 'from within'. In this way the sculpture is allowed to work on several levels: it can be seen as conflict between people in a social relationship or as an inner conflict between different parts of the self. The dispute between boyfriend and girlfriend might be felt as a family conflict, a political conflict, or an individual's struggle within themselves.

(Gobey, 1996: 29)

The facilitator does not allow judgements of 'right' or 'wrong' in discussion of the image from people participating and witnessing – the emphasis is on opening the image to the group for associations. If someone sees a mother-and-son conflict, the facilitator does not contradict this but encourages inclusion. The image might have meaning for the witness to explore and also the mother–son comment might open a new meaning for the person who created the sculpture. Gobey makes the important point that witnessing has effects for both those watching and those being watched:

No matter how much conflict and disintegration is going on, as long as it is going on 'on stage' – with a group of actors relating to each other – those watching have an integrated, and therefore comprehensible experience. The underlying message for all those involved is that conflict can be pictured, can be held, can be understood, without everything falling apart.

(Gobey, 1996: 30)

Here the notion is that being witnessed by another or others, if it occurs in a situation that can be experienced as supportive, can be important. In addition the experience for those witnessing in a group context can also be therapeutically important. This importance lies in the fact that the experience is shared and contained. The fear might be that the material cannot be expressed or seen without its being rejected, destructive or harmful. The experience of expressed material's being witnessed can be one of 'holding'. This means that the witness, whether this be fellow group members and therapist, or in one-to-one work with the therapist alone, can be a reparative experience or can be the first step in an exploration of material. For those witnessing in a group, or taking part in the sculpture, the act of being with the expressed material can also be important. This importance lies in the way material might connect to their own. Work done by one person might be done on behalf of someone else – messages, insight and relevance can connect people's situations. Through empathy someone might be connected to someone else's work, and this might have a direct effect on their experience of a parallel situation. In addition, the comments of witnesses might be useful and their connections might trigger further explorations.

In part this relates to the process of perspective described earlier – but it is a particular aspect – concerning the process of witnessing or being witnessed. This might also be part of a process related to other experiences of being witnessed – by a parent for example. Such connections might be re-enacted and explored through the therapy. This process is made more vivid by the art processes involved. For the client the creation of material and expressions enables them to witness aspects of themselves or their experience. At the same time it develops the witnessing part of themselves. In active expression the client puts himself or herself forward to be witnessed by another. The active role of the expressive art form is important in allowing the process of exploration of what it is to be witnessed. Feelings such as support or paranoia can be explored through the ways in which the experience of expression through the art form is encountered. In individual or group therapy, however, the key aspect of this process is how the client can shift to discover the value of being an active witness to the dance, movements, images, sound or roles they create: they see themselves and hear themselves. The witness part of themselves is brought to bear upon their life experiences. The role of art reflects this, and the products made are witnessed in an active way by their creator. McNiff describes this well when he says:

When I perceive the painting that I make, or the dream that I have as other than myself, I set the stage for dialogue. The painting might have something to say to me, and so I take on the role of listener rather than explainer . . . a sense of vitality emerges from these spontaneous expressions, unrestrained by habitual explanations.

(McNiff, 1994: 105–6)

Here are the links that the active witness function makes – the client sees himself or herself in and through the art form. At the same time, they are offered the opportunity within the arts therapy session to be a witness to themselves, their lives as reflected and processed within the art form and in the therapeutic relationship. They can also be witnessed – by themselves, by others and by the therapist.

CONCLUSION

In looking at the arts therapies as a whole, I would echo the position summarised by Smitskamp: their unique qualities spring from the ways in which 'they can elicit specific art-related healing processes, thereby expanding the range of possibilities offered by other psychotherapies' (Smitskamp, 1995: 182). Many of the key opportunities that the arts therapies offer concern these potentials: of the relationship between the client, therapist and art form. As the summaries within this chapter have shown, the ways in which this occurs can be described in a series of innovative, connected processes. Of course, dividing up the arts therapies in this way is an artificial construction around something that, in practice, is not separated into such categories. This was done in order to try to see more clearly the specific forces at work in creating original and exciting opportunities for client and therapist. The descriptions in this chapter have tried to isolate *particular aspects* of the ways the arts therapies work in order to try to see the *whole* more clearly, and to identify what makes the differences and innovations in the opportunities the arts therapies offer clients.

The arts therapies, as this book has shown, have largely developed organically. They did not arrive overnight, nor were they created by one individual. They are the product of many people in many places trying new ideas, exploring new territories and combinations. The arts therapies have emerged through a mixture of discovery, intuition and, later, structured investigation.

As we've seen, these innovations have emerged as practitioners from different areas and in different countries have challenged what health provision could be. Clarkson has described 'a characteristic of revolutionary change' as something that emerges unexpectedly, not 'out of the regions of probable predictions' (Clarkson, 1994: 10). Few would have predicted the radical advances made in the past fifty years to the situation described in Part II, where arts therapies are available throughout the world, and where established training, professionalisation and state recognition are becoming commonplace. What would have been seen as highly unlikely a century or so ago is now occurring: the arts therapies are an increasingly recognised presence as a mode of therapeutic change.

In talking about scientific revolutions, Kuhn says a common pattern is that: 'Led by a new paradigm, scientists . . . look in new places. Even more important, during revolutions scientists see new and different things when looking with familiar instruments in places they have looked before . . . familiar objects are seen in a different light and are joined by unfamiliar ones as well' (Kuhn, 1983: 111). He describes this as a new 'gestalt', as elements are put together in ways that are striking, new, and offering innovative ways of relating. As an example, he talks about the shift in perception and understanding from the Ptolemaic system that held the moon as a planet rather than a satellite of the earth: 'In the sciences . . . a perceptual switch accompanies paradigm changes . . ."I used to see a planet, but now I see a satellite" . . . a convert to the new astronomy says, "I once took the moon to be (or saw the moon as) a planet, but I was mistaken" ' (Kuhn, 1988: 111).

For those involved in the arts therapies, this recognition may seem familiar. For many the arts have been mainly seen as a diversion, a leisure activity, or a way of making profit from those who wish to consume art, drama, dance or music. The arts therapies, in their emergence, demand a shift in seeing the arts. This shift is one that must be made by clients, therapists and health organisations from local to international levels. It involves a perceptual shift such as Kuhn talks about: from seeing the arts as recreational, to seeing them as a force for change, healing or growth. The initial disbelief of a client, or professional, in the face of the idea of the arts therapies; the surprise or shock when, for the first time, the arts touch a client within therapy – these are traces of the shift that is necessary. From planet to satellite: from recreation to therapy. This may appear to be an exaggerated comparison, but, in terms of my encounters with clients in clinical situations, or my own experience as a client in art therapy, such a shift can be of enormous significance and have life-changing potential.

Smitskamp says that: 'A creative process can be described as a process in which one liberates oneself from rigid relationships with one's surroundings, and attempts to form new, original, and meaningful relationships with the world around one by entering into it' (Smitskamp, 1989: 33). The rigidities which kept therapy and the arts as separate are breaking, as we have seen. The many new possibilities opened by the connection of the two have been covered by the content of this book. The importance now is that the emerged arts therapies should not lose their sense of experimentation, challenge or difference. The new, original and meaningful relationships, described as characteristic of creativity by Smitskamp, must be held onto, as arts therapists work with clients in the various systems of established health provision. The first steps have been made, and are being consolidated: the next must keep the spirit and vigour and risk of the many innovators and initiators described in *The Arts Therapies*.

It can be a deeply moving process to see people fight free and emerge.

. . . both client and therapist are changed, through the process and the relationship.

Patsy Nowell Hall, in *Art Therapy: A Way of Healing the Split*
(1987:157)

Bibliography

Aiello, R. (1994) *Musical Perceptions*, Oxford: Oxford University Press.

Albers, J. (1934) 'Let Teaching Art Be Biological', Black Mountain College Papers, Carolina State Archives, Raleigh, 111.1.

Albers, J. (1935) 'Art As Experience', in *Progressive Education*, Vol. 12, October, 391–3.

Aldridge, D. (1996) *Music Therapy Research and Practice in Medicine*, London: Jessica Kingsley Publishers.

Aldridge, D., Gustorff, D. and Neugebauer, L. (1995) 'A Preliminary Study of Creative Music Therapy in the Treatment of Children with Developmental Delay', *The Arts in Psychotherapy*, Vol. 22, No. 3, 189–205.

Aldridge, F. (1998) 'Chocolate or Shit Aesthetics and Cultural Poverty in Art Therapy with Children', *Inscape*, Vol. 3, No. 1, 2–9.

Alibali, M.W. and Goldin-Meadow, S. (1993) 'Gesture–Speech Mismatch and Mechanisms of Learning: What the Hands Reveal about a Child's State of Mind', *Cognitive Psychology*, Vol. 25, 468–523.

Alvin, J. (1965) *Music Therapy*, London: John Clare Books, revised 1975.

Alvin, J. (1975) 'The Identity of Music Therapy', *British Journal of Music Therapy*, Vol. 6, No. 3, 14.

Amir, D. (1998) 'The Use of Israeli Folksongs in Dealing with Women's Bereavement and Loss in Music Therapy', in Dokter, D. (ed.), *Arts Therapies, Refugees and Migrants: Reaching Across Borders*, London: Jessica Kingsley Publishers.

Andersen-Warren, M. and Grainger, R. (2000) *Practical Approaches to Dramatherapy: The Shield of Perseus*, London: Jessica Kingsley Publishers.

Andsell, G. (1995) *Music for Life: Aspects of Creative Music Therapy with Adult Clients*, London: Jessica Kingsley Publishers.

Attar, F.U. (1954) *Conference of the Birds*, trans. C.S. Nott, London: Janus Press.

Axline, V. (1964) *Dibs: In Search of Self*, London: Penguin.

Baker, D. (1981) 'To Play or Not to Play', in McCaslin, N. (ed.), *Children and Drama*, New York: Longman.

Barber, V. and Campbell, J. (1999) 'Living Colour in Art Therapy', in Campbell, J., Liebmann, M., Brooks, F., Jones, J. and Ward, C. (eds), *Art Therapy, Race and Culture*, London: Jessica Kingsley Publishers.

Barkham, M. and Mellor-Clark, J. (2000) 'The Role of Practice-Based Evidence', in Rowland, N. and Goss, S. (eds), *Evidence-Based Counselling and Psychological Therapies*, London: Routledge.

Bateson, G. (1955) 'A Theory of Play and Fantasy', *Psychiatric Research Reports*, 2, 39–51.

Baudrillard, J. (1983) 'The Ecstasy of Communication', in Foster, H. (ed.), *Postmodern Culture*, London and Sydney: Pluto Press.

Birtchnell, J. (1984) 'Art Therapy as a Form of Psychotherapy', in Dalley, T. (ed.), *Art As Therapy*, London: Routledge.

Blair, D. (1987) 'The Basis of Music Therapy', *British Journal of Music Therapy*, Autumn, Vol. 14, No. 3, 2–5.

Blatner, A. (1997) *Acting In*, London: Free Association Books.

Blatner, A. and Blatner, A. (1988) *The Art of Play*, New York: Springer.

Bolton, G. (1981) 'Drama in Education – A Reappraisal', in McCaslin, N. (ed.), *Children and Drama*, New York: Longman.

Bondi, L. and Burman, E. (2001) 'Women and Mental Health: A Feminist Review', *Feminist Review*, Vol. 68, 6–33.

Boston, C.G. and Short, G.M. (1998) 'Art Therapy: An Afrocentric Approach', in Hiscox, A.R. and Calisch, A.C. (eds), *Tapestry of Cultural Issues in Art Therapy*, London: Jessica Kingsley Publishers.

Bourgeois, L. (2000) *Louise Bourgeois*, Catalogue, London: Tate Gallery Publishing.

Bourne, L.E. and Ekstrand, B.R. (1985) *Psychology: Its Principles and Meanings*, New York: Holt, Rinehart and Winston.

Bowlby, J. (1985) *Child Care and the Growth of Love*, London: Penguin.

Breton, A. (1972) *Surrealism and Painting*, Trans. S. Watson Taylor, New York: Helm.

Breton, A. (1987) *Mad Love*, Trans. A. Caws, Lincoln, Neb. and London: Pointer.

Bromberg, E.L. (2000) 'The Demographics and Practices of Art Therapists Working with Cancer Patients in the New York Metropolitan Area, Art Therapy Survey Results', AATA website..

Brown, D. and Peddar, J. (1979) *Introduction to Psychotherapy: An Outline of Psychodynamic Principles and Practice*, London: Routledge.

Brown, N.S., Curry, N.E. and Tittnich, E. (1971) 'How Groups of Children Deal with Common Stress Through Play', in Curry, N.E. and Arnaud, S. (eds), *Play: The Child Strives Towards Self Realization*, Washington DC: National Association for the Education of Young Children.

Budd, S. and Sharma, U. (eds) (1994) *The Healing Bond: The Patient–Practitioner Relationship and Therapeutic Responsibility*, London: Routledge.

Bunt, L. (1990) 'The Artist as Scientist: Is There a Synthesis?' in Kersner, M. (ed.), *The Art of Research, Proceedings*, Second Arts Therapies Research Conference.

Bunt, L. (1997) 'Clinical and Therapeutic Uses of Music', in Hargreaves, D.J. and North, A.C. (eds), *The Social Psychology of Music*, Oxford: Oxford University Press.

Bunt, L., Burns, S. and Turton, P. (2000) 'Variations on a Theme: The Evolution of a Music Therapy Research Programme at the Bristol Cancer Help Centre', *British Journal of Music Therapy*, Vol. 14, No. 2, 62–71.

Burt, H. (1997) 'Women, Art Therapy and Feminist Theories of Development', in Hogan, S. (ed.), *Feminist Approaches to Art Therapy*, London: Routledge.

Byrne, P. (1995) 'From the Depths to the Surface: Art Therapy as a Discursive Practice in the Post-Modern Era', *The Arts in Psychotherapy*, Vol. 22, No. 3, 235–9.

Callaghan, K. (1996) 'Torture – The Body in Conflict: The Role of Movement Psychotherapy', in Liebmann, M. (ed.), *Arts Approaches to Conflict*, London, Jessica Kingsley Publishers.

Cameron, D.F. (1996) 'Conflict Resolution through Art with Homeless People', in Liebmann, M. (ed.), *Arts Approaches to Conflict*, London: Jessica Kingsley Publishers.

Campbell, J. and Abra Gaga, D. (1997) 'Black on Black Art Therapy: Dreaming in Colour', in Hogan, S. (ed.), *Feminist Approaches to Art Therapy*, London: Routledge.

Campbell, J., Liebmann, M., Brooks, F., Jones, J. and Ward, C. (eds) (1996) *Art Therapy, Race and Culture*, London: Jessica Kingsley Publishers.

Carter, A. (1992) 'Stretto', *Journal of British Music Therapy*, Vol. 6, No. 1, 19.

Case, C. and Dalley, T. (1992) *The Handbook of Art Therapy*, London: Routledge.

Casson, J. (1997) 'The Therapeusis of Audience', in Jennings, S. (ed.), *Dramatherapy: Theory and Practice* 3, London: Routledge.

Casson, J. (2001) 'Dramatherapy, Psychodrama and Voices', *Dramatherapy*, Vol. 23, No. 2, 22–5.

Cattanach, A. (1992) *Drama for People with Special Needs*, London: A. and C. Black.

Cattanach, A. (1994) 'Dramatic Play with Children: The Interface of Dramatherapy and Play Therapy', in Jennings, S., Cattanach, A., Mitchell, S., Chesner, A. and Meldrum, B. (eds), *The Handbook of Dramatherapy*, London: Routledge.

Clarkson, P. (1994) *The Psychotherapeutic Relationship*, London: Whurr.

Clarkson, P. (ed.) (1998) *Counselling Psychology: Integrating Theory, Research, and Supervised Practice*, London: Routledge.

Clarkson, P. (2002a) *The Transpersonal Relationship in Psychotherapy*, London and Philadelphia: Whurr.

Clarkson, P. (2002b) *On Psychotherapy* 2, London and Philadelphia: Whurr.

Clarkson, P. and Nippoda, Y. (1998) 'Cross-Cultural Issues in Counselling Psychology Practice: A Qualitative Study of One Multicultural Training Organisation', in Clarkson, P. (ed.), *Counselling Psychology: Integrating Theory, Research, and Supervised Practice*, London: Routledge.

Clarkson, P. and Pokorny, M. (eds) (1994) *The Handbook of Psychotherapy*, London: Routledge.

Cohen, B.M. (1993) *The Diagnostic Drawing Test*, Virginia: Cohen.

Cohen, R. (1969) 'Play amongst European Kindergarten Girls in a Jerusalem Neighborhood', cited in Feitelson, D. (1977) 'Cross-Cultural Studies of Representational Play', in Tizard, B. and Haravey, D. (eds), *Biology and Play*, Philadelphia: Lippincott.

Conley, K. (2001) 'Anamorphic Love: The Surrealist Poetry of Desire', in Mundy, J. (ed.), *Surrealism: Desire Unbound*, London: Tate Publishing Ltd.

Conquergood, D. (2002) 'Performance Studies Interventions and Radical Research', in *The Drama Review*, Vol. 46, No. 2, 2002, New York University and the Massachusetts Institute of Technology, 145–57.

Cosgriff, V. (1986) 'Music and Parkinsonism', *British Journal of Music Therapy*, Autumn 1986, Vol. 17, No. 3, 13–18.

Couroucli-Robertson, K. (1997) 'The Tethered Goat and the Poppy Field: Dominant Symbols in Dramatherapy', in Jennings, S. (ed.), *Dramatherapy: Theory and Practice* 3, London: Routledge.

Courtney, R. (1988) *Re-Cognizing Richard Courtney*, in Booth, D. and Martin-Smith, A. (eds), Ontario: Pembroke Publishers.

Cox, M. (1978) *Coding the Therapeutic Process*, Oxford: Pergamon.

Cox, M. (1992) *Children's Drawings*, London: Penguin

Cubitt, S. (1993) *Videography: Video Media as Art and Culture*, London: Macmillan.

Dalley, T. (1984) *Art as Therapy: An Introduction to the Use of Art as a Technique*, London: Tavistock.

Dalley, T. (2000) 'Back to the Future: Thinking about Theoretical Developments in Art Therapy', in Gilroy, A. and McNeilly, G. (eds), *The Changing Shape of Art Therapy: New Developments in Theory and Practice*, London: Jessica Kingsley Publishers

Dalley, T., Rifkind, G. and Terry, K. (1993) *Three Voices of Art Therapy: Image, Client, Therapist*, London: Routledge

Danev, D. (1998) 'Library Project "Step to Recovery": Creative Sessions with Children in War and Post-War Time', in Dokter, D. (ed.), *Arts Therapies, Refugees and Migrants: Reaching across Borders*, London: Jessica Kingsley Publishers.

D'Ardenne, P. and Mahtani, A. (1989) *Transcultural Counselling in Action*, London: Sage.

Darnley-Smith, R. (1996) 'What do Music Therapists Hear?', unpublished paper presented at the 'Music and Psyche' Conference, London, City University.

Darrow, A.A., Gibbons, A.C. and Heller, G.N. (1985) 'Music Therapy Past Present and Future', *The American Music Teacher*, September–October, 18–20.

Dawes, S.A. (1987) 'The Role of Music Therapy in Caring in Huntingdon's Disease', *British Journal of Music Therapy*, Vol. 18, No. 1, 2–8.

Desmond, J. (1998) 'Embodying Difference: Issues in Dance and Cultural Studies', in Carter, A. (ed.), *The Routledge Dance Studies Reader*, London and New York: Routledge.

Dokter, D. (1996) *Arts Therapies and Clients with Eating Disorders: Fragile Board*, London: Jessica Kingsley Publishers.

Donaldson, M. (1992) *Human Minds: An Exploration*, London: Penguin.

Douglas, M. (1994) 'The Construction of the Physician: A Cultural Approach to Medical Fashions', in Budd, S. and Sharma, U. (eds), *The Healing Bond: The Patient–Practitioner Relationship and Therapeutic Responsibility*, London and New York: Routledge.

Dubowski, J. (ed.) (1984) *Art Therapy as a Psychotherapy with the Mentally Handicapped*, Hertfordshire College of Art and Design Conference Proceedings.

Duggan, M. and Grainger, R. (1997) *Imagination, Identification and Catharsis in Theatre and Therapy*, London: Jessica Kingsley Publishers.

Edinger, E. (1990) *The Living Psyche*, Wilmette, IL: Chiron.

Edwards, D. (1999) 'The Role of the Case Study in Art Therapy Research', *Inscape*, Vol. 4, No. 1, 2–9.

Edwards, J. (2002) 'Using the Evidence Based Medicine Framework to Support Music Therapy Posts in Healthcare Settings', *British Journal of Music Therapy*, Vol. 16, No. 1, 29–34.

Edwards, M. (1989) 'Art, Therapy and Romanticism', in Gilroy, A. and Dalley, T. (eds), *Pictures at an Exhibition: Selected Essays on Art and Art Therapy*, London: Routledge.

Elam, K. (1991) *The Semiotics of Theatre and Drama*, London: Methuen.

Emunah, R. (1983) 'The Impact of Theatrical Performance on the Self-Images of Psychioatric Patients', *The Arts in Psychotherapy*, Vol. 10, 233–9

Erkkila, J. (1997) 'From the Unconscious to the Conscious, Musical Improvisation and Drawings as Tools in the Music Therapy of Children', *Nordic Journal of Music Therapy*, Vol. 6, No. 2, 112–20.

Evans, J. (1982) 'Art Therapy at the Crossroads – Implications for Training', in Evans, J. (ed.), *Art Therapy and Dramatherapy*, Conference Proceedings, Hertfordshire College of Art and Design.

Evans, K. and Dubowski, J. (2001) *Art Therapy with Children on the Autistic Spectrum: Beyond Words*, London: Jessica Kingsley Publishers.

Feder, B. and Feder, E. (1998) *The Art and Science of Evaluation in the Arts Therapies: How Do You Know What's Working?*, Springfield: Charles C. Thomas.

Fernando, S. (1991) *Mental Health, Race and Culture*, London: Macmillan/MIND Publications.

Ferran, B. (1999) 'Arts Council of England Panel: "Nurturing Creativity" ' in Candy, L. and Edmonds, E.A. (eds), *Introducing Creativity to Cognition*, Conference proceedings, Loughborough University, Association for Computer Machinery Press.

Ferrara, N. (1991) 'Art As a Reflection of Child Development', *The American Journal of Art Therapy*, Vol. 30, Nov. 44–50.

Frayn, M. (1998) *Copenhagen*, London: Methuen.

Freud, A. (1965) *Normality and Pathology in Childhood*, London: Hogarth Press.

Frohne-Hagemann, I. (1998) 'The Musical Life Panorama (MLP) – A Facilitating Method in the Field of Clinical and Sociocultural Music Therapy', *Nordic Journal of Music Therapy*, Vol. 7, No. 2, 104–12.

Fryrear, J.L. and Fleshman, B. (1981) *The Arts Therapies*, New York: Charles C. Thomas.

Gale, C. and Matthews, R. (1998) 'Journey in Joint Working', in Rees, M. (ed.), *Drawing on Difference: Art Therapy with People Who Have Learning Difficulties*, London and New York: Routledge.

Gantt, L. and Tarbone, C. (1997) *The Formal Elements Art Therapy Scale (FEATS)*, New York: Gargoyle Press.

Gardner, H. (1973) *The Arts and Human Development*, New York: Wiley and Sons.

Garvey, C. (1977) *Play*, Cambridge, Mass.: Harvard University Press.

Garvey, C. (1984) *Children's Talk*, London: Fontana.

Ghiselin, B. (1952) *On The Creative Process, A Symposium*, New York: New English Library.

Gilroy, A. (1992) 'Research in Art Therapy', in Waller, D. and Gilroy, A. (eds), *Art Therapy: A Handbook*, Buckingham: Open University Press.

Gilroy, A. (1996) 'Our Own Kind of Evidence', *Inscape*, Vol. 1, 52–60.

Gilroy, A. and Lee, C. (eds) (1995) *Art and Music Therapy and Research*, London: Routledge.

Gilroy, A. and Skaife, S. (1997) 'Taking the Pulse of Art Therapy: A Report on the 27th Annual Conference of the American Art Therapy Association, November 13–17, 1996, Philadelphia', *Inscape*, Vol. 2, No. 2, 57–60.

Gobey, F. (1996) 'Conflict, Knowledge and Transformation: Three Drama Techniques', in Liebmann, M. (ed.), *Arts Approaches to Conflict*, London: Jessica Kingsley Publishers.

Goodman, P. (1951) 'Advance-Guard Writing, 1900–1950', *Kenyon Review*, Vol. 13, 376–81.

Goodman, P., Perls, F.S. and Hefferline, R.F. (1951) *Gestalt Therapy*, New York: Julian.

Goss, S. and Rowland, N. (2000) 'Getting Evidence into Practice', in Rowland, N. and Goss, S. (eds), *Evidence-Based Counselling and Psychological Therapies*, London: Routledge.

Gottman, J. and Parkhurst, J. (1977) 'Developing May Not Always Be Improving: A Developmental Study of Children's Best Friendships', paper presented to Biennial Meeting of Society for Research in Child Development, New Orleans.

Grainger, R. (1990) *Drama and Healing: The Roots of Dramatherapy*, London: Jessica Kingsley Publishers.

Grainger, R. (1999) *Researching the Arts Therapies*, London: Jessica Kingsley Publishers.

Grainger, R. (2000) 'A Synthesis of Dramatherapy Research', unpublished Ph.D, Leeds Metropolitan University.

Gregory, D. and Garner, R. (2000) 'Paradigms and Research: Examining the History and Future of Art Therapy', Artery International, *http://www.burleehost.com/artery/researchparadigm.htm*

Griffing, P. (1983) 'Encouraging Dramatic Play in Early Childhood', *Young Children*, Vol. 38, No. 4, 13–22.

Gruhn, N. (1960) 'Introduction to Music Therapy Conference on Music Therapy in the Education of the Child', Society for Music Therapy and Remedial Music, Conference Proceedings, University of London, Institute of Education.

Gunter, B. (1998) *The Effects of Video Games on Children: The Myth Unmasked*, Sheffield: Sheffield Academic Press.

Hagood, M.M. (1992) 'Art Therapy Research in England: Impressions of an American Art Therapist', *Arts in Psychotherapy*, Vol. 17, No. 1, 75–9.

Halley, P. (1988) *Collected Essays 1981–1987*, Zurich: Bruno Bischotberger Gallery.

Hamm, C. (1979) *Subculture: The Meaning of Style*, New York: Methuen and Co.

Haraway, D.J. (1991) *Simians, Cyborgs and Women: The Reinvention of Nature*, New York: Routledge.

Harris, J. (2001) *The New Art History*, London and New York: Routledge.

Harrison, C. and Wood, P. (1992) *Art in Theory*, Oxford: Blackwell.

Hayes, N. (1994) *Foundations of Psychology*, London: Routledge.

Helman, C.G. (1994) *Culture, Health and Illness*, Oxford: Butterworth-Heinemann.

Herrmann, U. (2000) 'Developing in Splendid Isolation? A Critical Analysis of German Art Therapy Approaches in Key Papers from 1990–1999', *Inscape*, Vol. 5, No. 1, 19–30.

Hickling, F. W. (1989) 'Sociodrama in the Rehabilitation of Chronic Mentally Ill Patients', *Hospital and Community Psychiatry*, Vol. 40, No. 4, 402–6.

Higgins, R (1993) *Approaches to Case Study*, London: Jessica Kingsley Publishers.

Hill, A. (1945) *Art versus Illness*, London: Allen and Unwin.

Hill, A. (1951) *Painting out Illness*, London: Williams and Northgate.

Hitchcock, D. (1987) 'The influence of Jung's Psychology on the Therapeutic Use of Music', *Journal of British Music Therapy*, Vol. 1, 17–21.

Hobbes, T. (1651) *Leviathan* (1968 edn), London: Penguin.

Hogan, S. (ed.) (1997) *Feminist Approaches to Art Therapy*, London: Routledge.

Holden, S. (1990) 'Moving Together: The Group Finds a Dance', *Group Analysis*, Vol. 23, 265–76 – 270, London: Sage.

Holland, E. (1988) 'Schizoanalysis: The Postmodern Contextualization of Psychoanalysis', in Nelson, C. and Grossberg, L. (eds), *Marxism and the Interpretation of Culture*, London: Macmillan.

Holmes, J. and Lindley, R. (1989) *The Values of Psychotherapy*, Oxford: Oxford University Press.

Hoskyns, S. (1982) 'An Investigation into the Value of Music Therapy in the Care of

Patients Suffering from Huntington's Chorea: Report on a Pilot Programme', Association to Combat Huntington's Chorea, UK.

Hoskyns, S. (1995) 'Observing Offenders: The Use of Simple Rating Scales to Assess Changes in Activities during Group Music Therapy', in Gilroy, A. and Lee, C. (eds), *Art and Music: Therapy and Research*, London: Routledge.

Howat, J. (1992) 'The Relationship between Music Therapy and Distinguishing Words from Music, Stretto', *Journal of British Music Therapy*, Vol. 6, No. 1, 22–3.

Hugo, M. (2002) 'Music Therapy in Uruguay: A Long and Winding Road', Voices: A World Forum for Music Therapy, http://www.voices.no/country/monthuruguay _july2002.html

Innes, C. (1993) *Avant Garde Theatre 1892–1992*, London: Routledge.

Jacobi, J. (1967) *The Way of Individuation*, London: Hodder and Stoughton.

James, J. (1998) 'Remembering: Intercultural Issues in Integrative Arts Psychotherapy', in Dokter, D. (ed.), *Arts Therapies, Refugees and Migrants: Reaching across Borders*, London: Jessica Kingsley Publishers.

Jarry, A. (1965) *The Ubu Plays*, trans. C. Connolly and S. Watson Taylor, London: Methuen and Co.

Jennings, S. (1973) *Remedial Drama*, London: Pitman.

Jennings, S. (1983) *Creative Therapy*, London: Kemble Press.

Jennings, S., Cattanach, A., Mitchell, S., Chesner, A. and Meldrum, B. (eds) (1994) *The Handbook of Dramatherapy*, London: Routledge.

Jennings, S. (1997) *Dramatherapy: Theory and Practice 3*, London: Routledge

John, D. (1992) 'Towards Music Psychotherapy', *Journal of British Music Therapy*, Vol. 6, 10–12.

Johnson, J.E. (1976) 'Relations of Divergent Thinking and Intelligence Test Scores with Social and Non-social Make Believe Play of Pre-school Children', *Child Development*, Vol. 47, 1200–3.

Johnson, R. (1999) 'The Use of Photographs in Mourning and Bereavement and the Anthropology of Art', *Anthropology and Medicine*, Vol. 6, No. 2, 231–41.

Johnson, S. (1987) in Murphy, J (1998) 'Art Therapy with Sexually Abused Children and Young People', *Inscape*, Vol. 3, No. 1, 10–20.

Jones, P. (1993) 'The Active Witness', in Payne, H. (ed.), *Handbook of Inquiry in the Arts Therapies: One River Many Currents*, London: Jessica Kingsley Publishers.

Jones, P. (1996) *Drama as Therapy: Theatre as Living*, London: Routledge.

Joyce, S. (1997) 'Feminist-Perspective Art Therapy: An Option for Women's Mental Health – An Australian Perspective', in Hogan, S. (ed.), *Feminist Approaches to Art Therapy*, London: Routledge.

Judges, A.V. (1960) 'Opening Address', Conference on Music Therapy in the Education of the Child, Society for Music Therapy and Remedial Music, Conference Proceedings, University of London Institute of Education.

Jung, C.G. (1931) 'The Practice of Psychotherapy', *Collected Works*, Vol. 16, pars 66–113, in *Jung on Active Imagination*, ed. J. Chodorow, London: Routledge (1997).

Jung, C.G. (1935) *Tavistock Lectures*, Lecture 3, London: Routledge, Kegan, Paul.

Jung, C.G. (1955) *Mysterium Coniunctionis*, Excerpt from *Collected Works*, Vol. 14, paras 705–11, in *Jung on Active Imagination*, ed. J. Chodorow, London: Routledge (1997).

Jung, C.G. (1959) *Archetypes and the Collective Unconscious*, *Collected Works*, Vol. 9, Part 1, Princeton: Bollingen.

Jung, C.G. (1961) *Memories, Dreams, Reflections*, New York: Random House.

Jung, C.G. (1997) *Jung on the Active Imagination*, London: Routledge.

Junge, M.B. and Asawa, P.P. (1994) *A History of Art Therapy in the United States*, Mundelein: The American Art Therapy Association.

Karkou, V. (1999a) 'Art Therapy in Education, Finding from a Nationwide Survey in Arts Therapies', *Inscape*, Vol. 4, No. 2, 62–70.

Karkou, V. (1999b) 'Who? Where? What? A Brief Description of DMT: Results from a Nationwide Study', *E-motion*, Vol. XI, No. 2, 5–10.

Killick, K. (2000) 'The Art Room as Container in Analytical Art Psychotherapy with Patients in Psychotic States', in Gilroy, A. and McNeilly, G. (eds), *The Changing Shape of Art Therapy: New Developments in Theory and Practice*, London: Jessica Kingsley Publishers

Killick, K. and Greenwood, H. (1995) 'Research into Art Therapy with People Who Have Psychotic Illnesses', in Gilroy, A. and Lee, C. (eds), *Art and Music Therapy and Research*, London: Routledge

Kim, J. (2002) 'Music Therapy in the Republic of Korea Voices: A World Forum for Music Therapy' *http://www.voices.no/country/monthkorea_december2002.html*

Klein, M. (1932) *The Psychoanalysis of Childhood*, London: Hogarth.

Klein, M. (1961) *Narrative of a Child Analysis*, London: Hogarth Press.

Klineberg, O. (1987) 'The Social Psychology of Cross Cultural Counselling', in Pedersen, P. (ed.), *Handbook of Cross-Cultural Counselling and Therapy*, New York: Praeger.

Kristeva, J. (1986) 'Interview with Catherine Francblin', in *Flash Art*, No. 126, Feb.–Mar. 44–7.

Kuhn, T.S. (1983) *The Structure of Scientific Revolutions*, Chicago: The University of Chicago Press.

Lacan, J. (1969) 'The Mirror Phase as Formative of the Function of the I', *New Left Review*, Vol. 27, September, 36–55.

Lacapra, D. (1983) *Rethinking Intellectual History: Texts, Contexts, Language*, Ithaca, New York: Cornell University Press.

Landy, R. (1986) *Drama Therapy Concepts and Practices*, Springfield: Charles C. Thomas.

Landy, R. (1993) *Persona and Performance: The Meaning of Role in Drama, Therapy, and Everyday Life*, London: Jessica Kingsley Publishers.

Landy, R. (1995) 'Isolation and Collaboration in the Creative Arts Therapies – The Implications of Crossing Borders', *The Arts in Psychotherapy*, Vol. 22, No. 2, 83–6

Landy, R. (1997) 'The Case of Sam: Application of the Taxonomy of Roles', in Jennings, S. (ed.), *Dramatherapy: Theory and Practice* 3, London: Routledge.

Landy, R. (2001) *New Essays in Drama Therapy*, Springfield: Charles C. Thomas.

Langer, S. (1952) *Philosophy in a New Key*, London: Oxford University Press.

Lanham, R. (1989) 'Is it Art or Art Therapy?', *Inscape*, Vol. 3, Spring, 18–22.

Lawes, M. (2001) 'Aesthetic Experience and the Healing Process: The Story of a Therapist's Rediscovery of Music', *British Journal of Music Therapy*, Vol. 15, No. 1, 22–6.

Lee, C. (1995) 'The Analysis of Therapeutic Improvisatory Music', in Gilroy, A. and Lee, C. (eds), *Art and Music: Therapy and Research*, London and New York: Routledge.

Levens, M. (1990) 'Borderline Aspects in Eating Disorders: Art Therapy's Contribution', *Group Analysis*, Vol. 23, 277–84, pp. 283–4.

Levine, R. and Levine, A. (1963) 'Nyansorgo: A Gusii Community in Kenya', in Whithing, B. (ed.), *Six Cultures: Studies in Childrearing*, New York: John Wiley.

Levine, S.K. and Levine, E.G. (eds) (1999) *Foundations of Expressive Arts Therapy: Theoretical and Clinical Perspectives*, London: Jessica Kingsley Publishers.

Levinge, A. (1996) 'Discord or Harmony: Issues of Conflict in Music Therapy', in Liebmann, M. (ed) *Arts Approaches to Conflict*, London: Jessica Kingsley Publishers.

Li, T.C. (1999) 'Who or What is Making the Music: Music Creation in a Machine Age', in Candy, L and Edmonds, E.A. (eds), *Introducing Creativity to Cognition*, Loughborough University, Association for Computer Machinery Press, New York Conference Proceeding.

Liebmann, M. (ed.) (1996) *Arts Approaches to Conflict*, London: Jessica Kingsley Publishers.

Loizos, C. (1969) 'Play Behaviour in Higher Primates: A Review', in Morris, D. (ed.), *Primate Ethology*, Garden City: Anchor.

Lomas, D. (2001) 'Surrealism, Psychoanalysis and Hysteria', in Mundy, J. (ed.), *Surrealism: Desire Unbound*, London: Tate Publishing Ltd.

Lyotard, J.F. (1983) *The Postmodern Condition: A Report on Knowledge*, Minneapolis: University of Minnesota Press.

McAlister, M. (1999) 'An Evaluation of Dramatherapy in a Forensic Setting', in Wigram, T. (ed.), *Assessment and Evaluation in the Art Therapies*, Radlett: Harper House Publications.

McClean, C. (1999) 'Mixed Metaphors–Dependency or Defence: Art Therapy as an Intervention within a Mother–Daughter Relationship', in Waller, D. and Mahony, J. (eds), *Treatment of Addiction: Current Issues for Arts Therapists*, London: Routledge.

McClelland, S. (1993) 'Pat and Ann, The Art of Science with Clients: Beginning Collaborative Enquiry in Process Work', in Payne, H. (ed.), *One River Many Currents*, London: Jessica Kingsley Publishers.

McCully, R.S. (1987) *Jung and Rorschach*, Dallas: Spring Publications.

McDougall, J. (1989) *Theatres of the Body: A Psychoanalytic Approach to Psychosomatic Illness*, London: W.W. Norton.

McFee, J.K. and Degge, R.M. (1977) *Art, Culture and Environment*, Belmont, California: Wadsworth Publishing Company.

Maclagan, D. (1989) 'Fantasy and the Figurative', in Gilroy, A. and Dalley, T. (eds), *Pictures at an Exhibition: Selected Essays on Art and Art Therapy*, London: Routledge.

McLeod, C. (1999) 'Empowering Creativity with Computer Assisted Art Therapy: An Introduction to Available Programmes and Techniques', *Art Therapy: Journal of the American Art Therapy Association*, Vol. 16, No. 4, 201–5.

MacLow, C. (1994) 'Dancing in Leaner Times', in Barnes, S. (ed.), *Writing Dancing in the Age of Postmodernism*, Middleton, CT: Wesleyan University Press.

McNiff, S. (1992) *Art as Medicine*, Boston: Shambhala.

McNiff, S. (1994) *Art as Medicine: Creating A Therapy of the Imagination*, London: Piatkus.

McNiff, S. (1998) *Art-Based Research*, London: Jessica Kingsley Press.

Malchiodi, C.A. (1993) 'Medical Art Therapy: Contributions to the Field of Arts Medicine', *International Journal of Arts Medicine*, Vol. 2, No. 2, 28–31.

Malchiodi, C.A. (1999a) *Medical Art Therapy with Adults*, London: Jessica Kingsley Publishers.

Malchiodi, C.A. (ed.) (1999b) *Medical Art Therapy with Children*, London: Jessica Kingsley Publishers.

Malchiodi, C.A. (2000) *Art Therapy and Computer Technology: A Virtual Studio of Possibilities*, London: Jessica Kingsley Publishers.

Males, J. and Males, B. (1982) 'Research on the Efficacy of Art Therapy–Behavioural Approaches', in Evans, J. (ed.), *Art Therapy and Dramatherapy*, Hertfordshire College of Art and Design Conference Proceedings.

Maslow, I. (1966) 'Comments on Dr Frankl's Paper', *Journal of Humanistic Psychology*, Vol. 6, No. 2, 107–12.

Massey, R. and Massey, J. (1987) *The Music of India*, New York: Taplinger.

Matthews, J. (1986) 'Children's Early Representation: The Construction of Meaning', *Inscape*, Winter, 12–17.

Mauro, M.K. (1998) 'The Use of Art Therapy in Identity Formation: A Latino Case Study', in Hiscox, A.R. and Calisch, A.C. (eds), *A Tapestry of Cultural Issues in Art Therapy*, London: Jessica Kingsley Publishers.

Meekums, B. (2002) *Dance Movement Therapy: A Creative Psychotherapeutic Approach*, London: Sage.

Merlin, D. (1993) 'Human Cognitive Evolution: What We Were, What We Are Becoming', *Social Research*, Vol. 60, No. 1, 143–70.

Merriam, A.P. (1964) *The Anthropology of Music*, Illinois: Northwestern University Press.

Mertens, M. (1996) *Kunsttherapie – Entwicklung eines Berufsbildes. Argumente für die Anerkennung durch die gesetzlichen Krankenversicherungen*, Hamburg: Kova Verlag.

Milioni, D. (2001) 'Social Construcionism and Dramatherapy: Creating Alternative Discourses', *Dramatherapy*, Vol. 23, No. 2, 10–17.

Milner, M. (1986) *A Life of One's Own*, London: Virago, first published, 1934, under pseudonym Joanna Field.

Minsky, R.K. (1996) *Psychoanalysis and Gender: An Introductory Reader*, London: Routledge.

Mitchell, S. (ed.) (1996) *Dramatherapy Clinical Studies*, London: Jessica Kingsley Publishers.

Mond, P. (1994) Interview, in Jennings, S. *et al.* (eds) *The Handbook of Dramatherapy*, London: Routledge.

Mundy, J. (ed.) (2001) *Surrealism: Desire Unbound*, London: Tate Publishing Ltd.

Murphy, J. (1998) 'Art Therapy with Sexually Abused Children and Young People', *Inscape*, Vol. 3, No. 1, 10–15.

Murphy, J (2001) *Art Therapy with Young Survivors of Sexual Abuse*, London: Brunner Routledge.

Nadirshaw, Z. (1992) 'Theory and Practice: Brief Report – Therapeutic Practice in Multiracial Britain', *Counselling Psychology Quarterly*, Vol. 5, No. 3, 257–61.

Naumburg, M. (1958) 'Case Illustration: Art Therapy with a Seventeen Year Old Girl', in Hammer, E.F. (ed.), *The Clinical Application of Projective Drawings*, Springfield: Charles Thomas.

Newham, P. (1997) *Therapeutic Voicework: Principles and Practice for the Use of Singing as a Therapy*, London: Jessica Kingsley Publishers.

Newham, P. (1999) 'Voicework as Therapy', in Levine, S.K. and Levine, E.G. (eds), *Foundations of Expressive Arts Therapy: Theoretical and Clinical Perspectives*, London: Jessica Kingsley Publishers.

Nordoff, P. and Robbins, C. (1971) *Therapy in Music for Handicapped Children*, London: Gollancz.

Nordoff, P. and Robbins, C. (1977) *Creative Music Therapy*, London: Gollancz.

North, M. (1972) *Personality Assessment through Movement*, Plymouth: MacDonald Evans.

Nowell Hall, P. (1987) 'Art Therapy: A Way of Healing the Split', in Dalley, T. (ed), *Images of Art Therapy*, London: Routledge.

Oatley, K. (1984) *Selves in Relation*, London and New York: Methuen.

Odell, H. (1989) 'Foreword', *Journal of British Music Therapy*, Vol. 3, No. 1, 3–4.

O'Hare, P. (1981) *The International Society for Psychopathic Art Meeting 1958*, Art and Psychiatry, Barcelona University Conference Proceedings.

Okazaki-Sakaue, K. (2003) 'Music Therapy in Japan', *Voices: A World Forum for Music Therapy* http://www.voices.no/country/monthjapan_may2003.html

Parry, G. (2000) 'Evidence-Based Psychotherapy', in Rowland, N. and Goss, S. (eds), *Evidence-Based Counselling and Psychological Therapies*, London: Routledge.

Pavlicevic, M. (1995) 'Growing into Sound and Sounding into Growth: Improvisation Groups with Adults', *The Arts in Psychotherapy*, Vol. 22, No. 4, 359–67.

Pavlicevic, M. (1997) *Music Therapy in Context: Music, Meaning and Relationship*, London: Jessica Kingsley Publishers.

Pavlicevic, M. (2001) 'A Child in Time and Health: Guiding Images in Music Therapy', *British Journal of Music Therapy*, Vol. 15, No. 1, 14–21.

Pavlicevic, M. (2003) *Groups in Music: Strategies from Music Therapy*, London: Jessica Kingsley Publishers

Payne, H. (1992) *Dance Movement Therapy: Theory and Practice*, London: Routledge.

Payne, H. (ed.) (1993) *Handbook of Inquiry in the Arts Therapies: One River Many Currents*, London: Jessica Kingsley Publishers.

Perls, F.S., Heffenline, R.F. and Goodman, P. (1951/1989) *Gestalt Therapy: Excitement and Growth in the Human Personality*, New York: Julian Press (first published 1951).

Peters, J. (1994) *The Patient–Therapist Relationship*, London: Croom Helm.

Petzold, H. and Ilse, O. (eds) (1990) *Die neuen Kreativitatstherapien, Handbuch der Kunsttherapie*, Vols 1 and 2, Paderborn: Junfermann-Verlag.

Piaget, J. (1962) *Play, Dreams and Imitation in Childhood*, New York: Norton.

Pickard, K. (1989) 'Shape', in Jones, P. (ed.), *Dramatherapy: State of the Art*, Hertfordshire College of Art and Design Conference Proceedings.

Picton, J. (1996) *West Africa and the Guinea Coast, in Africa: The Art of a Continent*, Munich, New York: Prestel.

Priestley, M. (1975) *Music Therapy in Action*, London: Constable.

Priestley, M. (1995) *Essays in Analytical Music Therapy*, Barcelona: Philedelphia.

Prinzhorn, H. (1922) *Bildnerei der Geisteskranken*, Berlin: Springer.

Prokofiev, F. (1997) 'A Painting Perspective', *Special*, Spring, pp. 31–3.

Rauschenberg, R. (1959) 'Statement', in Miller, D. (ed.), *Sixteen Americans*, New York: Museum of Modern Art.

Read Johnson, D. (1981) 'Some Diagnostic Implications of Dramatherapy', in Schattner, G. and Courtney, R. (eds), *Drama in Therapy*, Vol. 1, New York: Drama Book Specialists.

Read Johnson, D. (1982) 'Developmental Approaches to Drama Therapy', *The Arts in Psychotherapy*, Vol. 9, 183–90.

Read Johnson, D. (1998) 'On the Therapeutic Action of the Creative Arts Therapies: The Psychodynamic Model', *Arts in Psychotherapy*, 85–99.

Read Johnson, D. (1999) *Essays on the Creative Arts Therapies*, Springfield: Charles C. Thomas.

Reason, P. (1991) 'Power and Conflict in Multidisciplinary Collaboration', *Journal of Complementary Medical Research*, Vol. 5, No. 3, 144–50.

Rider, M. (1987) 'Treating Chronic Disease and Pain with Music-Mediated Imagery', *The Arts in Psychotherapy*, Vol. 14, 113–20.

Robb, M. (2001) 'The Changing Experience of Childhood', in Foley, P., Roche, J. and Tucker, S. (eds), *Children in Society: Contemporary Theory, Policy and Practice*, London: Palgrave.

Robbins, A. (1987) *The Artist as Therapist*, New York: Human Sciences Press Inc.

Roberts, S. and Bund, A. (1993) 'Good Medicine', Arts in Health in the West Midlands, Artservice/West Midlands Arts.

Rogers, P. (1993) 'Research in Music Therapy with Sexually Abused Clients', in Payne, H. (ed.), *Handbook of Inquiry in the Arts Therapies: One River Many Currents*, London: Jessica Kingsley Publishers.

Rosenbaum, M. (1993) *Children and the Environment*, London: National Children's Bureau.

Rowan, J. (1983) *The Reality Game*, London: Routledge and Kegan Paul.

Rust, M.J. (1998) 'Art Therapy in the Treatment of Women with Eating Disorders', in Sandle, D. (ed.), *Development and Diversity, New Applications in Art Therapy*, London: Free Association Books

Sackett, D.L., Rosenberg, W.M., Gray, J.A., Haynes, R.B. and Richardson, W.S. (1996) 'Evidence Based Medicine: What It Is and Isn't', *British Medical Journal*, Vol. 312, 71–2.

Sandle, D. (ed.) (1998) *Development and Diversity: New Applications in Art Therapy*, London: Free Association Books

Schaverien, J. (1992) *The Revealing Image: Analytical Art Psychotherapy in Theory and Practice*, London: Routledge.

Schaverien, J. (1995) 'Researching the Esoteric: Art Therapy Research', in Gilroy, A. and Lee, C. (eds), *Art and Music Therapy and Research*, London: Routledge.

Schechner, R. (1988) *Performance Theory*, New York: Routledge.

Senior, P. and Croall, J. (1993) *Helping to Heal: The Arts in Health Care*, London: Calouste Gulbenkian Foundation.

Sharma, U. (1994) 'The Equation of Responsibility', in Budd, S. and Sharma, U. (eds), *The Healing Bond*, London: Routledge.

Sheridan, M. D. (1999) *Play in Early Childhood*, revised and updated J. Harding and L. Meldon-Smith, London: Routledge.

Simmons, M. (2001) 'Music Therapy for Children on the Autistic Spectrum with Auriel Warwick Interviewed by Mary Simmons', *British Journal of Music Therapy*, Vol. 15, No. 2, 44–50.

Simpson, F. (2000) 'Speaking with Clients: Perspectives from Creative Music Therapy', *British Journal of Music Therapy*, Vol. 14, No. 2, 83–92.

Skaife, S. (1990) 'Self-Determination in Group-Analytic Art Therapy', *Group Analysis*, Vol. 23, 237–44.

Skaife, S. (1995) 'The Dialectics of Art Therapy', *Inscape*, Vol. 1, 2–7.

Skaife, S. (2000) 'Keeping the Balance: Further Thoughts on the Dialectics of

Art Therapy', in Gilroy, A. and McNeilly, G., *The Changing Shape of Art Therapy: New Developments in Theory*, London: Jessica Kingsley Publishers.

Skewes, K. (2002) 'Review of Music in the US: A Review of Current Practice in Group Music Therapy', *British Journal of Music Therapy*, Vol. 16, No. 1, 46–55.

Slade, P. (1995) *Child Play: Its Importance for Human Development*, London: Jessica Kingsley Publishers.

Smith, M.P. da Cruz (2003) 'Music Therapy in Brazil Music Therapy', in Brazil, Voices: A World Forum for Music Therapy, http://www.voices.no/copuntry/monthbrazil_april2003.html

Smitskamp, H. (1989) 'The Creative Process in Therapy', in Houben, J., Smitskamp, H. and te Velde, J. (eds), *The Creative Process, Vol. 1 Applications in Therapy and Education*, Culemborg: Phaedon.

Smitskamp, H. (1995) 'The Problem of Professional Diagnosis in the Arts Therapies', *The Arts in Psychotherapy*, Vol. 22, No. 3, 181–7.

Sobey, R. (1992) 'Stretto: The Relationship between Music Therapy and Psychotherapy', *Journal of British Music Therapy*, Vol. 6, No. 1, 19–21.

Solomon, A.P. (1950) 'Drama Therapy', in Dunton, W.R. (ed.), *Occupational Therapy: Principles and Practice*, Springfield, IL: Charles C. Thomas.

Souall, A.T. (1981) *Museums of Madness*, London: Sphere.

Standing Committee on the Arts in Prisons (SCAP) (1997) *Guidelines for Arts Therapists Working in Prisons*, Croydon: HM Prison Service.

Standing Committee of Arts Therapies Professions (1989) *Artists and Arts Therapists*, London: Carnegie UK Trust.

Stanton-Jones, K. (ed.) (1992) *An Introduction to Dance Movement Therapy in Psychiatry*, London: Routledge.

Steiner, M. (1992) 'Alternatives in Psychiatry: Dance Movement Therapy in the Community', in Stanton-Jones, K. (ed.), *An Introduction to Dance Movement Therapy in Psychiatry*, London: Routledge.

Stern, D. (1985) *The Interpersonal World of the Infant: A View from Psychoanalysis and Developmental Psychology*, New York: Basic Books.

Stevens, R. and Wetherell, M. (2000) 'The Self in the Modern World: Drawing together the Threads', in Stevens, R. (ed.) (1996) *Understanding the Self*, London: Sage.

Storr, A. (1972) *The Dynamics of Creation*, London: Penguin.

Tateno, K. and Ikuko, S. (1982) 'Music Therapy', *British Journal of Music Therapy*, Autumn, Vol. 13, No. 3, 2–10.

Taylor, S. (1998) 'There Is Light at the End of the Tunnel: Ways to Good "Clinical Effectiveness Research"', in Rees, M. (ed.), *Drawing on Difference: Art Therapy with People Who Have Learning Difficulties*, London and New York: Routledge.

Theilgaard, A. (1992) 'Performance and Projective Possibilities', in Cox, M. (ed.), *Shakespeare Comes to Broadmoor*, London: Jessica Kingsley Publishers,.

Thomas, K. (1996) 'The Defensive Self: A Psychodynamic Perspective', in Stevens, R. (ed.), *Understanding the Self*, London: Sage.

Torres, F. (1996) 'The Art of the Possible', in Hall, D. and Fifer, S.J. (eds), *Illuminating Video*, San Francisco: Aperture in association with Bay Area Video Coalition.

Tyler, H.M. (2000) 'The Music Therapy Profession in Modern Britain', in Horden, P. (ed.), *Music as Medicine*, Aldershot: Ashgate Publishers.

Ulman, E. (2001) 'Art Therapy: Problems of Definition', *American Journal of Art Therapy*, Vol. 40, August, 16–26.

Valente, L. and Fontana, D. (1993) 'Research into Dramatherapy Theory and Practice', in Payne, H. (ed.), *Handbook of Inquiry in the Arts Therapies: One River Many Currents*, London: Jessica Kingsley Publishers.

Valente, L. and Fontana, D. (1997) 'Assessing Client Progress in Dramatherapy', in Jennings, S. (ed.), *Dramatherapy: Theory and Practice*, 3, London: Routledge.

Van de Wall, W. and Liepmann, C.M. (1936) *Music in Institutions*, New York: Russell Sage Foundation.

Viola, B. (2002) 'Reasons for Knocking at an Empty House', *Writings 1973–1994*, London: Thames and Hudson.

Vygotsky, L. (1967) 'Consciousness of a Problem in the Psychology of Behaviour', *Soviet Psychiatry*, Vol. 17, No. 4, 3–35.

Wadeson, H. (1980) *Art Psychotherapy*, New York: Wiley.

Wald, J. (1999) 'The Role of Art Therapist in Post-Stroke Rehabilitation', in Malchiodi, C.A., *Medical Art Therapy with Adults*, London: Jessica Kingsley Publishers.

Walker, R. (1990) *Musical Beliefs, Psychoacoustic, Mythical and Educational Perspectives*, Columbia: Teachers College Press.

Waller, D. (1991) *Becoming a Profession: The History of Art Therapy in Britain, 1940–82*, London: Routledge.

Waller, D. (1995) 'Art Therapy in Bulgaria', in Gilroy, A. and Lee, C. (eds), *Art and Music Therapy and Research*, London: Routledge.

Waller, D. (1998) *Towards a European Art Therapy*, Buckingham and Philadelphia: Open University Press.

Warner, M. (1996) *The Inner Eye: Art Beyond the Visible*, Manchester: National Touring Exhibitions.

Warner, M. (2000) 'Nine Turns Round the Spindle: The Turbine Towers of Louise Bourgeois', *Louise Bourgeois: Catalogue*, London: Tate Gallery Publishing.

Watson-Gegeo, K. and Boggs, S. (1977) 'From Verbal Play to Talk Story: The Role of Routines in Speech Events among Hawaiian Children', in Ervin-Tripp, S. and Mitchell-Kernan, C. (eds), *Child Discourse*, New York: Academic Press.

Wigram, A. (1993) 'The Feeling of Sound – the Effect of Music and Low Frequency Sound in Reducing Anxiety in Challenging Clients with Learning Difficulties', in Payne, H. (ed.), *Handbook of Inquiry in the Arts Therapies: One River Many Currents*, London: Jessica Kingsley Publishers.

Wigram, T. (2002) 'Indications in Music Therapy', *British Journal of Music Therapy*, Vol. 16, No. 1, 11–28.

Williams, G.H. and Wood, M.M. (1977) *Developmental Art Therapy*, Baltimore: University Park Press.

Wils, L. (ed.) (1973) *Bij wijze van spelen*, Samson: Alphen a.d. Rijn.

Wilshire, B. (1982) *Role Playing and Identity*, Bloomington and Indianapolis: Indiana University Press.

Wingler, H. (1969) *The Bauhaus*, Cambridge, Massachusetts: MIT Press.

Winnicott, D.W. (1974) *Playing and Reality*, London: Pelican.

Wiser, S.L., Goldfried, M.R., Raue, P.J. and Vakoch, D.A. (1996) 'Cognitive Behavioural and Psychodynamic Therapies: A Comparison of Change Processes', in Dryden, W. (ed.), *Research in Counselling and Psychotherapy*, London: Sage.

Wood, C. (1990) 'The Beginnings and Endings of Art Therapy Relationships', *Inscape*, Winter, 7–13.

Wood, C. (2000) 'The Significance of Studios', *Inscape*, Vol. 5, No. 2, 40–50.

Wood, M.J.M. (1998) 'The Body as Art: Individual Session with a Man with Aids', in

Pratt, M. and Wood M.J.M. (eds), *Art Therapy in Palliative Care: The Creative Response*, London: Routledge.

Young, M. (1992) in Murphy, J. (1998) 'Art Therapy with Sexually Abused Children and Young People', *Inscape*, Vol. 3, No. 1, 10–15.

Zollar, J.W.J. (1994) 'Dancing in Leaner Times', in Barnes, S. (ed.), *Writing Dancing in the Age of Postmodernism*, Middleton, CT: Wesleyan University Press.

Selection of Arts Therapies Associations and Websites

Art therapy

The American Art Therapy Association (AATA)   http//www.arttherapy.org/
Art Therapy Association of Colorado (ATAC)
http://www.arttherapy-co.org/
Art Therapy in Canada Homepage (ATCH)   http://home.ican.net/
British Association of Art Therapists (BAAT)   http://www.baat.org/
Canadian Art Therapy Association/ L'Association canadienne d'art therapie
(CATA)   http://www.catainfo.ca/
Institut for Kunstterapi, Denmark   http://www.kunstterapi.dk/
Irish Association of Creative Arts Therapists (IACAT)
http://www.iacat.ie/arttherapy.html
Israeli Association of Creative and Expressive Therapies (YAHAT)
www. yahat.org/eng/
Northern Ireland Group for Art as Therapy (NIGAT)
http://www.geocities.com/nigat_uk/
PROFAC Centre de Psychologie Appliquée   http://www.arttherapie.com/
US National Coalition of Creative Arts Therapies Associations (NCCATA)
http://www.nccata.org
US National Expressive Therapy Association   www.expressivetherapy.com

Music therapy

Australian Music Therapy Association   http://www.austm.org.au
ADIMU Ambito de Docencia e Investigacion en Musicoterapia, Ambito de
Docencia e Investigacao em Musicoterapia ADIMU
http://geocities.com/Paris
American Music Therapy Association   www.musictherapy.org/
Association of Professional Music Therapists UK   www.apmt.org/
British Society for Music Therapy (BSMT)   http://www.bsmt.org/
mt-whatismt.htm
Canadian Association for Music Therapy/Association de Musicotherapie du
Canada   http://www.musictherapy.ca/

Florida Association for Music Therapy
http://www.floridamusictherapy. com/
The Mostar Music Centre
http://www.warchild.org/projects/centre/music
Music Therapy in Brazil, Voices
http://www.voices.no/country/monthbrazil_ april2003
Music Therapy in Japan, Voices: A World Forum for Music Therapy
www.voices.no/country/monthJapan_may2003
Netherlands Music Therapy   www.stinchtingmuziektherapie.nl/
New Zealand Society for Music Therapy (NZSMT)
www.musictherapy. org.nz/
Voices: A World Forum for Music Therapy
http://www.voices.no/ mainissues/ Voices .html
World Federation of Music Therapy
http://www.musictherapyworld.de/modules/wftm/w

Dance movement therapy

American Dance Therapy Association (ADTA)   www.adta.org/
Irish Association of Creative Arts Therapists (IACAT)
http://www.iacat.ie/dancetherapy
Japan Dance Therapy Association
http://www.jadta.net/dancebadth.ision.co.uk
UK Association for Dance Movement Therapy (ADMT)
http://www.admt.org.uk/

Dramatherapy

British Association for Dramatherapists (BADth)
http://www.badth.ision.co.uk
US National Association for Drama Therapy (NADT)   http://www.nadt.org/
Irish Association of Creative Arts Therapies (IACAT)
http://www.iacat.ie/dramatherapy

Others

European Consortium for Arts Therapies Education
http://www.uni-muenster.de/Ecarte
Israeli Association of Creative and Expressive Therapies
http://motetsrv.mofet.macam98.ac.U/
Kenvak Netherlands Centre of Expertise for the Arts Therapies, University
of Profernonel Education Zuyd http://www.kenvak.hszuyd.nl

Further reading

Cox, M. (1992) *Children's Drawings*, London: Penguin

Dalley, T. (2000) 'Back to the Future: Thinking about Theoretical Developments in Art Therapy', in Gilroy, A. and McNeilly, G. (eds), *The Changing Shape of Art Therapy: New Developments in Theory and Practice*, London: Jessica Kingsley Publishers

Dalley, T., Rifkind, G. and Terry, K. (1993) *Three Voices of Art Therapy: Image, Client, Therapist*, London: Routledge

Emunah, R. (1983) 'The Impact of Theatrical Performance on the Self-Images of Psychioatric Patients', *The Arts in Psychotherapy*, Vol. 10, 233–9

Jennings, S. (1997) *Dramatherapy: Theory and Practice* 3, London: Routledge

Killick, K. (2000) 'The Art Room as Container in Analytical Art Psychotherapy with Patients in Psychotic States', in Gilroy, A. and McNeilly, G. (eds), *The Changing Shape of Art Therapy: New Developments in Theory and Practice*, London: Jessica Kingsley Publishers

Killick, K. and Greenwood, H. (1995) 'Research into Art Therapy with People Who Have Psychotic Illnesses', in Gilroy, A. and Lee, C. (eds), *Art and Music Therapy and Research*, London: Routledge

Landy, R. (1995) 'Isolation and Collaboration in the Creative Arts Therapies – The Implications of Crossing Borders', *The Arts in Psychotherapy*, Vol. 22, No. 2, 83–6

Pavlicevic, M. (2003) *Groups in Music: Strategies from Music Therapy*, London: Jessica Kingsley Publishers

Rust, M.J. (1998) 'Art Therapy in the Treatment of Women with Eating Disorders', in Sandle, D. (ed.), *Development and Diversity, New Applications in Art Therapy*, London: Free Association Books

Art therapy

Campbell, J., Liebmann, M., Brook, F., Jones, J. and Ward, C. (eds) (1999) *Art Therapy, Race and Culture*, London: Jessica Kingsley Publishers

Case, C. and Dalley, T. (1992) *The Handbook of Art Therapy*, London: Routledge

Evans, K. and Dubowski, J. (2001) *Art Therapy with Children on the Autistic Spectrum*, London: Jessica Kingsley Publishers

Malchiodi, C.A. (ed.) (1999) *Medical Art Therapy with Children*, London: Jessica Kingsley Publishres

Rubin, J.A. (ed.) (2001) *Approaches to Art Therapy: Theory and Technique*, New York: Brunner Mazel

Sandle, D. (ed.) (1998) *Development and Diversity: New Applications in Art Therapy*, London: Free Association Books

Schaverien, J. (1992) *The Revealing Image: Analytical Art Psychotherapy in Theory and Practice*, London: Routledge

Waller, D. (1993) *Group Interactive Art Therapy: Its Use in Training and Treatment*, London: Routledge

Waller, D. and Gilroy, A. (eds) (1993) *Art Therapy: A Handbook*, Buckingham: Open University Press

Music therapy

Aldridge, D. (1996) *Music Therapy Research and Practice in Medicine*, London: Jessica Kingsley Publishers

Bruscia, K.E. (1991) *Case Studies in Music Therapy*, Gilsum: Barcelona

Bruscia, K.E. (1998) *Defining Music Therapy*, Gilsum: Barcelona

Bunt, L. and Hoskyns, S. (2002) *The Handbook of Music Therapy*, London: Routledge

Wigram, T. (2002) *A Comprehensive Guide to Music Therapy: Theory, Clinical Practice, Research and Training*, London: Jessica Kingsley Publishers

Dramatherapy

Andersen Warren, M. and Grainger, R. (2000) *Practical Approaches to Dramatherapy*, London: Jessica Kingsley Publishers

Casson, J. (2004) *Drama, Psychotherapy and Psychosis: Dramatherapy and Psychodrama with People who Hear Voices*, London: Routledge

Emunah, R. (1994) *Acting for Real: Dramatherapy Process, Technique and Performance*, New York: Brunner/Mazell

Gersie, A. (ed.) (1993) *Dramatic Approaches to Brief Therapy*, London: Jessica Kingsley Publishers

Jennings, S., Cattanach, A., Mitchell, S., Chesner, A. and Meldrum, B. (eds) (1994) *The Handbook of Dramatherapy*, London: Routledge

Jones, P. (1996) *Drama as Therapy: Theatre as Living*, London: Routledge

Landy, R. (1986) *Drama Therapy Concepts and Practices*, Springfield: Charles C. Thomas

Mitchell, S. (ed.) (1996) *Dramatherapy Clinical Studies*, London: Jessica Kingsley Publishers

Dance movement therapy

Behar-Horenstein, L.S. and Garnet-Sigel, J. (1999) *The Art and Practice of Dance/Movement Therapy*, New York: Pearson

Chodorow, J. (1991) *Dance Therapy and Depth Psychology*, London: Routledge

Levy, F. (ed.) (1995) *Dance and Other Expressive Arts Therapies*, London: Routledge

Meekums, B. (2002) *Dance Movement Therapy: A Psychotherapeutic Approach*, London: Sage

Payne, H. (1992) *Dance Movement Therapy: Theory and Practice*, London: Routledge
Stanton-Jones, K. (ed.) (1992) *An Introduction to Dance Movement Therapy in Psychiatry*, London: Routledge

Arts therapies

Gilroy, A. and Lee, C. (eds) (1995) *Art and Music: Therapy and Research*, London: Routledge
Grainger, R. (1999) *Researching the Arts Therapies*, London: Jessica Kingsley Publishers
Levine, S.K. and Levine, E.G. (1999) *Foundations of Expressive Arts Therapy: Theoretical and Clinical Perspectives*, London: Jessica Kingsley Publishers
McNiff, S. (1998) *Art-Based Research*, London: Jessica Kingsley Publishers
Read Johnson, D. (1999) *Essays on the Creative Arts Therapies*, Springfield: Charles C. Thomas

Author index

Subject index